CEYLON IN 1903
DESCRIBING
THE PROGRESS OF THE ISLAND SINCE 1803

MAVEN BOOKS

CEYLON IN 1903
DESCRIBING
THE PROGRESS OF THE ISLAND SINCE 1803

John Ferguson, C.M.G.

Editor of "Ceylon Oberver," "Tropical Agriculture,"
'Ceylon Handbook," etc.

Vice-President of the Ceylon Branch of the Royal Asiatic Society;

President of the Ceylon Christian Literature Society;

Honorary Corresponding Secretary of the Royal Colonial Institute.

MAVEN BOOKS

Chennai   **New Delhi**   **Tirunelveli**

MAVEN BOOKS

An Imprint of **MJP Pubishers**

ISBN 978-93-87488-52-6   **Maven Books**

All rights reserved   No. 44, Nallathambi Street,
Printed and bound in India   Triplicane, Chennai 600 005

MJP 401   © Publishers, 2018

Publisher: **C. Janarthanan**

PUBLISHER'S NOTE

The legacy of a country is in its varied cultural heritage, historical literature, developments in the field of economy and science. The top nations in the world are competing in the field of science, economy and literature. This vast legacy has to be conserved and documented so that it can be bestowed to the future generation. The knowledge of this legacy is slowly getting perished in the present generation due to lack of documentation.

Keeping this in mind, the concern with retrospective acquiring of rare books has been accented recently by the burgeoning reprint industry. Maven Books is gratified to retrieve the rare collections with a view to bring back those books that were landmarks in their time.

In this effort, a series of rare books would be republished under the banner, "Maven Books". The books in the reprint series have been carefully selected for their contemporary usefulness as well as their historical importance within the intellectual. We reconstruct the book with slight enhancements made for better presentation, without affecting the contents of the original edition.

Most of the works selected for republishing covers a huge range of subjects, from history to anthropology. We believe this reprint edition will be a service to the numerous researchers and practitioners active in this fascinating field. We allow readers to experience the wonder of peering into a scholarly work of the highest order and seminal significance.

Maven Books

PREFACE.

THE first edition of this work was published by Messrs. Sampson Low, Marston, & Co., as "Ceylon in 1883." A second edition, under the auspices of the same firm, was called for in a few months, and came out as "Ceylon in 1884." The latter volume was out of print for some time before a further issue could be made; but the Queen's Jubilee made it very appropriate that a third edition, much enlarged, should appear in 1887, (published by Messrs. John Haddon & Co.) as "Ceylon in the Jubilee Year." So favourably was this enlarged fourth publication received, that "out of print" was the only answer to numerous inquiries by 1890; and therefore a fifth Edition called "Ceylon in 1893" (also published in London) was prepared. This again has long ago been disposed of and so "CEYLON IN 1903" in a compact form, has been prepared at rather short notice to supply an urgent want for a popular, illustrated, up-to-date Handbook. The Author trusts that this succinct and popular account of what is the most important—whether population, trade, or resources be considered—of Her Majesty's Crown Colonies, will be once again found to supply a felt want. Thrown very much into the form of an Illustrated Handbook for Visitors, this volume will be found by all interested in Ceylon (whether officials, merchants, planters, or home residents with relatives in the island) to contain late and reliable information on a great variety of topics. The endeavour has been to bring all the chapters up vi *Preface.*

to date, while several have had considerable additions, and the closing chapter is quite new. The Appendix, again, with some eight divisions, is almost entirely new, and includes the Lectures which the Author was enabled to give before the Royal Colonial Institute and Society of Arts during 1899; a good deal of information about Uva and the new Camp at Diyatalawa organised by Sir West Ridgeway for the Boer prisoners and to be kept up for Military and Volunteer exercises, and for Military and Naval convalescents. There is also information as to the encouragement offered for new enterprises—Stock-raising, &c.—in the region to be opened up by Governor Ridgeway's great Northern Railway which will be completed by 1905. The main results of the Census of 1901 are given; a list of Native Names of Places with their meaning; and a Glossary of Native Terms from a paper compiled under official auspices, and revised,—all of which will be very useful for reference. A full Index makes all the main "facts and figures," as well as the general information, readily available.

Regarding "Ceylon in 1903" as an Illustrated Volume, a special feature of the present edition is the separate arrangement of most of the engravings (many of them new) on distinctive sheets. The map of the Island (which will be found in the pocket inside cover or bound in the volume if required) will be found fairly correct and convenient for reference.

Finally, the author has to express his pleasure that permission has been given him to dedicate the present edition to one of the ablest and most successful as well as prosperous in the long list of British Governors of Ceylon, and whose name will long be remembered in the annals of the island, as well as in those of the Isle of Man, of Ireland, of India and Afghanistan, in all

Preface.

of which countries, His Excellency Sir West Ridgeway has made his mark as an Administrator.

By way of postscript, it may be mentioned that if the "British Association for the Advancement of Science" accept the invitation of the Ceylon Government, sent home to the Council in July this year, to hold its annual meeting in Colombo during either 1907 or 1908, a new interest will be taken in scientific and literary circles all over the world, in this "first of British Crown Colonies," this "Eden of the Eastern Wave," with its interesting peoples of many races, its many attractions, industries and resources.

Colombo, 12th September, 1903.

CONTENTS.

CHAPTER I.
PAST HISTORY. PAGE.
The Ophir and Tarshish of Solomon—Northern and Southern Indian Dynasties—Chinese Invasion and Connection with the island in ancient and modern times—Portuguese and Dutch Rule—British Annexation. ... ...

CHAPTER II.
THE ISLAND IN 1796, 1815, AND EIGHTY-EIGHT YEARS LATER.
Extent and Topographical features—Condition of the island previous to, and after, eighty-eight years of British Rule contrasted ... ...

CHAPTER III.
SOCIAL PROGRESS IN THE CENTURY.
Population—Buildings—Postal and Telegraphic Services—Savings Bank—Banking and Currency—Police and Military Defence—Medical and Education Achievements—Laws and Crime 21

CHAPTER IV.
LEGISLATIVE AND GENERAL IMPROVEMENTS UNDER THE RULE OF SUCCESSIVE BRITISH GOVERNORS—THE NEED OF PROMOTING CO-OPERATION AND GOOD FEELING BETWEEN DIVERSE CLASSES AND RACES 31

CHAPTER V.
NATIVE AGRICULTURAL AND MANUFACTURING INTERESTS.
Paddy (Rice) Cultivation—Cinnamon—Coconut, Palmyra, Kitul, Arecanut and other Palms—Essential Oils—Tobacco Cotton—Sugarcane—Other Fruit-trees and Vegetables—Natural Pasture—Local Manufactures ... 44

CHAPTER VI.

THE ORIGIN AND RISE OF THE PLANTING INDUSTRY.
Coffee introduced in 1690, by the Dutch—First systematically cultivated in 1740—Extensive development in 1837—Highest level of prosperity reached in 1868-70—Appearance of Leaf Disease in 1869—Its disastrous effects. ... 60

CHAPTER VII.

THE ERA OF TEA, CACAO, RUBBER AND OTHER NEW PRODUCTS.
Tea—Cinchòna—Cacao—Indiarubber—Cardamoms—Liberian Coffee, &c. 67

CHAPTER VIII.

PRESENT POSITION OF AGRICULTURAL ENTERPRISE, LOCAL INDUSTRIES AND FOREIGN EXPORT AND IMPORT TRADE.
Exports of last decade—The Plumbago Trade—Gold and Iron—Native Industries generally flourishing—Tea and Cacao will make up for the deficiency in Coffee. 78

CHAPTER IX.

WHAT THE PLANTING INDUSTRY HAS DONE FOR THE MOTHER COUNTRY.
The swing of the pendulum: a Cycle of Prosperity from Tea—Previous years of depression considered—Planting profits absorbed in the past by Home Capitalists—Absence of Reserves of Local Wealth—The accumulated Profits of past years estimated. 81

CHAPTER X.

WHAT THE PLANTING INDUSTRY HAS DONE FOR CEYLON.
Population more than doubled—Revenue expanded eightfold—Trade sixteen to twenty fold—Employment afforded to natives—An El Dorado for the Indian immigrant—Coffee in the past, as Tea in the future, the mainstay of the island—The material progress in the Planting Districts 86

CHAPTER XI.

PRESENT PROSPECTS FOR CAPITALISTS IN CEYLON.
Ceylon still a good Field for Investment—Its freedom from Atmospheric Disturbances—Shipping conveniences at

the New Harbour of Colombo—Moderate Freights—Cheap and Unrivalled means of Transport—Certain Lands available for Tropical Culture in Coconut Palms, Rubber, Cotton, Tobacco, Fibres and other New Products —Openings for Young Men with capital—High Position taken by the Ceylon Planter—Facilities for personal Inspection of Investments. 94

CHAPTER XII.
ATTRACTIONS FOR THE TRAVELLER AND VISITOR.

The Voyage a Pleasure Trip—Historical Monuments, Vegetation, &c.—Variety of Climate—Colombo, the Capital—Kandy, the Highland Capital—Nuwara Eliya the Sanatorium—The Horton Plains—Adam's Peak—Uva and its long-delayed Railway—Ancient Cities of Anuradhapura and Polonnaruwa—Occasional Pearl Fisheries—Probable Expense of a Visit to Ceylon—The alleged inconveniences of Tropical Life. 100

CHAPTER XIII.
THE REVENUE AND EXPENDITURE OF CEYLON.

Chief Sources of Revenue :—Grain and Customs Dues, Sales of Crown Land and Railway Profits—Taxation and Revenue. 118

CHAPTER XIV.
WHAT ITS GOVERNMENT CAN DO FOR CEYLON.

Active and independent Administrators required—The obstruction to Progress offered in Downing Street—Railway Extensions—Law Reform needed—Technical, Industrial, and Agricultural Education needs encouraging—The Buddhist Temporalities Questions—Fiscal Reform of Road, Excise Laws, Salt Monopoly, Food Taxes and Customs Duties—The Duke of Buckingham's Ceylon and Southern India Railway Project—Ceylon and India—Waste Crown Lands. 121

CHAPTER XV.
SOCIAL LIFE AND CUSTOMS.

Social Life and Customs of the Natives of Ceylon—How little Colonists may know of Village Life—Domestic Servants—

	PAGE.
Caste Restrictions—Curious Occupations among the people	... 132

CHAPTER XVI.

FURTHER PROGRESS INDICATED AND A FEW REFORMS CALLED FOR. Relation and Importance of Ceylon to India—Progress of Christianity and Education—Statistics of Population—Need of Reform in the Legislative Council, and Sketch of a Scheme for the election of unofficial members—Loyalty of People to British Rule, as evinced during Royal Visits, and in connection with the Jubilees of the late Majesty the Queen Empress and of the Coronation of King Edward VII.—Progress of Ceylon since 1837. 141

CHAPTER XVII.

SIR WEST RIDGEWAY'S ADMINISTRATION : 1896–1903 ... 147

APPENDICES.

I.—GLOSSARY. ... ...

II.—DERIVATIONS AND MEANINGS of the Names of some of the Towns, Villages, Districts, Rivers, and Mountains in Ceylon. xl

III.—THE CEYLON CENSUS OF 1901 :—Christian by Sect ; Population by Nationality and Religion ; Education by Nationality and Religion ; Races in Ceylon ; Occupations or Means of Livelihood ; The Provinces of Ceylon ; Districts, Towns, Villages, Houses, Families and Males and Females ; Population of Ceylon by Religion ; Population of Ceylon by Race ; Districts and Towns in Ceylon by their Population, Area and Density ; Colombo—Area, Houses, Persons, &c ; Chief Towns and Villages in Ceylon.. xlvi

CHRISTIAN MISSIONS IN CEYLON—Review of the Decade, 1892-1902 : by J. Ferguson :—Roman Catholics, Baptist Mission, Wesleyan Mission, Church Mission, American Ceylon Mission, S. P. G. Mission, Salvation Army, Friends' Mission, Henaratgoda Mission, Independent Catholics, Bible and Christian Literature Societies. lxxxiii

(5)

	PAGE.
IV.—OLD AND NEW COLOMBO by J. Ferguson. ...	... ciii
V.—CEYLON IN 1899—by J. Ferguson. ...	... cxli
Meteorological Conditions in North Central and North-East Ceylon	...clxii
VI.—TYPES OF RACES AND AMUSING CHARACTERS IN CEYLON	clxiv
VII.—UPPER UVA, Ceylon, as a Station for British Troops.	clxxiii
VIII.—TREE-GROWING at a High Elevation in Ceylon—The Best-wooded Plantation in the Island. ...	clxxx
IX.—NORTH CENTRAL CEYLON : How is the Wastelands opened by the Railway to be utilised?—Cattle Stations and Stock-raising suggested beyond the Tank-served Ricelands.	clxxxvi

GENERAL INDEX.

A.

	PAGE.
Abbotsford Estate	60
Acrobats, Native	139
Actors, Native	... 139
Adam's Bridge	 7
———— Peak	63, 112, clxxvii (*Illustration*)
Administration of Ceylon	 121
———— of Justice	... 30, clii
African Palm Oil Nut	76
Agricultural Education	... 55, 124
———— Enterprise of Ceylon	78
Agriculture, Native	... 45, cxliv
———— Tropical, Manuals on	98
———— under the Dutch	5
Agriculturist, Tropical	98
Agri-Horticultural Exhibitions	124
Alagala Peak (*Illustration*)	clv
Altitudes of Mountains	8
———— suited to Coffee	... 64, 70
Ambalangoda	106
American Mission	xcv
Amusing Characters in Ceylon	... clxiv
Animals, Wild	115
Annotto Dye Plant	... 77
Anuradhapura	... 4, 33, 114
———— Ruins (*Illustrations*)	108, 114, 115, 138
Apprentices to Tea Planters	... 97
Arabi and the Egyptian Exiles	... 2, 40, *Illustration* (144)
Arabs, Cinnamon known to	... 49
———— Coffee Introduced by	61
Archæological Survey	130
Area of Ceylon	7
Areca Palm	54

	PAGE.
Army—See MILITARY.	
Arrack	51
———, Illicit Sales of	124
——— Rents	124
Astrologers	139
Asylums in Ceylon	26
Ætagala	109
Atmospheric Disturbances, Freedom of Ceylon from	94
Attractions for Travellers and Visitors	100
Australia to Ceylon	126
Authorities on Ceylon	140, cxxxi
Avissawella	108

B.

Backwaters	8, 19
Badulla (*Illustration*)	clxxiii
Baker, Sir Samuel	102
Balangoda	109
Bandarawela	113
——— Railway Extension	38
Bank Notes	23
——— of Ceylon	32
Banking Facilities	23
Banyan Tree (*Illustrations*)	80, 81
Baptist Mission	lxxxix
Baptists, Number of	xlvii
Barbers	139
Bark, Cinnamon—See CINNAMON.	
———, Cinchona—See CINCHONA.	
Barnes, Governor Sir Edward	11
——— ——— ———, Statue of (*Illustration*)	21
Batticaloa	44, 116
Beef Supply of Ceylon	57
Beggars	139
Bentota	106
Bhang Licenses	38
Bible Society	ci
Bibliography of Ceylon	140, cxxxi
Births, Registration of	33

		PAGE.
Boats, Bridge of	...	11, 35 (*Illustration*)
Boer Camp	...	113
——— Prisoners of War in Ceylon	...	40
Books on Ceylon		140
Botanic Gardens, Ceylon	...	40, 110
Breadfruit-tree	...	55
Breakwater, Colombo		34, 39, cxxii, cliii
Brides, Native	...	137
Bridge of Boats	...	11, 35 (*Illustration*)
Bridges	..	... 12, 14, 15
British Governors of Ceylon	...	*Illustration* (1), 7-20, 153
——— Rule in Ceylon	.	7—20, 145, 153
Buddhism	...	136, 142
——— and Caste		136
——— and State		32
Buddhist Fishermen, Hypocrisy of	... ...	138
——— Priests	...	127, 139
——— Sects	... ...	139
——— Shrines (*Illustrations*)		101, 109, 114, 115, 130, 134, 138
——— Temples	... ...	3, 109
——— Temporalities	...	29, 35, 127
Buddhists	..	142
———, Number of		xlvi
Buildings in Ceylon		22
Bullock Carts		19
Bullocks, Imported		57
Burghers, Status of	..	141
Burmese Pilgrims at Kandy (*Illustration*)		134
Burnside, Sir Bruce, Chief Justice	...	30

C.

Cacao Acreage in Ceylon		151
——— Cultivation		74
——— Exports	...	74, 151
——— Plantations, Finest		111
——— Prices	.	98
——— Tree and Pods (*Illustrations*)	...	74, 76
Cambodia, Presents from King of	. .	3
Cameron, Mr. C. A.		103
———, Mrs. Julia		103

(10)

	PAGE.
Canals made by Dutch	5, 19
———, Mileage of	19
Canoe, Stone (*Illustration*)	51
Caoutchouc—See INDIA-RUBBER.	
Capital and Returns	82-84
Capitalists, Prospects for	94
Cardamom Acreage in Ceylon	151
——— Cultivation	75
——— Exports	76, 151
Carpenters, Sinhalese	58
Carriage of Produce	99
Carrier-Pigeons	32
Cart Registration	30
——— Roads	10
Carts and Carriages	19
Caryota Urens	53
Cassia Auriculata	67
Caste	19,36,134,135,136
Cattle-rearing	57
——— in Ceylon, No. of	11
——— (*Illustration*) Proposed	clxxxiv
Ceara Rubber Tree	61
Census of Ceylon	21, 33, xlvi
Centipedes	117
Central Province, Chief Towns and Villages in	lxxix
——————— Gazetteer of the	39
——————— Population, of	lxviii
Ceylon a Central Military Station	126
——— a Good Field for Investment	94
——— a Huge Tropical Garden	101
———, A Lecture on	40
———, Ancient History of	1, 2, 101
——— an El Dorado for Indian Immigrants	87
——— and King of Cambodia	3
——— and Muhammadans	2
——— Antiquities	108,114,115,138
———, Area of	7
——— a Training Ground for Tropical Agriculturists	97
———, Bibliography of	140, cxxxi
Ceylon, Buddhist Temples in	3
———, Chinese Invasion of	3

	PAGE.
Ceylon, Civilisation in	3
———, Commerce of	5, 86
——— Company, Limited	24
———, Configuration of	7
——— Contingents	40, 41
———, Cost of Living in	116
———, Expenditure of	42,118
———, First King of	2
———, Freedom of, from Atmospheric Disturbances	94
———, Greek and Roman Appellations of	2
——— in 1899—Paper by John Ferguson, Esq.	cxli
———, its Relation and Importance to India	141
———, Last King of	2
——— Medical College	27, 33
———, Names of	2,101
———, Natural Features of	8, 101
——— Observer	68,98
———, Progress in	9, 145
———, Prospects for Capitalists in	94
———, Public Debt of	42
———, Revenue of	42, 118
——— Rifle Regiment	25, 30
——— Steamship Company	115
———, Topographical Features of	7
——— Trade, Value of	86
———, Types of Races and Amusing Characters in (Illustrations)	clxiv
——— vs. India as a Tea-growing Country	96
———, What its Government can do for it	121
———, Writers on	140, cxxxi
Changes of European Element	82
Characters in Ceylon, Amusing (Illustrations)	clxiv
Charitable Allowances	10
Chartered Bank of India, &c.	24
Cheetah Hunting	115
Chicago Exhibition	38
Chilaw	108
China, Buddhist Temples in	3
——— Tea	70
Chinese in Ceylon	3
Chocolate Tree	74

(12)

	PAGE.
Chocho	55
Christian Literature Society	ci
—— Missions in Ceylon	27, 133, lxxxiii
Christianity and Caste	136
—— in Ceylon	139, 142, lxxxiii
Christians, Number of	xlvi
Church of England Members, Number of	xlvii
—— Mission	40, xciii
Cinchona, Acreage of	69
—— Branch (Illustration)	68
—— Cultivation	68
—— Exports	69
——, Introduction of	68
Cinnamon Cultivation	44, 49
—— Monopoly	4, 5
—— Oll	56
—— Preparation of (Illustrations)	48
Citronella Oil	55
Civilisation and Roads	15
—— in Ceylon	3
——, European	139
Civil Laws, Codification of	124
—— Procedure Code	30
—— Servants in British Colonies	121
—— Service, Ceylon Subordinate	130
—— —— of India and Ceylon	129
Climate of Ceylon	96
Climbers, Coconut and Areca Tree	(Illustrations) 91, cxv
Clothing of Natives	91
Clubs	36
Coal in Ceylon, Absence of	79
Coast, Palms around the	50
Cobden Club and Food Taxes in Ceylon	128
Cocoa—See CACAO.	
Coconut and Areca Palms	(Illustrations) 70, 91, cxv
—— Climber (Illustration)	cxv
—— Desiccated	52
—— Exports	52
—— Fibre	52,93
—— Palm	50
—— Plantation (Illustration)	50

	PAGE.
Coconut Plantations, Tax on	128
———, Products of the	52
Code, Penal and Civil	30
Coffee, Altitudes suitable for	64, 70
——— Bush (*Illustrations*)	68, 75
———, Capital and Profits	83
——— Crops, Total	83
——— Cultivation	60
——— Exports	60, 61, 66, 80
——— Gardens, Sinhalese	62
———, Introduction of	60
——— Land, Prices of	64
——— Leaf Disease	63, 64
———, Native-grown	85
——— Plantations, Profits from	83
———, Prices of	83
——— Stores and "Barbacues" (*Illustration*)	cxiv
———, Total Quantity produced in Ceylon	83
Coir Fibre	52, 93
———, Export of	52
Colombo, Academy	32
——— and the British Association	cxxix
———, Area of	lxxvi
———, Attractions of	103
———, Benefit of making it a Free Port	129
———, Bibliography of	140, cxxxi
——— Breakwater	34, 39
———, Climate of	105, 109
———, Density in	lxxvi
——— Described	107
———, Distances from	126
——— Drainage	39, 105
——— Electric Tramways	105, cxxi
——— Flagstaff (*Illustration*)	21
——— Graving Dock	39
——— Harbour Works	34, 39, cxxii, clii
———, Houses in	lxxvi
——— in the Dutch Era	cv
——— in the Portuguese Era	civ
———, Iron Works and Foundries	cxxvi
——— Lake	107

	PAGE
Colombo, Means of Locomotion in	105
——— Merchant's Seaside Mansion (*Illustration*)	20
———, Modern	cii, cxii
——— Museum (*Illustrations*)	33, 34
———, Old	40, cii
——— Passengers to	117
——— Pettah (*Illustration*)	cxx
———, Population of	9, 103, lxxvi, cxx
——— Queen's House (*Illustration*)	21
———, Railways and Tramways	105, cxxi
——— Railway Terminus (*Illustration*)	cxliv
——— Roadstead	95, cxxv
——— Sanitation of	cxx
———, Shipping Conveniences at	95
——— "Stores"	90
——— Street Scene (*Illustration*)	102
——— the Port for South India	cxxv
——— under British Rule	cvii
——— Vegetation	107
——— *versus* Trincomalee	34
———, Visitors to	cxxvii
——— Waterworks	105
Colonial Office	121
Commerce of Ceylon	5
Communication, Means of	11, 14, 15
Commutation, Rice	119
Compulsory Labour	31
Congregationalists, Number of	xlvii
Conjurors, No. of	139
Conservation of Forests	33
Coode, Sir John, and Colombo Harbour Works	11
Coolies Earnings of	87
———, How they talk English	135
——— on Estates	133
Cooly Girl Picking Tea Leaves (*Illustration*)	70
Copleston, Most Rev. Dr. R. S.	41
———, Rt. Rev. A. E.	41
Copra, Export of	52
Coral Reefs	106
Cordiner, Rev. James	14
Cost of living in Ceylon	119

(15)

	PAGE.
Cotton Cultivation	56
——— Mills, Colombo	56
——— Spinners	56
Council Reform	31, 144
Cricket and Sinhalese Lads (*Illustration*)	133
Crime in Ceylon	30, clii
Crocodiles	117
Crown Colonies	1, 121
——— Land along Northern Railway	130
——— —— Sales	43, 119
Croton Oil Seeds	76
Crucibles, Plumbago for	78
Cruelty to Animals	138
Cultivated Areas	11, 44–59
Currency, Decimal	24
——— Notes	23
——— of Ceylon	141
Customs Duties	119
——— and Social Life	132
Cycles of Depression	81

D.

Dagobas in Ceylon	101, 108, 114, 138 (*Illustrations*)
Dancers, Native	139
Deaths by Accidents	30
———, Registration of	33
Debt of Ceylon	42
Decimal Currency	141
Deerhorns, Trade in	79
Defences See MILITARY	
Delft Island	57
Density in Ceylon	lxxvi
Dependents in Ceylon	lxiii
Depression, Financial	82
Derivations of Place Names	xl
De Soysa, Mr. C. H.	27
Devil-dancers	(*Illustration*) 139
Dhobies	(*Illustration*) 139
Diamond Jubilee Celebrations	40
Dairy Farm in Colombo	57

(16)

	PAGE.
Dikoya	63
Dimbula District	63
——— Plantation (*Illustration*)	60
Disease, Coffee—See COFFEE LEAF DISEASE.	
Disestablishment in Ceylon	32, 84, lxxxiv
Dispensaries in Ceylon	10, 26
Distances from Colombo	126
Districts of Ceylon	lxiv, lxxiv
Diyatalawa	113
——— as a Military and Naval Sanitarium	126
Dock, Graving—See GRAVING DOCK.	
Dolosbage, Tea in	67
Domestic Servants	134
Dress of Natives	
Drinking Habits among People	125
Dumbara	109
Dutch Rule in Ceylon	4
———, Taxation by the	128
Duties and Taxes	118
Dyeing Substances	79

E.

Earners in Ceylon	lxiii
Earthquakes	
Eastern Province, Chief Towns and Villages in	lxxx
Eastern Province, Population of	lxx
East India Naval Station Headquarters	126
Ebony, Export of	79
Edinburgh, Duke of	33, 144
Education	27, 33, 133, 139, 141
Education among Christians	lxxxv
Education by Nationality and Religion	xlix, l
Egyptian Exiles and *Illustration*	40, 144
Electric Tramways	105
Elective Principle, Introduction of	143
Elephant-keepers	139
Elephant Kraals	115
Elephants, (Illustration)	
——— in Ceylon	79
Elephant-shooting in Ceylon	115

(17)

	PAGE.
Elevations suited for planting—See ALTITUDES.	
Elk Hunting	115
Ella Pass	114
Elliot, Mr. E., on Paddy Cultivation	45
Endowments, Buddhist—See BUDDHIST TEMPORALITIES	
English as spoken by Domestic Servants	134
——— Education in Ceylon	133
Essential Oils	55
Estate Coolies	133
——— Property, Value of	64
Eucalypts in Ceylon	clxxxi
Eurasians, Number of	xlvi
———, Status of	141
European Civilisation in Ceylon	139
——————— Element, Changes of	82
Europeans in Ceylon, Number of	xlvi
Exchange Facilities	23
Executive Council, Enlargement of	144
Expenditure of Ceylon	42, 118
Experimental Stations	55
Export Duties, Abolition of	33
——— Trade of Ceylon	78, 152
Exports of Ceylon	93
——— under the Dutch	5
Extension of Railways—See RAILWAYS.	
Eye Hospital and Blind Asylum	41

F.

Facilities for Travel	98
Factories, Government	58
Fakirs	139
Families in Ceylon, No. of	lxiv, lxxvi
Famine and Roads	15
Fa-hien, the Chinese Traveller	4
Faviell, Mr. W. F.	16
Farming, Stock	130
Female Education	27
Females in Ceylon	lxiv
Ferguson, A. M., C. M. G. (*Illustration.*)	98
Ferguson, Hon. John, C. M. G. (*Illustration.*)	99

(18)

	Page.
Ferguson Memorial Hall	40
"Ferguson's View" from Railway Incline (*Illustration*)	clvi
Fibre, Coir—See COIR FIBRE.	
Fibre, Kitul—See KITUL FIBRE.	
Ficus Indica (*Illustration*)	81
Financial Crises	81
Fiscal System	128,142
Fish Tax	32,128
Flagstaff, Colombo (*Illustration*.)	21
Fodder Grasses	57
Food Consumption	44, 89
—— Taxes in Ceylon and Cobden Club	128
Forced Labour in Ceylon	5, 31, 49
Foreign Invasions of Ceylon	3
Forest Conservation	33
Forestland, Price of	64
Forest Reserves	119
Fortune-tellers	139
Freights in Ceylon	96
Friend-in-Need Societies	93
Friends' Mission	c
Fruit Trees in Ceylon	55
Fungus, Coffee Leaf—See COFFEE LEAF-DISEASE.	

G.

Galle	106, 116
—— Harbour (*Illustration*)	cxxxviii
———— Landing Jetty (*Illustration*)	40
—— Lighthouse (*Illustration*)	136
Game Preservation	33, 79
Gambling	125
Gampola	111
————, Sinnapittia Estate (*Illustration*)	71
Gaols in Ceylon	30, 33
Gangaroowa Experimental Station	40
————, View of (*Illustration*)	
Gansabhawas—See VILLAGE COUNCILS	
Gas-lighting	34
Garden Cultivation	45, 48
Gem-digging Pits	108

(19)

	PAGE.
Gems in Ceylon	79, 104, cxvi
Geography of Ceylon	7
Geological Survey	130
George Wall Library and Clock-Tower	40
Giffard, Sir Hardinge	122
Glossary	i
Gneiss in Ceylon	130
Gold Currency	24, 41
——— in Ceylon	79
Gordon Gardens	37
———, Lady Hamilton	37
———, Governor Sir Arthur	11, 35
Governor, An Ideal	123
Governors of Ceylon, British—(*Illustration*)	
———————————, Salaries of	35
Grain—See RICE	
Graphite—See PLUMBAGO	130
Grant-in-aid System of Education	27, 32
Grass-cutter, Tamil (*Illustration*)	49
Grass-land in Ceylon	57
Gravelled Roads	10, 14
Graving Dock, Colombo	39
Green, Dr., American Missionary	27
——— Tea Leaf, Weighing of—(*Illustration*)	77
——— Tea, Public Sale of	40
Gregory, Governor Sir William—13,33, 38, 88; also *Illustration* (33)	
——— Lake	111
Guavas	55
Guests at the Governor's	37
Guinea Grass	57
Gunmakers, Sinhalese	58

H.

Hakgala Botanic Gardens	112
——— — Peak (*Illustration*)	113
Halsbury, Lord Chancellor	122
Hambantota	113, 116
Haputale	109, 113
————— Waterfalls	114
————— Extension—See RAILWAYS.	
——— — Pass	114

	PAGE.
Harbour, Colombo (*Illustration*)	cxxii
———— Works, Colombo	cxxii, cliii
Hardy, Rev. Spence, on Ceylon	91
Harvesting Tea and Coffee	70
Hatton	112
Havelock, Governor Sir Arthur	37
Headmen (native) and Revenue Officers	124
Headman, Professor	41
Head Quarters of the East India Naval Station	126
Health in Ceylon	88
Healthiness of Colombo	105
Healthiness of Uva	114, clxxiii
Heathenism in Ceylon	134
Heber's Hymn	49
Heights of Mountains	8
Hemileia vastatrix	33, 64, 66
Henaratgoda Mission	ci
Hides and Skins, Export of	79
Hill Stations—See NUWARA ELIYA.	
Hindus	142
————, Number of	xlvi
Historical Monuments of Ceylon—See MONUMENTS.	
H. M. King Edward VII	144
Holidays and Natives	135
Homicides in Ceylon	30
Hongkong and Shanghai Bank	24
Hoolooganga Falls (*Illustration*)	112
Horses in Ceylon	20, 79
Horton Plains	112
Hospitals in Ceylon	10, 26
Hotels in Colombo	104
———— in Nuwara Eliya	111
Houses in Ceylon	lxiv, lxxvi
————, No. of	22
Hurricanes in Ceylon	95

Idulgashena	114
Immigration Route	15
Import Duties	125

	PAGE.
Import Trade of Ceylon	78
Imports of Grain—See RICE	
———— Value of	9
Improvement in Ceylon	86-93
Improvements, Legislative and Social ..	123
Independent Catholics, Number of	xlvii
——————— Catholics	ci
India and Ceylon Tea Compared	72
Indian Dynasties in Ceylon	2
———— Famine Relief	40
India-rubber Cultivation	40
———————— Tree—(*Illustration*)	83
Indolence of Natives	135
Industrial Education	124
Industries of Ceylon	78
Insect Life in Ceylon	117
Inspection of Investments	98
Intoxicants	51
Invalids Visiting Ceylon	102
Investments, Ceylon a good field for	94-99
Iron in Ceylon	79
Ironworks, Colombo	58
Irrigation Board	47
——————— Works, Expenditure on	46, 47
Ivory Carvers	139

J.

Jaffna	116
Jaggery Sugar	53, 54
———— Palm	53
Jails in Ceylon—SEE GAOLS	
Jak-tree	55
Java and Liquor	51
———— Ceylon Compared	95
Jewsbury, Miss, on Ceylon	104
Jinrikshaws	106
Jubilee Celebrations in Ceylon	144
Juries and Caste in Ceylon	31
Jury, Trial by	81
Justice, Administration of	30
————, Charter of	31

K.

	PAGE.
Kaffirs, First Arrival of	104
Kalawewa Tank	47
Kalutara	106
———— Railway—See RAILWAY	
Kandy	109
———— Girls' Industrial School	39
————, No. of Houses in	22
———— Railway—See Railway	
———— Temple—(*Illustration*)	
———— Victoria Commemoration Buildings	40
Kandyan Chieftain (*Illustration*)—	
———— Disturbance	32
———— Marriage Laws	32
Kandyans, Number of	xlvi
Kapok	56
Kelani River Bridged	11
———— Tea District	108
Keolin for Pottery	3
Kings of Ceylon, Ancient	3, 127
Kitul Fibre—See FIBRE	
———— Palm	53
Knox, Robert	140
Kraal, Elephant—See ELEPHANT KRAAL	
Kurunegala	109
————————, Cacao in	74
Kyle, Mr. John, and Colombo Harbour Works	13

L.

Labour, Compulsory, Abolished	
———— on Roads	32
———— Supply (Tamil Coolies)	62
Lady Havelock Hospital	26, 39
———— Horton's Walk	109
Lakes and Lagoons	8, 19
Land Sales, Crown	119
———— Tax, A General	124
Languages Spoken in Ceylon	28, 133
Lapidaries	139
Laterite in Ceylon	130
Laws of Ceylon	99

(23)

	PAGE
Layard, Sir C. P. on Rice Cultivation ...	38
———————— on Paddy Cultivation	45
Leaf Disease—See COFFEE LEAF DISEASE	
Leeches in Ceylon ...	116
Legislative Council ...	142
————— Council, Establishment of ...	31
————— Council, First Meeting in Kandy	41
————— Improvements ...	123
————— Reforms	141
Lemongrass Oil	55
Lepers in Ceylon	38
Liberian Coffee ...	66, 76
Libraries and Reading Rooms	127
Licenses	116
————, Liquor	125
Lightning Conductors, Ancient ..	58
Litigation and Sinhalese ...	29
Liquor Traffic ...	51, 119
Llandoff, Lord	122
Llewellyn, Mr., and Assam Tea	67
Local Boards	33
———— Option and Liquor Licenses ..	125
Longden, Governor Sir James	84
Loyalty of Ceylon, Marks of	144
Lunatic Asylum	34

M.

MacCarthy, Governor Sir Chas. ...	13
Madras Bank	24
Madulsima	114
Mahaweliganga River	8
Mail Coach, First, in Asia	12
Malabar Incursions of Ceylon	4
Malay Servants	135
Malays ...	25, 135
————, Number of	xlvi
Maldive Islands	51
Males in Ceylon	lxiv
Maligawa, Kandy	109
Manchester Goods	56

	PAGE.
Mango	55
Manuals on Planting &c.	98
Manufacture, Native	58
Marawila	108
Markham, Mr. Clements	68
Marriages and Caste	135
————, Registration of	33
Maskeliya	62
Masons in Ceylon	58
Matale	16, 74, 111
Matara	1'6, 116
———— Tea Plant	67
Mathews Mr., Home Secretary	122
Maturata	113
Mauritius and Ceylon	8
———— Grass	57
Meteorological Conditions in North-Central and North-East Ceylon	clxii
Military Roads	12
Meanings of Place Names	xl
Meat supply of Ceylon	57
Medical College, Ceylon	27, 33
———— Expenditure and Hospitals	10, 25
Melons	55
Mercantile Bank of India, Ltd.	24
Military Expenditure	25
———— Strength of Ceylon	24, 86, 126
———— Station, Ceylon a Central	126
Mines, Plumbago	78
Mining Industry of Ceylon	78
Missionaries in Ceylon	133
Missions in Ceylon	
Molesworth, Sir G. L.	16
Monopoly, Cinnamon, &c., —See CINNAMON	
Moonlight in Ceylon	117
Monsoons	102,105
Monuments, Historical	33,115
Moorman Tamby (*Illustration*)	
Moors, Number of	xlvi
Moratuwa	106
Morgan, Sir Richard	29

(25)

	Page.
Mosquitoes	117
Mountains, Highest	8, 112
———— reached by Train	113
Muhammadans	142
———— and Ceylon	2
Muhammadan Marriage Registration	35
————, Number of	xlvi
Municipal Institutions	142
Municipalities	3,3
Murders in Ceylon	30
Museum, Colombo	34
Mutton supply of Ceylon	57
Mt. Lavinia	106

N.

Names, Ceylon, Derivations and Meanings of	xl
Nanu-oya	16, 111
National Bank of India, Ltd.	24
Nationalities in Ceylon	133
Native Agriculture	44
———— Characteristics	125, 135
———— Food Products	44
———— Manufactures	58
———— Occupations—See Occupations	
———— Products, Exports of	85
———— Social Life and Customs	133
———— Trade	80
———— Weddings	137
Natives, Employment for	32, 86, 90, 139
———— as Lawyers	29
———— and Taxation	120
————, Indolent Habits of	135
————, Status of	141
————, Treatment of	37
———— and Wages	87
———— under British Rule	7-20, 120-131
Natural History of Ceylon	101
Nautch Girls	139
Nawalapitiya	108, 111

	PAGE.
Navigation round the Island	115
Negombo	108
New Galway	112
——— Oriental Bank Corporation	24
——— Products Introduced	34, 67
——— Vegetables Introduced	55
Nilwala Ganga	106
North-Central Ceylon	clxxxiv
————————— Province, Creation of	33
———————————, Chief Towns and Villages in	lxxxii
———————————, Resources of the	clvi
———————————, Meteorological Conditions of the	clxii
———————————, Farming in the	clxxxvi
———————————, Poppulation of	lxix
North-Western Province, Chief Towns and Villages in	lxxxii
————————————, Population of	lxx
Northern Province, Population of	lxix
———————————, Chief Towns and Villages in	lxxix
——————— Railway, Crown Land along	130
Note Issue, Government	23
Nuwara Eliya	111
——————————, Climate of	102

O.

Observer, Ceylon—See CEYLON OBSERVER	
Occupations in Ceylon	lii
——————— of Natives	139
Oil, Coconut	52
——— Mills and Crushers	52
Oil-cake—See POONAC	
Oils, Essential	55
Orange	55
Ophir of Solomon	1
Opium Licenses	38
———, Restrictions of	125
Openings for men with Capital	94
Orchella Weed	
Oriental Bank Corporation	23
——————— Failure of	35
Oysters, Pearl—See PEARL OYSTERS	

P.

	PAGE
Paddy Cultivation— See RICE	
—— Tax, Abolition of	38
—— Tax or Rent	119
Palm and Fruit Trees, Area of	55
—— Coconut	49
——, Cultivation in Ceylon	49
—— Oil	51
——, Talipot	55
Palms at Peradeniya Botanic Gardens	110
——, Group of—(*Illustration*)	
—— Planted by forced labour	6
Palmyra Palm	52
———— Wood, Export of	79
Panadure	106
Pansala or Buddhist Schools	28
Papaws	55
Paris Exhibition	40
Parliament and Crown Colonies	122
Parsnip in Ceylon	55
Passage, Cost of	116
Passengers to Colombo	117
Pasturage	57, 113
Pasture in Ceylon	57
Patana Grass	57
Pattipola	113
Paumben Channel	115
Pavilion, The	109
Pearl Fisheries	5, 41, 79, 115
—— Fishery Receipts	120
Pearls	5, 79
—— in Ceylon	cxviii
Pelmadulla	108
Penal Code, Ceylon	30
Penny Postage, Introduction of	32
Pensioners in Ceylon	129
People of Ceylon	133, cl
Peradeniya Botanic Gardens	110
—— —— Group of Palms (*Illustration*)	
Pidurutalagala	8, 112
Pigeon Service, Carrier	32
Pilgrimages in Ceylon	34
Pine-apples	55
Pioneers of Planting in Ceylon	88
Plague in Bombay	93

(28)

	PAGE.
Plantains	55
Plantation Companies	24
Planters of Ceylon	96
Planting Districts, Climate of	103
——— Districts, Material Change in	90
——— Districts, Material Progress in the	60-77
——— Enterprise	cxlii
——— Industry : benefit to the Northern Country	81
——— Industry : what it has done for Ceylon	86
——— Industry, Origin and Rise of the	60
——— Profits	82
Plumbago Industry	cxv
——— Mines	108
——— Trade	78
Point Pedro	116
Polgahawela	109
Police in Ceylon	10
Political Reforms in Ceylon	31
Polonnaruwa	114
Polyandry, Abolition of	33
Pony-breeding in Ceylon	57
Poonac	52
Population	9, 21
——— of Ceylon	x'vi 86
——— by Nationality and Religion	xlvii, lxxiii
——— in Tank Region	21
Portuguese, Taxation by the	128
——— Rule in Ceylon	4
Postal Savings Banks	23
——— Service	22
Post and Telegraph Office, General	39
Pottery, Kaolin for	
Poverty in Ceylon	39
Prairie Grass	57
Prakrama Bahu, King	3
Precious Stones	79
Presbyterians	xcix
———, Number of	xlvii
Press in Ceylon, The	31, 33, 98
Price of Land in Ceylon	
Priests and Education	127
Products of Ceylon	5, 44-59
———, New	67-78
Profits from Planting Coffee	82
Progress of Ceylon in 107 years	7, 9

	PAGE.
Prospects for Capitalists	94
Prosperity of Ceylon	86
Protestant Christians	142
Provinces of Ceylon	lxiv
Pussellawa	112
Puttalam	108

Q.

Queen Victoria, Jubilee of	37
———— ————, Death of	40
Quinine—See CINCHONA	

R.

Races in Ceylon	104, li, lxxiii
———— in Ceylon, Types of	clxiv
Railway, Colombo, Kandy	16, 33
———— —— Extension to Haputale	16
————————, Indo-Ceylon	7, 39, 129
————————, Kelani Valley	17
————————, Northern	17, 109
————————, No. of Passengers carried by	18
———————— Receipts	120
———————— Ride to Uva	103
————————, Seaside	17, 35, 106
———————— Statistics	17
———————— to Bandarawela	38, 39
———————— to Jaffna	41
———————— to Kurunegala	39
———————— to Nanuoya	34
———————— to Nuwara Eliya	41
———————— to Yatiyantota	41
————————, Udapussellawa	17
Railways	cliv
————————, Benefit of	15
Rain in Ceylon—See MONSOONS	
Rakwana	108
Ramboda Falls (*Illustration*)	
———————— Pass	112
Rameswaram Temple	116
———————— Island	7
Ratnapura, Extension to	108
Reading Rooms and Libraries	127
Rebellions of 1848	12
Reform of Laws—See LAW REFORM	
Reforms, Political and Social	141

	PAGE.
Regiments in Ceylon—See MILITARY	
Registration of Marriages	33
———— of Titles to Land	33
Religion and Employment	5
——— and State Aid	32, 34
——— and State	142
Religions in Ceylon, Population according to	lxxxvii
Rents or Land Tax	120
Returns—See PROFITS	
Revenue Offices and Native Headmen	121
——— of Ceylon	42, 86, 118
Rice Cultivation	33, 45
———, Import Duty on	118
——— Tax, Abolition of	38
Ridgeway, Governor Sir J. West	39, 41, 147
——— ——— Golf Links	39
Rifle Regiment, Ceylon	25
River Scenery (*Illustration*)	
Rivers in Ceylon	8
——— and Lagoons	8, 19
Road Ordinance Levy	127
——— Tax	32
Roads	11, 14, 15
——— and Famine	153
——— in Planting Districts	91
Robinson, Governor Sir Hercules	13, 33
Roman Catholics	142, xlvii, lxxxviii
——— Catholics and Fishermen	128
——— Catholics in Ceylon	4
Romans and Cinnamon	49
Royal Family, Events connected with the	153
——— Visits to Ceylon	144
Ruanweliseya Dagoba	58
Rubies—See PRECIOUS STONES	
Rubber Acreage in Ceylon	151
——— Exports	151
Ruins of Ceylon	014
Rupee Currency	24
Russian Firms in Colombo	10

S.

Sabaragamuwa Province, Chief Towns and Villages in	lxxxi
——— ——— ———, Creation of	35
——— ——— ———, Population of	lxxii

	PAGE.
Sago	53
Salt Monopoly and Tax	119
—— Tax, Abolition Advocated	127
Salvation Army	
Salvationists, Number of	xlvii
Sanatorium—See NUWARA ELIYA	
Sapanwood, Exports	
Sapphires	79
Satinwood, Export of	79
Savings Bank	32
—— Banks, Postal	10
Scenery of Ceylon	100-117
Schools	139
—— in Ceylon—See EDUCATION	
Scorpions	117
Scotch the Pioneers of Planting	96
Seasons, Dry and Wet—See MONSOONS	
Secretary of State	122
Self-Government—See LEGISLATIVE REFORM	
Serendib, Term for Ceylon	2
Servants, Domestic	134
—— —— Registration	30
Service Tenures, Temple	34
Sharks	117
Sheep Imported	57
Shipping Conveniences at Colombo	95
—— ——, Tonnage of	10
Shooting in Ceylon	115
Siamese King and Ceylon	3
Silversmiths	cxix
Sindbad's Adventures	2
Singers, Native	139
Sinhalese and Litigation	29
—— —— and Caste	
—— —— and Planting Industry	86
—— —— as Tea Planters	73
—— ——, Status of	141
—— ——, Improvements among	91-93
—— —— Man and Woman *(Illustration)*	
—— —— not a Warlike Nation	125
—— ——, Number of	xlvi
—— —— Plumbago Miners	78
—— —— Servants	134
Skins, Export of	79
Slavery, Abolition of	32

	PAGE.
Snakes	116
Snipe	114
Social Improvements	123
—— Life and Customs	132
—— Reforms in Ceylon	31
Soils	72, 94, 114
Sources of Revenue	118
Southern India, Exports to	49, 51, 54, 56
——————, Imports from	44, 48, 57, 129
——————, Labour from	62, 87
——————, Railway from Ceylon to	129
Southern Province, Chief Towns and Villages in	lxxx
——————, Population of	lxx
Spence Hardy on Ceylon—See HARDY, REV. SPENCE	
Spiders	117
S. P. G. Misson	xcviii
"Spolia Zeylanica"	40
Sport in Ceylon	115
Sports for the People	124
Stamp Duties	
Steam Navigation round the Island	32
Steamer Companies	95
—— —— Rates	116
Steamers calling at Colombo—See SHIPPING	
Stewart-Mackenzie, Governor J. A.	32
Stock-raising in Ceylon	...clxxxiv, 57
Storms—See MONSOONS	
Street Riots in Colombo	125
Sugar-cane Cultivation	56
Superstition in Ceylon	134
Supreme Court, Appointment of a Fourth Judge to	40

T.

Talipot Palm	55
———— Palm (*Illustration*)	
Tamarind Wood	80
——————, Export of	79
Tamby Moorman (*Illustration*)	
Tamil Coolies	72, 87
———— Coolies and Planting Industry	86
———— Cooly Mission	87, 133
———— Servants	134
Tamils in Ceylon	4, 46
——.—, Number of	xlvi

	PAGE.
Tangalla	100
Tanks, Artificial	8
———, Restoration of	33
———. Village	46
Tanning in Ceylon	79
Taprobane of Greeks and Romans	
Tarshish of Solomon	1
Taxes and Duties	118
Taxation in Ceylon	41, 121-9
———— in Ceylon and India	129
————, Incidence of	120
Tea Acreage in Ceylon	151
——, Altitudes suitable for	70
—— Area Cultivated	71
——, Assam	67, 70
—— Bush (*Illustration*)	
——, China and Hybrid	70
——, Ceylon, Quality of	72
——, Ceylon *v.* Indian or China	— 71, 72
—— Consumption	73
—— Cultivation	67, 69
—— Duty	71
—— Exports	71, 151
—— Gardens, Native	72
——, Green	71
——, Introduction of	67
——, Labour for	72
——, Labour for—See COOLIES	
—— in London Market	72
—— Machinery	73
—— Plant (*Illustration*)	
—— Planting Students	97
Technical College	124
———— — Education	124
Telegraphic Service	23, 32
Temple Endowments	34
———— Service Tenures	34
Temporalities, Buddhist	34
Temperance in Ceylon	34, 51
Temperature of Colombo	
Theobroma Cacao	74, (*Illustration*)
Thoroughfares Ordinance Levy	127
Thwaites, Dr. G.H.K.,F.R.S.	63, 66
Timber Trade	79

		PAGE.
Titles to land, Registration of		33
Tobacco Cultivation		53
Toddy	...	52, 56
Tom-tom-beaters	...	139
—...———-beater (*Illustration*)		
Tomato	..	55
Tonnage of Shipping entered and cleared	...	10
Topari Tank (*Illustration*	..	
Topographical Features		7
Tortoise-shell Workers		139
Tortoises and Cruelty	...	138
Torture. Abolition of	...	31
Towns of Ceylon	...	91, lxiv, lxxv, lxxvii
Trade and Planting Enterprise	...	81
——— of Ceylon, Value of		9
Traffic, Wheeled		19
Training School	...	129
Tramways, Electric		
Transport Facilities	...	96, 99
Travellers, Attractions for	...	100
Tree-growing at High Elevations in Ceylon,	...	clxxx
———, Tomato, Introduced	...	55
Trees, Fruit		55
Trincomalee	...	116
—————— Harbour (*Illustration*)	...	
Tropical Agriculturist		98
Trips to Ceylon,		98
—·— from Colombo	..	106
Troops in Ceylon —See MILITARY.		
Tytler, Mr. Robert Boyd	...	61, 7

U.

Udapussellawa	...	112
Uva, Climate of	..	113
———Province	...	114
—————, Chief Towns and Villages in ..	...	lxxxii
——————, Creation of	...	35
——————, Population of	...	lxxii
——— Upper, as a Station for British Troops	...	clxxiii
———, Valley of	...	113

V.

Van Imhoff, Dutch Governor		6
Veddahs, Number of	..	xlvi

	PAGE.
Vegetables in Ceylon	55
Vegetation in Ceylon	100, 101
Vernacular Schools—See SCHOOLS and EDUCATION	
Victoria Bridge	39
Victoria Buildings, Kandy	40
Victoria Memorial Eye Hospital	41
Village Councils	29, 33
——— Life in Ceylon	133
Villages of Ceylon	lxiv, lxxvi, lxxvii
Visitors, Attractions for	100
Volunteer Corps	34
Volunteers in Ceylon	26, 125

W.

Wages of Natives	87
Wales, Prince of	34
———, Prince and Princess of	40, 144
War in South Africa	40
Ward, Governor Sir Henry	13, 32
Washers or Dhobies, 139, (*Illustration*)—	
Wasteland Used by the Dutch	
Water Supply of Colombo	33, 105
Waterfalls (*Illustration*)	
Wealth of Ceylon—See, PROSPERITY	
Weddings, Native	137
Weligama	106
Wesleyan Methodists, Number of	xlvii
——— Mission	xc
Western Province, Chief Towns and Villages in	lxxvii
——— Province, Population of	lxvii
Wheeled Traffic	19
Wijaya Bahu III.	127
Wilderness of the Peak	62
Willey, Dr.	40
Wilmot-Norton, Governor Sir Robert	32
Wodehouse, Sir Philip	127
Works on Ceylon	140
Worms, Messrs, and Tea	67
Writers in Ceylon	140

Y.

Yatiyantota	108
Yodi-ela	47

ILLUSTRATIONS.

H. E. the Rt. Hon. Sir West Ridgeway, G.C.M.G., K.C.B., K.C.S.I., —*Frontispiece*	
Most of the British Governors of Ceylon ...	1
Railway Bridge over the Mahaweliganga, Peradeniya	8
"Dark Arches" on the Railway Incline at Kadugannawa	9
A Merchant's Seaside Mansion : Mutwal, Colombo	20
Signal Tower, Flagstaff and Battery, Colombo	21
Queen's House, Colombo, and Sir Edward Barnes' Statue	21
Hon. Sir Arthur Hamilton Gordon, G.C.M.G.	32
Statue of the Rt. Hon. Sir Wm. Gregory, K.C.M.G., in front of the Colombo Museum	33
Colombo Museum	34
Bridge of Boats near Colombo (now removed)	35
Landing Jetty at Point-de-Galle	40
Kandy--Lake and Town	40
The Pavilion (Governor's Residence) Kandy	41
A Cinnamon Drying Ground	48
Tying the Cinnamon in Bundles for Exportation	48
Stretching the Cinnamon Bark	48
Cleaning the Cinnamon on Boards	48
Cutting the Cinnamon into Lengths	48
Peeling the Cinnamon Sticks	48
Cutting the Cinnamon Sticks	48
Tamil Grass Cutter	49
Coconut and Areca Palms	50
A Stone Cave or Rice-feeding Receptacle	51
Abbotsford Estate, Dimbula	60
Ceara Rubber Tree	61
Adam's Peak from Maskeliya Bridge	63
Dhobies at Work	64
Liberian Coffee	68
Cinchona Succirubra (Genuine Red Bark)	68
Talipot Palm in Flower	69
Tea Plant	69
Tamil Cooly Girl Picking Tea Leaves	70

	PAGE
Sinnapittia Estate, Gampola	71
Cacao Tree	74
Coffee Tree	75
Cacao Pods	76
Weighing Green Tea Leaf on a Tea Estate	77
Union of the Banyan Tree and the Palmyra Palm	80
Banyan Tree (Ficus Indica)	81
R. E. Lewis, Merchant, Planter, and Editor	87
Major Skinner, C.M.G.	88
Views on the Mahaweliganga near Kandy	90
Natives Climbing Arecanut Trees	91
A. M. Ferguson, Esq., C.M.G.	98
Hon. Mr. John Ferguson, C.M.G.	99
Shrine of the Sacred Tooth, Kandy	100
A Buddhist Shrine	101
A Colombo Street Scene	102
An Up-country Tea Estate	103
Colombo Rickshaw	106
Young Tamil Married Woman	107
Ruins of Thuparama Dagoba, Anuradhapura	108
Kandy Maligawa or the Temple of the Tooth	109
Remains of the Old Temple Gateway, Dondrahead	109
Group of Palms and Allied Plants in the Royal Botanic Gardens, Peradeniya	110
Entrance to the Royal Botanic Gardens, Peradeniya	111
Hoolooganga Falls, Kelebokke Valley	112
Nuwara Eliya and Hakgala Peaks from Ramboda Pass	113
Ruins of the Ruanwelie Dagoba, Anuradhapura	114
Sacred Bo-tree, Anuradhapura	115
Trincomalee Harbour	116
Trincomalee	117
Ruins of Jetawanarama, Polonnaruwa	130
—— of Polonnaruwa	131
Sinhalese Lads at Cricket	133
Burmese Pilgrims at Maligawa, Kandy	134
Lighthouse at Galle	136
Mount Lavinia	136
Sinhalese Village	137
A Ruined Dagoba	138
Sinhalese Devil-Dancers	139
Dhobies at Work	140

	PAGE.
A Gem-diggers Hut in Ceylon	141
Arabi and the other Egyptian Eixles to Ceylon	144
Coffee Stores and "Barbacues" (Drying Grounds)	cxiv
A Coconut Climber	cxv
Colombo: Pettah across Lake	cxx
Railway Terminus Approach, Colombo	cxxi
Colombo Harbour	cxxii
Part of Galle Harbour	cxxxviii
Falls of the Hoolooganga : Knuckles Road	cxxxix
Railway Terminus, Colombo	cxliv
View of the Satinwood Bridge at Peradeniya	cxliii
View of the Mahaweliganga at Gangaruwa near Kandy	cxlviii
Devon Falls, Dimbula	cxlix
"Sensation Rock" on the Ceylon Railway Incline	cliv
View of Alagala Peak from the Railway on the Kadugannawa Incline	clv
"Ferguson's View" looking towards Kurunegala from No. 2 Tunnel on the Town Part of the Railway Incline	clvi
Scene on the Nilwalaganga, Southern Province	clvii
Veddahs at Kallodai	clxi
Types of Races and Amusing Characters in Ceylon	clxiv
Badulla, the Capital of the Ancient Principality of Uva	clxxiii
Falls on the Diyalumaoya, near Naula, Eastern Haputale	clxxiv
Topare Tank, near the Ruins of Polonnaruwa	clxxv
Falls of Ramboda	clxxvi
View of Adam's Peak from Woodstock Estate, Maskeliya	clxxvii

Hon. F. North, Earl of Guilford.   General Sir Robert Brownrigg.   Lt.-General Sir Edward Barnes.

Sir Robert Wilmot Horton.   Rt. Hon. J. A. Stewart Mackenzie.   Sir James Emerson Tennent.

Sir Henry George Ward.   Sir Charles J. MacCarthy.   Major-General T. O'Brien.

Sir Hercules G. R. Robinson.   Sir A. N. Birch.   Rt. Hon. Sir W. H. Gregory.

Sir J. R. Longden.   Sir Arthur H. Gordon.   Sir A. E. Havelock.

MOST OF THE BRITISH GOVERNORS OF CEYLON

CHAPTER I.

PAST HISTORY.

The Ophir and Tarshish of Solomon—Northern and Southern Indian dynasties—Chinese invasion and connection with the island in ancient and modern times—Portuguese and Dutch rule—British annexation.

I TAKE it for granted that the readers of this work will have some general acquaintance with the position, history, and condition of Ceylon. Until the establishment of Orange River Colony and Transvaal—whose destiny is to be merged in a South African Federation—Ceylon was the largest, most populous, and most important of his Britannic Majesty's Crown Colonies, which are so called because the administration of their affairs is under the direct control of the Colonial Office.

Ceylon has long been
> Confess'd the best and brightest gem
> In Britain's orient diadem.

There can be no danger nowadays of a member of Parliament getting up in his place to protest against British troops being stationed in Ceylon on account of the deadly climate of "this part of West Africa," the "utmost Indian isle" being thus confounded with *Sierra Leone!*

Known to ancient voyagers as far back as the time of King Solomon (of whose Ophir and Tarshish many believe Ceylon to have formed a part), the story of its beauty, its jewels, and its spices was familiar to the Greeks and Romans, who called it *Taprobane*, and to the Arab traders who first introduced the coffee plant into this island, and who placed in *Serendib* the scene of many of Sindbad's adventures. It was also known to the Mohammedan world at large, who to this day regard the island as the elysium provided for Adam and Eve to console them for the loss of Paradise, a tradition used as a solatium by Arabi and his co-Egyptian exiles some years ago, when deported from their native land. To the people of India, to the Burmese, Siamese, and Chinese, Lanka, "the resplendent," was equally an object of interest and admiration, so that it has been well said that no island in the world, Great Britain itself not excepted, has attracted the attention of authors in so many different countries as has Ceylon.

There is no land, either, which can tell so much of its past history, not merely in songs and legends, but in records which have been verified by monuments, inscriptions, and coins; some of the structures in and around the ancient capitals of the Sinhalese are more than 2,100 years old, and only second to those of Egypt in vastness of extent and architectural interest.* Between 543 B.C., when Wijaya, a prince from Northern India, is said to have invaded Ceylon, conquered its native rulers, and made himself king, and the middle of the year 1815, when the last king of Kandy, a cruel monster, was deposed and banished by the British, the Sinhalese chronicles present us with a list of well-nigh 170 kings and queens, the history of whose administrations is of the most varied and interesting character, indicating the attainment of a degree of civilisation and material progress very unusual in the East at that remote age. Long, peaceful, and prosperous reigns—such as that of the

---

* *See* "Buried Cities of Ceylon," by S. M Burrows, c.c.s., published by A. M. & J. Ferguson.

famous king Tissa, contemporary with the North Indian emperor Asoka, 250 B.C.—were interspersed with other administrations chiefly distinguished by civil dissensions and foreign invasions. The kings of Ceylon, however, had given sufficient provocation to foreign rulers when in the zenith of their power. In the twelfth century the celebrated king Prakrama Bahu not only defeated the rulers of Southern Indian States, but sent an army against the king of Cambodia, which, proving victorious, made that distant land tributary to Ceylon.* On the other hand, in retaliation for the plundering of a Chinese vessel in a Sinhalese port, a Chinese army, early in the fifteenth century, penetrated to the heart of the hill-country, and, defeating the Sinhalese forces at the then royal capital, Gampola, captured the king, and took him away to China; † and the island had for some time to pay an annual tribute to the country. At that time the Chinese imported from Ceylon a certain quantity of *kaolin* for pottery, which still abounds in the island. The close connection in early times between the island and the great Eastern empire constitutes a very interesting

---

* The king of Cambodia (Siam) even in the present day is a tribute-offerer to Lanká, as the following paragraph from a Sinhalese paper in 1886 will show :—

"PRESENTS FROM THE KING OF CAMBODIA TO THE BUDDHIST COLLEGE, MALIGAKANDA, COLOMBO.—Several gold images, an excellent umbrella, ornamented with precious stones, and a brush made of the king's hair, to be kept for use (sweeping) in the place where Buddha's image is placed, have been sent by the king of Cambodia to the high-priest in charge of the college. Two or three priests have also come down to receive instruction in Pali, etc., etc. —*Lakrivikirana*, April 19."

During a visit to China in 1884 nothing struck the author more than the exact resemblance between a Buddhist temple in Canton and one in Ceylon ; the appearance of the priests, their worship and ceremonies, all were alike. *Outside*, in that Mongolian world, all was so different ; the country, the towns, the customs, and the people with their pigtails, their oval eyes, and loose dress, everything was strange and novel ; but *inside* this Canton temple, before the shaven, yellow-robed monks, one felt for a moment carried back to "Lanká," and its numerous Buddhist temples.

† Of this defeat and capture no mention is made in the Sinhalese History, the Mahawanso ; it was only by referring to the archives at Pekin that the facts were brought out.

episode. Fa-hien, the Chinese monk-traveller, visited Ceylon in search of Buddhist books about 400 A.D., and abode two years in the island. He gives a glowing account, still extant, of the splendour of the capital Anuradhapura, then in its zenith, with its brazen (brass-covered) palace, great shrines and monasteries, with "thousands" of monks, dagabas, and of the splendours of the Perahera (Procession of the Tooth).

Ceylon was, however, exposed chiefly to incursions of Malabar princes and adventurers with their followers, from Southern India, who waged a constant and generally successful contest with the Sinhalese. The northern and eastern portions of the island at length became permanently occupied by the Tamils, who placed a prince of their own on the Kandyan throne; and so far had the ancient power of the kingdom declined, that when the Portuguese first appeared in Ceylon, in 1505, the island was divided under no less than seven separate rulers. Ceylon, in the Middle Ages, was "the Tyre of Eastern and Southern Asia."

For 150 years the Portuguese occupied and controlled the maritime districts of Ceylon, but it was more of a military occupation than a regular government, and martial law chiefly prevailed. The army of Roman Catholic ecclesiastics, introduced under Portuguese auspices, alone made any permanent impression on a people who were only too ready to embrace a religion which gave them high-sounding honorific baptismal names, and interfered seldom, if at all, with their continued observance of Buddhistic feasts and ceremonies. The Portuguese established royal monopolies in cinnamon, pepper, and musk; exporting, besides cardamoms, sapan-wood, areca-nuts, ebony, elephants, ivory, gems, pearls, and small quantities of tobacco, silk, and tree cotton (the "kapok" of modern times).

The Dutch, who by 1656 had finally expelled the Portuguese rulers from the island, which the Lisbon authorities had said "they had rather lose all India than imperil," pursued a far more progressive administrative policy, though, as regards commerce, their policy was selfish and oppressive. Still confined to the low-country (the king of Kandy defying the new, as he had done the previous, European invaders), the Dutch did much to develop cultivation and to improve the means of communication—more especially by canals in their own maritime territory—while establishing a lucrative trade with the interior. The education of the people occupied a good deal of official attention, as also their Christianisation through a staff of Dutch chaplains; but the system of requiring a profession of the Protestant religion before giving employment to any of the people speedily confirmed the native love of dissimulation, and created a nation of hypocrites, so that the term "Government Christian," or "Buddhist Christian," is common in some districts of Ceylon to this day.

The first care of the Dutch, however, was to establish a lucrative commerce with Holland, and their vessels were sent not only to Europe, but also to Persia, India, and the Far East ports. *Cinnamon* was the great staple of export;* next came *pearls* (in the years which gave successful pearl-oyster fisheries in the Gulf of Mannar); then followed elephants, pepper, areca or betel nuts, jaggery-sugar, sapan-wood and timber generally, arrack spirit, choya-roots (a substitute for madder), cardamoms, cinnamon oil, etc. The cultivation of coffee and indigo was begun, but not carried on to such an extent as to benefit the exports.

Agriculture was promoted by the Dutch for an essentially selfish purpose, but nevertheless good resulted to the people from the system of forced labour,

---

* The peeling of cinnamon, the selling or exporting of a single stick, save by the appointed officers, or even the wilful injury of a cinnamon plant, were made crimes punishable by death by the Dutch. *See* the Index for the Cinnamon Industry.

as in the case of the planting of coconut palms along the western coast, from Colombo southwards, which, so late as 1740, was described by Governor Van Imhoff as waste-land to be surveyed and divided among the people, who were bound to plant it up. At the end of last century, when the British superseded the Dutch in the possession of the maritime provinces of Ceylon, the whole of the south-western shore, for nearly 100 miles, presented the unbroken grove palms which is seen to this day.

From 1797 to 1802 Ceylon was placed under the East India Company, who administered it from Fort St. George, Madras; but in the latter year it was made a Crown Colony; the Hon. F. North, afterwards Earl of Guilford, continued as administrator, and was therefore the first governor of Ceylon. It soon became evident there could be no settled peace until the tyrant king on the Kandyan throne—hated by his own Nobility and Countrymen—was deposed, and the whole island brought into subjection to the British Crown. This was accomplished in 1815, when, at the instigation of the Kandyan Chiefs and people themselves, Wikkrama Rája Sinha, the last king, was captured and deposed, and exiled by the British to Southern India.

So great was the value attached to Ceylon as the "*key* of India" owing to the grand harbour of Trincomalee, as well as to its supposed fabulous wealth in precious stones and valuable produce, that, at the general peace, Britain chose to give up Java to the Dutch, and retained this little island, although inferior in area, population, and natural resources.

CHAPTER II.

THE ISLAND IN 1796, 1815, AND EIGHTY-EIGHT YEARS LATER.

Extent and topographical features – Condition of the island previous to, and after, eighty-eight years of British rule contrasted.

HAVING now arrived at the British period, it may be well to give some idea of the condition of Ceylon and its people in the early part of this century, and to compare the same with what is realised after British government has been established for eighty-eight years throughout the whole island.

The position of Ceylon as a "pearl-drop on the brow of India" with which continent it is almost connected by the island of Ramisseram and the coral reef called Adam's Bridge *, is familiar to all who have ever glanced at a map of Asia. To that great continent it may be said to be related as great Britain is to Europe, or Madagascar to Africa. In extent it comprises nearly sixteen million acres, or 24,702 square miles, apart from certain dependent islands, such as the Maldives. The total area is about five-sixths of that of Ireland, but is equal to nearly thirty-seven times the

* An Indo-Ceylon connecting Railway was first brought before the British public by the author in a paper read before the London Chamber of Commerce on April 15th, 1897. It was treated as a chimerical scheme at the time, but some years later was discussed at a Meeting of the Imperial Institute; and the Viceroy of India, Lord Curzon, has lately (December 1902) appointed a Commission to consider the railway gauges in Southern India and Ceylon with reference to future connections. At present an Indian metre gauge line is made to Paumben, and it is proposed to carry it over to Ramisseram (there is also some talk of opening a new port near Paumben); while in Ceylon, the 5½-feet gauge runs to Anuradhapura and Jaffna.

superficial extent of the island of Mauritius, which sometimes contests with Ceylon the title of the "Gem of the Indian Ocean." One-sixth of this area, or about 4,000 square miles, is comprised in the hilly and mountainous zone which is situated about the centre of the south of the island, while the maritime districts are generally level, and the northern end of the island is broken up into a flat, narrow peninsula and small islets. Within the central zone there are 150 mountains or ranges between 3,000 and 7,000 feet in altitude, with ten peaks rising over the latter limit. There are about 250 recorded Trigonometrical points over 1,000 feet in altitude in the island. The highest mountain is Pidurutalágala (8,296 feet, or nearly 1,000 feet higher than Adam's Peak, 7,353 feet), which was long considered the highest, because to voyagers approaching the coast it was always the most conspicuous, mountain of Ceylon.

The longest river, the Mahaweliganga (the Ganges of Ptolemy's maps), has a course of nearly 200 (190) miles, draining about one-sixth of the area of the island before it reaches the sea at Trincomalee on the east coast. There are twelve other large rivers (large especially in the rainy season) running to the west, east and south, (besides numerous tributaries and smaller streams); but none of these exceed 90 miles in length. The course of the Kelani Ganga, the large river near Colombo, is about 60 miles, and that is also the length of the Kaiuganga near Kalutara. The rivers are not favourable for navigation, save near the sea, where they expand into backwaters, which were taken advantage of by the Dutch for the construction of their system of canals all round the western and southern coasts. Steamers ply between Colombo and Negombo along this narrow canal and lake. A similar service on the Kaluganga has not proved a success.

There are no natural inland lakes, save what remains of magnificent artificial tanks in the north and east of the island, and the backwaters referred to on the coast. The lakes which add to the beauty of Colombo

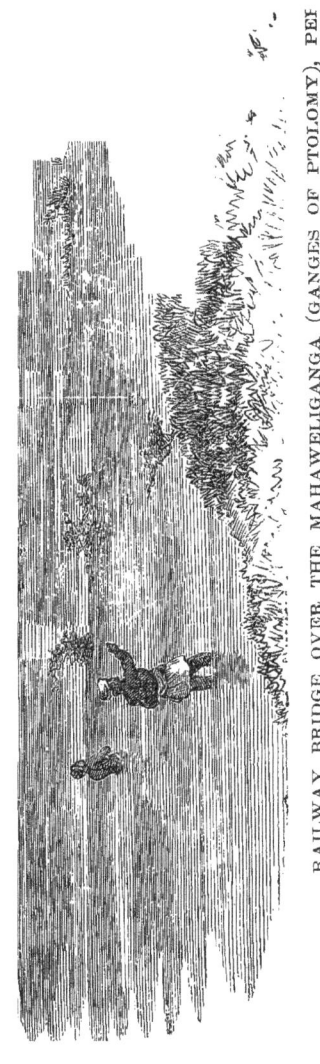

RAILWAY BRIDGE OVER THE MAHAWELIGANGA (GANGES OF PTOLOMY), PEI

THE "DARK ARCHES," ON THE RAILWAY INCLINE AT KADUGANNAWA.

(416 acres), Kandy (45½ acres) Lake Gregory, Nuwara Eliya (142 acres), and Kurunegala (104 acres), are artificial or partly so. Giant's Tank is said to have an area of 6,380 acres and Minnery and Kalawewa each exceed 4,000 acres.

Most of the above description of mountain, river and tank, was true of Ceylon at the beginning of the century even as it is now; but in other respects how altered! It is impossible to get full and exact information as to the condition in which the British found the island and its people in the early years, and up to the subjugation of the Kandyan division in 1815. But from the best authorities at our command we have compiled the following tabular statement to show at a glance a few of the salient points in which the change is most striking, by far the greater part of the change having taken place within the reign of Queen Victoria :—

CEYLON.

	In 1796—1815.	In 1903.
Population	From ¾ to 1 million	3,650,000
No. of houses	20,000 (tiled)	600,000
Population of the Capital, Colombo..	28,000	159,000
Military force	6,000	2,366
Cost of ditto	£160,000	£140,000
Imperial share	£160,000	£40,000
Volunteer corps	nil	2,436
Cost	nil	£18,000
Police	nil	2,000
Cost	nil	£60,000
Revenue	£226,000	£1,803,000*
Expenditure	£320,000	£1,798,000
Trade :—		
Imports—value	£266,790	£7,508,500 ⎫ †
Exports— ,,	£206,583	£6,000,000 ⎭
		(local Customs' value really worth much more)

* More properly Rupees 27,045,000.

† In 1901 the total values in local currency were—Imports, R112,627,000; Exports, R89,909,000.

	In 1796—1815.	In 1903.
Roads	Sand and gravel tracks	Metalled, 2,600 miles Gravelled, 660 miles Natural, 400 miles
Bridges	none	Too numerous to mention
Railways	none	367 miles *
Canals	120 miles	170 miles
Tonnage of Shipping entered and cleared	75,000 tons	9,030,000 tons
Government Savings Bank :—	nil	1
Deposits	nil	£270,000
No. of Depositors	nil	27,700
Post Office Savings Banks	nil	150
No. of Depositors	nil	55,000
Exchange and Deposit Bank Offices	nil	14
Annual volume of business in Colombo Banks' Clearing house	nil	about £13,300,000
Govt. note issue	nil	£1,000,000
Educational expenditure	£3,000 (for schools and clergy)	£66,000
No. of schools	170	4,000
No. of scholars	4,500	220,000
The press	Govt. Gazette only	45 newspapers and periodicals
Medical expenditure	£1,000	£90,000
No. of civil hospitals and dispensaries	nil	375
Covenanted { Civil servants : Revenue officers,	6	48
judges, magistrates, etc.	6	42
Charitable allowances from general revenue	£3,000 No Poor Law	£8,000 Friend in Need Society for Voluntary Relief, £2,000. No Poor Law
Post offices	4	340
Total No. of letters	not known	22,000,000
No. of printed matter despatched	nil	4,548,386
Money order offices	nil	150
Telegraph wires	nil	2,100 miles

* Besides about 200 miles more under construction and about 90 miles of line, being surveyed or enquired into.

The Island in 1796, 1815, and in 1903

	In 1796—1815.	In 1903.
Area cultivated (exclusive of natural pasture)	400,000 acres	4,900,000 acres
Live stock:— Horses,* cattle, sheep, goats, swine, etc.	250,000	1,900,000
Carts and carriages..	50	30,000

[For a fuller statistical statement, and for more detailed information still, see the latest edition of Ferguson's "Ceylon Handbook and Directory for 1903-4."]

There is, of course, an immense amount of improvement which cannot be tabulated, even if we extended our comparison in this form to much greater length. The greatest material change from the Ceylon of pre-British days to the Ceylon of the present time is most certainly in respect of means of internal communication. If, according to Sir Authur Gordon (now Lord Stanmore) as quoted by Charles Kingsley in "At Last"— the first and most potent means of extending civilisation is found in roads, the second in roads, the third again in roads, Sir Edward Barnes, when Governor of Ceylon (1824 to 1831), was a ruler who well understood his duty to the people, and he was followed at intervals by worthy successors.

When the English landed in Ceylon in 1796, there was not in the whole island a single practicable road, and troops, in their toilsome marches between the fortresses on the coast, dragged their cannon through deep sand along the shore. Before Sir Edward Barnes resigned his government in 1831, every town of importance was approached by a carriage-road. He had carried a first-class macadamised road from Colombo to Kandy, throwing a "bridge of boats"

---

* Of 21,000 horses imported between 1862 and 1903, the greater portion has been bought by native gentlemen, traders, coach-owners, etc.

(which was, only in 1893, superseded by an iron bridge) over the Kelani river near Colombo, erecting other bridges and culverts too numerous to mention *en route*, and constructing, through the skill of General Fraser, a beautiful satin-wood bridge of a single span across the Mahaweliganga (the largest river in Ceylon) at Peradeniya, near Kandy. On this road (72 miles in length) on the 1st of February, 1832, the Colombo and Kandy mail-coach—the first mail-coach in Asia—was started; and it continued to run successfully till the road was superseded by the railway in 1867.

There can be no doubt that the permanent conquest of the Kandyan country and people, which had baffled the Portuguese and Dutch for 300 years, was effected through Sir Edward Barnes' military roads. A Kandyan tradition, that their conquerors were to be a people who should make a road through a rocky hill, was shrewdly turned to account, and tunnels formed features on two of the cart-routes into the previously almost impenetrable hill-country. The spirit of the Highland chiefs of Ceylon, as of Scotland seventy years earlier, was effectually broken by means of military roads into their districts; and although the military garrison of Ceylon has gone down from 6,000 troops to 2,300, and, indeed, although for months together the island has been left with not more than a couple of hundred of artillerymen, no serious trouble has been given for about eighty-five years by the previously warlike Kandyans or the Ceylonese generally. The so-called " rebellion " of 1848 is not deserving of mention, since it was so easily quieted that not a single British soldier received a scratch from the Sinhalese rabble during the brief compaign.

So much for the value of opening up the country from a military point of view. Governor Barnes, however, left an immense deal to do in bridging the rivers, in the interior, and in constructing and extending district roads; but of this not much was attempted until the arrival of his worthiest successor, Sir Henry Ward. This governor, with but limited means, did a great deal to open up remote districts, and to bridge the Mahaweliganga at Gampola and Katugastota, as well as many other rivers which in the wet season were well-nigh impassable. He thus gave a great impetus to the planting enterprise, which may be said practically to have taken its rise in the year of Queen's Victoria's accession (1837). For the restoration and construction of irrigation works to benefit the rice cultivation of the Sinhalese and Tamils, Sir Henry Ward also did more than any of his predecessors. He, too, began the railway to Kandy, which was successfully completed in the time of his successors, Sir Charles MacCarthy and Sir Hercules Robinson.

In Sir Hercules Robinson, Ceylon was fortunate enough to secure one of the most active and energetic governors that ever ruled a Crown colony. He came to Ceylon in his prime and left his mark in every province and nearly every district of the country, in new roads, bridges, public buildings, and especially in the repair of irrigation tanks and channels and the provision of sluices. He extended the railway from Peradeniya to Gampola and Nawalapitya, some seventeen miles; and he laid the foundation of the scheme through which, under his successor, the late Sir William Gregory, the Colombo Breakwater was begun. By this great undertaking, through the engineering skill of Sir John Coode and the firm of Messrs Coode, Son & Matthews and their local representatives, Messrs. Kyle Sr. and Bostock, there has been secured for the capital of Ceylon one of the safest, most convenient and commodious artificial harbours in the world.

To Sir William Gregory belongs the distinction of having spent more revenue on reproductive public works than any previous governor of Ceylon. The roads in the north and east of the island, which were chiefly gravel and sand tracks, were completed in a permanent form, and nearly every river was bridged. The North-Central Province, a purely Sinhalese rice-growing division of the country, was called into existence; and large amounts were invested in tanks and roads; planting roads were extended; about fifty miles were added to the railway system, and preliminary arrangements made for a further extension of some sixty-seven miles. When Governor Gregory left in 1877, there were few rivers of any importance left unbridged, a large extent of previously unoccupied country had been opened up for cultivation, and an impetus given to both natives and the European colonists in the extension of cultivation, especially of new products, which alone saved the island from a serious collapse in the years of commercial depression and blight on coffee which followed. After 1877 not many miles of new road were added by Sir James Longden; but Governor Gordon greatly improved existing roads, and made several extensions besides constructing some important bridges, especially in the new and rising Kelani Valley tea district. Later on, we shall see what progress was made between 1890 and 1903. It is a great matter to be able to say that, whereas the the Rev. James Cordiner, chaplain to the Governor of Ceylon in 1807, could write "Strictly speaking, there are no roads in Ceylon," now, after a century of British rule, about 2,600 miles of first-class metalled roads, equal to any in the world, have been constructed, besides about 660 miles of gravelled roads for light traffic, supplemented by 400 miles of natural tracks available in dry weather to traverse districts where as yet there is little or no traffic. The main roads are those from Colombo to Batticaloa viá Ratnapura, Haputalé, and Badulla, right across the island; from Colombo to Trincomalee viá Kandy, and another branch viá Kurunegala, also right across the breadth of the island, but north instead of south of the Central Province; from Jaffna southwards through the centre of the island to Kandy, and thence to Nuwara Eliya and Badulla, and by a less frequented route to Hambantota on the south coast; from Kandy to Mannár on the north-west coast—the great immigration route; and the main roads on the coast, Colombo to Galle and Hambantota, and north to Mannár and almost to Jaffna. Subsidiary first-class roads, especially in the Central Province, are too numerous to mention.

The benefit which this network of roads has conferred on the people it is impossible to over-estimate. Secluded districts have been opened up, and markets afforded for produce which previously was too often left to waste; settlements, villages, and even large towns, have sprung up, within the last sixty-five years alongside roads where previously all was jungle and desolation, and means of employment have been afforded to a people who had scarcely ever seen a coin.

As in India, so on a smaller scale in Ceylon, it is a recognised fact that there is no more effectual preventive of famine than internal means of communication, whether by road, rail, canal, or navigable river. There has probably never been a year in which India, within its widely extended borders, did not produce enough food to supply all its population; but unfortunately there has been no means of getting the superabundance of one district transferred to the famine area in another part of the continent. So in Ceylon, in years gone by, there has been great scarcity and mortality in remote districts without the central Government at Colombo being made properly aware of the fact, or being able to supply prompt relief. The mortality from fever and food scarcity in some parts of the country must thus have been very great before British times.

Roads, again, are great educators, but in this they are surpassed by railways in an Oriental land. The railways in India and Ceylon are doing more in these modern days to level caste and destroy superstition than all the force of missionaries and schoolmasters, much as these latter aid in this good work. They also greatly help to promote migration from overcrowded to unoccupied districts and in this education is a great help.

The railway between Colombo and Kandy, projected originally about sixty years ago, was not seriously taken in hand till the time of Sir Henry Ward. After many mistakes and alterations of plans, it was successfully completed under the skilful engineering guidance of Mr. (now Sir) G. L. Molesworth, K.C.S.I. (afterwards consulting engineer to the Government of India), the late Mr. W. F. Faviell being the successful contractor. The total length is 74¼ miles, and, including a good deal of money unavoidably wasted in dissolving and paying off a Company, it cost the colony, from first to last, as much as £1,738,413 ; but the line (on the broad Indian gauge of 5 ft. 6 in.) is most substantially constructed, including steel rails on inclines, iron-girder bridges, viaducts; a series of tunnels, and an incline rising 1 in 45 for 12 miles into the mountain zone, which gives this railway a prominent place among the remarkable lines of the world.

Between 1867 and 1877, the railway was extended by Sir Hercules Robinson, on the same gauge, for 17 miles from Pérádeniya to Gampola and Náwalapitiya, rising towns in the Central Province ; and by Sir William Gregory for 17½ miles from Kandy to Mátalé, a town on the borders of the Central Province ; while in low country the latter governor constructed a seaside line from Colombo, through a very populous district, to Kalutara (27½ miles), and also some 3½ miles of wharf and breakwater branches.

To Governor Gregory's time also belongs the inception and practical commencement of the extension from Náwalapitiya to the principality of Uva (67 miles), of which 41½ to Nánu-oya were commenced in 1880, and finished in 1885. This line includes two long inclines, with gradients of 1 in 44, a tunnel 614 yards long, and the end of the section at Nanu-oya is 5,600 feet above sea-level, within four miles of the sanitarium and town of Nuwara Eliya (6,200 feet above sea-level).

The Island in 1796, 1815, and in 1903.

This extension, however, only touched the borders of Uva, one of the richest parts of the country, an ancient principality, which Sir Arthur Gordon separated from the Central and constituted into a separate province. Governor Gordon, after some doubt and delay at first, became thoroughly convinced of the importance of the work of extending the railway from Nanu-oya into Uva as far as Haputale or Bandarawela (for 25 to 29 miles), as originally suggested in 1872 in the memorial drawn up by the author of this volume and presented to Sir William Gregory. It took some years of hard work on Sir A. Gordon's part to overcome the objections of the Colonial Office, but at length sanction was obtained for the Haputale section, and a commencement made in December 1888, while the spring of 1893 saw the opening of the line to Bandarawela. Sir West Ridgeway's administration will always be connected with the great Northern Railway of 200 miles from Kurunegala to Jaffna and the coast; as also with the introduction of light narrow-gauge (2½ feet) lines to Kelani Valley, Nuwara Eliya and Udapussellawa.

In all there are now about 367 miles of railway open in Ceylon, besides the 12 miles to Yatiyantota and 19 to Udapussellawa nearly completed. Then there is the remainder of the line to Jaffna (165 miles), with the light line 19¼ miles to Nuwara Eliya and Udapussellawa from Nanuoya about to opened. This will give a total of about 563 miles due to be complete by the beginning of 1905 * ; but only the main line to the hill districts and that from Colombo to Matara may be said

---

* The following note will be useful for reference :—

RAILWAYS OPEN :—	MILES	UNDER CONSTRUCTION :—	MILES
Colombo-Kandy	74½	Awissawella-Yatiyantota	12
Peradeniya-Bandarawela	91	Pallai-Kurunegala	165
Kandy-Matale	17½	Nanuoya-Udapussellawa	19
Polgahawela-Kurunegala	13	Total	196
Colombo-Matara	9¾	Grand Total	562¾
Breakwater & Wharf	2½	BEING SURVEYED :—	
Kangesanturai-Pallai	83	Awissawella to Ratnapura (about)	20
Colombo-Awissawella	86¾	UNDER COMMISSION OF ENQUIRY :—	
Total	366¾	Colombo to Negombo-Chilaw Puttalam	60

to have been working long enough to afford a fair test of the traffic and the benefit to colonists, natives, and the country generally. The seaside line, however, has a wonderfully large passenger traffic, and it also secures profitable freight. Altogether 122 miles of railway are the free property of the colony ; while the debt on the remaining 440 miles will not much exceed two-and-a-half millions sterling, if allowance is made for contributions to sinking fund up to date and for the amounts paid from surplus revenue.

The main line to Kandy has more than repaid its cost in direct profit, apart from the immense benefits it has conferred. It is sometimes said that this railway and other lines in Ceylon, constructed as they were mainly for the planting enterprise and with the planters' money, confer far more benefit on the Europeans than on the native population. An answer to this statement, and an evidence of the immense educating power of our railways, is found in the fact that during the past thirty-five years over three-hundred millions of passengers have been carried over the lines, of whom all but an infinitesimal proportion were natives (Sinhalese and Tamils chiefly). On the Kandy line alone it would have taken the old coach, travelling both ways twice daily and filled each time, several hundred years to carry the above number of passengers. There was scarcely a Kandyan chief or priest who had ever seen, or, at any rate stood by, the sea until the railway into the hill country was opened in 1867, whereas, for some time after the opening, the interesting sight was often presented to Colombo residents of groups of Kandyans standing by the sea-shore in silent awe and admiration of the vast ocean stretched out before them and the wonderful vessels of all descriptions in Colombo harbour. This experience will probably be repeated next year in the case of grey-bearded Kandyans from the secluded glens of the Wanni and North-Central Province. As regards further Railway Extension, besides the light lines to Ratnapura and Puttalam, the connection of Trincomalee and Batticaloa in the low-country and of Badulla in the hill country, with our Railway system, deserves attention.

In pointing out that the Dutch (equally with the Portuguese) constructed no roads, we must not forget that the former, true to their home experience, constructed and utilised a system of canals through the maritime provinces along the western and south-western coast. In this they were greatly aided by the backwaters, or lagoons, which are a feature on the Ceylon coast, formed through the mouths of the rivers becoming blocked up, and the waters finding an outlet to the sea at different points, often miles away from the line of the main stream. The canals handed over by the Dutch at first fell into comparative disuse, but within the last fifty years they have been repaired and utilised, and there are now about 175 miles of canal in the island. In some parts, however, as between Colombo and Puttalam, the canal, being crossed by many rivers which in monsoon time bring down much silt, gives much trouble and the delay in traffic is so great that a light railway (alongside for passengers and light traffic especially) is now being urged. On the other hand, at Batticaloa, the re-opening of an old Dutch Canal is called for.

With the construction of roads wheeled traffic became possible, and a large number of the Sinhalese speedily found very profitable employment, in connection with the planting industry mainly, as owners and drivers of bullock carts, of which there must be from 15,000 to 20,000 in the island, besides single bullock-hackeries for passenger traffic, not to speak of the numerous jinrickshaws (man-power carriages, introduce first in 1884 from Japan) in all the towns. In nothing is the increase of wealth among the natives more seen, in the Western, Central, and Southern Provinces, than in the number of horses and carriages now owned by them. Forty-five to fifty years ago to see a Ceylonese with a horse and conveyance of his own was rare indeed; *now* the number driving their own carriages, in the towns especially, is very remarkable. The greater number of the horses imported during the past forty years—the imports during that time numbering 20,000—have certainly passed to the people of the country.

A MERCHANT'S SEA-SIDE MANSION: MUTWAL, COLOMBO.

QUEEN'S HOUSE, COLOMBO AND SIR EDWARD BARNES STATUE.

SIGNAL TOWER, FLAGSTAFF AND BATTERY, COLOMBO.

CHAPTER III.

SOCIAL PROGRESS IN THE CENTURY.

Population—Buildings—Postal and Telegraphic Services—Savings Bank—Banking and Currency—Police and Military Defence—Medical and Education Achievements—Laws and Crime..

HAVING thus described more particularly the vast change effected in British times by the construction of communications all over the island, we must touch briefly on the evidences of social progress given in our table (pages 9, 10).

The increase in population speaks for itself. It is very difficult, however, to arrive at a correct estimate of what the population was at the beginning of the century, as the Dutch could have no complete returns, not having any control over the Kandyan provinces. The first attempt at accurate numbering was in 1824, by Governor Barnes, and the result was a total of 851,440, or, making allowance for omissions due to the hiding of people through fear of taxation, etc., say about a million of both sexes and all ages. As regards the large estimate of the ancient population of Ceylon located in the nothern, north-central, and eastern districts, now almost entirely deserted, we are by no means inclined, with the recollection of the famous essay on "Populousness of Ancient Nations," to accept the estimates published by Sir Emerson Tennent and other enthusiastic writers. There can be no doubt, however, that a very considerable population found means of existence in and around the ancient capitals of Ceylon, and in the great Tank region of the north and east, a region which affords scope for a great, though gradual, extension of cultivation by both Sinhalese and Tamils in the future. At present it must be remembered that fully two-thirds of the population are found in the south-western districts and mountain zone, occupying a good deal less than half the area of the island, and that there are large divisions, once the best-cultivated with rice, with *now* perhaps only half a dozen souls to the square mile.*

As regards the number of inhabited houses, in 1824 there were not more than 20,000 with tiled roofs in the island ; that number has multiplied manifold, but the 600,000 now given refer to all descriptions of inhabited houses, some of these being huts roofed with coconut leaves. The improvement in the residences of a very large proportion of the people is, however, very marked : and the contrast between the old and modern homes has been well described as being as great as that between a begrimed native chatty (clay-vessel) and a bright English tea-kettle.

In the town of Kandy, which has now about 4,800 dwelling-houses—the large majority substantially built, many of two stories—ninety years ago no one but the tyrant-king was allowed to have a tiled roof, or any residence better than a hut. In all the towns, and many of the villages of the island, substantial, public buildings have been erected ; revenue offices, court-houses, hospitals and dispensaries, prisons, schools, and post and telegraph offices. A great change for the better in respect of these institutions was effected by Governors Robinson and Gregory, and still more has been done by some of their successors notably since 1896 by Governor Ridgeway.

Further evidences of the good done through a liberal and enlightened administration we find in an admirable internal postal service, made possible by the roads through which every town and village of any

---

* The Superintendent of the Census of 1901 in his Report bases an estimate on ancient records which works out a population for Ceylon of 10 million in 1301 A.D.

Social Progress in the Century. 23

consequence is served; the total number of post-offices is 340 supplemented by nearly 85 telegraph stations, there being 2,100 miles of telegraph wire in the island; while, in addition, the Postal-Telegraph Department has opened over 150 postal savings-banks in all the towns and important villages, with 50,000 to 60,000 accounts. This is apart from a long-existing Government savings bank, with about 28,000 depositors, owning deposits to the amount of perhaps four million rupees. There were about 510,000 telegraphic messages sent from Ceylon in 1901, and 22,000,000 of letters were received in and despatched from Ceylon in 1901. In the Post and Telegraph Departments altogether there are nearly 1,100 employees.

With the rise of local trade and foreign commerce, chiefly through the export of planting products, came the need of banking and exchange facilities, and the call for these led to the establishment of a local Bank nearly sixty years ago. This was superseded, however, soon after, by the Oriental Bank Corporation, which gradually secured by far the larger share of local business, so that the Ceylon branches became among the most important and profitable of this well-known Eastern bank. This gradually tempted its managers to depart from legitimate business by lending its capital too freely on planting, produce, and estates, and when this bank closed its doors in March 1884, nowhere was the shock more widely or acutely felt than in Ceylon. The effect and distrust among the natives would have been greatly aggravated were it not for the bold step taken by Governor Sir Arthur Gordon in extending an official guarantee to the bank's note issue, which eventuated in a reform long advocated by the author, namely, a Government note issue, much to the advantage of the people and the local exchequer. For, now, the circulation of Government notes approximates to fourteen millions of rupees. Nor was any loss sustained from taking up the notes of the Oriental Bank, which, in fact, ought never to have closed its doors. The gradual liquidation of its affairs showed its solvency. The New Orienta Bank Corporation, founded upon the old Bank, prospered for some years, until owing to losses in Australia, Persia, the Straits, etc., it had to close in June 1892. The plantations that fell to the Oriental Bank creditors were mainly taken over by a Limited Company, and have been worked at a profit. Ceylon credit suffered a good deal in the coffee era from plantation companies, chiefly through the "Ceylon Company, Limited," which, though so named, was really founded to take up bad business in Mauritius, where its heaviest losses were sustained.—Other banks and agencies working and generally prospering in Ceylon are those of the Mercantile Bank of India Ltd. (which as the Chartered Mercantile Bank of London, India and China, opened in Ceylon in 1854); the Bank of Madras, (dating here from 1867); the National Bank of India, from 1881 in Ceylon; and (opened in 1892 on the fall of the New Oriental Bank) the Chartered Bank of India, London and Australia, and the Hongkong and Shanghai Banking Corporation. It may be mentioned that Sir Hercules Robinson gave Ceylon, in 1872, the benefit of a decimal currency in rupees and cents of a rupee, thus placing it in advance of India, where the cumbrous subdivisions of the rupee into annas, pice, and pies still prevail; in this respect Ceylon is indeed in advance of the mother-country. Next by an Ordinance passed in 1902 gold was made legal tender at 15 rupees to the sovereign; and with reference to a scarcity of silver which resulted, a Currency Commission has been consulted as to whether we should have a Ceylon rupee as well as an increase of subsidiary coinage supplied.

We need scarcely say that, at the beginning of British rule, there was no post-office, and for many years after the service was of the most primitive, although expensive kind; nor were there police or volunteer corps in those days; but there was an army corps (infantry, artillery, and even cavalry, altogether 5,000 to 6,000 men) kept up for many years, out of all proportion to the necessities of the case. The home authorities had the idea hundred years ago that the hidden wealth* of Ceylon would enable a handsome annual subsidy to be paid to the treasury of the mother-country after all local expenses of Government were defrayed. In place of that, so long as Ceylon remained a mere military dependency, it was a dead loss to, and drain on, the imperial treasury. By degrees, however, it was seen that four British and as many native (Malay, Tamil, and Kaffir) regiments were not required, and, the force being cut down, it was decided by a Commission, appointed by the Secretary of State in 1865, that Ceylon should bear all the military expenditure within its bounds, the local force being fixed at one regiment of British infantry, one of native (the Ceylon Rifles), and one brigade of artillery, with a Major-General and staff. The Ceylon Rifles again were disbanded a few years later, in 1873. The island, therefore, has cost the Home Government very little— most years nothing at all—since 1865. On the other hand, the military force in Ceylon has been utilised very frequently for imperial and inter-colonial purposes. This will be alluded to later on, but we may mention here that Governor Gordon, in 1883, was instrumental, in view of the depression of revenue resulting from the failure of coffee, in getting the annual military contribution reduced to 600,000 rupees in place of about a million formerly paid. The smaller amount was a very fair appraisement of the responsibility of Ceylon, considering that no internal trouble beyond the capacity of the large body of police and volunteers can be feared. But with returning prosperity, through tea cultivation, to Ceylon came a renewed demand for an increased contribution, and in 1892 this was fixed at £81,000 per annum, subject to revision after 1896, and so in 1897-8, an Ordinance (No. 2 of 1898) was passed, making the contribution

* In her Pearl Fisheries, Mines and Gem-pits.

9¼ p. c. of the General Revenue, less Land Sales and Railway Charges (working expenses and interest and sinking fund)—but never to exceed three-fourths of total cost of the Garrison estimated at £151,250. The Colony is also liable for any buildings or land required by the Military outside of Trincomalee, less any land or buildings given up or not required which may be sold and a fund formed. At the same time, the charge for Volunteers, including Artillery, Light Infantry, Mounted Infantry, and Planters' Rifle Corps, or about 2,500 strong, exceeds 260,000 rupees and the total expenditure for Military exceeds two million rupees. The colony might now, so far as her own necessity is concerned, dispense with a British Regiment, though retaining a battery of Royal Artillery always in Colombo. This would save the Colony—even after doing full justice to the Local Forces—quite a million of rupees a year which would enable many very desirable important and urgent public works to be effected. At the same time a British Regiment or more could not be more conveniently stationed in the East for Imperial purposes, than in Ceylon

In no direction has more satisfactory work been done in Ceylon by the British Government than through its Medical and Educational Departments. Here are branches which give the natives a vivid idea of the superiority of English over Portuguese or Dutch rule, and, to judge by the way in which hospitals, dispensaries, and schools are made use of, it is evident that the Sinhalese and Tamils value their privileges.

Of civil, lying-in, (Lady Havelock Hospital for women), gaol, contagious diseases, and an Eye Hospital and Asylum being built (1903) at the initiation of Lady Ridgeway as a Queen Victoria Memorial, and other hospitals, with lunatic and leper and incurable asylums, and outdoor dispensaries, there are now quite 500 in the island, in or at which over a million persons are treated annually, more than three-fourths being, of course, for trifling ailments at the dispensaries. There

Social Progress in the Century.

are about 500 Colonial surgeons, assistants, health officers, vaccinators, etc., on the Government staff under the control and direction of an Inspector-General and Principal Civil Medical Officer.

In this connection, the Ceylon Medical College, founded by Sir Hercules Robinson in 1870, most heartily supported by his successor, Governor Gregory, and liberally endowed and extended by two wealthy Sinhalese gentlemen, Messrs. De Soysa and Rajapakse, and further improved by additions to the staff by Governor Ridgeway, is worthy of mention. Out of some 500 Ceylonese students entered, about 150 have qualified and obtained licences to practise medicine and surgery; about as many more are hospital assistants and dispensers; some have taken service under the Straits Government; while others have gone home to qualify for degrees of British Universities. The college has a Principal, a Registrar, and nearly a dozen lecturers with a qualified lady tutor for female students; and the Ceylonese have already shown a peculiar aptitude for the profession, surgeons of special, even of European eminence, having come from their ranks. We must mention here the good work done by the late Samuel Fisk Green, M.D., of the American Mission, in his Medical classes for native students long before the Government College was founded, and in his translation and compilation of medical text-books, treatises, etc., in Tamil. In this way 87 natives were trained as medical practitioners by Dr. Green; while his works upblish in Tamil covered 4,500 pages octavo.

In Education, generally, although there is still an immense deal to do, Ceylon is far in advance as compared with India. This has been chiefly through the agency of the several Christian Missions at work in the island which have done a noble work, more especially in female education; but Sir Hercules Robinson gave a great impetus to education by the establishment of an admirable grant-in-aid system, while Sir W. Gregory and his successors, more specially Sir West Ridgeway extended the work, multiplying especially Government vernacular schools. Latterly special attention has been given to agricultural and technical education: a Technical College and Training College has been established and in connection with Experimental Gardens (under the auspices of the separate Botanic Gardens Departments) in different parts of the country, much good is likely to be effected. The great improvements in the educational, as well as in some other special, departments of recent years, is very much owing to the employment, as their heads, of public servants with local experience, in place of importing "fresh blood," a penchant which has cost the colony a great deal up to fifteen years ago. Under the previous system a half-pay naval officer has been sent out by the Colonial Office as Director of Prisons. and an impracticable theorist as Director of Public Instruction, while other departments have similarly suffered. At present the proportion in Ceylon is one pupil to every fourteen of population; in India it is about one to every 120, while in Great Britain it is, we suppose, one to every five or six. In other words, while practically all children of school-going age are being served educationally in Great Britain, only three-fifths of those in Ceylon get some education, while two-fifths of the children get no instruction whatever at present.

Visitors always remark on the large number of the people in Ceylon, of the domestic servants especially, who understand and speak English, as compared with their experience on the continent of India. In ancient times each Buddhist temple had its pansala or school; but although such pansalas are still kept up in some low-country districts, in the Kandyan country for many years the priests have neglected their duty in teaching and other respects. They are entirely independent of the people through the endowments in land left by the Kandyan Kings, and these have in this case proved a curse instead of a blessing to the priests themselves, as well as to the people. Sir

Arthur Gordon in place of, boldly making the attempt to utilise a large portion of these "Buddhist Temporalities," hitherto worse than wasted, for popular vernacular and agricultural instruction, devised an ordinance to secure a check on the priests and lay managers; but not much result has followed and further legislation has been required. It is to be hoped that most of the property will someday be utilised by express ordinance for the benefit of the mass of the people in promoting vernacular education. Stirred-up, however, by the work of the Missionaries, the Buddhist and Hindus have of years established Colleges and Schools of their own in Colombo, Jaffna and at several outstations. In the low-country there are few temple endowments.

Educated Ceylonese are now, in many cases, finding it difficult to secure openings in life suited to their taste; the legal profession has hitherto been the most popular, it being occupied almost entirely by them as notaries, attorneys or solicitors, advocates, barristers, and even judges. In this way Sir Richard Morgan, born and educated in Ceylon, rose to be attorney-general, chief justice, and knight. In 1892 Sir Harry Dias, a Sinhalese Barrister, retired as judge of the Supreme Court after many years' service; Sir Samuel Grenier, knight, followed Sir R. Morgan to high office, and other Ceylonese fill important offices at present as Judges of the Supreme, Kandy and other Courts, Crown counsel, district judges, magistrates, leading barristers, and solicitors, as well as physicians.

The fondness of the Sinhalese for litigation is proverbial and has come down from the time of Dutch: their cases in court abound, even to disputing about the fractional part of a coconut-tree. The revival of native Village Councils (Gansabawa) by Sir Hercules Robinson, has done much to prevent litigation in the expensive law courts, with which many hundred of advocates and proctors are connected. Crim generally is represented by a daily average of about 2,500 convicted prisoners in the goals of the island, a large number being for petty thefts and assaults, but many for serious crime, through the rash use of the knife under passionate impulse. Homicides are still far too common among the Sinhalese in rural districts from this cause. Four to six times as many murders are committed every year in Ceylon—a Buddhist country!—as are committed in the United Kingdom in proportion to population. The total of convictions in all the courts is now about 30,000 a year. Not 1 per cent of these are women, the explanation being that the native women do not "drink" or 'gamble," the two chief causes of crime among the Sinhalese and Tamils. The wearing of open knives (now forbidden by law) and the habit of perjury aggravate crime among the Sinhalese. About 150 natives lose their lives annually from snake-bites and wild beasts —bears, cheetahs, elephants, buffaloes, etc.; while more than that number are killed by falling from trees— coconut palms chiefly. The cost of the administration of justice for the criminal class—police, courts, gaols, etc.—cannot be less than Rupees 2,400,000 or £160,000 per annum. A penal code after the fashion of that of India was arranged for by Sir Bruce Burnside, as Chief Justice of the island, and successfully introduced in 1885; and a Civil Procedure Code was passed in 1889. A successful system of Cart and Servants' Registration is at work, the credit of which is due to Sir G. W. R. Campbell, K.C.M.G., who also reorganised the police to take the place of the Ceylon Rifle Regiment disbanded in Governor Robinson's time.

CHAPTER IV.

LEGISLATIVE AND GENERAL IMPROVEMENTS UNDER THE RULE OF SUCCESSIVE BRITISH GOVERNORS—THE NEED OF PROMOTING CO-OPERATION AND GOOD FEELING BETWEEN DIVERSE CLASSES AND RACES.

AMONG the political and social reforms introduced into Ceylon by the British during the present century may be mentioned the abolition by the first Governor, the Hon. F. North, of torture and other barbarous punishments abhorrent to English feeling, and the relaxation during the time of his successor of the severe laws against Romanists; this was twenty years before Catholic Emancipation was granted in England. Trial by jury was first introduced by a new charter of justice in 1811; but it was not till 1844 that all caste and clan distinctions in the jury-box and all slavery were finally abolished.

A new and much improved charter of justice, the establishment of a Legislative Council with ten official to six unofficial members,* an order in Council abolishing compulsory labour, the establishment of a

---

* Sir Arthur Gordon in 1889 got the number of unofficials increased to eight, their term of office not usually to last beyond five years, so as to extend the educating process of assisting in legislation among the Ceylonese; the members are nominated by the Governor with the aid of various public bodies and opinions, through the press, to represent (1) the Low-country Sinhalese, (2) the Kandyan Sinhalese, (3) the Tamils, (4) the "Moormen" (Arab descendants, etc.), (5) the Eurasians (Burghers), (6) the Planters, (7) the Merchants, and (8) the General European community. Now the time has arrived for adding two more unofficial members and for including one or two unofficials in the Executive Council, besides generally liberalizing the Legislature after the pattern shown in India and other Dependencies.

Legislative and General Improvements.

free press, the relinquishment of the cinnamon monopoly, the institution of a Government savings-bank and the Colombo Academy, all served to mark the years between 1830 and 1840, when such enlightened Governors as Sir Robert Wilmot-Horton, and the Right Hon. J. A. Stewart-Mackenzie, administered Ceylon affairs.

During the next decade a tax on fishermen of onetithe of all the fish taken was abolished; the bonds of slavery were finally removed; great efforts were made to extend education and medical relief to the masses, and the important planting industry took its first start; a wise and most useful law for the improvement of roads, exacting six days' labour per annum, or its value, from all able-bodied males between eighteen and fifty-five years of age, was passed; the last attempt at disturbance by some of the Kandyans was quickly suppressed without the loss of a single life; the colony passed through a commercial and financial crisis, and on the ruins of the Bank of Ceylon the Oriental Bank Corporation arose.

In 1850 there was commenced in Ceylon the most successful service with carrier-pigeons ever known in connection with the press. The *Ceylon Observer* carrier-pigeons travelled regularly between Galle (the mail port) and Colombo with budgets of news, including Crimean and Indian Mutiny war news, for over seven years, till 1857, when they were superseded by the telegraph. All official connection between the British Government and Buddhism was closed in 1855, the year in which Sir Henry Ward commenced to rule, and a new impetus was given to native and European industry by useful legislation. The restoration of irrigation works, the construction of roads, the commencement of a railway, the reorganisation of the public service, the introduction of penny postage (with a halfpenny rate for newspapers), the establishment of steam navigation round the island and of telegraph communication between the principal towns, the reform of the Kandyan

THE HON. SIR ARTHUR HAMILTON GORDON, G.C.M.G
GOVERNOR OF CEYLON, 1883-1890.

THE RT. HON. SIR WILLIAM GREGORY, K.C.M.G., GOVERNOR OF CEYLON, 1872-77.

Erected by the inhabitants of the Island in front of the Colombo Museum, in commemoration of the many benefits conferred by him upon the colony during his administration of the Government.

marriage laws, and the abolition of polyandry, also marked this period.

The following decade, 1860-70, is chiefly distinguished for Governor Sir Hercules Robinson's energetic and most useful administration, with measures for the civil registration of marriages, births, and deaths, and of titles to land; the opening of the railway to Kandy; the publication by the people of Sinhalese and Tamil newspapers; the formation of the towns of Colombo, Kandy, and Galle into municipalities, with Boards composed of elected and official members; the revival of gansabhawas, or village councils; the adoption of a grant-in-aid scheme for promoting the education of the people; the abolition of export duties; the founding of the Ceylon Medical College; and the visit in 1870 of H. R. H. the Duke of Edinburgh.

The next decade in the history of Ceylon has its interest in the very prosperous, busy, and successful Government of Sir William Gregory. The first systematic census of the population was taken in 1871. Measures were adopted for the conservation of forests and for preventing the extinction of elk, deer, elephants, etc.; the registration of titles was provided for; Colombo, Kandy, and Galle were much improved, arrangements for a good water-supply to each town being made; while for the sanatorium (Nuwara Eliya) and seven other minor towns a bill was passed establishing Local Boards on the elective principle; the gansabhawas, or village councils, were improved and encouraged; an immense impetus was given to rice cultivation, 100 village tanks being repaired every year, besides larger works; the North-Central Province, in purely native interests, was formed, and the great lines of communication between the north and east were permanently opened; Anuradhapura, the ancient capital, was cleared of jungle, and rendered a healthy revenue station; gaols, hospitals, and schools were greatly improved, gaol discipline being put on a new footing;

pilgrimages on a large scale injuriously affecting public health were discouraged and practically stopped; scientific education was provided for; temperance was promoted by the reduction of the number of licences granted to grog-shops; gas lighting was introduced into Colombo; the stoppage of all payments from the revenue in aid of religion ("Disestablishment") was arranged for; the industry in the growth of new products—tea, cinchona, and cacao—took its first systematic start; an enactment dealing with service tenures in connection with temples was passed; road and railway extension were actively taken in hand; a public museum was erected and well filled at Colombo; and in 1875 H. R. H. the Prince of Wales visited the island, and laid the first stone of the Colombo Breakwater designed and constructed by Sir John Coode, and since successfully completed (in 1886) by the resident engineer, Mr. Kyle. A Northern Arm and Graving-dock for the Imperial Navy (in supersession partly of Trincomalee), as well as for commercial purposes, has been fully supported by the Admiralty, who bear half the cost. A good deal of work upon it has now been done (1903).

Soon after Sir James Longden assumed the reins of government, a period of depression, owing to the failure of coffee, set in, though in 1877-9 very large revenues were collected. A Volunteer Corps was established under Governor Longden's patronage; and the first section of the Uva railway to Nanu-oya was commenced by means of a public loan; but almost the only important work undertaken out of revenue during this Governor's rule of six years was an extensive lunatic asylum costing R600,000, and deemed beyond the requirements of the colony, being built on a scale likely rather to astonish than benefit poor rural Sinhalese lunatics, when taken from jungle huts to be lodged in brick and mortar palaces. An increase to the fixed expenditure of the Colony made in 1878 in Governor Longden's time,

COLOMBO MUSEUM.

BRIDGE OF BOATS NEAR COLOMBO, (NOW REMOVED.)

included an addition of R10,000 to his own salary.*

Sir Arthur Gordon assumed the Government of Ceylon at the end of 1883, and continued to direct affairs till the middle of 1890. A period of renewed activity in useful legislation and material improvement was eagerly anticipated; but the new Governor, indefatigable in his work, was much hampered by financial depression. Still, no less than one hundred and sixty-three ordinances were added to the local statute-book in the six years, though only a few of these were of first-class importance, and two of them—a Muhammadan (Polygamous) Marriage Registration Act, and the Buddhist Temporalities Measure—were decidedly backward steps in their conception and carrying out; but the great acts and works of this Governor are found in his persistent advocacy of Railway extension into Uva; his guaranteeing the Oriental Bank notes and so preventing a financial crisis, and his establishment of a Government note issue which is every year becoming a greater financial success, now giving an income of over R200,000 a year. Quite as noteworthy was Sir Arthur Gordon's Administration for an unprecedented expenditure on Irrigation Works, and liberal votes for roads (two hundred and sixty-one miles opened), bridges, hospitals, public instruction, and for railway extension in the lowcountry along the sea-side to Bentota. The province of Uva was created out of the Central Province in 1886, and in 1889 Sabaragamua was separated from the Western and (rather unwisely) made a new province. The Colombo Breakwater, on Sir John Coode's admirable design, was completed, and the Harbour has since been fully utilised as the great steamer-calling and coaling port of the East.

A failure appertaining to Sir Arthur Gordon was in not promoting and cementing that good feeling be-

* Making the salary of the Governor of Ceylon R80,000 per annum. Rather a contrast to that of the Dutch Governors, which was £30 per month (besides rations and allowances), but then they were expected to make a fortune in other, not to say corrupt and secret, ways!

tween the governing and governed classes, and especially between the different races and ranks, embraced in the very varied community of Ceylon, which Sir William Gregory, above all his predecessors, was successful in fostering. In the time of the latter Governor, Europeans, Burghers (European descendants), and natives, co-operated more cordially, and supported the Government more trustfully, than at any period before or since. His successor (Sir James Longden) was too antiquated and sleepy in his ideas to promote this desirable state of feeling, or any other movement beyond the bounds of red-tape official routine ; while Governor Gordon, by his favour of ceremonial supported by high-caste natives and by ill-judged special patronage of Buddhist priests at his levees, etc., created distrust, and undid much of the good effected during 1872-77. A frank, genial, straightforward administrator, free of all official prejudice or predilection for outward ("caste") show, recognising merit wherever it is to be found, and good work for the benefit of the body-politic, no matter by whom promoted, has nowhere a more encouraging or fruitful field to work in than Ceylon, and this is why, as has often been said, a governor, straight from "the free air of the British House of Commons," generally proves a bright success, socially if not administratively, in this first and most important of Crown Colonies. It may not be known to people in England, interested in our tropical dependencies, how much evil cliques—official and otherwise—promoted to some extent by "club" life, are working, and are likely still further to work, in India and Ceylon. The Englishman carries his "club" with him—it has been said—wherever he goes, and has the undoubted right to do so; but it is a question whether in Crown dependencies, "public servants," not excluding the King's Representative, drawing their salaries and pensions from taxes paid by the people at large, have the right to patronise clubs which practically exclude His Majesty's native-born subjects, without exception, no matter what their merit or degree ;* and still more whether occult influences should dictate (through aide-de-camps and private secretaries) who are to be honoured, if not received at "Queen's House." It was to the credit of Sir William Gregory that he never allowed himself to be restricted by the sneers of would-be colonial "society" dictators, but sought out and marked by his attentions merit and good work, wherever he found them. In this way Sinhalese, Tamils, and Burghers (and not merely a few "high caste" families favoured by narrow-minded officials) found their industry and integrity noticed by the Governor, who again had at his table, as honoured guests, the heads and chief workers in the various Missions and principal Educational Institutions, whether Christian or secular, Hindu or Buddhist, showing his personal interest in every thing or person calculated to advance the colony and people committed to his care by Her Most Gracious Majesty the Queen. This was following the example of such Governors as Sir Robert Brownrigg, Sir R. Wilmot Horton and Sir Stewart Mackenzie in earlier years.

Sir Arthur Gordon's Administration was marked by one very notable event in the Queen's Jubilee, which was fittingly observed with due ceremonial in June 1887 (as fully related in the 1893 edition of this book). The death, early in 1889, of Lady Gordon, universally esteemed as she was, excited deep regret in the Colony. The "Gordon Gardens," inaugurated in the Fort Ward, Colombo, will keep alive the memory of Sir Arthur and Lady Hamilton Gordon in Ceylon for many years to come.

Sir Arthur Elibank Havelock, K.C.M.G., succeeded to the Government of Ceylon in May 1890, and while

---

* This was written in 1887, and since then (1891-92) some of the chief authorities in India have expressed views similar to the above in respect of public servants and institutions which are regulated by distinctions of race.

38 Legislative and General Improvements.

continuing the active beneficial policy of his predecessor in respect of Railway extension and other desirable public works His Excellency, after a few months' experience, chose to recommend the abolition of the "Paddy" rent or tax, the only branch of Land Revenue in the island. Unfortunately, this levy on rice cultivation was removed without touching the corresponding Customs duty on imported rice, so establishing Protection in its worst form. This abolition was given effect to by Lord Knutsford as Secretary of State, in opposition to the opinion of nearly the whole Civil Service and four previous Governors of Ceylon, the last of whom, Sir Arthur Gordon, had prepared the way for the removal of all the obnoxious features of the Paddy tax without destroying the just principle of an internal rice levy balancing the Customs duty. So that since 1892, a large proportion—from three-eighths to one-half— of the population have been eating rice free of tax, while the majority including the estate coolies, some of the poorest of our public in the towns and villages, pay 10 per cent *ad valorem*; and this arrangement was approved of by the Cobden Club.

In 1891 it was estimated there were from 1,500 to 2,000 lepers in Ceylon; but Dr. Jonathan Hutchinson's "bad fish" theory is not generally accepted by local medical men. The sanction of Railway Extension to Bandarawela was received this year. The Colony made a great show in the Chicago Universal Exhibition in 1892. The death in London of Sir Wm. Gregory, as also in 1893 of Sir C. P. Layard, senr., were greatly regretted. The evil of the Government system of licensing opium and bhang shops led to a memorable public meeting supported by representatives of all races in October 1893, eventuating in the most numerously signed Memorial ever seen in Ceylon, 28,000 persons all writing their own names calling for restrictions. Afterwards in 1897, Sir West Ridgeway granted a Commission of Enquiry, and this led to legislation of a repressive character—forbidding

Ceylon in 1903.

the importation of bhang and doubling the customs duty on opium, but still maintaining licensed opium shops, through which local consumption rapidly increased; and it became evident that the same regulations as in England should apply in Ceylon for a people who never used opium until within the past 50 years of British rule. The Railway Extension to Kurunegala was opened on 14th February, and of the Bandarawela section on 3rd September, 1894. Active operations towards the construction of Northern Breakwaters for Colombo Harbour were begun this season. Early in 1895 the foundation was laid of the "Lady Havelock Hospital for Women" and the opening of the Victoria Bridge over the Kelani river in May and the occupation of the new General Post and Telegraph Office in August, were two notable events in 1895. Sir Arthur Havelock's term of Government ceased in September and Sir J. West Ridgeway arrived in the succeeding February.

The Administration of 1896-1903 is the subject of a special closing chapter; but we may mention a few of the principal events here. Lady Ridgeway opened the new Hospital for Women on October 12th, 1896, and the foundation of a Kandy Girls' Industrial School and Home was laid in November, while the "Ridgeway Golf Links" in Colombo were inaugurated in Dec. The Bubonic Plague in Bombay occupied much attention and a Commission was appointed early in 1897. Mr. Mansergh, ex-President of the Institute of C. E., arrived in January to report on Colombo Drainage; the first volume of Mr. Justice Laurie's "Gazetteer of the Central Province" appeared; and the construction of a Graving Dock at Colombo to cost £318,000—divided between Ceylon and the Admiralty—was settled. In April a paper by Mr. J. Ferguson on a proposed Railway to connect India and Ceylon was read before the London Chamber of Commerce; and it was afterwards read before the Imperial Institute in April 1898. The despatch of an

Legislative and General Improvemets.

Address to the Queen-Empress and the celebration of the Diamond Jubilee occupied much attention in June. The establishment of two Russian Firms in Colombo in March 1898, opened a new era in the trade in Ceylon tea for Russia. A Commission to consider an Agricultural Department for Ceylon resulted in a Mycologist, Entomologist, advising Analytical Chemist, and Experimental Station Curator being added to the Royal Botanic Gardens' Staff, Peradeniya, and besides useful Circulars, the publication of quarterly "Annals of the Royal Botanic Gardens, Peradeniya," was commenced. Later on a Mineralogist or Geologist was appointed and Dr. Willey, F.R.S., becoming Director of the Colombo Museum (in May 1902) soon began the issue of a quarterly entitled "Spolia Zeylanica." The cultivation of India-rubber secured much attention from 1899 onwards. The Centenary of the Church Mission was celebrated in April. Preparation for the Ceylon Court at the Paris Exhibition and the War in South Africa occupied attention. A Lecture on "Ceylon" before the Royal Colonial Institute and on "Old Colombo" before the Society of Arts, both in November, by Mr. J. Ferguson, attracted attention. The first Ceylon Contingent was despatched to South Africa for the War, February 1st, 1900. The opening of the Planters' Victoria Commemoration Buildings, including "Ferguson Memorial Hall" and "George Wall Library and Tower," took place on February 17th. Boer prisoners, eventually numbering close on 6,000, arrive at Diyatalawa from August onwards. The first public sale of Green Tea in Colombo took place in October; and the Ceylon Relief Fund for the Indian Famine closed at about R210,000. Memorial services in connection with the death of the Queen-Empress took place in January-February 1901; while the visit of the Prince and Princess of Wales in April excited much enthusiasm. Appointment of a Fourth Judge to the Supreme Court was sanctioned in August. Last of the Egyptian

LANDING JETTY AT POINT-DE-GALLE

KANDY—LAKE AND TOWN.

"THE PAVILION" (GOVERNOR'S RESIDENCE) KANDY.

Exiles was pardoned and Arabi Pasha and family allowed to return to Egypt, September 1901. The gold sovereign was declared legal tender in Ceylon at R15 in October; and a Commission appointed to enquire into "Incidence of Taxation" in November. In January 1902, arrived Professor Herdman, F.R.S., invited by Governor Ridgeway, to investigate our Pearl-oyster fisheries and advise as to conservation and culture of the oysters. Governor Ridgeway opened the first section of the Jaffna Railway on March 10th, and on 17th presided at a Public Meeting in the Council Chamber to promote an Eye Hospital and Blind Asylum as memorials to Queen Victoria. A second Contingent of 100 infantry for South Africa left April 22nd. Dr. Copleston, Bishop of Colombo, was transferred to Calcutta as Metropolitan Bishop in May 1902, and his brother, the Rev. E. A. Copleston, was consecrated as his successor in the Bishopric of Colombo, 30th August 1903. The first section of the Kelani Valley, and second section of Jaffna Railway were opened on September 15th, 1902. An extension by the Secretary of State of the term of office of Sir West Ridgeway till October 1903 gave general satisfaction. On 8th May, 1903, a meeting of the Legislative Council took place for the first time in the Pavilion, Kandy: and in March the Governor accompanied by his Executive and Legislative Councillors and staff together with Lord Crewe and several visitors, inspected the Pearl Fishery in progress at Madawachchi, and then went on to Paumben and Tataparai Cooly Immigration Depôts. Some important public matters were dealt with in the Legislative Council in June and July and it was determined to send an invitation to the British Association to visit Colombo in 1907 or 1908. The foundation-stone of the Victoria Memorial Eye Hospital was laid by Lady Ridgeway (who had initiated the Memorial) on 6th August. The railway to Nuwara Eliya was opened for goods in August and for passengers a little later. The railway to Yatiyantota

F

42 *Legislative and General Improvements.*

was opened by the Governor in September. In an elaborate state document Sir West Ridgeway reviewed his Administration in opening the Legislative Council in October; and in November he gave up the reins of Government and returned to Europe. Handsome farewell souvenirs were presented to Lady Ridgeway by the ladies of the Ceylonese and European communities.

It is interesting to compare the Revenue, Expenditure, Public Debt incurred, and Sale of Crown Lands under successive governors. The periods of activity and energetic administration were those of Governors Ward, Robinson, Gregory, and Gordon. The returns are as follows :—

REVENUE AND DEBT FOR SUCCESSIVE GOVERNORS.

	Annual Revenue.		Public Debt.
	Minimum.	Maximum.	Imposed.
	£	£	
1850-54 Sir G. Anderson	408,000	429,000	—
1855-60 Sir H. Ward	476,000	767,000	—
1861-65 Sir C. MacCarthy	752,000	978,000	£800,000
1866-71 Sir H. Robinson	925,000	1,124,000	250,000
1872-76 Sir W. Gregory	1,174,000	1,467,000	600,000
1877-82 Sir J. Longden	1,216,000	1,702,000	1,250,000
1883-89 Sir A. Gordon	1,240,000	1,540,000	750,000
1890-95 Sir A. E. Havelock	1,529,988	2,098,281	1,750,000
1896-03 Sir W. Ridgeway	2,197,457	2,843,516	1,400,000

Here more particularly is the total amount of revenue received within each administration :—

TOTAL REVENUE COLLECTED BY SUCCESSIVE GOVERNORS.

	R.
Sir Henry Ward (1854-60)	30,600,000
Sir Hercules Robinson (1865-71)	60,400,000
Sir Wm. Gregory (1872-77)	80.750,000
Sir Jas. Longden (1878-83)	85,619,310
Sir Arthur Gordon (1884-89)	79,668,991
Sir A. E. Havelock (1890-95)	127,449,505
Sir J. W. Ridgeway (1896-1903)	206,275,475

Here, finally, is how the alienation of CROWN LANDS, under successive Governors, compares :—

	Acres	£	Average. Per Acre.
Governor Sir H. Ward in six years, 1855 to 1860, sold	111,596 for 199,884		1 15 9¾
Governor Sir Charles MacCarthy and General O'Brien in five years, 1861 to 1865, sold	156,893 for 3C7,117		1 19 1¾
Governor Sir Hercules Robinson in six years, 1866 to 1871, sold	226,926 for 341,562		1 10 1
Governor Rt. Hon. Sir W. H. Gregory in six years, 1872 to 1877 sold	269,905 for 612,036		2 5 4
Governor Sir Jas. Longden in six years, 1878 to 1883 sold,	148,836 for 375,395		2 10 5¼
Governor Sir Arthur Gordon in 1884-89, sold	114,828 for 217,911		1 18 0
Governor Sir A. E. Havelock in six years. 1890-5 sold	87,327 for 231,041		2 12 11
Governor Sir J. West Ridgeway in seven years, 1896-1902 sold	185,313 for 408,526		2 4 1
Total: acres	£1,301,624	£2,693,832	£2 0 6½

CHAPTER V.

NATIVE AGRICULTURAL AND MANUFACTURING INTERESTS.

Paddy (Rice) Cultivation—Cinnamon—Coconut, Palmyra, Kitul, Arecanut, and other Palms—Essential Oils—Tobacco—Cotton—Sugarcane—Other Fruit-trees and Vegetables—Natural Pasture—Local Manufactures.

WHETHER or not Ceylon was in ancient times the granary of South-Eastern Asia, certain it is that long before the Portuguese or Dutch, not to speak of the British, era, that condition had lapsed, and so far from the island having a surplus of food products, the British, like their European predecessors, had to import a certain quantity of rice from Southern India to feed their troops and the population of the capital and other chief towns.* There can be no doubt as to the large quantity of rice which could be grown around the network of tanks in the north and east, which have been lying for centuries broken and unused in the midst of unoccupied territory, and are now being gradually restored with a Railway, shortly to be opened from Kurunegala to Jaffna, under the enlightened policy of Sir West Ridgeway, as sanctioned by Mr. Chamberlain.

Driven from the northern plains by the conquering Tamils, the Sinhalese, taking refuge in the mountain zone more to the south and west, found a country in many respects less suited for rice than for fruit and root culture; but yet, under British

* Old Sinhalese records show that rice was imported into Ceylon from the Coromandel Coast in the second century before Christ.

as under native rule, *rice* or *paddy-growing* continues to be the one most general and favourite occupation of the Sinhalese people, as indeed it is of the Ceylon Tamils in the north and east of the island. Agriculture, in their opinion, is the most honourable of callings; and although in many districts fruit and root— that is, garden—culture would prove more profitable, yet the paddy field is more generally popular.

Nowhere in Ceylon are there tracts of alluvial lands so extensive as those which mark the banks and deltas of rivers in India, and the average return of rice per acre in Ceylon, under the most favourable circumstances, is considerably below the Indian average. It was the opinion of one of the most experienced of Ceylon civil servants—Sir Charles P. Layard, who served in the island from 1829 to 1879— that the "cultivation of paddy is now the least profitable pursuit to which a native can apply himself; it is persevered in from habit, and because the value of time and labour never enters into his calculations." This view has since been contested (in 1885) by an experienced revenue officer, Mr. E. Elliott, who shows that rice cultivation is fairly profitable; but his calculations refer chiefly to select districts, rather than to the island generally. In some parts of the Western, in the Matara division of the Southern, and in the Batticaloa district of the Eastern provinces, profitable rice fields may be the rule, and large crops are also grown under irrigation in the North-Central Province; but an experiment made under European auspices during recent years near Tangalla in the South has not been a success. On the principle, therefore, of buying in the cheapest and selling in the dearest market, it would appear that many of the rice cultivators in Ceylon could more profitably turn their attention to plantation and garden products, such as coconuts, areca or betel-nuts, pepper, cinnamon, nutmeg, cacao, tea, cardamoms, and fruits of all tropical kinds (putting tea on one side for the present)

46 Native Agricultural & Manufacturing Interest.

then, selling the produce to advantage, they could buy rice from southern and northern India and Burmah more cheaply than they can produce it. But it is impossible, even if it were politic—which we doubt—to revolutionise the habits of a very conservative people in this way; and, therefore, so soon as the sale of forest land to planters, and the introduction of capital for the planting enterprise, put the Government in possession of surplus revenue, Sir Henry Ward acted wisely in turning his attention to the restoration and repair of such irrigation works in the neighbourhood of population as he felt would at once be utilised for the increased production of grain. In this way he changed a large extent of waste land into an expanse of perennial rice culture, for the benefit of the industrious Mohammedans and Hindus of the Batticaloa district in the Eastern Province. Similarly, he spent large sums for the benefit of the Sinhalese rice cultivators in the southern districts.

Sir Hercules Robinson conceived a statesmanlike law, by which expenditure on irrigation works, chiefly village tanks, on terms far more liberal to the people than any offered in India, formed a part of the annual budget. Most cordially was this policy supported by his successor, Sir William Gregory, who, moreover, entered on an undertaking of greater magnitude than any previously recorded in British times: namely, the formation of a new province around the ancient capital of Ceylon, and the restoration of tanks and completion of roads and bridges within its bounds, sufficient to give the sparse Sinhalese population every advantage in making a start in the race of prosperity. At a considerable expenditure, spread over four or five years, this was accomplished, and a population of of some 60,000 Sinhalese and Tamils were thereby more directly benefited than they had been by any of their rulers, native or European, for several centuries back. Curiously enough, not the Sinhalese but the Tamils— who have been called " the Scotchmen of the East," from their enterprise in migrating and colonising —have been taking chief advantage of the expenditure in this north-central region—an expenditure continued by Governor Longden, and to a still more marked degree by Governor Gordon, who entered on very large and important works in restoring the Kalawewa and Yodi-ela Irrigation tanks and channels. The formation of a permanent Irrigation Board for the colony, with a settled income in a proportion of the land revenue, was another step of the last mentioned governor in the interests of rice culture—commendable so long as the Paddy tax was continued, but quite indefensible in the form adopted by Governor Havelock, who having no land revenue, takes his Irrigation votes out of the Customs duty paid chiefly by townspeople and plantation coolies. More justifiable is the course adopted by Sir West Ridgeway, by order of Mr. Chamberlain, of spending by degrees R500,000 on Irrigation Tanks, out of a public loan partly to be covered by surplus revenue. The amount expended on Irrigation Works during the thirty-six years, 1867 to 1903, the end of Sir West Ridgeway's term of government, is nearly as follows:—

SPENT ON IRRIGATION WORKS BY GOVERNORS.

Sir H. Robinson	1867-71	R630,921
Sir W. Gregory	1872 77	R1,650,944
Sir J. Longden	1878-83	R1,379,947
Sir A. Gordon	1884-90	R3,200,000
Sir A. Havelock	1891-95	R2,012,283
Sir West Ridgeway	1896-1903	R4,162,990
	Total in 36 years	R13,037,085

Before its abolition, Governor Gordon expended all the net proceeds of the Paddy rent or tax on Irrigation Works. Special encouragement to other branches of agriculture in certain districts would do much good; and this is what Governor Ridgeway has aimed at, as may be seen further on. Revenue officers should establish annual district Agricultural Shows for produce and stock, with suitable prizes.

The effect of the liberal policy above described, of successive governors, from Sir Henry Ward on to Sir

48 Native Agricultural & Manufacturing Interest.

West Ridgeway, has undoubtedly been to bring a far larger area under grain cultivation now than was the case at the beginning of the century, but it is impossible, in the absence of a cadastral survey, to give the exact extent. This is, however, now being carried out, thanks to our present Governor's enlightened policy.

It is estimated that there are now 620,000 acres under rice or paddy, and about 120,000 under dry grain, Indian corn, and other cereals. And the striking fact is that, so far from the import of grain decreasing as the local production has extended, the reverse has been the case. In this, however, is seen the influence of the expanding planting enterprise: sixty years ago, when coffee planting was just beginning in Ceylon, the total quantity of grain required from India was an annual import of 650,000 bushels; now, it is as high as between nine and ten million bushels. The import in 1877, the year of the Madras famine, when Ceylon planters had to provide for 170,000 fugitives from Southern India, besides their usual coolie labour force, amounted to 6,800,000 bushels; but in 1900, with an increased population, it was 9,600,000 bushels.

The disposal of the increasing local production simultaneously with these imports is explained by the rapidly increased population in the rural districts, and the much larger quantity of food consumed in a time of prosperity. In the early part of the century the average Sinhalese countryman consumed, probably, only half the quantity of rice (supplemented by fruit and vegetables) which he is now able to afford. Our calculation is that about two-fifths of the grain constmed is locally produced against three-fifths imported.*

Turning from the main staple of native agriculture to garden produce, we have to note that, while the Dutch

---

* For further information see paper on "Food Supply of Ceylon," by the author, in 'Ferguson's Ceylon Handbook and Directory " and also papers on "Grain Taxation in Ceylon," quoted by Sir William Gregory in despatches to Earl Carnarvon.

PEELING THE STICKS.

STRETCHING THE CINNAMON BARK.

CLEANING THE CINNAMON ON BOARDS.

CUTTING THE CINNAMON INTO LENGTHS.

A CINNAMON DRYING GROUND.

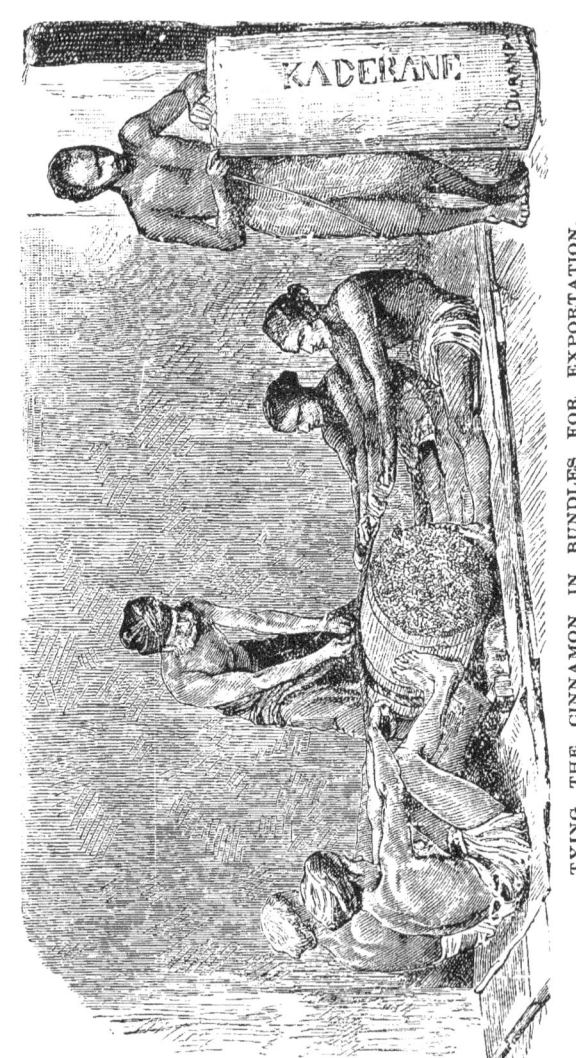

TYING THE CINNAMON IN BUNDLES FOR EXPORTATION.

CUTTING CINNAMON STICKS.

TAMIL GRASS-CUTTER.

monopolies in cinnamon, pepper, etc., were probably worked at a loss to the Government, even with forced labour at their command, the export of the cinnamon spice was insignificant as compared with what it has become under the free British system. There can be no doubt that Ceylon *cinnamon* is the finest in the world, celebrated from the middle of the fourteenth century according to authentic records, and one of the few products of importance indigenous to the island. It was known through Arab caravans to the Romans, who paid in Rome the equivalent of £8 sterling per pound for the fragrant spice. Ceylon (called by De Barras the " mother of cinnamon") has, therefore, well earned the name " Cinnamon Isle," whatever may be said of its " spicy breezes," a term originally applied by Bishop Heber, in his well-known hymn, to Java rather than to Ceylon. The maximum export, attained by the Dutch was in 1738, when 600,000 lb., valued at from 8s. 4d. to 17s. 8d. per lb., was sent to India, Persia, and Europe from Ceylon. In the commercial season, 1881-82, Ceylon sent into the markets of the world, almost entirely through London, as much as 1,600,000 lb. of cinnamon quill bark, and nearly 400,000 lb. of chips, the finest bark being purchasable at the London sales for from 2s. 6d. to 3s. per lb.; while in season 1885-86 the export was 1,630,000 lb. quill and 550,000 lb. of chips, and the price had fallen almost 50 per cent, in six years. In 1902, the export of cinnamon was as high as 2,555,313 lb. in bales and 1,763,679 lbs. in chips, but the London price is so low as to leave only a small margin for the cultivator. The above quantity is yielded by an area of about 45,000 acres, cultivated entirely, and almost entirely owned, by the people of Ceylon.

Of far greater importance now to the people, as well as to the export trade of the island, is its *Palm cultivation*, which has enormously extended since the time of the Dutch, especially in the maritime districts. European capital has done much in turning waste land into coconut plantations; but there is, also, no more favourite mode of investment for the native mercantile, trading, and industrial classes of the people (Sinhalese and Tamils), who have greatly increased in wealth during the past sixty years, than in gardens and estates of coconuts, arecas, palmyras, and other palms and fruit trees. Within the Dutch and British periods a great portion of the coastline of Ceylon (on the west, south, and east), for a breadth varying from a quarter of a mile to several miles, and extending to a length of 150 miles, has been planted with coconut palms. Afterwards in British times, a great extension of planting took place on the coast of the North-Western Province, and in the nothern and eastern coast districts. Then, thirty to forty years ago, attention in Colombo was turned to inland districts, such as the delta of the Maha-oya (river), and these have been planted with coconuts as far as thirty to forty miles from the coast. More recently, a great deal of coconut cultivation has taken place from Madampe and Chilaw to Puttalam on the north-west, and around Anuradhapura in the North-Central Province, where there are now several hundreds of thousands of palms planted, nearly half of them in bearing, thanks very much to Mr. Ievers' energetic encouragement of native agriculture in all forms; while Sir West Ridgeway's term is distinguished by the opening of a quite new coconut district at Tirukovil in south Batticaloa where 5,000 acres have been planted. In the Jaffna peninsula, the natives have chiefly planted the equally useful palmyra. One or two palms, together with a little rice and a piece of cotton cloth, are capable supplying most of the wants of a family.

It has been commonly remarked that the uses of the coconut palm * are as numerous as the days of the year. Percival, early in this century, relates that a small

---

* See "All about the Coconut Palm," published by A. M. & J. Ferguson, Colombo.

COCONUT AND ARECA PALMS.

A STONE CAVE OR RICE FEEDING RECEPTACLE,
Built of Granite Slabs 62 ft. 9 in. by 4 ft. 4 in. Inside.

ship from the Maldive Islands arrived at Galle which was entirely built, rigged, provisioned, and laden with the produce of the coco-palm.* Food, drink, domestic utensils, materials for building and thatching, wine, sugar, and oil are amongst the many gifts to man of these munificent trees. Unlike the other trade staples (tea, cacao, rubber, cinchona bark, and cinnamon) by far the largest proportion of the products of the cocounut palm—nuts, oil, arrack (intoxicating spirit), leaves for thatch, fences, mats and baskets, timber, etc.—are locally utilised.

Arrack (in varying quantities, according the demand in the Madras Presidency) is exported, but the export is not to be compared with the large local consumption, which unfortunately increases with the increasing wealth of the people. The British are blamed for regulating and protecting the arrack and liquor traffic, but the consumption was pretty general before the British came to Ceylon. It is evident, though, that here taverns have been too freely established—and still worse, under the "renting" system, illicit selling of arrack, winked at—and the Ceylon authorities should take a leaf out of the Dutch policy in Java, where the consumption of intoxicating liquors among natives is very rigidly restricted. Our calculation is that 9 to 10 millions of rupees are spent by the people of Ceylon on intoxicants, against not much more than a fifth of this amount devoted to education by the people, missions, and the Government. Legislation to place the sale of such drugs as opium under the same restrictions as in England, is urgently required in Ceylon. A good many millions of coconuts are annually exported, but the chief trade is in coir fibre from the husk, and still

---

* The food value of the coconut is not generally understood: some years back the crew of a wrecked vessel cast away on a South Sea island subsisted for several months on no other food than coconuts and broiled fish, and added to their weight in that time.

52 Native Agricultural & Manufacturing Interests.

more in the oil expressed from the kernel of the nut, used in Europe as a lubricator, for soap-making, and dressing cloths, and (partially) for candle-making and lighting purposes: African palm oil and petroleum are its great rivals. The maximum value of the products of coconut palm exported may be taken at about the following figures: oil, £500,000; coir, £15,000; arrack, £2,000; "copra" (the dried kernel sent to Europe to be expressed), £260,000; "poonac" (the refuse of the oil, or oil-cake, used for cattle food), £50,000; nuts, £50,000; miscellaneous products, £5,000; making a total of over £1,000,000; while the value of produce locally consumed must be nearly one and a half million sterling per annum, and the market value of the area covered with coconuts rather over than under fifteen millions sterling. The local use of coconuts is sure to increase with railway extension and the development of the interior of the island. There are perhaps fifty millions of coconut palms cultivated in Ceylon, covering about 650,000 acres, all but about 100,000 acres being owned by natives themselves. The annual yield of nuts cannot be much under 1,000 millions, allowing for trees devoted to "arrack," the sap being collected to ferment into the spirit rather than allowed to form fruit. The largest oil-expressing mills in the world are in Colombo with splendid hydraulic presses. There are nearly 2,000 native oil-crushers driven by bullocks, apart from steam establishments in Colombo, Negombo, etc., owned by natives as well as Europeans, while the preparation of the fibre affords occupation to a large number of the people. A new industry of recent years is desiccating coconut for confectionery purposes, and 50 million nuts are now annually used in about a dozen mills to prepare 16 millions lb. of the desiccated product exported to Europe, America, Australia, etc.

After the coconut tree, the palmyra (*Borassus flabelliformis*) has been regarded as the richest plant in the

East. Both require from eight to twelve years to come into bearing, but they are supposed to live from 150 to 300 years.* By many the palmyra is thought a richer tree than the coconut, and it is especially adapted to the drier regions of the north and east of the island. It is estimated there are eight millions of palmyras owned by the people in the Jaffna peninsula, the edible products of which supply one-fourth of the food of 300,000 inhabitants. The Tamil poets describe 800 different purposes to which the palmyra can be applied, and their proverb says "it lives for a lac † of years after planting, and lasts for a lac of years when felled." The timber is prized for house-building purposes, especially for rafters, being hard and durable. Besides there being a large local consumption, as much as £8,000 worth is sometimes annually exported from Ceylon; while of jaggery sugar about 20,000 cwt. are made and there is also a fibre got from this palm, the cultilvation of which covers 40,000 acres, yielding perhaps over a hundred millions of nuts annually; this nut is much smaller than the coconut. The cultivation of the palmyra by the natives or by prison labour under Government auspices on the sandy wastes in the north, north-west, and south-east of the island has been strongly advocated: it is very easy and inexpensive; an outlay of fourteen rupees per acre for ten years would be sufficient, and then the jaggery would begin to yield returns. A beginning has been made in the Hambantota district and the North-Central Province.

The kitul or jaggery palm (*Caryota urens*), known also as the bastard sago, is another very valuable tree common in Ceylon. Jaggery sugar and toddy wine are prepared from the sap, the best trees yielding 100 pints of sap in twenty-four hours. Sago is manufactured from the pith, and fibre from the

---
* See William Ferguson's Monograph on "The Palmyra Palm."
† A lac or lakh equals 100,000.

leaves for fishing-lines and bow-strings, the fibre from the leaf-stalks being made into rope for tying wild elephants. Of the fibre, from £3,000 to £7,000 value is exported annually; of the jaggery sugar, £2,000 worth. The quantity used in the country is very great. This palm is found round every Kandyan's hut; indeed it has been said by Emerson Tennent that a single tree in Ambagamuwa district afforded the support of a Kandyan, his wife, and children. The area covered is, perhaps, equal to 30,000 acres. The trunk timber is used for rafters, being hard and durable.

The cultivation of the *Areca catechu* (which is compared to "an arrow shot from heaven" by the Hindu poets) was always one of the chief sources of the Ceylon trade in ante-British times. In the Portuguese era great quantities of the nuts were exported, and these formed the chief medium of exchange for the proportion of grain which the natives of Ceylon have for centuries drawn from Southern India. The Dutch esteemed the areca-nut a very great source of revenue, and they made an exclusive trade of it. They exported yearly about 35,000 cwt. About the same quantity was annually shipped between 1806 and 1813. Twenty years as many as 150,000 cwt. of nuts were shipped in one year; but latterly 100,000 cwt. is the maximum. The export is almost entirely to Southern India. An areca-nut tree requires six years to come into full bearing. It grows all over the low-country and in the hills up to an elevation above sea-level of between 2,000 and 3,000 feet. Some coffee estate proprietors around Kandy in the early days planted areca-nuts along their boundaries, thereby forming a capital division line, and the cultivation has anew attracted the attention of colonists in recent years, especially in the Matale and Udagama districts. The chief areca gardens owned by natives are, however, to be found in the Kegalla district. The home consump-

Ceylon in 1903.

tion is very large, and the area covered by the palm must be equal to 70,000 acres. The annual value of the exports of areca-nut produce is from £60,000 to £100,000.

There are numerous other palms, more especially the magnificent talipot *(Corypha umbraculifera)*, which flowers once (a grand crown of cream-coloured, wheat-like blossom twenty feet high) after sixty or eighty years, and then dies, and which is freely used for native huts, umbrellas, books, etc.; the heart also being, like that of the sago palm, good for human food.

The bread-fruit tree, the jak, orange, and mango, as well as gardens of plantains and pine-apples, melons, guavas, papaws, etc., might be mentioned among products cultivated and of great use to the people of Ceylon ; in fact, there is scarcely a native land-owner or cultivator in the country who does not possess a garden of palms or other fruit trees, besides paddy fields. The total area cultivated with palms and fruit trees cannot be less than from 1,000,000 to 1,100,000 acres (in addition to 100,000 acres under garden vegetables, yams, sweet and ordinary potatoes, roots, cassava, etc.); and although by far the major portion, perhaps four-fifths, of the produce is consumed by the people, yet the annual value of the export trade in its various forms, from this source, averages well over a million sterling, against less than £90,000 at the beginning of the century. Among food products recently added to the list of easily grown fruits and vegetables, are the tree-tomato, chocho, a parsnip, and a small yam, all introduced from the West Indies, and already very popular with the Sinhalese, especially of the Uva Province. Mr. Nock, of the Hakgala Gardens, has also introduced several new English varieties of potatoes and other vegetables. Agricultural Schools and the Experimental Station—all established by Sir West Ridgeway—are sure to benefit the native horticulture and agriculture.

Besides coconut oil, there is an export of essential oils expressed from citronella and lemon-grass, from

56 Native Agricultural & Manufacturing Interests.

cinnamon and cinnamon leaf, which, valued at £25,000 to £30,000, is of some importance to a section of the community.

Of more importance to the people is their tobacco, of which about 25,000 acres are cultivated, the greater part of the crop being consumed locally, though as much as 50,000 cwt. of unmanufactured leaf, valued at £150,000, have been exported to India, in one year. Of late years European planters have given some attention to the cultivation of tobacco, as well as cotton, but without much success.

The natives have always grown a little cotton in certain districts, and at one time a good deal of cotton cloth was manufactured at Batticaloa, but the industry has almost entirely ceased, being driven out by the cheapness of Manchester goods. The establishment of cotton mills at Colombo, and the consequent local demand for the raw material, gave an impetus for a time to the cutivation of the plant, and a good deal was done by the late Dr. Trimen and the District Agents of Government to encourage the natives in cotton-growing 10 years ago. Now (in 1903) the Government has begun experiments in its gardens with special cotton seed, and Mr. Willis, the present director, is hopeful of seeing a successful industry follow along the Northern Railway. A new industry which has sprung up of recent years, however, is the collection of the short-stapled cotton from the pods of the silk-cotton tree (*Bombax Malabaricum*), exported under the name of "Kapok' (a Malay term) to Australia and Europe, to stuff chairs, mattresses, etc. As much as 2,000 cwt., worth £3,000, is exported of late years. A small quantity of this tree cotton was annually exported from Ceylon so a r back as the time of the Portuguese.

Sugar-cane is largely grown in native gardens for use as a vegetable, the cane being sold in the bazaars, and the pith eaten as the stalk of a cabbage would be. At one time the eastern and southern districts of the island were thought to be admirably adapted for systematic sugar cultivation ; but after plantations on an extensive scale had been opened by experienced colonists and a large amount of capital sunk, it was found that, while the cane grew luxuriantly, the moist climate and soil did not permit of the sap crystallising or yielding a sufficiency of crystallisable material There is, however, still one plantation and manufactory of sugar and molasses in European hands, near Galle.

Before leaving the branches of agriculture more particulary in native hands, we may refer to the large expanse of patana grass and natural pasturage, especially in the Uva and eastern districts, which is utilised by the Sinhalese for their cattle, a certain number of which supply the meat consumed in the Central Province. By far the greater portion, however, of the beef and mutton required in the large towns of the island is (like rice, flour, potatoes, and other food requisites) imported in the shape of cattle and sheep, to the value of £100,000, from India. In some years the return has been over £140,000, but that was chiefly through the demand for Indian bullocks for draught purposes. There is no doubt scope for the energy of the people of Ceylon to meet the local demand for such food supplies, although the natural pasturage is, as a rule, rather poor. But this difficulty can be met by the cultivation of other grasses. Guinea and Mauritius grass, which grow freely with a little attention, are some of the best fodder grasses in the world and are easily cultivated in Ceylon. At high elevations, the "prairie grass" (of Australia) is successfully grown. Stock-raising experiments along the Northern Railway have been urged of late and a dairy farm in Colombo and pony-breeding establishment in the island of Delft are steps in the right direction by Government.

H

58 *Native Agricultural & Manufacturing Interests.*

NATIVE MANUFACTURES.

Of *Manufacturing Industries* Ceylon has a very poor show. The Sinhalese are good carpenters, and supply furniture and carved work in abundance; both they and the Tamils make good artisans; witness the roll of workmen in the Government Public Works and Railway Factories of Colombo, and the Colombo Ironworks, where ocean-going steamers are repaired, as well as a great variety of machinery is turned out, such as steam-engines, water-motors and tea, coffee, and oil-preparing machines. The Sinhalese were distinguished as ironworkers in very ancient days; they knew nothing about firearms until the Portuguese era, and yet they soon excelled European gunmakers in the beautifully-worked muskets they turned out for their king. Even now there are ironsmiths who make muskets in the villages, within 20 miles of Colombo, for some 35 to 40 rupees (say £2 10s.), which can scarcely remunerate for the time given to them in their primitive mode of working. They were early workers in brass and glass, as their ancient ruins show, and they must have known a little about electricity, for it is related in the *Mahawansa* that King Sanghatissa, A. D. 234, placed a glass pinnacle on the Ruanwelli Dagoba, to serve as a protection against lightning. Of late years, the natives have watched with interest the introduction of railways, the electric telegraph, telephone, and light, as well as bicycles and rickshaws, both of which are now freely made locally; and when suitable electric motors are made available, and the numerous and splendid streams and waterfalls of the hillcountry afford ready force for utilisation, they will be still more delighted. Any contrivance for saving human labour has a great attraction to the Sinhalese Buddhists. Native cotton spinners and weavers were at one time common, but the industry is dying out; very little tobacco is manufactured; the making of mats, baskets, and coir-rope gives some employment. The masons of the country are now chiefly Moormen; though the Sinhalese must have done much in the building of tanks and other huge erections in ancient times. Fishing and mining plumbago and search for precious gems, as well as hunting, afford a good deal of employment. Workers in ebony, tortoiseshell, and porcupine quills, and in primitive pottery, are also numerous among the Sinhalese.

CHAPTER VI.

THE ORIGIN AND RISE OF THE PLANTING INDUSTRY.

Coffee introduced in 1690, by the Dutch—First systematically cultivated in 1740—Extensive development in 1837—Hightest level of Prosperity reached in 1868-70—Appearance of Leaf Disease in 1869—Its disastrous effects.

WE now turn to the great planting industry which began in coffee, and has been succeeded by tea (now by far the most important staple), cacao, the chocolate or cocoa plant, not to be confounded with the coconut palm, rubber trees, cardamoms, cinchona, etc. : to these the past rapid development and prosperity of the island are mainly due, and on them its future position as a leading colony must still chiefly depend.

It was long supposed, and Emerson Tennent adopted the opinion, that the Arabs first introduced coffee into India and Ceylon, and that the shrub was grown in the latter before the arrival of the Portuguese or Dutch, though the preparation of a beverage from its berries was unknown to the Sinhalese, who were said only to use the young coffee leaves for their curries, and the delicate jasmine-like coffee flowers for ornamenting the shrines of Buddha. But the late Dr. Trimen, F.R.S., the accomplished Director of the Ceylon Royal Botanic Gardens, shewed conclusively that coffee was unknown in tropical Asia until the Dutch introduced it in to Java in 1690 : it was brought thence by them to Ceylon probably about the same year.

The first attempt at systematic cultivation was made by the Dutch in 1740, but, being confined to the low

GENERAL VIEW OF YOUNG DIMBULA PLANTATION (ABBOTSFORD.)

Tea and cinchona nurseries foreground; rows of coffee around buildings in centre; felled and standing forest beyond

THE CEARA RUBBER TREE.

A specimen of rapid growth in Ceylon (Simbawattie Estate); 17 ft. high 10 in. in circumference, and only nine months old.

country, it did not succeed, and they seem never to have exported more than 1,000 cwt. in a year. The Moormen (Arab) traders and Sinhalese, having once discovered the use of coffee, kept up the cultivation and trade; but when the British took Ceylon, and up to 1812, the annual export had never exceeded 3,000 cwt. So it continued until the master-mind of Sir Edward Barnes designed and opened road communication between the hill country and the coast, and began to consider how the planting industry could be extended, and the revenues of the country developed. The Governor himself led the way, in opening a coffee plantation near Kandy, in 1825, just one year after the first systematic coffee estate was formed by Mr. George Bird, near Gampola. These examples were speedily followed, but still the] progress was slow, for in 1837, twelve years after, the total export of coffee did not exceed 30,000 cwt.

It is usual to date the rise of the coffee planting enterprise from this year, which witnessed a great rush of investments, and the introduction of the West India system of cultivation by Robert Boyd Tytler, usually regarded as the "father" of Ceylon planters. An immense extension of cultivation took place up to 1845, by which time the trade had developed to an export of close on 200,000 cwt. Then came a financial explosion in Great Britain, which speedily extended its destructive influence to Ceylon, and led to a stoppage of the supplies required to plant and cultivate young plantations. Much land opened was abandoned, and for three years the enterprise was paralysed; but nevertheless the export continued to increase, and by the time Governor Sir Henry Ward appeared, in 1855, confidence had been restored, and all was ready for the great impetus his energetic administration was to give; thus in twenty years, the coffee enterprise had come to be regarded as the backbone of the agricultural industry of the island, and the mainstay of the revenue. The Sinhalese soon followed the example set them by the European planters, and so widely and rapidly developed their coffee gardens throughout the hill-country, that between 1849 and 1869 from one-third to one-fourth of the total quantity of coffee shipped year by year was "native coffee."

The opening of the "Wilderness of the Peak"—Dimbula, Dikoya, and Maskeliya—under the auspices of Sir Hercules Robinson, led to the highest level of prosperity being reached in 1868, 1869, and 1870, in each of which years the exports slightly exceeded a million cwt., of a value in European markets of not less than four millions sterling, against 34,000 cwt., valued at £120,000, exported in 1837: a marvellous development in thirty years of a tropical industry!

In 1869 the total extent cultivated on plantations (apart from native gardens) was 176,000 acres, and the return from the land in full bearing averaged over 5 cwt. an acre, a return which should, under favourable circumstances, give a profit of from £7 to £10 an acre, or from twenty to twenty-five per cent. on the capital invested. Nothing could be brighter than the prospects of the colony and its main enterprise in 1869: Sir Hercules Robinson's administration, then in mid-course, was most beneficial; the railway between Colombo and Kandy, two years open, was a grand success; and with an unfailing supply of cheap free labour from Southern India, remarkable facilities for transport, and a splendid climate, the stability of the great coffee enterprise seemed to be assured.

Its importance was fully realised through the statistics of the actual extent cultivated which were for the first time compiled, in full detail (by the author), and although it began to be felt that the good land at the most suitable altitude had all been taken up, and most of it brought under cultivation, yet no one doubted the comparative permanency of such plantations under a liberal, scientific system of cultivation,

But in this same year there first appeared an enemy, most insignificant in appearance, which in less than a dozen years was fated to bring down the export of the great staple to one-fifth, and a few years later to onetwelfth, of its then dimensions, and that notwithstanding a wide extension of the area under cultivation. This enemy was a minute fungus on the leaf, new to science, and named by the greatest fungoid authorities *Hemileia vastatrix*, from its destructive powers, now popularly known as " coffee-leaf disease."

First appearing in one of the youngest districts, at a remote corner, it rapidly spread all over the coffee zone, being easily distinguished by the appearance of bright orange spots on the leaves, which subsequently wither and drop off. At first it was treated as a matter of little moment by all but the late Dr. Thwaites, F. R. S., the Director of the Ceylon Botanic Gardens, and for several years it apparently did little harm, crops being only slightly affected, and any decrease being attributed to seasonal in fluences rather than to a minute pest which, it was supposed, only served to remind the planter of the necessity of more liberal cultivation. Another cause, moreover, served most effectually to blind the eyes of all concerned to the insidious progress of the pest, and the gradual but sure falling-off of crops, namely, a sudden and unprecedented rise in the value of coffee in Europe and America—a rise equivalent. in a few years, to more than fifty per cent. This great access of value to his returns more than sufficed to compensate the Ceylon planter for any diminution of crop. It did more : it stimulated the vast extension of cultivation already referred to, into the largest remaining reserve, known as the Wilderness of the Peak, extending from Nuwara Eliya thorough a succession of upland valleys in Dimbula, Dikoya, and Maskeliya, to the Adam's Peak range, an area of forest, covering some 400 square miles, having the most delightful climate in the world, but until this time (1868-69) regarded as too high and wet for coffee. This region had been previously utilised as a hunting-ground by an occasional party of Europeans or Kandyans; the pilgrims' paths to Adam's Peak, winding their way through the dense jungle, and intercepted by a succession of large unbridged rivers, were then the only lines of communication. The rush into this El Dorado had begun in the time of Sir Hercules Robinson, who energetically aided the development by extending roads and bridging rivers, thus untilising some of the large surpluses which the sale of the lands and the increased customs and railway revenues afforded him.

A cycle of favourable—that is, comparatively dry—seasons still further contributed to the success of the young high districts, so that coffee (which had previously been supposed to find its suitable limit at 4,000 or 4,500 feet) was planted and cultivated pro fitably up to 5,000 and even 5,500 feet. All through Governor Gregory's administration the high price of coffee and the active extension of the cultivated area continued, the competition becoming so keen that forest-land, which ten or twenty years before would not fetch as much as £2 an acre, was sold as high as £15, £20, and even £28 an acre. Even at this price planters calculated on profitable results; but there can be no doubt that speculation, rather than the teachings of experience, guided their calculations.

Between 1869 and 1879 over 400,000 acres of Crown land were sold by the Ceylon Government, bringing in more than a million sterling to the revenue, and of this 100,000 acres were brought into cultivation with coffee, at an outlay of not less than from two to two and a-half millions sterling, almost entirely in the upland districts referred to.

Meanwhile the insidious leaf-fungus pest had been working deadly mischief. High cultivation, with manure of various descriptions, failing to arrest its progress, the aid of science was called in, special investigations took place, its life-history was written; but the practical result was no more satisfactory to the coffee planter than have similar investigations proved to the potato cultivator, the wheat farmer fighting with rust, or the vine grower who is baffled by the fatal *phylloxera*. Less deadly than the *phylloxera*, the leaf-fungus had nevertheless so affected the Ceylon coffee enterprise that, in the ten years during which cultivation had extended more than fifty per cent., the annual export had fallen to three-fourths of the million cwt. The same fungus had extended to the coffee districts of India and Java, with similar results in devastated crops, but in the greatest coffee country of all—Brazil—the impetus to an extension of cultivation which the high prices from 1873 onwards had given was not checked by the presence of this fungoid, or other coffee diseases, and from thence soon began to pour into the markets of the world such crops as speedily brought prices to their old level reacting disastrously on the Ceylon enterprise, which had at the same time to encounter the monetary depression caused by the collapse of the City of Glasgow Bank and other financial failures in Britain. Misfortunes never come singly, and accordingly a series of wet seasons crowned the evils befalling the planters in the young high districts, while the older coffee lower down began to be neglected, so enfeebled had it become in many places under the repeated visits of the fungus. This so disheartened the coffee planter that he turned his attention to new products, more especially cinchona, and later, tea, planted among and in supersession of the coffee, as well as in new land. Tea especially succeeded so well, as will be fully related farther on, that coffee over a large area has been entirely taken out, and the area cultivated has been reduced from the maximum of 275,000 acres in 1878 to not much more than 5,000 acres in 1903! The result is that in the present season (1903), in place of the million cwt. exported thirty-two years ago, the total shipments of coffee from Ceylon will not exceed 10,000 cwt., and it is impossible to revive the industry in the face of the leaf-fungus which always fastens on any young coffee if planted. All this refers to the cultivation of the Arabian species of coffee (*Coffee Arabica*); the industry in the Liberian variety came after, and is dealt with under "New Products." The mitigation of the disaster—the silver lining to the dark cloud which came over the prospects of the majority of Ceylon coffee planters—is dealt with in the next chapter.

At an early stage in the history of coffee leaf disease in Ceylon, one cause, and that perhaps the chief, of the visitation had become apparent in the limitation of cultivation to one plant, and one only, over hundreds of square miles of country which had previously been covered with the most varied vegetation. Nature had revenged herself, just as she had done on Ireland when potatoes threatened to become the universal crop, as well as on extensive wheat fields elsewhere, and on the French vineyards. The *hemileia vastatrix* was described by Dr. Thwaites as peculiar to a jungle plant, and finding coffee leaves a suitable food in 1869 it multiplied and spread indefinitely. It could not be said that the fungus thus burst out in Ceylon because of coffee being worn out or badly cultivated, for it first appeared in a young district upon vigorous coffee, and it afterwards attacked old and young, vigorous and weak trees, with absolute impartiality. The true remedy, then, for the loss occasioned by this pest—apart from the wisdom of the old adage not to have all one's eggs in one basket—lay in the introduction of *New Products*.

CHAPTER VII.

THE ERA OF TEA, CACAO, RUBBER AND NEW PRODUCTS.

Tea—Cinchona—Cacao—Indiarubber—Cardamoms—Liberian Coffee, etc

TEA cultivation was said to be tried in Ceylon in the time of the Dutch, but there is no reliable evidence of this tradition, and Dr. Trimen did not believe it;* for although there is a wild plant (*Cassia auriculata*), called the Matara tea plant, from which the Sinhalese in the south of the island are accustomed to make an infusion, yet nothing was done with the true tea plant till long after coffee was established. Between 1839 and 1842, under the auspices of Governor Stewart-Mackenzie and others, experiments were made with the Assam tea plant at Peradeniya and Nuwara Eliya, but without permanent results. A little later, the Messrs. Worms (cousins of the Rothschilds, who did an immense deal in developing Ceylon) introduced the China plant, and, planting up a field on the Ramboda Pass, proved that tea would grow well in the island. Mr. Llewellyn about the same time introduced the Assam plant again into Dolosbage

---

* The late Dr. Trimen was kind enough to report to me (September 1892) as follows:—" Bennett, in his 'Ceylon and its Capabilities,' gives a figure, a good one, of the real tea plant which, he says, was collected near Batticaloa (I think in 1826), but from the text he clearly confused it with our Matara tea, the leaves of the 'Ranawara' (*Cassia auriculata*). Still I think true tea may have been grown in some gardens in Ceylon, as it was certainly in the Botanic Gardens at Kalutara before 1824, the date of Morris's Catalogue. Assam tea was sent from Calcutta as early as 1836, and planted at Nuwara Eliya.'

district, but no commercial result came from these ventures. Attention was, however, frequently called to this product, and in 1867 a Ceylon planter was commissioned to report on the tea-planting industry in India. In that same year the attention of planters was also first turned to the cinchona plant, which had been introduced six years earlier to India and Ceylon by Mr. Clements Markham. The Director of the Botanic Garden, Dr. Thwaites, however, found great difficulty in getting any planter to care about cultivating a "medicine plant," and when the great rise in prices for coffee came, all thought of tea and inchona was cast to the winds, and the one old profitable product, which everybody—planters and coolies alike—understood, was alone planted.

Very early in his administration, Sir William Gregory, to his special credit be it said, saw the necessity for new products, and he used all his personal and official influence to secure their development, introducing a new feature into the Governor's annual speech to the Legislative Council in special notices of the progress of tea, cinchona, cacao, Liberian coffee, and rubber cultivation. The influence of the principal journal in the colony (the *Ceylon Observer*) was earnestly cast into the same scale, and practical information to aid the planter of new products was collected for it from all quarters, more especially from the tropical belt of the earth's surface.*

Cinchona.

When Governor Gregory arrived in 1872 only 500 acres of cinchona had been planted, but before he left in 1877 not only had these increased to 6,000 acres, but the planters had begun thoroughly to appreciate the value of the new product, its suitableness for the hill-country

---

* In June 1881 the monthly periodical, *The Tropical Agriculturist*, was started by the author from the *Ceylon Observer* Press for the special purpose of meeting the requirements of planters. It circulates all round the tropical belt of the world, and has received high encomiums in Britain, United States, West Indies, South America and Australia.

LIBERIAN COFFEE.

CINCHONA SUCCIRUTRA (GENUINE RED BARK.)

TALIPOT PALM IN FLOWER.

THE TEA PLANT.

and climate of Ceylon, and the profits to be made from judicious cultivation. The great rush, however, took place on the failure of coffee in 1879 and the next three years, so that by 1883 the area covered by this plant could not be less than 60,000 acres. The enormous bark exports which followed from Ceylon so lowered the price (involving the great blessing of cheap quinine) that it became no longer profitable to cut bark in the native South American cinchona groves, or to plant further in Ceylon or India. (In Java alone, with its rich soil, did cinchona planters persevere, carefully using seed only from the very best trees as per analysis of barks.) Attention, therefore, in Ceylon began in 1884 to be diverted from cinchona; nevertheless the exports from the existing area continued high, and the area still under cinchona, making allowance for what was planted throughout the tea and coffee plantations, continued up to 1887 at not less than 30,000 acres with several (perhaps forty) million trees above two or three years, of all descriptions of cinchona, growing thereon. The export of bark, which was 11,547 lb. in 1872, rose to 15,892,078 lb. in 1887; but since then, with the great reduction in price (quinine falling in fourteen years from 12s. to 1s. an ounce), the cultivation began to be superseded by tea, and the export has fallen down to less than half a million lb. in 1902. If only the price of bark were sufficient, Ceylon could continue to grow cinchona bark; but Java is now the great source of supply, and its bark, for the reason already given, is much richer. Very great mistakes were locally made at first in cinchona-planting in the use of immature seed and by the choice of unsuitable species and unsuitable soil, but the Ceylon planters rapidly qualified themselves to be successful cinchona growers, if only prices of bark had kept up; and a few still try to supplement their staple (tea) with fields or belts of cinchona.

Tea.

It had long been the conviction of many who have studied the climate and the character of Ceylon soils that the country is far more fitted to become a great tea producer than ever it was to grow coffee. It is now realised, too, that a large proportion of the area opened with the latter product—apart from the appearance of leaf fungus altogether—would have done much better under tea. Unlike India, there is never in the low country, western and south-western, or in the central (the hilly) portions of Ceylon, a month of the year without some rain, the annual fall in this region ranging from 80 to 200 inches, while the alternate tropical sunshine and moisture form the perfection of climate for the leaf-yielding tea-shrub. Untimely downpours, which so often wrecked the blossoms and the hopes of the coffee planter, do no harm to the leaf crop of the tea planter. Not only so, but the harvesting of tea leaf is spread over eight or even ten months of the year. If a fresh flush of young leaf fails from any cause this month, the planter has generally only a few weeks to wait for another chance, and, save for the "pruning" and the very wet season in Ceylon, the tea planter can look for some returns nearly all the year round. Very different was the case with coffee, the crop of which for a whole year was often dependent on the weather during a single month; or even a week's (or a day's) untimely rain or drought might destroy the chance of an adequate return for a whole year's labour. Even in the favoured Uva districts there were only two periods of harvesting coffee in the year. Again, while the zone suitable for the growth of coffee ranged from 1,500 or 2,000 to 4,500 or 5,000 feet above sea-level, tea seems to flourish equally well (the Assam indigenous kind, or good hybrid) at sea-level and up to 4,000 feet, and (a hardy hybrid or China kind) at from 3,000 to 6,000 and even to close on 7,000 feet above sea-level. The tea shrub is found to be altogether hardier and generally far more suitable to the comparatively poor soil of Ceylon than ever coffee was, and indeed the Sinhalese regard it as "a jungle plant." Nevertheless it took many years to convince Ceylon planters of the wisdom of looking

TAMIL COOLY-GIRL PICKING TEA-LEAVES.

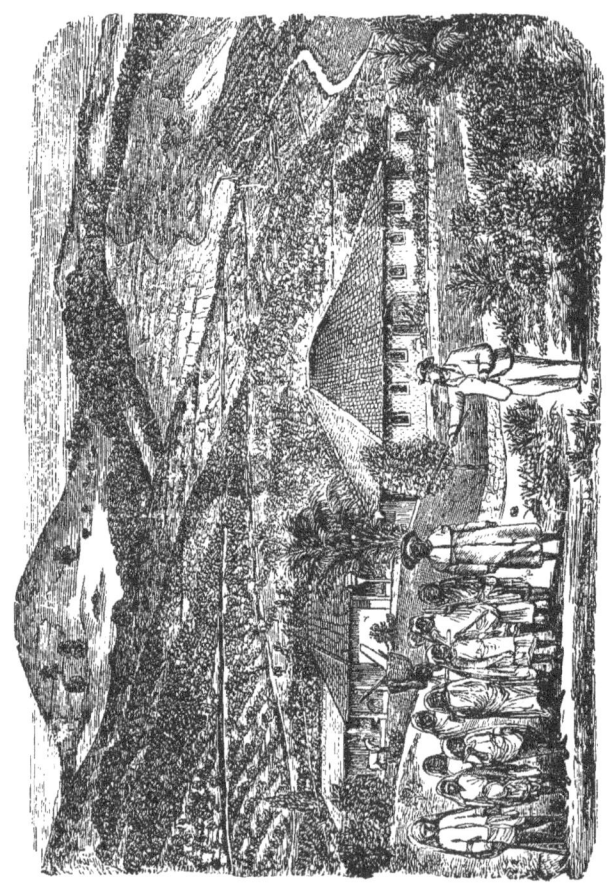

THE SINNAPITIA COFFEE ESTATE NEAR GAMPOLA.

New Products.

to tea; and for some years even after it was gone into in earnest, much less progress was made than in the case of cinchona. There were good reasons for this in the greater cost of tea seed, and the much greater trouble entailed in the preparation of the produce for the market. Beginning from 1873 with an extent planted of 250 acres, in ten years this area increased to about 85,000 acres, while in the succeeding year, 1884, this was doubled, as much being also added in 1885, and a large extent in 1886, so that before the Jubilee Year of Queen Victoria's reign closed, there were not less than 150,000 acres covered with the tea plant in Ceylon. Five years more added over another 100,000 acres, so that in 1893 the industry extended to 255,000 acres in all; while in the next decade, although a check came to planting in 1900, through low prices, the total extent covered with tea is not under 385,000 acres. The tea export from Ceylon of 23 lb. in 1876 rose to 7,849,886 lb. in 1886, to over 78,000,000 in 1892, and to over 149 millions lb. in 1902; while for 1903, the estimate is 154 millions for black and green tea together. There are still considerable reserves of Crown land suitable for tea, for, as already said, it is found to produce profitable crops on land a few hundred feet above sea-level, as well as at all altitudes up to the neighbourhood of Nuwara Eliya, approximating to 7,000 feet; while the Sinhalese may be expected to grow tea in their own gardens, at any rate for local consumption. But all this depends on a profitable price: at present there is no encouragement to plant another acre in Ceylon or India. Consumption has been checked by the high customs duty in Britain—6d a lb. —on what is practically a purely British Industry; while the United States has no duty! When Russia and England reduce their customs' levies consumption will certainly increase, and there may be a need to plant more; but not so at present. The manufacture of Green Teas for the American market begun in 1899 grew to an export of nearly 2,800,000 lb. in 1902 and is likely to be 11 or 12 millions lb. in 1903.

The rapid development of the tea-planting industry in Ceylon during the past fifteen to seventeen years constitutes the most interesting and important fact in the recent history of the island. The future of the colony depends upon this staple now far more than on any other branch of agriculture, and so far the promise is that the industry will be a comparatively permanent though only moderately profitable one. On favoured plantations, with comparatively flat land and good soil (tea loves a flat as coffee did a sloping hill-side) tea crops have already been gathered in Ceylon for some years in succession in excess almost of anything known in India. With unequalled means of communication by railway and first-class roads—with well-trained, easily-managed, and fairly intelligent labourers in the Tamil coolies*, with a suitable climate and soil, and, above all, with a planting community of exceptional intelligence and energy in pushing a product that is once shown to be suitable for cultivation, the rapid development of our tea enterprise from the infant of 1876-80 to the giant of 1893-1903 may be more easily understood. Ceylon teas have been received with exceptional favour in the London market. The teas are of a high character and fine flavour, perfectly pure, which is more than can be said of a large proportion of China and Japan teas. It was therefore expected by competent authorities that as the taste for the good teas of Ceylon and India spread—one never enjoys a common or adulterated tea after getting accustomed to one of good flavour—the China teas, to a great extent, would fall out of use. This has been fully realised, Ceylon and Indian teas having now driven China almost entirely out of consumption in the United Kingdom.

---

* One risk in regard to the future is with reference to a sufficiency of immigrant labour from Southern India to cope with the requirements of tea, cacao, cardamoms, and rubber. Only in a few districts do the Sinhalese come to the help of the planter,

The great danger, as already mentioned, is of prices falling too low to be remunerative. Still, if there is to be a struggle, there can be little doubt that the average Ceylon tea planter can hold his own. The consumption of his staple is spreading every year, and if the English-speaking people of the United States, Canada, and South Africa only did equal justice to the tea with their brethren in the United Kingdom and Australia, and if Russia's requirements increase year by year, the demand would then be fully up to the supply. Moreover, tea can be delivered more cheaply from Ceylon allowing for quality, than from either India or China As was the case with coffee, the preparation of the new staple in Ceylon is in a fair way to be brought to perfection. Improved machinery has already been invented by local planters and others to save labour to counteract the effect of unsuitable weather (for withering the leaf, etc.), or to turn out teas with better flavour; and yet the industry cannot be said properly to be more than a quarter of a century in the island. Its beneficial influence on local business, export trade, and revenue has been, of course, widely felt. The Sinhalese, in a few districts, are working for the tea planters, and native tea-gardens were freely planted up on low-country roadsides, until the fall in price came. But to meet a local consumption, the process may go on until there is a wide area covered with tea under native auspices. The cultivators will probably often sell their leaf to central factories owned by colonists; but there is no reason why, as times run on, they should not manufacture for themselves, the product being chiefly used for local consumption. The atmosphere of planting, business, and even official circles in Ceylon just now is highly charged with "tea," and the number of Tea Patents (for preparing machines), of Tea publications,* Tea Brokers, Tea

---

* *See* the "Ceylon Tea Planters' Manual," Tea and other New Products, "Planters' Note Book," "Tea Tables," and *Tropical Agriculturist*, [Published] by A. M. & J. Ferguson, Colombo.

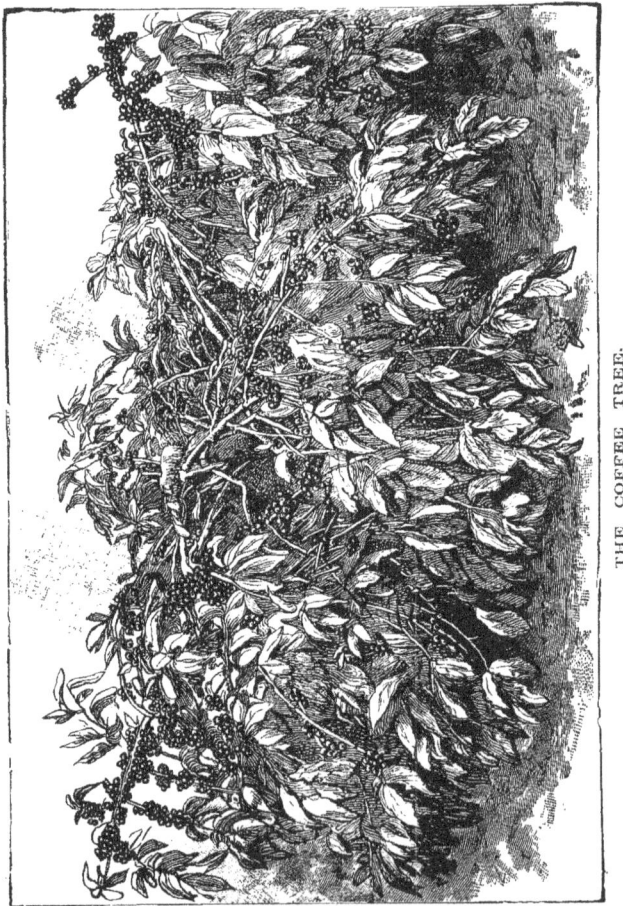

THE COFFEE TREE.

New Products.

of preparing the bean for the London market, and further improvements are under consideration.* The mycologist at Peradeniya has done good service in investigating and checking canker in cacao trees. There is fair encouragement in prices and demand to continue cacao cultivation; but further planting in West Indies and West Africa may lead to overproduction.

Cardamoms spice is another product, the cultivation of which has benefited a good many Ceylon planters, the export rising from 14,000 lb. in 1878 to 422,109 lb. in 1891, and 616,000 in 1902, until here again "overproduction" is the cry. The greater portion used to be sent to India, where there is a large demand in the Presidency towns; but now the quantity sent to the United Kingdom is three times as much and sufficient to seriously affect the price in the London market. It is, indeed, a significant fact that, in respect of several products, practically receiving no attention from our planters twenty five years ago, Ceylon has assumed a prominent if not a leading position in the markets of the world. We refer to tea, cacao, and cardamoms (by and bye, we trust) for the supply of which, as of cinnamon, coconut oil, and plumbago, this colony is pre-eminent. †

The *Caoutchouc*, or indiarubber trees of commerce, from South America and Eastern Africa, are of recent introduction, but their cultivation and growth in certain of the planting districts of Ceylon—Kalutara Udugama, Matale and Kelani Valley especially—have so far given very satisfactory results. The growth of the trees of the Para and Castilloa kinds has been excellent, and much is now known

---

* *See* pamphlets on "Cacao Cultivation," published by A. M. & J Ferguson, Colombo. Also in Appendix No. II. Mr. J. Ferguson s Paper before the London Chamber of Commerce, 25th June, 1892

† *See* Mr. J. Ferguson's Paper before London Chamber of Commerce, June 25th, 1892; Pamphlet on Cardamoms Cultivation, etc.," has been published by A. M & J. Ferguson, Colombo.

Ceylon in 1903.

about the mode of harvesting the rubber and the industry has in a small way been proved to be profitable.* There is an enormous demand for rubber in arts and manufactures in the United States as in Europe, and much encouragement therefore to give attention to this product. In 1903, it is estimated that the equivalent of 12,000 acres are planted with rubber trees, and the largest export yet made is of 21,168 lb. in 1902; but the first half of 1903 showed 22,533 lb. sent away, and prices for Ceylon biscuit Para rubber have been as high as 4s. 6d. a lb.

Among minor new products Liberian coffee was introduced from the West African Republic of that name (in 1875-79 chiefly), in the hope that its large size and strong habit would enable it, at the low elevation in which it grows, to resist the leaf-fungus; but this hope has not been realised, and although the acreage planted (615 acres in 1903) is giving fair crops, there is no attempt to extend this area for the present.† Coffee trees in bearing were not long ago reported in the Wanni of the Northern Province, and an experiment is likely to be made by the European planters on a grant of land eastward of Minneri Lake. Experiments with hybridised coffee plants are being made in the Peradeniya Gardens; but there is not much hope of a coffee industry ever springing up again.

Cotton (room for a large industry if experiments by Government with special seed succeed along our great Northern Railway), tobacco (exciting the attention of Europeans), areca, coconut palms, pepper, camphor (very promising in a small way) African palm-oil nut, nutmegs, cloves, croton oil seeds, coca, kola,

---
* *See* Mr. J. Ferguson's Paper before London Chamber of Commerce, June 25th, 1892; and "All About Rubber," third edition, published by A. M. & Ferguson, Colombo.

† *See* Mr. J. Ferguson's Paper before London Chamber of Commerce, June 25th, 1892; and "Liberian Coffee," illustrated, published by A. M. & J. Ferguson, Colombo.

THE CACAO POD.
Each containing twenty-four seeds in pulp, which, when prepared, give the Chocolate of Commerce.

WEIGHING-IN GREEN TEA-LEAF ON A TEA ESTATE.

New Products.

and annotto dye plant are among the other products to which, by reason of the reverse in coffee, and depression in tea, planters in the hill and low country of Ceylon have been turning their attention in isolated cases, with results more or less satisfactory. In the variety of all the industries detailed in the foregoing pages, it is felt there is sufficient guarantee to warrant the belief that the coffee leaf-fungus will prove eventually, if it has not already proved, a blessing in disguise to the island, its colonists, and native people. The latter suffered with their European brethren, not only through the disease affecting their coffee gardens, but much more through the absence of employment in so many branches which the prosperous coffee enterprise opened out to them. Some years back, Dr. Conan Doyle in one of his stories dealing with Ceylon, referred to the great crisis which overtook its coffee-planting industry and led to cinchona, cacao and tea as substitutes, in these words:—"Not often is it that men have the heart, when their one great industry is withered, to rear up in a few years another as rich to take its place, and the tea fields of Ceylon are as true a monument to courage as is the lion at Waterloo. My story concerns the royal days of coffee-planting in Ceylon, before a rooting fungus drove a whole community through years of despair to one of the greatest commercial victories which pluck and ingenuity have ever won." Tea plantations are now filling up the blanks left by coffee, so far as field and picking work is concerned; while many of the natives, led by their chiefs and intelligent headmen and villagers, are themselves planting new products—tea and cacao especially—and so following the example of the European planters. In this way the Planting enterprise in all its ramifications in Ceylon is fraught with the promise of a greater and more reliable prosperity than ever appertained to coffee alone in its palmiest days.

CHAPTER VIII.

PRESENT POSITION OF AGRICULTURAL ENTERPRISE, LOCAL INDUSTRIES, AND FOREIGN EXPORT AND IMPORT TRADE.

Exports of last decade—The Plumbago Trade—Gold and Iron—Native Industries generally flourishing—Tea and Cacao will make up for the Deficiency in Coffee.

TO sum up and show at a glance the present position of the export trade arising from our agricultural enterprise and local industry, we give opposite a tabular statement of the *staple exports* and their distribution for 1893-1902.

There are a few headings in this export table that we have not touched on yet, and the principal one of these is *plumbago*, or graphite. This is the only mineral of commercial importance exported from Ceylon. The mining industry is entirely in the hands of the Sinhalese; mines of from 100 to 200 and even 300 feet depth are worked in a primitive fashion, and the finest plumbago in the world for crucible purposes is obtained. Wars and rumours of war influence greatly the demand for plumbago and activity in British, American and other arsenals in 1900-1 created a great boom in Ceylon plumbago which nearly doubled in price for a time; but the reaction was not pleasant. However the industry has taken a great start of recent years, the average export increasing about 50 per cent. within the decade; the value of the trade averages about £700,000 per annum, and this mining industry has sprung up entirely within the last fifty-five years. *

---
* *See* Monograph on "Plumbago," by A. M. Ferguson contributed to the Royal Asiatic Society's Journal (Ceylon) in 1885.'

Position of Agriculture and Trade.

Mention may be made of the precious stones found in Ceylon and exported in certain quantities, the chief being rubies and sapphires and cat's-eyes. "Pearls" are included in the customs returns with "precious stones," and the total value of all recorded in any one year for exports has never exceeded £9,000; but the large proportion of both pearls and precious stones taken out of the island, on the persons of natives or others leaving, would not be entered at all in the customs returns. A successful Pearl Fishery in 1903, yielding perhaps £30,000 to £40,000 net to Government, is expected to be followed by a series in successive years; and much is expected in oyster culture of Professor Herdman and Mr. Hornell.

Gold is freely distributed in the primary rocks of Ceylon, but it has not been found in paying quantities. Rich iron ore is very abundant, but there is no coal. Native arrivals show that there were at one time 60 gold and 16 silver mines in Ceylon, but they must have been on a very small scale.

Of other minor exports affording some trade to native huntsmen are deer-horns, the trade in which indicates a considerable destruction of deer, so that a law has been passed to protect them as well as other game and elephants. Of elephants in forty years, Ceylon has sent away about 2,217, chiefly to India, for service, or show at the Rajahs' courts. The highest return was 271 in 1865; latterly, however, few have been exported. As some compensation, about 21,124 horses have been imported into Ceylon in the past forty years. The export of "hides and skins" is considerable, and might be more important were it not for the Sinhalese habits of cutting and marking the hides of their cattle. The local industry in tanning is very limited, though the materials are at hand to extend it considerably. There is also much scope for the export of dyeing (as well as tanning) substances. The export trade in timber—apart from ebony—is considerable, such as satinwood, palmyra, tamarind, etc., to a total average value of £20,000 per annum.

It will be observed that the branches of trade more particularly in the hands of the natives—the products of the coconut palm, cinnamon, and minor exports—are in a sound, flourishing and progressive condition. The case is very different with coffee, and the significance of the change will be understood when it is remembered that between 1865 and 1878 the average export of coffee shipped was equal in value to more than double of all the other exports put together. But instead of four or five millions of pounds' worth of coffee, we are now reduced to a value of less than £100,000. Here, however, come in the new products, tea, cocoa, cardamoms, rubber; while to tea belongs the honour of representing our planting enterprise *par excellence*, by as great a value in export as was ever reached by coffee; while the other products now tried, help to place us in a stronger position than in coffee days—apart from the great lowcountry industry in coconut and other palms.

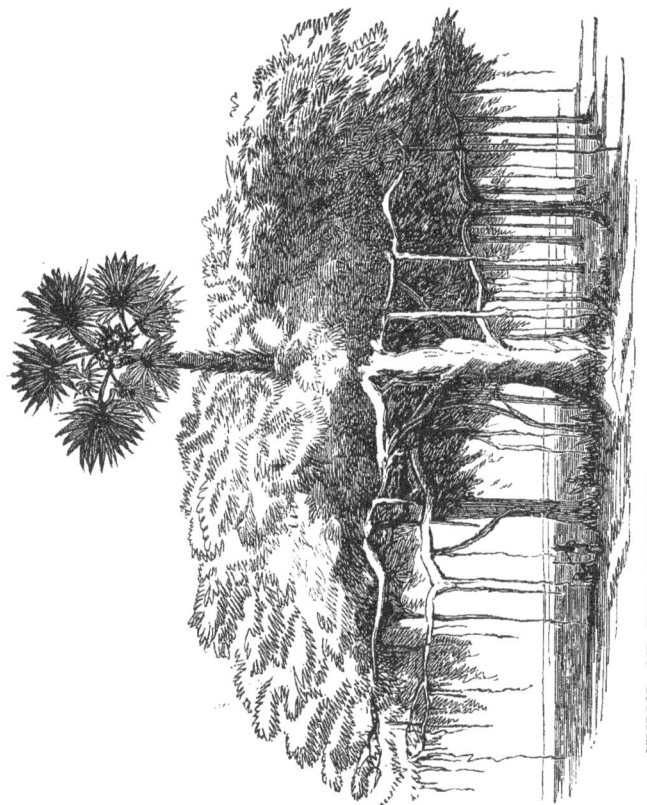

UNION OF THE BANYAN TREE AND THE PALMYRA PALM.

THE BANYAN TREE (FICUS INDICA).

CHAPTER IX.

WHAT THE PLANTING INDUSTRY HAS DONE FOR THE MOTHER-COUNTRY.

The swing of the pendulum: a Cycle of Prosperity from Tea—Previous Years of Depression considered—Planting profits absorbed IN THE PAST by Home Capitalists—Absence of Reserves of Local Wealth—The accumulated Profits of past years estimated.

SINCE 1888, when the success of the tea-planting enterprise became fully established, Ceylon has entered on a period of comparative prosperity, as indicated by her trade and revenue statistics. How long it may last is another question. In tropical experience the alternate swing of the pendulum from bad times to good times and *vice versâ* is fully recognised. For ten or eleven years previous to 1889 financial depression and scarcity of capital prevailed, and this result can readily be understood when a succession of bad coffee seasons, involving a deficiency in the planters' harvests of that product equal to many millions of pounds sterling, is taken into consideration. There have been periods of depression before in the history of the Ceylon planting enterprise, and these, curiously enough, have been noted to come round in cycles in eleven years Thus, in 1845, wild speculation in opening plantations, followed by a great fall in the price of coffee and a collapse of credit, arrested progress for a time; in 1856-57, a sharp financial shock affected the course of prosperity which had set in; and again, in 1866-67, the fortunes of coffee fell to so low an ebb that a London capitalist, who visited the island, said the most striking picture of woe-begone misery he saw was the typical "man who owned a coffee estate." Yet this was followed by good seasons and bounteous coffee harvests.

The depression which set in during 1879 was, however, the most prolonged and trying. True, agriculture nearly all over the world had been suffering from a succession of bad harvests, more particularly in the mother-country; but there are certain grave distinctions between the conditions of a tropical colony and lands in a temperate zone. In Ceylon a generation among European colonists has usually been considered not to exceed ten years—not at all on account of mortality, for the hills of Ceylon have the perfection of a healthy climate, but from the constant changes in the elements of the European community—the coming and going which in the past made such a distinct change in the broad elements of society every ten or certainly every fifteen years.

Those colonists who made fortunes in "coffee" in the island—only 10 per cent. of the whole body of planters, however—did not think of making it their permanent home. The capitalist who sent out his money for investment got it back as soon as possible, where, as in many cases, he did not lose it altogether. The "accumulated profits," made during the time of prosperity, which at home form a reserve fund of local wealth to enable the sufferer from present adversity to benefit by past earnings, were, so far as the planters were concerned, wanting in Ceylon. We had no reserve fund of past profits to fall back upon, no class of wealthy Europeans enriched by former times of prosperity living amongst us and circulating the liquidated products of former industry, when the period of adversity and depression arrived.

Ceylon, in fact, in the best coffee days, used to be a sort of "incubator" to which capitalists sent

The Benefit to the Mother-Country. 83

their eggs to be hatched, and whence a good many of them received from time to time an abundant brood, leaving sometimes but the shells for our local portion. Money was sent out to Ceylon to fill its forests and plant them with coffee, and it was returned in the shape of copious harvests to the home capitalist, leaving in some cases the bare hillsides from whence their rich harvests were drawn. Had the profits from the abundant coffee crops in those past days been located here and invested in the country and its soil, a fund of local wealth might have existed when the lean years came, manufactures might now have been flourishing, a number of wealthy citizens of European origin might have been living in affluence, and we might have possessed resources to help us over the time of adversity and depression.

The total amount of coffee raised on the plantations of Ceylon since 1849 is about 22,500,000 cwt., and there were produced previously (excluding native coffee in both cases) about 1,000,000 cwt. at the least, making a grand total of coffee of 23,500,000 cwt. as the produce of imported capital. Including interest and all items of local cost, we may safely say that this coffee has been produced for £2 5s. per cwt., and has realised at the least £3 net on an average; it has therefore earned a net profit of £17,000,000. The coffee so produced has been yielded by plantations of not more than 320,000 acres in the aggregate, after including a due allowance for lands abandoned; and the average cost of the estates, including the purchase of the land, has certainly not exceeded £25 per acre, involving a total capital of £8,000,000. There should, therefore, have been a sum of £9,000,000 of liquidated profit returned to the capitalist, besides the refund of his principal, and there would still remain the existing plant of say 200,000 acres of land under cultivation by means of the said capital, worth at least £10 per acre, or altogether £2,000,000—thus showing a total profit of £11,000,000.—Looking at some tracts of land which have been relegated to weeds and waste—tracts which for long years poured forth rich harvests for their owners— the question will force itself upon us : What would now have been the conditions of these lands if their owners had been settled on them, and their families, homesteads, and accumulated profits had remained to enrich the island? Fortunately, tea has enabled most of this waste land to be profitably replanted. It is strange that, though Ceylon can show many outward and visible signs of material wealth since the establishment of the planting enterprise, in a greatly increased revenue, big public works, railways, roads, harbour works, tanks, irrigation canals, and public buildings, and in a native population greatly raised in the scale of civilisation and in personal and home comforts, yet there are few, if any, wealthy Europeans in the island. There are not a few natives, however, who have amassed fortunes. In the case of Europeans, riches, if they have been heaped up, have gone elsewhere— that is, to the Mother-country out of Ceylon; while there were no large local incomes (save among a limited number of natives) to meet the era of short crops and financial disasters which began in 1879.

Of course, we are now looking at the Ceylon planting enterprise from the colonial point of view. When a financial crisis comes, and home capitalists find they cannot realise and sell their property through the absence of local purchasers, they are apt to speak disparagingly of the colony which has done so much for their brethren, if not for themselves, in years gone by, and which will yet give a good return on capital invested in the future.

Fortunately, within the past generation, a considerable change has taken place in the conditions of planting in Ceylon. An unusually large number of younger sons, and others with a certain amount of capital of their own, have settled in the higher and healthier districts—possessing in fact one of the finest

The Benefit to the Mother-Country.

climates in the world—and have formed comparatively permanent homes, in the midst of their tea as well as coffee and cinchona fields. The number of resident proprietary and of married planters has largely increased within the past twenty years, notwithstanding depression and difficulty, and with the return of prosperity through tea, further settlement in this way may be anticipated.

As regards the native cultivation of exportable articles, the profits from six or seven million cwt. of native-grown coffee shipped, and from coir, coconut oil, plumbago, cinnamon, etc., have, of course, come back and enriched the people in a way which is visible on all sides, and is more particularly striking to old colonists. There is a very large number of wealthy native gentlemen enriched by trade and agriculture within British times, and nearly all the property in the large towns, as well as extensive planted areas, belong to them; while, as regards the labouring classes, the artisans and carters, the benefit conferred by planting expenditure will be more particularly referred to in our next chapter.

CHAPTER X.

WHAT THE PLANTING INDUSTRY HAS DONE FOR CEYLON.

Population more than doubled—Revenue expanded eightfold—Trade sixteen to twenty fold—Employment afforded to Natives—An El Dorado for the Indian immigrant—Coffee in the past, as Tea in the future, the mainstay of the Island—The Material Progress in the Planting Districts.

WHAT British capital and the planting enterprise have done for Ceylon would require an essay in itself to describe adequately. In 1837, when the pioneer coffee planters began work, Ceylon was a mere military dependency, with a revenue amounting to £372,000, or less than the expenditure, costing the Mother-country a good round sum every year, the total population not exceeding one and a half million, but requiring well-nigh 6,000 British and native troops to keep the peace.

Now we have the population increased to over three and a half millions, with only about 1,500 troops (apart from 2,500 Volunteers) largely paid for out of a revenue averaging £2,000,000, and a people far better housed, clothed, and fed, better educated and cared for in every way. The total import and export trade since planting began has expanded from half a million sterling in value to from eight to ten millions sterling, according to the harvests. During the sixty-five years referred to some fifty to fifty-five millions sterling have been paid away in wages earned in connection with plantations to Kandyan axemen, Tamil coolies, Sinhalese carpenters, domestic servants, and carters.

R. E. LEWIS, MERCHANT, PLANTER, AND EDITOR, 1841-1870.

MAJOR SKINNER C.M.G
(The great "Roadmaker" of Ceylon where he worked over 50 years.

The Planting Industry and Ceylon.

A great proportion of this has gone to benefit Southern India, the home of the Tamil coolies, of whom
close on 200,000 over and above the usual labour
supply were saved from starvation in Ceylon during
the Madras famine, 1877-8. In fact, Ceylon at that
time, mainly through its planters, contributed nearly
as much aid to her big neighbour as the total of
the "Mansion House Fund" subscribed in the
United Kingdom.

According to official papers there are several millions
of people in Southern India whose annual earnings,
taking grain, etc., at its full value, do not average
per family of five more than £3 12s., or 1s. 6d.
per month—equal to ½d. per head per day. Incredible
as this may appear, it is true, although with better
times now perhaps 1d. would be a safe rate *per caput.*
Half-a-crown a week is enough to keep an Indian
peasant with wife and two or three children in
comfort; but there are eight millions people who
cannot get this, or even 2s., perhaps only 1s. 6d., for
each family per week. No wonder that to such a
people the planting country of Ceylon, when all is
prosperous, is an El Dorado, for each family can there
earn from 12s. per week, and save from half to three-
quarters the amount. The immigrant coolie labourers
suffered from the short crops of coffee and depression
like their masters; but of late years, with the revival
of profitable industry through tea, with medical care
provided, cheap food, comfortable huts, and vegetable
gardens, few labouring classes in the world are better
off. Nor ought we to forget the Tamil Cooly Mission,
which is doing a good work in educating and Christian-
ising many among the Tamil coolies, mainly supported
as it is by the planters.

Our calculation is that from each acre of tea, cacao,
or coffee land kept in full cultivation in Ceylon five natives (men, women, and children) directly or indirectly
derive their means of subsistence. It is no wonder then

that, with a population increased in Ceylon within the planting era by one hundred per cent., four to five times the quantity of cotton cloth is consumed, and ten times the quantity of food-stuffs imported into Ceylon. As a contrast must be mentioned a calculation made respecting the British pioneers of planting—the men who worked say from 1837 to 1870—which showed that only one-tenth of these benefited themselves materially by coming to Ceylon. Ninety per cent. lost their money, health, or even life itself. Latterly the experience is not so sad, especially in respect of health.

The British governors of Ceylon have repeatedly acknowledged that the planting enterprise is the mainstay of the island. None have more forcibly shown this than Governor Sir William Gregory, who, in answer to the remark that the general revenue of the colony was being burdened with charges for railway extension and harbour works, benefiting chiefly the planting industry, said: "What, I would ask, is the basis of the whole property of Ceylon but the planting enterprise? What gave me the surplus revenues, by which I was able to make roads and bridges all over the island, causeways at Mannár and Jaffna, to make grants for education and to take measures to educate the masses—in short, to promote the general industry and enterprise of the island from Jaffna to Galle— but the results of the capital and energy engaged in the cultivation of coffee? It follows, therefore, that, in encouraging the great planting enterprise, I shall be furthering the general interests of the colony." Sir William Gregory was able to create a new province in Ceylon, entirely occupied by the poorest and previously most neglected class of natives—namely, the North-Central Province—with roads, bridges, buildings, forest clearings, and irrigation works, solely by the surplus revenues obtained from the planting enterprise.

The pioneer planter introduces into regions all but unknown to man a host of contractors, who

The Planting Industry and Ceylon.

in their turn bring in a train of pedlars, tavern-keepers, and others, eager to profit by the expenditure about to take place. To the contractors succeed the Malabar coolies, the working bees of the colony, who plant and cultivate the coffee, and at a subsequent period reap the crop. Each of these coolies consumes monthly a bushel of rice, a quantity of salt and other condiments, and occasionally cloth, arrack, etc., the import, transport, and purchase of which find employment for the merchant, the retail dealer, the carrier, and their servants; and, again, the wants of these functionaries raise around them a race of shopkeepers, domestics, and others, who, but for the success of coffee planting, would have been unable to find equally profitable employment.

Nor are the results bounded by the limits of the colony. The import of articles consumed, as well as of products exported, gives employment to hundreds of seamen and to thousands of tons of shipping that, but for this increased trade, would never have been built. The larger demand for rice stimulates and cheers the toil of the Indian ryot; the extended use of clothing benefits the Manchester spinners and weavers and all dependent on them; a host of employees and middlemen are busy furnishing tinned and other provisions in food-stuffs for a planting colony; while the increased demand for the implements of labour tells on Birmingham and Sheffield, which also benefit, as regards the tea industry, by the demand for varied machinery, for sheet lead, hoop iron, and a host of other requisites. Who shall say where the links of the chain terminate, affecting as they do indirectly all the great branches of the human family?

Then again, when plantations become productive, how many different agencies are called into operation. Tea and cocoa require a host of manipulators in the factories where, as a rule, all is prepared for shipment; but there is transport to, and handling at, the shipping port. Coffee requires far more attention at the seaport, for on arrival in Colombo the parchment of coffee has to be peeled, winnowed, and sized by the aid of steam machinery; cardamoms are picked and sorted; cinchona bark is packed by hydraulic machines; and sometimes tea is re-bulked and re-fired: all these, agencies provide employment for engineers, smiths, stokers, wood-cutters, etc.

Colombo "stores" in their best days (mainly through the drying, picking, and sorting of coffee) gave occupation to thousands (estimated at 20,000) of the industrious poor natives, and enabled them to support an expenditure for food, clothing, and other necessaries, the supply of which further furnished profitable employment to the shopkeeper, merchant seaman, etc. This is, of course, still true to a certain extent. In fact, it is impossible to pursue in all their ramifications the benefits derived from the cultivation of the fragrant berry which was once the staple product of Ceylon. Other results, too, there are—moral ones—such as must sooner or later arise from the infusion of Anglo-Saxon energy and spirit into an Eastern people, from the spread of the English language, and, what is of more importance still, the extension of civilisation and Christianity.

The material change in the planting districts and the Central Province of Ceylon within the last sixty-five years has been marvellous. Villages and towns have appeared where all was barren waste or thick jungle; roads have been cut in all directions; and prosperous villages have sprung up like magic in "The Wilderness of the Peak." Gampola, Badulla, Nuwara Eliya, and Mátalé, which each consisted of a rest-house and a few huts, and Náwalapitiya, which had no existence at all in 1837, are now populous towns; while Hatton, Talawakele, Lindula, Nanuoya, Panwila, Teldeniya, Madulkele, Deltota, Haldummulla, Lunu-

VIEW ON THE MAHAWELI GANGA: THE LEWELLE FERRY NEAR KANDY.

VIEW ON MAHAWELI GANGA NEAR KANDY.

NATIVES CLIMBING ARECANUT TREES.

The Planting Industry and Ceylon.

gala, Passara, Welimada, Balangoda, Rattota, Rakwana, Yatiyantota, etc., are more than villages.

Some of the planting grant-in-aid roads, carried through what was dense forest or waste land, are lined for miles with native houses and boutiques, as also with native cultivation in gardens or fields. The change cannot be better described than in the words of the Rev. Spence Hardy, of the Wesleyan Mission, who, after spending twenty-two years in Ceylon, between 1825 and 1847, returned to England, and revisited the island in 1862. Mr. Hardy was accustomed to travel through nearly all the Sinhalese districts. Writing in 1864, he says:—"Were some Sinhalese *appuhami* to arise, who had gone down to the grave fifty years ago, and from that time remained unconscious, he would not know his own land or people; and when told where he was he would scarcely believe his eyes, and would have some difficulty with his ears; for though there would be the old language, even that would be mixed with many words that to him would be utterly unintelligible. Looking at his own countrymen, he would say that in his time both the head and the feet were uncovered, but that now they cover both; or perhaps he would think that the youths whom he saw with stockings and shoes and caps were of some other nation. He would be shocked at the heedlessness with which *appus* and *naidas* and everybody else roll along in their bullock-bandies; passing even the carriage of the white man whenever they are able by dint of tail-pulling or hard blows; and when he saw the horsekeepers riding by the side of their masters and sitting on the same seat, there would be some expression of strong indignation. He would listen in vain for the *ho-he-yoh* of the palanquin-bearers and their loud shouts, and would look in vain for the tomjohns and doolies, and for the old lascoreens with their talipots and formal dress. He would be surprised at seeing so many women walking in the road and laughing and talking together like men, but

with no burdens on their heads and nothing in their
hands, and their clothes not clean enough for them
to be going to the temple. He would perhaps complain of the hard road, as we have heard a native
gentleman from Kalpitiya do, and say that soft sand
was much better. He would wonder where all the
tiles come from for so many houses, and would think
that the high-caste families must have multiplied
amazingly for them to require so many stately
mansions; and the porticoes, and the round white
pillars, and the trees growing in the compound, bearing
nothing but long thin thorns, or with pale yellow leaves
instead of green ones, would be objects of great
attraction. He would fancy that the Moormen must
have increased at a great rate, as he would take the
tall chimneys of the coffee stores to be the minarets
of mosques, until he saw the smoke proceeding from
them, and then he would be puzzled to know what
they could be. In the bazaar he would stare at the
policemen and the potatoes and the loaves of bread,
and a hundred other things that no bazaar ever saw
in his day. And the talk about planters and barbacues,
coolie immigration, and the overland and penny postage,
and bishops and agents of Government, and the
legislative council and banks, newspapers and mailcoaches, would confuse him by the strangeness of the
terms. He would listen incredulously when told that
there is no rajakariya, or forced labour, no fish tax:
and that there are no slaves, and that you can cut
down a cinnamon tree in your own garden without
having to pay a heavy fine. Remembering that when
Governor North made the tour of the island, he was
accompanied by 160 palanquin-bearers, 400 coolies, 2
elephants. and 50 lascoreens, and that when the adigar
Æhælapola visited Colombo he had with him a retinue
of a thousand retainers, and several elephants, he
would think it impossible that the governor could go
on a tour of inspection, or a judge on circuit, without
white olas lining the roadside, and triumphal arches,

and javelin men, and tomtoms, and a vast array of attendants. He would ask, perhaps, what king now reigns in Kandy, and whether he had mutilated any more of the subjects of Britain. From these supposed surprises, we may learn something of the changes that have taken place in the island, but we cannot tell a tithe of the whole."

If this was true when the veteran missionary wrote in 1862, the picture might well be heightened and intensified by the experiences of 1903, for the progress in the second half our late good Queen's reign ; and the beginning of King Edward VII.'s reign among the people of Ceylon is not less remarkable than it was between 1837 and 1862.

As to the comparative freedom from poverty and suffering which distinguishes the lower classes, the vast masses of the natives of Ceylon, more especially in the rural districts where nearly all have an interest in field or garden, it must be remembered that they live as a rule in the most genial of climates, where suffering from cold is impossible and the pangs of hunger are almost unknown, little more than a few plantains a day being sufficient to support life in idleness, if so chosen. Sir Edward Creasy, in his "History of England," says: "I have seen more human misery in a single winter's day in London than I have seen during my nine years' stay in Ceylon." In the larger towns, there are, of course, a good many very poor people, for whom some provision is made through Friend-in-Need Societies,— there being no poor law or rates. Occasionally, special subscriptions are raised for the poor among the merchants and planters, while the Government makes grants to the Societies and has certain charitable votes.

CHAPTER XI.

PRESENT PROSPECTS FOR CAPITALISTS IN CEYLON.

Ceylon still a good Field for Investment—Its Freedom from Atmospheric Disturbances—Shipping Conveniences at the New Harbour of Colombo—Moderate Freights—Cheap and Unrivalled Means of Transport—Certain Lands available for Tropical Culture in Coconut Palms, Rubber, Cotton, Tobacco, Fibres and other new Products—Openings for Young Men with Capital—High Position taken by the Ceylon Planter—Facilities for personal Inspection of Investments.

WHAT we have said in the previous chapter will show the value of the planting enterprise to the settled inhabitants and to the government of Ceylon. We have also pointed out the immense advantages gained in commerce and profits by the Mother-country. The British Capitalist, who, during the period of deficient coffee crops, grievously lost confidence in Ceylon, has within the past sixteen years found cogent reason to forbear condemnation, and to look still on this colony as still in the lead of British dependencies for the judicious investment of capital.

The situation of Ceylon in the Eastern World is peculiarly favoured in certain respects. The atmospheric disturbances which periodically agitate the Bay of Bengal, and carry, in hurricanes and cyclones, destruction to the shipping in the exposed Madras roadstead and the deviated Hooghly, seldom or never approach the north-eastern shores of this island. If Java and the rest of the Eastern Archipelago boast of a far richer soil than is to be found in Ceylon, it is owing to the volcanic agency which makes itself known at frequent intervals by eruptions and earthquakes, the utmsot verge of whose waves just touches the eastern coast of the island at Batticaloa and Trincomalee in scarcely perceptible undulations. On the west, again, Ceylon is equally beyond the region of the hurricanes which, extending from the Mozambique Channel, visit so often and so disastrously the coasts of Madagascar, Mauritius, and Zanzibar. The wind and rain-storms which usher in periodically the south-west and north-east monsoons sometimes inflict slight damage on the coffee and rice crops, but there is no comparison between the risks attaching to cultivation in Ceylon and those experienced by planters in Java and Mauritius.

The same absence of risk holds good with reference to the formerly opened roadstead of Colombo, and the island shipping trade, which has for years been nearly all centred there.

Except for an occasional gale from the south-west, there was no special danger to be guarded against, and the risks to vessels lying at Colombo were much less than to those at Calcutta, Madras or Bombay. But the delay in the transaction of shipping business, owing to the prevalence of a heavy surf and a stiff breeze during monsoon months, was more than sufficient to justify the very substantial breakwaters, graving dock, and allied harbour works which are now successfully drawing to full completion at Colombo. The capital of Ceylon is now the great central mail and commercial steamer port of the East. All the large steamers of the P. & O. Company, Orient, the British India, Star, Ducal, and most of the Messageries, Nord-Deutscher Lloyds, Austro-Hungarian Lloyds, Rubattino, the Clan, Glen, City, Ocean, Anchor, Holts, and other lines for Europe, India, China, the Straits, and Australia, call at Colombo regularly. One consequence of this, valuable to the merchant and planter, is the regular and comparatively moderate freight offered to most of the world's markets.

There is no tropical land—indeed there are few countries anywhere—so thoroughly served by railways and roads, canals and navigable streams, as are the principal districts of Ceylon at the present day. The means of cheap transport between the interior and the coast (a few remote districts only excepted) are unequalled in the tropics. Indian tea planters confess that their Ceylon brethren have a great advantage over them in this respect, and still more so in the abundant supply of good, steady, cheap labour, trained by long experience to plantation work. A more forcing climate, too, than that of Ceylon does not exist under the sun; while now that the country is fully opened, the risks to health are infinitesimal compared with those of pioneers in new countries or of the tea planters in the Terai of India. Whatever may be said of the inimical effects of bad seasons on coffee—too much rain at blossoming time—there can be no doubt of the advantage of abundance of moisture and heat for *tea*, and it is in respect of the fitness of large tracts of undeveloped country for tea production that we would especially ask for the attention of British capitalists.

Indian tea planters, who have come to see how tea is growing in Ceylon, confess that we are bound to rival Northern India. Tea, of as good quality as that from Assam, can be placed on board ship at Colombo for less per pound than Indian tea on board ship at Calcutta. But tea (although the principal) is only one among a list of valuable tropical products which Ceylon is well fitted to grow.

As a body, Ceylon planters are the most intelligent, gentlemanly, and hospitable of any colonists in British dependencies. The rough work of pioneering in the early days before there were district roads, villages, supplies, doctors, or other comforts of civilisation, was chiefly done by hard-headed Scots: men bivouacked in the trackless jungle with the scantiest accommodation under tropical rains lasting for weeks together, with rivers swollen to flood-level and impassable while food supplies often ran short, as none could be got across the wide torrents. All these and many other similar experiences are of the past in the settled planting districts of Ceylon, although there are outlying parts where pioneers can still rough it to their hearts' content. In the hill-country the pioneers about twenty years ago began to be succeeded by quite a different class of men. Younger sons with a capital, present or prospective, of a few thousand pounds, educated at public schools, and many of them University men, found an opening in life on Ceylon plantations far more congenial than that of the Australian bush or the backwoods of Canada. Of course, some of these did not succeed as planters, as they probably would not have succeeded at anything in the colonies; but for well-inclined young men of the right stamp, not afraid of hard work, Ceylon still presents an opening as planters of tea, Liberian coffee, cacao, coconut palms, etc., provided the indispensable capital is available.

The usual mode, and the safe one, is to send the young man fresh from home, through the introduction of some London or Colombo firm to study his business as a planter, and to learn the colloquial Tamil spoken by the coolies, under an experienced planter two or three years. In prosperous times such young assistants were taught and boarded free in return for their help, and began to earn a salary after a year or so. Now a fee for board and teaching (£50, or at most £100 for a year) may be needful; but only capitalists or young men who are to pioneer elsewhere should at present (1903) come to the island, the situations for working planters being all fully taken up. At the same time nowhere in the whole wide world can young men learn so thoroughly the management of native free labourers, the mysteries of tea, coffee, cacao cinchona, palm planting, etc., or be so well equipped as *tropical* agriculturists as in Ceylon. Ceylon planters and machinists have taught the rest of the tropics how to grow and prepare coffee properly; more is known in it about the mysteries of cinchona bark culture than anywhere else; the Ceylon tea planter had made his mark in the production of fine teas. Ceylon "cocoa" has already fetched the highest prices in the London market, just as she sends thither the finest cinnamon, cardamoms, coconut-oil, coir, etc. It may truly be said that the *Press* of Ceylon has greatly aided the planters in acquiring this pre-eminence. The *Ceylon Observer* has sent special correspondents to report on the tea regions of Assam and Darjeeling; on the cinchona gardens of the Nilgiris and of Java ; to West Africa to learn all about Liberian coffee, and to South and Central America to ascertain the progress of coffee; while its manuals on coffee, tea, cinchona, cacao, indiarubber, coconuts and areca palms, cardamoms and cinnamon planting, on gold and gems, are known throughout the tropics. Of late years, since 1881, a monthly periodical, the *Tropical Agriculturist*, published at the same office, has been effectually bringing together all the information and experience available in reference to everything that concerns agriculture in tropical and sub-tropical regions. This is merely mentioned, *en passant*, in part explanation of the high position taken by the Ceylon-trained planter, wherever he goes.

After the depression of 1879 many Ceylon plantation managers and assistant superintendents had to seek their fortunes elsewhere ; and, indeed, the planting districts of Southern India may be said to be offshoot settlements from Ceylon, while in Fiji, Northern Australia, the Straits Settlements, Burmah, North Borneo, East, Central and West Africa, there are Ceylon planters pioneering and building up a planting enterprise.

The convenience afforded by quick passages in large steamers *via* the Suez Canal, and by railways and roads in Ceylon, is such that capitalists can now

THE LATE A. M. FERGUSON C.M.G., COLOMBO, CEYLON.
The oldest Newspaper Editor in Asia—Editor of the "Ceylon Observer."

HON. MR. JOHN FERGUSON, C.M.G.
Editor of the "Ceylon Observer" &c., &c.
General European Representative in the Ceylon Legislative Council.

inspect their property in Ceylon with as much ease and pleasure as they would have in a two months' trip to the Highlands of Scotland or to the South of Europe; and it is becoming quite a common thing for the retired proprietor or business man to run out to Ceylon for the winter months. How different the case was thirty years ago! We remember a Glasgow capitalist owning a property worth £100,000 in Ceylon, coming out to see it, and after getting to Nuwara Eliya, within forty miles of the property, refusing to go further, so bad were the roads; and he, a man of sixty-eight or seventy, returned home without ever having seen the plantation; he ultimately sold his interests to a Limited Company at a considerable profit!

The carriage of produce from the estates to Colombo, from 100 to 200 miles, used often to take as much time and cost as much as the freight 15,000 miles round the Cape. From the remotest planting districts to Colombo carriage sometimes still costs in time and money as much as freight to London *via* the Canal; but, as a whole, Ceylon is magnificently roaded, has a very considerable proportion of railways, especially of first-class mountain lines, with an ample supply of cheap labour, and a particularly favourable climate.

Finally, let the capitalist know that obnoxious *laws* connected with land and commerce, based on the Roman-Dutch system, have either been or are shortly to be reformed. Codes have been framed, and antiquated laws bearing on mortgages and other business transactions will be superseded.

CHAPTER XII.

ATTRACTIONS FOR THE TRAVELLER AND VISITOR.

The Voyage a Pleasure Trip—Historical Monuments, Vegetation, etc. —Variety of Climate—Colombo, the Capital—Kandy, the Highland Capital—Nuwara Eliya the Sanatorium—The Horton Plains —Adam's Peak—Uva and its long-delayed Railway—Ancient Cities of Anuradhapura and Polonnaruwa—Occasional Pearl Fisheries—Probable Expense of a Visit to Ceylon—The Alleged Inconveniences of Tropical Life.

TO the traveller and visitor Ceylon offers more attractions even than to the capitalist and would-be planter. It is a joke with disappointed men that the stranger can see on the hills of Ceylon the graves of more British sovereigns than of Kandyan Kings! But the latter are not wanting, and no dependency of Britain—India not excepted—presents more attractions than Ceylon to the intelligent traveller, to the botanist, the antiquarian or the man of science, the orientalist, or even to the politician and the sociologist. Visitors from America and North India have said that Ceylon, for natural beauty, historical and social interest, is the "show-place of the universe," and that, as such, it might well in these days of travelling sightseers, be leased by either a Barnum or Cook! The voyage of twenty-one to twenty-five days from London to Colombo (of fourteen to eighteen from Brindisi or Marseilles) on a first-class steamer of any of half a dozen lines competing at from £50 to £55 for the single, or less than double for the return passage, is at the proper season of the year—September to March or April—a pleasure trip of the most

SHRINE OF THE SACRED TOOTH: INTERIOR OF THE DALADA MALIGAWA, KANDY.

A BUDDHIST SHRINE.

Attractions for the Traveller and Visitor. 101

enjoyable and instructive kind. The calling by some steamers at Gibraltar, Malta, Port Said, Suez, and Aden affords instruction and pleasuse of a high order; while the beauty of Ceylon vegetation and scenery the interest attaching to her people, towns, and ancient cities and monuments, amply reward even the worst sea traveller for the unpleasantness of a voyage. Tennent well says that Ceylon, from whatever direction it may be approached, unfolds a scene of loveliness and grandeur unsurpassed, if it be rivalled, by any land in the universe. Its names—"Lanka, the resplendent," of the Brahmins; the "pearl-drop on the brow of Ind," of the Buddhists; "the island of jewels," of the Chinese; the land of the hyacinth and ruby," of the Greeks; and "the home of Adam and Eve after losing Paradise," according to the Mohammedans—as Arabi and his fellow-exiles said soon after their arrival—will show the high esteem in which it has been held both in the East and the West.

As for its history, as already mentioned, no region between Chaldea and China can tell so much of its past deeds as Ceylon, while the ruins of its ancient capitals in palaces, temples, dágobas, and tanks are only second to those of Egypt. These ruins are all now rendered accessible in a few days' trip by railway, coach, and other conveyance from Colombo, without risk or incovenience, and at very little expense to the traveller.*

As to vegetation and natural history generally, Ceylon is one huge tropical garden, presenting objects of intense interest to the botanist and zoologist, from the coral reef and pearl oyster banks around its coasts, and the palms and creepers bending down to meet "the leaguelong rollers thundering on its shores," to the grassy pathways

* *See* Burrows' "Guide to the Buried Cities of Ceylon"; also Guides to Colombo. to Kandy, Nuwara Eliya, and Kurunegala published by A. M. &. J. Ferguson.

running up to hills clothed to their summit with the most varied forest trees, or to the plateaux of Nuwara Eliya and the surrounding plains—"the Elysium of Ceylon"—where, at an elevation of over 6,000 feet in grass, and flowers, and trees, a bit of

"Europe amid Asia smiles."

There, is snug cottages, wood fires and blankets are often required to keep away the cold. In one day the visitor can pass from Colombo, with its average temperature of 81°, to the sanatorium, with its wintry comforts, and temperature falling to freezing-point occasionally, but averaging 57°; or, now that the Uva railway is open—he can pass on the same evening to a nearly perfect climate at an average temperature of 63° on the Haputale range. During March, April, and May—"the season" at the sanatorium —the weather is very equable, comparatively dry, and delightful. September, and part of August and October, are very pleasant, and often January and February, as well as December sometimes; but thin ice on the water, and hoar frost on the herbage, are then not uncommon. The very wet months are June, July, and December. Sir Samuel Baker lived eight years continuously at Nuwara Eliya, and speaks very highly of its healthfulness.* Indian civilians and other residents declare that Nuwara Eliya is more pleasantly accessible to them than most of their own hill-stations, the short sea-voyage from Calcutta or Bombay being an additional benefit to many who come from the hot dry plains of Central India. For invalids, the marine boarding-house at Mount Lavinia, as well as the Colombo seaside hotels, are very safe and suitable places of resort.

The perfection of climate, in an average of 65° all the year round, is found at 5,000 feet, among the bungalows

---

* *See* Sir Samuel Baker's "Eight Years" and "Rifle and Hound in Ceylon."

of Dimbula, Dikoya and Maskeliya, or of Uva, with its
drier and at times more pleasant climate. The wet
season of the south-west monsoon (June and July) is
sometimes rather trying to residents in the districts
west of Nuwara Eliya. With the Uva railway open,
visitors are now able to pass easily to the ancient
principality, now province of Uva, where the weather
is bright and dry in these months. It is no
wonder then that parents and others, with their
sons, daughters, or other relatives settled in Ceylon,
should have begun to visit it in order to escape the
trying winter and spring months in England. Not a
few who used to winter in Egypt find it nearly as
convenient and more interesting to come on to Ceylon.
The late Mr. C. A. Cameron and his wife, Mrs. Julia
Cameron (the well-known artist and friend of Tennyson),
even when in advanced years (approaching in Mr.
Cameron's case to or over fourscore), made the voyage
across more than once to visit and stay for considerable
periods with their sons settled in the island. One
London lady past middle life, who ventured to visit her
daughter in Ceylon, dreaded the voyage so much that
her leave-taking was of the most solemn and desponding
character; but her experience was so entirely pleasant
that she has since repeated the winter visit several
times, and now declares that the trip to "the city" from
her residence in a cab is more dangerous and trying to
the nerves than the voyage from the Thames to Colombo
in a first-class steamer. Of late years winter visitors
from Europe and hot-weather refugees from India have
been numerous, apart from "globe-trotters" calling
in; while the large number of passengers by the mail
and commercial steamers to and from Australia, China,
India, etc., who land for a day or more, give Colombo,
and sometimes Kandy, a very busy appearance.

Colombo, the capital, a city of close on 160,000 inhabitants, with its fine artificial harbour (projected by Sir Hercules Robinson and continued by Sir William Gregory
and Sir West Ridgeway) has much to interest the visitor

in its beauitful drives over the smoothest of roads through the "Cinnamon Gardens"; its lake, and the Kelani river, although Sir Edward Barnes's bridge of boats has been recently superseded by a modern iron screwpile bridge; its public museum, erected by Sir William Gregory, and containing objects of interest from all parts of the island; the old Dutch church, containing the tombs and monuments of Dutch governors; the bungalows and gardens of the Europeans; its hospitals and other public institutions; still more unique are the crowded native parts of the town, teeming with every variety of oriental race and costume—the effeminate light brown Sinhalese, the men as well as women wearing their hair tied behind in knots (the former patronising combs, the latter elaborate hairpins), the darker and more manly Tamils, Hindus of every caste and dress, Moormen or Arab descendants, Afghan traders, Malay policemen, a few Parsees and Chinese, Kaffir mixed descendants,* besides the Eurasians of Dutch, or Portuguese, or English and native descent.

Colombo has three first-class, besides minor hotels, and the stranger is soon surrounded by native pedlars, especially jewellers with their supply of gems, from rare cat's-eyes, rubies, sapphires, and pearls to firstclass Birmingham imitations.

The scene to the new-comer is bewilderingly interesting; visions of the "Arabian Nights" are conjured up, for, as Miss Jewsbury sang after her visit some fifty years ago:—

"Ceylon! Ceylon! 'tis nought to me
How thou wert known or named of old,
As Ophir, or Taprobané,
By Hebrew king, or Grecian bold:—

---

* Kaffirs first arrived in Ceylon as a company of soldiers sent from Goa to help the Portuguese against the Sinhalese in 1636-40. The first British Governor (the Hon. F. North) actually *purchased* a body of Kaffir soldiers from the Portuguese Government at Goa, besides sending an officer to try and "crib" Malays from the eastward (Straits and Java)! Major Skinner went on a legitimate recruiting expedition to the Straits and Java in the early "thirties" to get Malays for the Ceylon Rifles, but was not successful.

Attractions for the Traveller and Visitor.

> "To me thy spicy-wooded vales,
> Thy dusky sons, and jewels bright,
> But image forth the far-famed tales—
> But seem a new Arabian night.
>
> "And when engirdled figures crave
> Heed to thy bosom's glittering store—
> I see Aladdin in his cave;
> I follow Sinbad on the shore."

Although the mean temperature of Colombo is nearly as high as that of any station in the world as yet recorded, yet the climate is one of the healthiest and safest for Europeans, because of the slight range between night and day, and between the so-called "seasons," of which, however, nothing is known there, it being one perpetual summer varied only by the heavy rains of the monsoon months—May, June, October, and November. But in the wettest months it rarely happens that it rains continuously even for two whole days and nights; as a rule, it clears up for some hours each day.

Waterworks have been constructed, at a heavy cost, to convey water from mountain streams, distant thirty miles, to serve Colombo. When the works and distribution over the city are completed —an additional pipe to increase the supply is now being laid—and when the drainage (now taken in hand by Mr. Mansergh) is complete, Colombo will more than ever be entitled to its reputation of being one of the healthiest (as well as most beautiful) cities in the tropics, or indeed in the world. A convenient system of electric tramways is worked over two long and populous routes affording one of the best and easiest means of seeing the city and people; while, besides the railway through one side of the town, there are numerous conveyances of different descriptions for hire at very moderate rates, more especially "Jinirickshaws" (man-power carriages), peculiar to Japan and the Far East.*

There are several places of interest in the neighbourhood of Colombo that are well worth a visit.

A seaside railway line runs for 98½ miles as far as Mátara, which may erelong be extended 24 miles to Tangalla. This passes through several interesting stations and towns:—Mount Lavinia, with its commanding hotel, originally erected as a Governor's residence; Moratuwa, the scene of a flourishing church in connection with the Wesleyan Mission; Pánaduré, with its backwater and fishing; Kalutara, the Richmond of Ceylon; Bentota, the old half-way station, famous for its oysters and river; Ambalangoda, for its sea-bathing; Galle, for its picturesque harbour and surroundings; Weligama for the bay and village so dear to Haeckel; and Mátara, with its star-fort and blue river, the Nilwaláganga. The railway runs nearly all the way under an avenue of coconut palms, diversified here and there by jak, bread-fruit, and other fruit trees, and close to the seashore with the waves breaking over coral reefs and a cool breeze generally blowing. The enjoyment of the scene to a lover of natural beauty is indescribable : the cool shade of the palm groves, the fresh verdure of the grass, the bright tints of the flowering trees, with occasional glimpses through openings in the dense wood of the mountains of the interior, the purple zone of hills above which the sacred mountain of Adam's Peak is sometimes seen, all

* "Jinirickshaws," which have become very popular in Ceylon towns, in Colombo, Kandy, and Nuwara Eliya especially, were freely introduced in 1884, on the suggestion of the author, after a visit to the Straits, China, and Japan, where he noted the "'rickshaws" and wrote of their peculiar fitness for Colombo roads. Mr. Whittall, an ex-Hong Kong resident, introduced the first "'rickshaw" some time before, but little notice was taken of it till after the letters appeared. Bicycles have of late years become very common and are freely used even by Sinhalese wearing "comboys" or petticoats.

COLOMBO PRIVATE "RICKSHAW."

YOUNG TAMIL MARRIED WOMAN

Attractions for the Traveller and Visitor.

combine to form a landscape, which, in novelty and beauty, is unsurpassed:—

> "So fair a scene, so green a sod,
> Our English fairies never trod."

Returning to Colombo, we may remark on the great variety of vegetation presented to the visitor, apart from the palms (coconut, areca, kitul, dwarf, etc.), the shrubs, such as cinnamon, the crotons, hibiscus and cabbage trees, the aloes and other plants, or the many fruit trees of the gardens. The winding, ubiquitous lake, too, adds much to the beauty and health of the city.

As Miss Martineau wrote, fifty years ago, in her political romance, "Cinnamon and Pearls":—"The Blue Lake of Colombo, whether gleaming in the sunrise or darkening in the storms of the monsoon, never loses its charm. The mountain range in the distance is an object for the eye to rest lovingly upon, whether clearly outlined against the glowing sky, or dressed in soft clouds, from which Adam's Peak alone stands aloft, like a dark island in the waters above the firmament."

Nor is Edward Carpenter writing in 1891 ("Adam's Peak to Elephanta") less complimentary, when he says:—"Everywhere are trees and flowering shrubs and, as one approaches the outskirts of the town, the plentiful broad leaves of coco-palms and bananas overshadowing the roads. Nor in any description of Colombo should the fresh-water lake be forgotten, which ramifying and winding in most intricate fashion through the town, and in one place coming within a hundred yards of the sea, surprises one continually with enchanting glimpses. I don't know any more delightful view of its kind—all the more delightful because so unexpected—than that which greets the eye on entering the Fort Railway Station at Colombo. You pass through the booking-office and find yourself on a platform which, except for the line of rails between, might be a terrace on the lake itself; a large expanse of water with wooded shores and islands, interspersed with villas, cottages and cabins lies before you; white-sailed boats are going to and fro; groups of dark figures, waist-deep in water, are washing clothes; children are playing and swimming in the water; and when, as I saw it once, the evening sun is shining through the transparent, green fringe of banana palms which occupies the immediate foreground, and the calm lake beyond reflects like a mirror the gorgeous hues of sky and cloud, the scene is one which, for effect of colour, can hardly be surpassed."

A delightful country to pass through for vegetation, river, lake and plantation scenery is that between Colombo and Negombo and on to Chilaw and Puttalam, some 80 miles; but the coach journey is not very comfortable, although its early supersession by a railway is hoped for. The vegetation up to Negombo, and indeed Márawila, is about the richest in the island. Some of the finest cinnamon and coconut plantations are *en route*. A great many Roman Catholic churches are noted, many of the people being descendants of the converts of Francis Xavier.

An interesting excursion from Colombo is by railway and coach for 60 miles to Ratnapura, " the City of Gems," running for the first 37 miles by narrow-gauge railway which, at Avissawella, enters into one of the most extensive tea-growing districts, although the coach for the " City of Gems " has to go 24 miles further. Railway extension from Avissawella to Ratnapura is looked for erelong. If the traveller chooses he can pass from Avissawella through this Kelani tea district by rail to Yatiyantota and drive by carriage thence to join the railway at Nawalapitiya. When he goes on by coach to Ratnapura, Pelmadulla, and Rakwána, he ought to see all about " gem-digging "

RUINS OF THE THUPARAMA DAGOBA, ANURADHAPURA.

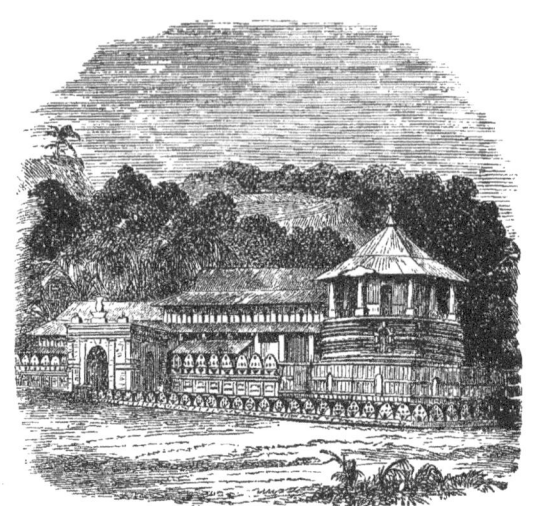

KANDY MALIGAWA, OR TEMPLE OF THE TOOTH.

REMAINS OF THE OLD TEMPLE GATEWAY, DONDRA HEAD, CEYLON.

Attractions for the Traveller and Visitor. 109

pits and plumbago mines, and he can also see the plantations; while, should he pass on by road via Balangoda to Haputale, he will pass through magnificent scenery and come to very fine tea and coffee fields.

The mildness of the climate of Colombo, the murmur of cricket and insect life at night, and the brilliancy of the moonlight, strike the stranger, although the closeness of the atmosphere then is sometimes felt to be oppressive, and the attention of mosquitoes at certain seasons is far from pleasant. But the low-country can easily be exchanged for the hills. In four hours one passes from Colombo by a splendid railway running through interesting country,* surmounting an incline which is one of the greatest railway ascents in the (at least, tropical) world, 1,600 feet above sea-level, to the last capital of the native kings of the island—Kandy—a town of 27,000 people. Kandy is uniquely beautiful: the most charming little town in the world, travellers usually describe it. It is situated in a valley surrounded by hills, and boasts an artificial lake, Buddhist and Hindu temples, including the Máligáwa, the most sacred Buddhist temple in the world; this contains the so-called relic of Buddha's tooth, to which the kings and priests of Burmah, Siam, and Cambodia send occasional offerings, and which is held in reverence in portions of India, Thibet, and even China and Japan. "The Pavilion," one of the three official residences of the Governor in the island, with its gardens and grounds, surmounted by the public "Lady Horton's Walk" on a hill-range overlooking the Dumbara valley, will attract attention. The view of the town

---
* From Polgahawela, the half-way station, a railway is also open to Kurunegala, the capital of the North-Western Province, the residence of the kings of Ceylon from 1319 to 1347 A. D., and romantically situated under the shade of Ætagalla (the Rock of the Tusked Elephant), 600 feet high. The North-Western Province is a favourite field for sportsmen, and the great Northern Railway of Ceylon begins at Kurunegala and, passing by Anuradhapura, runs for nearly 200 miles to the coast beyond Jaffna at Kangesanturai.

from any of the hillsides surrounding it is surpassingly interesting.*

Between Colombo and Kandy extensive paddy or rice cultivation can be seen in the low-country; also plantations of coconut palms; and more inland fields of tea, with some of Liberian coffee and chocolate trees; while higher up the Kandyans' terraced rice-fields may be noted.

The Botanical Gardens at Pérádeniya, three miles from Kandy, "beautiful for situation exceedingly," as well as full of interest in the vegetation, are well worth a visit.†

The group of palms at the entrance has always been an object of admiration to strangers, and it shows how well adapted Ceylon is to be the home of this family. We print an engraving of this group, and append here the—

NAMES OF PALMS, ETC., IN GROUP.

(See List of Illustrations.)

1. Corypha umbraculifera (Talipot)—highest plant in the centre.
2. Phytelephas macrocarpa (Ivory-nut Palm)—in front of foregoing, and behind native servant.
3. Cycas circinális (called erroneously "Sago Palm")—immediately to the left of preceding, in front.
4. Areca Catechu—directly behind the Cycas, and with its head of leaves amongst those of the Talipot.
5. Yucca gloriosa—a cluster of shoots of this in front; to the left of the Cycas.
6. Cocos nucifera (Coconut)—immediately behind the Yucca.
7. Oncosperma fasciculata ("Kattoo Kittool")—behind, between the Talipot and Coconut.
8. Acrocomia sclerocarpa—behind the Yucca, and with its trunk a little to the left of that of the Coconut.
9. Livistona sp.—at the extreme left of the group.
10. Livistona Chinensis ("Mauritius Palm")—behind and directly to the right of the Talipot.

---

* *See* Skeen's and Burrows' Guides to Kandy, etc., published by A. M. & J. Ferguson.
† An interesting little guide-book and list of plants, etc., have been prepared by the late director, Dr. Trimen, and improved by his successor, and are available.

GROUP OF PALMS AND ALLIED PLANTS (INDIGENOUS AND EXOTIC) IN THE ROYAL BOTANIC GARDENS, PERADENIYA, NEAR KANDY.

ENTRANCE TO THE ROYAL BOTANIC GARDENS,
PERADENIYA, NEAR KANDY.

Attractions for the Traveller and Visitor.

11. Livistona sp.—immediately to the right of the coolie, in front.
12. Oreodoxa regia (Cabbage Palm)—directly behind No. 11; trunk large, smooth, bulged above the middle.
13. Sabal Palmetto ("Palmetto" of the Southern States of America)—to the right of the group, in front.
14. Eloesis Guineensis ("Palm Oil Palm" of Africa)—with numerous long spreading leaves; behind and overtopping No. 13, and to the extreme right of the group.

From Kandy a visit to the Dumbara valley, five or six miles by road, or to Mátalé, twenty miles by railway, will show some of the finest cacao (chocolate) plantations; while $south_{h}war_{d}$, the railway journey to Gampola and Náwalapitiya, for 17 miles, and then on for forty-two miles, rising by successive inclines to a point 5,290 feet above sea-level at Nánu-oya, near Nuwara Eliya, will carry the visitor through long stretches of tea plantations, with a sprinkling here and there of cinchona trees and some coffee fields. These are placed amidst enchanting mountain scenery, with rivers, forests, waterfalls and gorges that nothing can surpass. Altogether, the railway ride from Colombo to Nánu-oya, nearly 130 miles, and rising from sea-level fully one mile in the air, is one of the most varied and interesting in the world.* The journey is made by a first-class broad-gauge railway, with a refreshment car attached, in seven to eight hours, without any change of train or carriage.

Nánu-oya is only about four miles from Nuwara Eliya, by a fine road, but there is now a light 2½-feet gauge railway running up to the heart of the sanatorium. There is good hotel and boarding-house accommodation; the "Gregory Lake," due to Sir William Gregory, is a fine feature; a grand golf links, racing, tennis, croquet and hockey grounds; public park and garden, and Hill and United Clubs, reading rooms and libraries are available. Sir West Ridgeway has done an immense deal for Nuwara Eliya: its water

* See "Guide to Ceylon Railways and Railway Extensions, with Notice of the Sanatorium," compiled and published by A. M, & J. Ferguson, and Burrows' "Guide to Nuwara Eliya."

supply, lighting, conservancy, roads and buildings. Plantations of tea and cinchona, and the finely situated and admirably kept Hakgala experimental gardens, are in the neighbourhood. The summit of the highest mountain in Ceylon, Pidurutalágala, 8,296 feet, or 2,000 feet above the Plains, can be easily attained in a walk before breakfast; while a trip to the top of the far more interesting Adam's Peak (sacred alike to Buddhists, Hindus, Mohammedans, and even Roman Catholics) can be readily arranged by leaving the railway at Hatton. Thence a good road runs to a point on the mountain breast about 3,000 feet from the summit, which is 7,353 feet high. The climb up Adam's Peak is a stiff one, particularly the last portion, where steps are cut out, and even chains fixed in the rock, to prevent the climber from slipping or being blown down the side of the precipice in stormy seasons. The view from the top in clear weather is ample reward for all trouble, and the projection of the shadow across the low-country to the sea as the sun rises is a sight, once seen, never to be forgotten.

Another interesting trip is the drive from Nuwara Eliya down the old mail-coach road by Ramboda Pass, famous for its waterfalls and outlook, through Pussellawa to Gampola,. From Nuwara Eliya, too, excursions can be made to Udapussellawa and Maturata districts or to New Galway, calling at Hakgala on the way. Again, from Nuwara Eliya a day's ride suffices to reach the Horton Plains, 1,000 feet higher; and there, as well as between these two points, is a large extent of upland in a delightful climate, well suited for comparative settlement by Europeans. At any rate their children could be kept here in rude health until twelve to fourteen years of age; and the soil is well fitted for small farms and vegetable gardens, as well as for growing cinchona and the finer qualities of tea. Cricket, tennis, as well as other sports, and shooting

HOOLOOGANGA FALLS, KELLEBOKKA VALLEY.

NUWARA ELIYA AND HAKGALA PEAKS FROM RAMBODA PASS.

Attractions for the Traveller and Visitor. 113

trips enliven the planter's labours. As a sanatorium for British troops, this site is unequalled, both for climate and accessibility.

Already the surrounding districts, served by road and Railway, and having villages, stores, churches, clergymen, and doctors, are beginning to be regarded as the comparatively permanent homes of many of the planters. Nuwara Eliya and the Horton Plains border on the Uva Principality, with its comparatively dry upland climate, where so deliciously pleasant and health-giving is the air that to breathe it has been compared to a draught of the pure juice of the grape. This country is now most readily approached by first-class railway rising from Nanuoya until at Pattipola summit level is reached in 6,200 feet, and then traversing tunnels and winding down until at Haputale the elevation is 4,500 feet and a grand view of the low-country to the seaside at Hambantota is obtained; at Diyatalawa the old camp of the Boer prisoners (now a camp for military and naval convalescents) is noted; while at the terminus at Bandárawela, about 4,200 feet above sea-level, 160 miles from Colombo, the perfection of climate in Ceylon is reached. Probably there is not such an attractive railway ride in the world of its length as that from Colombo into Uva. The railway journey through the dividing mountain range and the burst into the grand Uva amphitheatre of mountain range, embracing rolling patanas (grassy plains), rich, cultivated valleys with sparkling streams and glistening irrigation channels, will be full of an interest of its own to travellers. The effect of the tunnels and the open spaces between, when trains are running, will be most striking. Emerging from a tunnel, travellers will suddenly behold spread out as a vast panorama the grassy prairies, the green rice fields, the glancing rivers and the grand mountain ranges, of the valley of Uva; a marked contrast to the alternating tea cultivation and forest expanses of the western side of the range. The scene will repeatedly appear and disappear as if at the command of a magician, until the series of tunnels and of wooded hills give place to the open and precipitous ranges which stretch from Idulgashena to the Haputale Pass, whence the sea will be visible on the eastern side of island. A waterfall in Eastern Haputale, one of the divisions of Uva, is supposed to be the highest in Ceylon, though in Maturata and Madulsima there are rivals, while the Ella Pass and the view of the low-country and sea coast from the hill range is very striking.* The Province of Uva too, perhaps more than any other in Ceylon, will offer attractions and opportunities to the planting settler and capitalist for investment, its soil and climate being generally considered the best in the island for the staple products of the colonist as well as for the fruits and vegetables cultivated by the natives. In the park country division of the province, there is also rich pasturage for feeding cattle, while opportunities for sport, from snipe to elephants, are presented on all sides. As already stated, civil and military officers, merchants and others, from India, are now beginning to regard Ceylon, with its seaside boarding-establishments, and its comfortable accommodation at Nuwara Eliya sanatorium, as more desirable than Indian hill-stations during the hot season.

From Kandy the trip to the ancient capitals of Anuradhapura and Polonnaruwa, from ninety to sixty miles to the north and east, can easily be arranged

* "Perhaps there is not a scene in the world which combines sublimity and beauty in a more extraordinary degree than that which is presented at the Pass of Ella, where, through an opening in the chain of mountains, the road from Badulla descends rapidly to the lowlands, over which it is carried for upwards of seventy miles, to Hambantota, on the south coast of the island. The ride to Ella passes for ten or twelve miles along the base of hills thickly wooded, except on those spots where the forest has been cleared for planting coffee. The view is therefore obstructed, and at one point appears to terminate in an impassable glen, but on reaching this the traveller is startled on discovering a ravine through which a torrent has forced its way, disclosing a passage to the plains below, over which; for more than sixty miles, the prospect extends, unbroken by a single eminence, till, far in the distance, the eye discerns a line of light, which marks where the sunbeams are flashing on the waters of the Indian Ocean."—*Emerson Tennent.*

RUINS OF THE RUANWELI DAGOBA, ANURADHAPURA.

THE SACRED BO-TREE, THE OLDEST HISTORICAL TREE IN THE WORLD, FIRST PLANTED FROM A CUTTING IN CEYLON 2,133 YEARS AGO.

Attractions for the Traveller and Visitor. 115

for the visitor; and from amid the ruins of Anurádhapura (2,000 years old) one can despatch a telegram to
friends at home in England or America, or post a
budget of news. Very shortly (by 1905) the visitor
can pass from Colombo to Anurádhapura all the way
by railway, and in the following year go on if he pleases
by the same locomotive train to Jaffna.

For sportsmen there is elephant shooting in the far
south in the Hambantota district, or in the Eastern Province, or outlying northern districts; elk hunting round
Nuwara Eliya; or wild buffalo, bear, boar, or wild
hog, and cheetah hunting in the forests of the north
and east.*

We have already alluded to the prospect of successive pearl-oyster fisheries off the north-west coast, for
which Ceylon has been famous from time immemorial;
and which can be readily visited, as steamers fly to and
fro during the fishery. A very successful one of nearly
44,000,000 oysters, bringing in nearly 1,223,355 rupees
to the Ceylon Government, was held early in April-
May 1903. The primitive mode of diving for and
gathering the oysters by a particular caste of native
divers (who are paid by one-third of the oysters taken),
their sale by Government auction, and the business
in pearls with thousands of dealers and their followers,
who collect from all parts of India in the hope of a
good fishery taking place,—all this is full of novelty.†

A further interesting trip to the visitor, is that
round the island by one of the well-found steamers
of the Ceylon Steam Navigation Company; a week
suffices for this, including the passage northward
through Paumben Channel, with a visit to the far-

---

*.-Elephant kraals—a system of capturing elephants peculiar
to Ceylon—are now of rare occurrence, being organised only on
special occasions. Herds of as many as 200 elephants and 100 wild
hogs have been seen at one time in Ceylon.

† For particulars of the "Pearl Fisheries" see Ferguson's
"Ceylon Handbook and Directory," for successive years. Also see
"Gold, Gems and Pearls" compiled by J. Ferguson.

famed Rameswaram temple, to Jaffna and its gardenpeninsula and interesting mission-stations; to Point Pedro, the *ultima thule*; Trincomalee, the naval headquarters in the Indian Ocean, with its magnificent harbour; Batticaloa, with its fine lake (singing-fish), coconut and rice culture; Hambantota and its salt pans; perhaps Mátara, and its three rivers as well as beautiful surroundings; and Point-de-Galle.

The cost of living in Ceylon at hotels ranges from 8s. or 10s. per day upwards, board and comfortable accommodation by the month being available at from £8 to £10 for each adult. A lady and gentleman leaving England early in November, and returning by the 1st of May, spending four clear months in a comfortably-furnished bungalow in the hill-country of Ceylon, could do so for a total cost of from £250 to £300, including cost of trips to the points of interest in the island; the greater portion of this amount being for passage-money to and fro, which now ranges from £60 to £90 for return tickets. An individual visitor could, of course, do the trip for less. With further competition there can be no doubt—for the steamers' margin of profit allows of a considerable reduction*—that the day is not far distant when £35 should secure a first-class passage between Ceylon and England, and £50 a return ticket extending over six months. Before the Suez Canal opened £100 was the single rate of the overland route.

It may be averred that little has been said about the *drawbacks* to life in, or even to a visit to, Ceylon. The tropical heat in the low-country must be endured; but, if found trying, a single day's journey will carry the visitor to a cool region. As to the detestable leeches described by Tennent as infesting every country pathway, and the poisonous snakes, the visitor

---

* A first-class passage by mail steamer can at present be obtained for Melbourne or Sydney for very little more than to Colombo, which is only half way; this is an anomaly which must shortly be removed.

TRINCOMALEE.

Attractions for the Traveller and Visitor. 117

may be months, or even years, in Ceylon without ever seeing the one or the other, being no more troubled by them than by the enormous crocodiles in the river or the voracious sharks round the coast. Repulsive insects, such as centipedes, scorpions, and large spiders, are also rare in any well-ordered bungalow; while mosquitoes are only occasionally troublesome, and that chiefly in the low-country. The hum of insect life, as soon as day closes, in the moist, warm, low-country at once arrests the ears of new-comers, though local residents become so accustomed to it as not to hear it until their attention is specially directed to it. The brilliancy of moon-lit nights, especially of a full moon, in the tropics is generally a great treat to strangers; so also are the stars and constellations of the Southern Hemisphere, including the bright fixed star Canopus and the interesting as well as brilliant constellation of the Southern Cross. The monotony of perpetual summer, and of days and nights of about the same length all the year round, affords one point of strong contrast to England, but is pleasing, rather than otherwise, to the visitor.

No less than from 25,000 to 30,000 passengers call at Colombo during each year, bound to England, Europe generally or America, or to Australia, India, the Straits, or China.

CHAPTER XIII.

THE REVENUE AND EXPENDITURE OF CEYLON.

Chief Sources of Revenue:—Grain and Customs Dues, Sales of Crown Land and Railway Profits—Taxation and Revenue.

UNTIL 1828 there was an annual excess of expenditure over revenue in Ceylon: but between 1829 and 1836 the balance was on the right side, owing chiefly to a series of successful pearl fisheries. From 1837 to 1842, and again from 1846 to 1849, expenditure once more exceeded revenue; but from that time there was a surplus, and the amount of revenue quadrupled within twenty-five years, owing to the rapid development of the planting enterprise—the sale of Crown forest lands largely contributing—until in 1877 it attained a maximum of R17,026,190. After that, owing to the falling off in the coffee crops, the revenue went down, until in 1882 it reached R12,161,570. Then a gradual recovery set in, but there was no marked improvement until the Tea enterprise became fully established in 1887-8. Since then the improvement has been most marked, so that for 1902 the revenue reached the unprecedented amount of R28,435,000.

The main sources of the Ceylon General Revenue are found in import duties on the rice imported from India for feeding the coolies and others directly or indirectly connected with the great planting enterprise of Ceylon, including a large proportion of the urban population. This import duty also bears on all the population of the big towns, and on a considerable proportion of that of the villages. The Sinhalese and Tamil rice

The Revenue and Expenditure of Ceylon. 119

cultivators barely grow enough grain to support themselves and their dependents. To balance this import duty (or rather previous to its existence) there was up to 1892 an excise collection on locally-grown grain by means of a Government levy, the remains of the old tithe or rent paid to the native kings. This rent had been greatly reduced by the application of commutation, so that the import duty on grain had become decidedly protective of local industry. But not content with this, it pleased Lord Knutsford, as Secretary of State, and Sir Arthur Havelock to abolish the internal grain levy or "paddy" rent altogether from January 1st, 1893, without, however, touching the corresponding Customs duty; and this was approved by the Cobden Club. The other most productive import duties are those on wines, spirits, hardware, and cotton goods. Altogether the Customs bring in between a quarter and a fifth of the entire revenue. The annual income from the railways, all held by the Government (and 122 out of 368, shortly to be over 600, miles the free property of the Colony), now makes up more of the general revenue than do Customs duties or nearly one-fifth of the entire revenue. "Licences" (to sell intoxicating drinks, chiefly arrack) unfortunately yield between one-eighth and one-ninth of the total; and the "Salt-tax" and "Stamps" together make up one-seventh of the general revenue. Sales of Crown lands, chiefly to planters, used occasionally in former years to be as productive as the Customs; but latterly the extent of land offered for sale, and the consequent revenue, have greatly fallen of. Among the rules guiding the Forest Department formed of recent years is one prohibiting the the sale of Crown forest land 5,000 feet above sea-level and upwards, or on the ridges of mountains or banks of rivers below that height.

It is now felt that a great mistake was made sixty years ago in not keeping the proceeds of land sales in a separate fund as capital to be expended in reproductive public works, apart from the general revenue. The same may be said of the surplus of the large railway receipts after providing for working expenses and interest on debt with sinking fund. Had this been done, the expenditure on fixed establishments would not have been allowed to increase year by year, as if the general revenue from Customs, land sales, and railway profits dependent on the planting enterprise, were a permanent source of income. The railway profits were for many years almost entirely due to the carriage of coffee from the interior to Colombo, and of rice, general goods, and manure for the plantations. Now tea (and tea requisites), with cocoa, cardamoms, coconuts and other new products, make up the main freight on the line, In addition to the Customs the railway profits, land sales, the excise on the sale of spirits, stamp duties, and the monopoly or tax on salt, as the main sources of revenue, we have an occasional contribution of from R100,000 to R1,000,000 from a pearl fishery. The latter is one of the most acceptable, but one of the most uncertain, sources of Ceylon wealth. We trust the series of Fisheries begun in 1903 will long continue.— A commission to consider the incidence of taxation in Ceylon, appointed by Governor Sir West Ridgeway, is now sitting, and we trust, as the result of its report, that the taxation of the Colony will be placed on a wise, equitable and permanent footing.

CHAPTER XIV.

WHAT ITS GOVERNMENT CAN DO FOR CEYLON.

Active and Independent Administrators required—The Obstruction to Progress offered in Downing Street—Railway Extensions —Law reform needed—Technical, Industrial, and Agricultural Education needs encouraging—The Buddhist Temporalities Questions—Fiscal Reform of Road, Excise Laws, Salt Monopoly, Food Taxes and Customs Duties—The Duke of Buckingham's Ceylon and Southern India Railway Project—Ceylon and India— Waste Crown Lands.

AS regards the wants of Ceylon, its government is a paternal despotism; and the Governor and Secretary of State (with his Colonial Office advisers) being to a great extent irresponsible rulers, much depends on their treatment of the island. There can be no doubt that in the past progress has been made in spite of, rather than with, the prompt, zealous co-operation of Downing Street. In support of this view we would quote from a review in the London *Spectator* of a recent work on the "Crown Colonies of Great Britain":—

"The system of Crown Colonies is supposed to be that of a benevolent despotism, a paternal autocracy. It is in many cases that of a narrow and selfish oligarchy. It is supposed that the Colonial Office exercises a beneficial supervision, and is everywhere the guardian angel of the bulk of the population in all the British Colonies. The supposition that a few Civil Servants, most of whom have never lived out of England, or engaged in any trade or business but that of clerks in the Colonial Office, could really exercise any such power,

P

is extravagant on the face of it. There are more than thirty Crown Colonies, as various and widely scattered as Hong Kong, Fiji, Cyprus, Malta, Heligoland, Jamaica, Honduras, Ceylon, and Sierra Leone. How could any body of officials in London, however large, highly educated, and capable, adequately exercise any form of real control or intelligent supervision over such a mixed lot of *disjecta membra*? As for the Secretary of State, who is changed, on the average, once a year, it is impossible that he can be more than a figure-head, or have any real voice in the determination of anything except large questions of policy when there is Colonial trouble. Parliament is, however, supposed to exercise a control." But this control is limited to questions put from time to time in the House of Commons, the answers to which are supplied in the first instance by the same Colonial Office clerks, and in the last resort by the people who are to be controlled, the actual administrators of the various Colonies.[*]

An active, energetic, independent Governor, however, exercises an immense influence, especially if he is at the same time frank, free from a weakness to connect his name with showy, but hasty legislation, risky and unsound though apparently beneficial revenue changes, is opposed to inquisitorial, underhand proceedings, and is inflexibly just. Every department of the public service, indeed almost every individual officer, feels the effect of such a ruler's presence, just as the whole administrative machinery goes to rest and rust in this tropical isle when the fountain-head of authority

---

[*] A curious circumstance in connection with the last Unionist Government was that two of its prominent members were either born in or had close relations with Ceylon. Lord Chancellor Halsbury still in the Ministry) is a nephew of Chief Justice Sir Hardinge Giffard, who administered Justice in Ceylon in 1820-27 and whose portrait in oils Lord Halsbury has sent out for our Supreme Court; while Mr. Mathews, Home Secretary, now Lord Llandaff, was born in Colombo, where his father lived and died as Advocate-Fiscal (Attorney-General) and Judge about the same time, the son lately erecting a memorial brass to his father's memory in St. Peters' Church, Colombo.

and honour is found to be somnolent and indifferent himself.

Statesmen bred in the free air of the House of Commons, as a rule, make the best governors of Crown Colonies; at least three or four in the Ceylon list— Governors Wilmot Horton, Stewart Mackenzie, Sir Henry Ward, and Sir William Gregory—had such a training, and stand out pre-eminently as among our best administrators, although equally able and useful were some others—Governors Sir Edward Barnes, Sir Hercules Robinson, and Sir Arthur Hamilton Gordon— who had no parliamentary experience. To the latter category may be added Sir J. West Ridgeway, certainly one of the best sovereign representatives and administrators Ceylon has ever had.

Ceylon wants a governor who has his whole heart in his work, is ready to sympathise with all classes and races, to see provinces, districts, and public works for himself—by journeys on horseback where necessary —open to receive counsel as to proposed legislation from the most diverse quarters, while deciding for himself after giving it due consideration; a Governor, moreover, not easily led away in his councils or provinces by officers, it may be of long experience but with special "hobbies," nor by oriental gossip or suspicion, which if once listened to leads into one quagmire after another. Such an administrator will always be the best gift that Britain can offer to the natives and colonists of Ceylon, provided that his hands are not tied by the Colonial Office in Downing Street.

The only large public works at present under construction in Ceylon may be said to be the Ratnapura Railway extension, the Railway from Colombo to Chilaw and, if possible, Puttalam; an extension from Matara to Tangalla; and several light railways in the planting districts, as well as roads there and in the low-country.

In legislative, administrative and social improvements there is still a good deal to do: law reform in improved Mortgage, Bankruptcy, Registration, and other measures—in fact, a complete codification of our Civil Laws—is urgently wanted; while education, especially in the vernacular, has to be promoted.

Still more needful is the extension of the system of technical, industrial, and agricultural instruction. Something has been done by the establishment of a Technical College as well as a Training School, and of agricultural instruction and inspectors; but we can only speak of this as "a beginning."* It is felt by many that Ceylon junior civil servants, like those of Java, should pass at an agricultural college and spend one or two years on arrival in the island at Government experimental gardens or plantations.† The influence of the personal example and precept of the revenue officers of Government over the headmen and people in getting them to try new products or extend cultivation is immense; experimental gardens to supply the natives with plants and seeds, and to show them how to cultivate the same, ought to be multiplied, and bonuses offered for the growth of certain qualities of new products in different districts. One advantage of a general land levy would be that official attention would be given to a variety of products. Another beneficial reform would be the official establishment of an agri-horticultural exhibition, with holidays and sports for the people, in connection with each Kachchéri (district revenue station) in the island.

In Administration, much good may be done by the discouragement, indeed stern suppression, of illicit sale of arrack and the substitution of the "Still"

---

* "I believe that the most important thing you can do for education in India [and Ceylon] is to throw as much weight as you can into the Scientific as against the Literary scale."—*Sir E. M. Grant-Duff*.

† Lecturing in August 1903 in Colombo, upon "Early British Rule in Ceylon" and the great success of military-political administrators, we recommended that Civil Service cadets should be made to study and pass an examination in the lines and work of such men as Skinner, Campbell, Forbes, Stewart, Davy, &c,

for the "Renting" System ; also the suppression of gambling among the natives, a common concomitant of drunken lazy habits, indeed of assaults, theft, burglary, and other crimes, There is sufficient legislation perhaps ; it is the strict and impartial administration of the law towards Europeans and natives alike that is required. Gambling being a chief obstacle to the progress and well-doing of large numbers of the Sinhalese, Tamils, Malays, etc., all public servants, at the very least, should be instructed to be most careful personally, as well as administratively, to discourage betting, lotteries, and gambling among all classes. Both Governor and Secretary of State should see to this. There is also need for official discouragement of drinking habits among the people by a refusal to open any new liquor shops or arrack taverns, by decreasing the number now is existence, and by experimenting with, if not sanctioning, a modified form of "local option" in certain districts. There are other evil arrangements after European precedent, bearing on public morality, which ought to be suppressed and kept out of Ceylon.

A step of much practical importance in legislation is the placing of opium under the same restrictions in Ceylon as in Europe; and Ceylon is quite ripe for a legislative and administrative experiment of this kind.

The people of Ceylon are perhaps the least warlike of any nation under British rule: not a soldier has sustained a scratch here since 1817, when the Kandyan kingdom was finally subdued. Street riots in Colombo through religious feuds or dearness of rice, at rare intervals, only require the sight of a red-coat to subside ; a few artillerymen (a picked company of the local volunteers would do) with a light field-gun would be sufficient to cope with the most formidable gathering that could possibly take place as a breach of the peace. There are now 2,500 Volunteers of all arms in Ceylon costing R200,000 a year ; while the Military

Contribution for less than 1,500 is two millions rupees. An abatement of this contribution in view of the largely increased local Force should have important results.

Nevertheless, it is important to note that, for imperial purposes, Ceylon is a most central and useful station for even more than one regiment of infantry with a good staff. This will be readily seen from what has happened during the past thirty-five years, Sir Henry Ward sent the 37th Regiment at a day's notice to Calcutta in 1857 to the aid of Lord Canning against the mutineers, those troops being the first to arrive; in 1863 the troopship *Himalaya* took the 50th Regiment from Ceylon to New Zealand to aid in suppressing the Maoris; later on, part of the Ceylon garrison did good service in China, the Straits, and Labuan; in 1879 the 57th Regiment was despatched at short notice to Natal; and, with equal expedition, the 102nd was sent thither in 1881, when the colony was practically denuded of infantry without the slightest inconvenience.

Ceylon is by far the most central British military garrison in the East; its first-class port, Colombo, is distant 900 miles from Bombay, 600 from Madras, 1,400 from Calcutta, 1,200 from Rangoon (Burma), 1,600 from Singapore, 2,500 from Mauritius, a little more from Madagascar, about 4,000 from Natal, 3,000 from Hong Kong, 3,000 from Fremantle or Western Australia, and about 2,200 from Aden. Its value, therefore, as a station from whence troops can, at the shortest notice, be transferred to any one of these points, should make it the Malta of the Eastern Seas; indeed its hill station at Diyatalawa in a perfect climate (see Appendix No. VII) served by railway, as already mentioned, might be made the sanatorium for troops in Southern India. It is now to be a convalescent station for naval as well as military invalids from all Eastern stations.

It is generally felt—and in this view high naval as well as military authorities agree—that the headquarters of the East India naval station might well

What its Government can do for Ceylon. 127

be removed from Trincomalee to Colombo, since firstclass harbour works have been constructed at the latter; and this would probably be done now that the construction of a Northern Arm to the Breakwater, and of a Graving Dock are taken in hand.

There are reforms urgently needed in connection with the wide area of lands (much lying waste and unutilised) with which certain Buddhist temples are endowed, and revenues of which are now comparatively wasted without benefit to the people, the majority of whom would gladly vote for their appropriation to the promotion of vernacular and technical, especially agricultural, education in each district. It is recorded that King Wijayo Bahu III., who reigned in Ceylon in 1240 A.D., established a school in every village, and charged the priests who superintended them to take nothing from the pupils, promising that he himself would reward them for their trouble. This was probably done by temple endowments now by no means usefully employed very often*. The multiplication of Reading Rooms and Libraries in the island is desirable, as also a Free Public Library in Colombo. The small annual levy under the Roads or Thoroughfares Ordinance on every able-bodied man between eighteen and fifty-five in the island (the Governor, Buddhist priests, and a few more, alone excepted) has been productive of much good—in providing a net work of district roads—since it was drafted by the late Sir Philip Wodehouse over fifty years ago. But in some districts, the tax, small as it is, leads to a good deal of trouble and expense through defaulters; and its collection is everywhere, even in the towns, attended with a certain amount of corruption and oppression. This will, however, grow less as education advances. A liberal modification, if not abolition, of the Salt tax would

---

* The land belonging to the temples is very considerable, but generally unremunerative, being mostly jungle: the temples are said to have insufficient capital to cultivate or exploit the land. —*Mr. H. L. Crawford's Report for 1903.*

be a great boon. This tax, though not felt by the prosperous, undoubtedly presses hard on many poor persons, while it debars agricultural improvement in certain directions,—salt is rich in soda, a most valuable article of manure—and affects the health of the people in the remoter districts.

In the estimation of the reformers of the Cobden Club there used to be a financial reform of greater importance than any of these, namely, the abolition of the "Foodtaxes of Ceylon," or the levy made on locally-grown grain crops, and the customs duty imposed on imported rice. But while the internal tax, inherited from the Sinhalese rulers as a *rent*, has been abolished, the Cobden Club to its shame says nothing now about the one-sided, unjust and protective customs duty on rice. The only substitute possible for both this and the customs duty is a general land-levy, and to that complexion it must come at last, unpopular though it may be with the natives, when the Cadastral Survey is finally completed.

The fiscal reformers of 1892 would have done well to have studied, before abolishing the paddy rent, the history of the fish-tax established by the Portuguese, continued by the Dutch, superseded by the British by a licence for boats, which nearly stopped fishing altogether. The old form had to be resumed, but the tax was reduced again and again, without in the least benefiting the industry, for the fishermen simply caught less, having no longer duty to pay, and when the tax was finally abolished by Government, the Roman Catholic priests stepped in, and continued it, without demur from the fishermen, who are mostly of that Church. In the same way, grain cultivators who have had their tax or rent remitted, have been known to allow a portion of their fields to go out of cultivation in view of no rent to pay—so much less work to do was their idea of the benefit of remission of taxation—while in a large number of cases, the cultivator, the goyiya, has had no advantage from the remission of the rent or paddy-tax, the proceeds going to the Moormen and other creditors, headmen and comparatively well-to-do landowners.

Of course, the removal of all customs duties and the inauguration of Colombo as a free port will add immensely to the importance of Colombo and the colony. And no doubt the day is fast approaching when, in this respect, the system of taxation in Ceylon and India must approximate. In people, in trade, and other important respects, the two countries are closely allied; and they will be further identified when the grand scheme which the Duke of Buckingham, as Governor of Madras, propounded to Sir William Gregory, of connecting the railway systems of Ceylon and Southern India, is carried out; the object is to serve the very large passenger traffic in coolies and traders, as well as to carry the produce of Southern India to the safe and commodious Colombo harbour—the Madras harbour works being a great failure. The Indian railway system now reaches to Paumben and will shortly cross to Rameswaram: the Ceylon railway will soon be open to Madawachchi—the connecting line should not be long in coming (see papers by J. Ferguson on Indo-Ceylon Railway read before the London Chamber of Commerce and Imperial Institute). One great difference between the two countries is the much larger Covenanted Civil Service, and number of European officials generally, in Ceylon, in proportion to population and area, than in India. Of course, the individual salaries are much lower here, but it is a question whether the island has not too many public servants of the higher ranks, and whether there is not room for reform in the system of administration such as was referred to by Sir Emerson Tennent in his Financial Reports over fifty years ago. The pension list of Ceylon is becoming a serious burden to the colony, and some steps are urgently called for to prevent a continuance of growth such as has been experienced of recent years.

Sir West Ridgeway's scheme for an uncovenanted subordinate service has done much good. At the same time, in a country situated like Ceylon, agriculture in one of its many forms ought to be kept steadily before educated burghers and natives alike, as the one sure means of affording a livelihood. Tea planting, we are glad to think, has done much for young men of these classes; in the tea factories room has been found for a large number of intelligent young men of the country, as tea makers, clerks, etc., and many of the natives cultivate tea-gardens of their own, besides trying other new and profitable products.

A reform tending to extend local industry would be the throwing open, at a merely nominal price, of Crown waste lands, at present unsaleable, along the Northern Railway, or the leasing of large blocks at nominal rents for experiments in cotton, tobacco fibre and stock-raising.

The exploration and clearing of the "Buried Cities"—Polonnaruwa as well as Anurádhapura, both ancient capitals of the Sinhalese kings—has latterly been done much more energetically. Mr. H. C. P. Bell, the Government Archæologist in charge of the exploration, is decidely the right man, but he should be liberally supported.

A geological survey of Ceylon is much required in the interests of industry—mines of plumbago as well as gemming and other branches—as well as of science. Sir West Ridgeway tried hard to get a survey staff, but so far has only secured a mineralogist.

Two of the most mysterious rocks in our earth's crust are abundant here, laterite and graphite. Where the iron of the one came from and the carbon of the other, even the most accomplished geologists would be chary of dogmatically affirming. About low level laterite we are able to say something, but gneiss or other rock passing into laterite on the top of a hill

RUINS OF THE JAYTAWANARAMA, POLONNARUA.

A SCENE AMONG THE RUINS OF POLONNARUA, ONE OF THE ANCIENT CAPITALS OF CEYLON.

is another question. Equally difficult is it to say whether graphite was deposited from water or solidified from gas; and why the mineral should have so strong an affinity to quartz, is, we believe, amongst the as yet unsolved problems of a science, the scope and definiteness of which have been, respectively, greatly expanded and largely settled by the Indian department.

CHAPTER XV.

SOCIAL LIFE AND CUSTOMS.

Social Life and Customs of the Natives of Ceylon—How Little Colonists may know of Village Life—Domestic Servants—Caste Restrictions—Curious Occupations among the People.

THE variety of race, colour, physiognomy, and costume among the people in the busy streets of Colombo—especially the Pettah, or native market-place—at once arrests the attention of the stranger. But, save what he sees in the public highways, and may learn from his servants, the ordinary colonist may live many years in the island without learning much of the every-day life and habits of the people of the land, whether Sinhalese or Tamils, in their own villages and homes. There is a beaten track now for the European to follow, be he merchant or planter, and there is so much of western civilisation and education on the surface that the new comer is apt to forget very soon that he is in the midst of a people with an ancient civilization and authentic history of their own, extending far beyond that of the majority of European nations; and with social customs and modes of life, when separate from foreign influences, entirely distinct from anything to which he has been accustomed. The foreigners who see somewhat of this inner life of the people, especially in the rural districts, are the civil servants and other public officers of Government, and the missionaries. Now, as regards the work of the latter, the average European planter or merchant returning home after six, ten, aye, or even twenty

SINHALESE LADS AT CRICKET.

Social Life and Customs. 133

years in Ceylon, too often declares that the missionaries are making no way in Ceylon, that they live comfortably in the towns, and content themselves with ordinary pastoral duties in their immediate neighbourhood, and in fact, that they (the colonists) never saw any evidence of mission work or progress among the natives, unless it were through the catechists and other agents of the Tamil Cooly Mission visiting the plantations. Now the way to meet such a negative statement would be by an inquiry as to whether the colonist had ever interviewed a missionary to the Tamils or Sinhalese, whether in Colombo, Kandy, or Galle, to go no further, and had asked to accompany him to his stations. Had he done so, he could have been taken to village after village, with its little church and good, if not full, attendance of members, presided over in many cases by pastors of their own people and in some instances supported by themselves. He would have seen schools of all grades—mission boarding-schools for native girls and lads, and training institutions for the ministry. Now, just as this branch of work in the rural districts of Ceylon is unknown to many scores, if not hundreds, of European colonists who never trouble their heads about anything beyond their own round of immediate duties or pleasures; so it is, for an even wider circle, in reference to the social life and customs of the natives.

Education has made such strides that, in the towns, English is rapidly becoming the predominant language among all classes. In India all foreigners learn a native language, and domestic servants never think of speaking English, even if some few of them understand it. Here, in Ceylon, English is almost universally in domestic use, and there is scarcely a roadside village in Ceylon now where the traveller could not find some person to speak English, or interpret for him. The coolies on the plantations are different; with few exceptions they only know Tamil, and the planters have to learn that language colloquially.

Civil servants pass examinations in the languages. Very amusing are some of the servants, occasionally, who are only beginning to acquire English, or who try to show a command beyond their depth; like the Sinhalese "appu" (butler) who, one day, on being remonstrated with by his Christian mistress for attending some tomfooleries of ceremonies at a temple, replied, Yes, he knew better, but he only did it "to please the womens" (his wife and daughters!), the hold of superstition and heathenism in Ceylon, as elsewhere, being strongest on the female portion of the household. On another occasion a horsekeeper (Tamil groom), coming to report to his master that his horse had gone lame, expressed himself thus, holding up his fingers in illustration, "Sar, three legs very good; one leg very bad!" Some of the letters and petitions in English of budding clerks, or warehousemen, or other applicants for situations, are often comical in the extreme. Both Sinhalese and Tamils make the most docile and industrious of domestic servants. Of course, there are exceptions, but ladies who have been for some years in Ceylon, after visiting "home" again, or especially after going to Australasia or America, are usually glad to get back to their native servants.

Caste in Ceylon has not so much hold on the people as it has in India, and in respect of domestic service, only one-half to one-third the number of men-servants is required here, in consequence of one man making no objection to different kinds of work. Sinhalese "appus" and "boys," with their often smooth cheeks, and hair done up in a knot, surmounted by a comb, and with white jackets and long "comboys" (long petticoats), are frequently taken for female servants, the latter having no comb, but a silver or other pin in their hair, and only taking service as ayah (nurse), or lady's attendant. In the hotels passengers frequently make the mistake of supposing they are attended by maid, instead of men, servants. The

Social Life and Customs.

Sinhalese have, indeed, been called the women of the human race, and the story is that in trying to make soldiers of them, the British instructors in the early days never could get them not to fire away their ramrods!

Of course there are some bad native servants, but they are the exceptions; at any rate a good master and mistress generally get good service. But sometimes robberies do occur in households, and usually then some one or other of the servants has been conspiring with outside thieves. A few colonists prefer Malay servants.

The demand for holidays is often a nuisance, and the saying is that native servants must have half a dozen grandfathers each from the number of funerals of grandfathers they have to attend. The fact is that the Western habit of constant work does not suit the Oriental taste at all, the proverbial saying of the Buddhist Sinhalese being, "Better to walk than to run, to sit down than walk, and best of all to go to sleep."

We have said that caste has not a great hold in Ceylon; but in one point of social life it is still almost universally observed,—there can be no marriage between persons of different castes. Your servant may be a man of higher caste than your wealthy native neighbour driving his carriage, and yet the "appu" would probably never consent to allow his daughter to marry the son of the rich, lower caste man. Christianity is working against caste, and among native Christians there are many cases of caste being disregarded; but on the other hand, when the Duke of Edinburgh was entertained by a Sinhalese gentleman of medium caste, it was stated that Sinhalese officials (including a Christian chaplain) of the Vellala (agricultural) caste absented themselves from the entertainment where all were expected to appear, because they could not enter the grounds or house of a man of the Fisher caste. The most striking case in recent times in Ceylon was that of a young girl of good family in a Kandyan village, who fell in love with the son of a trader in the same village, of greater wealth but lower caste than her father, who was a decayed Chief. The lad and girl had seen each other in school days, and acquaintance had ripened into more than friendship, and they were bent on defying caste, family opposition, and any other obstacle to their marriage. But a young brother of the girl haughtily forbade the courtship, threatening his sister with vengeance if ever he saw her with the young trader. The lovers planned a clandestine match, so far that (being both Buddhists) they should get married by civil registration before the magistrate. They stole away one morning, and were mixing in the crowd usually awaiting the opening of the magistrate's court in county towns, when the young chief, finding out what had happened, rushed up and peremptorily ordered his sister home. She refused and clung to her lover, when the brother suddenly drew a knife from his girdle and stabbed her to the heart. She fell dead on the spot; the murderer holding the knife aloft and shouting, in Sinhalese, "Thus I defend the honour of my family," and going to the scaffold a few weeks after exulting in his deed. Education and the railway are, however, aiding Christianity to weaken the hold of caste, and the people of Ceylon will, before many generations have gone by, have learned that—

> "Honour and shame from no condition rise,
> Act well your part, there all the honour lies";

and that—

> "From yon blue heavens above us bent,
> The grand old gardener and his wife,
> Smile at the claims of long (or caste) descent."

It is a striking evidence of the slight influence of Buddhism that here, in its sacred or holy land, where

LIGHTHOUSE AT GALLE.

MOUNT LAVINIA.

SINHALESE VILLAGE.

Social Life and Customs.

it has prevailed for over two-thousand years, caste, which was thought to be condemned by its founder and its tenets, still exercises a baneful influence over the Sinhalese people. All castes, however low, were supposed to be eligible to Buddha's priesthood; but in Ceylon ordination gradually became the privilege of the Vellála caste alone, until a Sinhalese of a lower caste went to Burmah and got ordained, the second priestly order being open to three castes outside the Vellalas, but refusing any of other castes—so making two castes of priests in the island! In other Buddhist countries, Burmah, Siam and Thibet, caste does not exist in any similar form. A stanza from a Ceylon Buddhist work runs as follows—

> "A man does not become low caste by birth,
> Nor by birth does one become high caste;
> High caste is the result of high action—
> And by actions does a man degrade himself to a caste that is low."

Native weddings, with the peculiarities of each race—Sinhalese, Tamil, or Moormen (Mahommedan)—are sometimes very curious, and, as the parties are generally rather proud than otherwise of Europeans being present, there is no difficulty about getting an invitation. The youthfulness of the bride—perhaps thirteen to fifteen years—and the quantity of jewellery, literally weighing her down (collected and borrowed from all the family circle of relatives for the occasion), are two peculiarities. There are scarcely any unmarried native women, and, as is always the case in a naturally ordered community, the males exceed the females in number. The Sinhalese have no army or navy or flow of emigration to supply, and no artificial customs to interfere with or delay the marriage of their daughters. Of the influence of the Buddhist and Hindu religions upon the people, enough is said elsewhere; but we may just refer here to the fact that a people bred under the influence of tenets (Buddhist) forbidding the taking of life, have developed

R

some of the most cruel and exquisite forms of torture known to history in reference to the lower animals. A law had to be passed forbidding the roasting of tortoises alive, in order to get the tortoise-shell of a finer lustre than if taken from the dead animal; and only the other day a military officer discovered in Colombo that native cooks were in the habit of cutting out the tongues of the living turkeys, in order that the flesh, when cooked, might be the more tender. But a long list of such instances might be given, as well as illustrations of the hypocrisy which makes Buddhist fishermen say: "We do not kill the fish, we take them out of the water and they die of themselves!" Householders put out the old dog or at on the highway for the wheel of a passing vehicle to go over and kill, so that they may have no sin; or shut up the deadly snake in wicker-work on the river to be carried to the sea; while early in the present century it was the custom to expose old and helpless human beings in the jungle, each with a bowl of rice and chatty of water, to die without troubling their relatives, or to be devoured, as was often the case, by beasts of prey. And all this in one of the most bigoted of Buddhist districts—Matara—in the south of the island. It was in the same district a veteran missionary demonstrated the hypocrisy of a catechist, of whom he had authentic accounts that, while professing to be doing certain work as a Christian teacher for the sake of a salary, he was in heart a Buddhist, attending all the temple ceremonies. In a remote village there was no check, and on being questioned by the missonary, while sitting in a room together, he utterly denied that he had any belief in Buddhism. Taking a small brass image of Buddha from his pocket, the missionary placed it on the table, when immediately (as all Buddhists should do) the would-be catechist sprang to his feet, placed his hands before his forehead with a low obeisance towards the image, and then slunk from the room discomfited!

A RUINED DAGOBA.

SINHALESE DEVIL DANCERS.

Social Life and Customs. 139

Among the more curious occupations of the people, as related in the census, are such novelties as 1,753 devil-dancers, 121 exhibitors of trained animals, 224 conjurors and fortune-tellers, 216 actors, dancers and singers, 10 acrobats, 1,325 tom-tom beaters, 9 nautch girls, 276 astrologers, 20,849 (8,224 women) dhobies or washers, 2,763 barbers, 156 elephant-keepers and trainers, about 102 fakirs and devotee-beggars, 411 lapidaries, 3 ivory carvers, 39 workers in tortoise-shell, and 410 in jewellery, etc. The census of 1901 showed there were 7,331 Buddhists priests in Ceylon, but of three different sects—the Siamese ordination, Amarapara or Burmese, and Ramanya or reformers.*

European civilisation and Christianity are both taking a firm hold of the people. Education is desired by the natives, perhaps not yet for its own sake, but as a means of advancement, as very few good posts are to be obtained in which English is not needed. Boarding schools for native boys and girls are the very best educational and mission agency, and ought to be greatly multiplied.

Once in our Government or Mission schools (and education, especially in the villages, is mainly in the hands of the missionaries) children acquire new habits of industry and perseverance and in time come to regard truthfulness as desirable and care for others, whether of their own blood or not, as a duty. Though Buddha led a most self-denying life and taught others to do the same, yet his example had made small impression on his followers, and philanthropy was not regarded as a duty by the Sinhalese or their priests. Now it is different. Each of our missions can quote many instances of noble generosity and hearty zeal for the welfare of the people.

We have merely touched the skirts of topics in this chapter, which might well require for their

* The main results of the census of 1901 will be found tabulated in Appendix III.

treatment a volume in themselves. Those interested in the subject may be referred to good old Robert Knox's veracious account of his sojourn, as a prisoner among the Kandyan people for twenty years—1659 to 1680—or to more modern books, in Percival's, Cordiner's, Davy's, Selkirk's, Forbes's, Pridham's, or Emerson Tennent's histories, with Spence Hardy's "Eastern Monachism," "Jubilee Memorials," and "Legends of the Buddhists."

DHOBIES AT WORK.

A GEM-DIGGER'S HUT IN CEYLON.

CHAPTER XVI.

FURTHER PROGRESS INDICATED AND A FEW REFORMS CALLED FOR.

Relation and Importance of Ceylon to India—Progress of Christianity and Education—Statistics of Population—Need of Reform in the Legislative Council, and Sketch of a Scheme for the Election of Unofficial Members—Loyalty of People to British Rule, as evinced during Royal Visits, and in connection with the Jubilees of Her late Majesty the Queen-Empress and of the Coronation of King Edward VII.--Progress of Ceylon since 1837,

CEYLON, in a social and political way, bears the same relation to India and the Far East that England has done to the European continent. Mr. Laing, when Finance Minister for India, confessed it was most valuable to law-makers and administrators in the Indian Presidencies to have Ceylon under a separate form of Government, and to have experiments in administrative and legislative reforms tried here, which served as an example or a warning to the big neighbouring continent, the peoples being allied in so many respects. There is, for instance, no distinction made between native and European judges and magistrates in Ceylon; and the acting Chief Justice, lately, was a Eurasian, a Sinhalese barrister only retired eleven years ago from being Judge of the Supreme Court after fifteen years' service, while the second Puisne Justice is now (1903) a Dutch descendant; and other Ceylonese fill the responsible offices of Solicitor-General and Crown Counsel as well as District Judges and Magistrates of the Colony. Again, in Ceylon, we have a decimal system of currency, a great step in advance of the cumbrous Indian system, and we have entire freedom of all religions (including Christianity) from State patronage and control. On the other hand, Ceylon is now much behind India in its fiscal system, the unwise action of Lord Knutsford and Sir Arthur Havelock giving us Protection and discriminating taxation on rice—the staple food of the people—in their worst form.

The progress of Christianity and education among the people is greater than in any other Eastern State, and should Buddhism, the religion of over two millions of Sinhalese, fall here, it would have a great effect on the millions of Burmah, Siam, and even China, who look to Ceylon as the sacred home of Buddhism. The kings of Burmah and Siam especially continue to take an interest in, and make offerings to, the Buddhist "temple of the tooth" at Kandy. Roman Catholicism has been propagated since the arrival of the Portuguese in the sixteenth century; while English Protestant missions have worked in Ceylon since 1811. The Roman Catholic number about 288,000, the Protestants 62,000, against 2,142,000 Buddhists and demon worshippers, 827,000 Hindus, and 246,000 Muhammadans.

Some allusion should be made to more than one local movement in Ceylon for a reform in the system of government, and more especially in the liberalising of the Legislative Council. Sir Hercules Robinson, while opposing this claim, originated municipal institutions in the three principal towns, as a means of training the people in the art of self-government. The working of these has, however, unfortunately, not been so successful as was hoped, and one reason is a curiously Oriental one, namely, that respectable Ceylonese consider it derogatory to go and ask the people below them—often ignorant and poor franchise-holders—for "the honour of their votes." "Honour comes from above, not from below," they say; and so the better classes of natives abstained from the Municipal Boards, and left many disreputable men to get in. A reformed and restrictive municipal constitution law, just passed, may work better. But as regards the Legislature, the occupation of one of the seats allotted to the Ceylonese by nomination of the Governor has always been greatly coveted, and an object of ambition to every rising man in the country. Sir Arthur Gordon very liberally got two additional native seats provided--one for the Kandyan Sinhalese and one for the "Moormen" (chiefly Arab descendants). He also secured a reform in the old practice of granting what was practically life seats, by limiting the term of office for unofficial members to five years, at the option of the Governor—it ought to be permanently fixed. A change of membership in this way cannot fail to be beneficial to the community, by educating and testing an increasing number of Ceylonese for public life. There is no reason, however, why even two more unofficial seats should not be added to the Legislative Board. Indeed, the elective principle might, under due safeguards, be applied in the nine provinces of the island,—under a severely restricted franchise to begin with,—so giving nine elected unofficial members, to whom might be added two or four nominees of the Governor, from among the trading or other native classes not adequately served by the elections; while the planting and mercantile nominated memberships continued. Elections and nominations could take place every six years, or on the advent of each new Governor, and a few more privileges might be accorded to the members, such as the right of initiating proposals, even where such involved the expenditure of public money up to a certain moderate limit. The Governor, for the time being, could always command a majority against any unwise scheme, and his own veto, as well as that of the Secretary of State, would continue operative. Some such improvement of the Legislative Council—which has continued without change for about seventy years, or since the days of Governor Sir Robert Wilmot Horton in 1833— cannot long be delayed, and if asked for on broad grounds by a united community, it might well be granted before the close of the century. A movement in the Legislative Council in 1903 may lead to reform.

Another practical reform of importance would be the ensuring that four out of the six members of the Executive Council—that is, the Colonial Secretary, Attorney-General, Auditor-General, and Treasurer—should always be trained public servants of the colony, with local experience. The farce has been seen even in recent years of a Governor and his five Executive advisers in Ceylon, not counting half a dozen years of local experience between them. Then, one if not two of the unofficial members of the Legislative Council should be added to the Executive Council. We must also plead, as we have personally urged on the Secretary of State, that (now especially there are four Judges) one Judge of the Supreme Court of the Colony should always be taken from among the senior Judicial Civil Servants, who, trained from the magisterial to the highest district benches, not only know the language and laws, but also the habits and local customs of the people, far better than any Colombo lawyers or English judges that can be selected.

Ceylon was honoured with a visit from H.R.H. the Duke of Edinburgh in 1870, from H.R.H. the Prince of Wales (now King Edward the VII.) in 1875, from the young Princes Albert and George of Wales in 1881, and again from the present Prince and Princess of Wales in 1901. On each occasion the loyalty and devotion of the people to the British Crown, and their warm personal interest in the happiness and welfare of their sovereign, were very conspicuous. This was still more shown in connection with the Jubilees of Her late Most Gracious Majesty the Queen-Empress Victoria, and on the Coronation of the new King-Emperor, when

THE EGYPTIAN EXILES.

all classes and races vied with each other in the endeavour to do honour to the occasion. Liberal support has been given to the Imperial Institute, dear to the late Queen ; while, as a local memento of Her Majesty, a Home for Incurables and an Eye Hospital are established in Colombo.

From the official record of British progress in fifty years, prepared by Governor Gordon on the occasion of the Jubilee celebrations in 1887, we quote the few items referring to Ceylon :—

In 1838 the Legislative Council of the Colony, created but not completed in 1833, received its full complement of members.

In 1844 the last remains of Slavery were wholly abolished.

In 1848 a slight insurrectionary movement took place in a part of the Kandyan districts, which is only worthy of mention in order to contrast it with the loyalty of all classes ten years later on which the Governor of Ceylon was able safely to rely when in 1857 he sent all the available troops in this Island to assist in the suppression of the Indian Mutiny.

In 1856 Sir Henry Ward commenced the restoration of the long-neglected Irrigation System of the Island ; and in 1857 the ancient Village Councils were revived, chiefly with a view to the promotion and enforcement of Irrigation Works.

In the same year the first sod was cut of the first Railway in Ceylon.

In 1858 Ceylon was united with India by the Electric Telegraph.

In 1865 the Municipalities of Colombo and Kandy were established.

In 1868 the general scheme of Public Education now in force was adopted by the Legislature.

In 1870 legislative measures enabling the tenants of Temple Lands to commute their services were adopted and in the same year the Ceylon Medical School was established.

In 1871 the powers of Village Councils were largely extended and Village Tribunals instituted.

In 1875 the first stone of the Colombo Breakwater was laid by His Royal Highness the Prince of Wales.

In 1881 an Ordinance, which however did not come fully into effect until 1886, was passed, withdrawing pecuniary aid, saving in the case of vested life-interests, from all Ecclesiastical Bodies.

In 1883 a Code of Criminal Law and Procedure was passed which came into operation at the beginning of 1885.

In 1885 Currency Notes were first issued by the Government.

In 1886 the Colombo Breakwater was completed.

The Population of Ceylon, which in 1837 was estimated at 1,243,066, and on the first census taken in 1871 was found to be 2,405,287, in 1887 amounted to about 3,000,000. [In 1903 it is over 3,600,000.]

The Revenue, which in 1837 was £371,993, amounted in 1867 to £969,936, and in 1886 to Rs. 12,682,549. [In 1903 about Rs 28,000,000.]

The number of miles of Main Roads open in 1837 was about 450; in 1887 it was 3,343. [In 1903 about 5,700 miles.]

The number of Estates in the hands of European Settlers in 1837 probably did not exceed 50; in 1887 [and 1903] it was over 1,500. The development of Agricultural Industry which these figures denote is, in itself, the most remarkable feature in the History of Ceylon during Her Majesty's reign. It is a development which has changed the physical appearance of the country, and profoundly modified its social condition, and which is due to the energy and perseverance of men who have shown that they can bear adversity with fortitude as they sustained prosperity with credit.

CHAPTER XVII.

SIR WEST RIDGEWAY'S ADMINISTRATION :—1896-1903.

GOVERNOR Ridgeway will long be remembered in Ceylon for his extended, prosperous and successful administration. Only two previous British Governors—both military men—ruled as long, namely, Sir Robert Brownrigg, 1812-1820; and Sir Edward Barnes, 1820 or, more properly, 1824-1831. If the last-mentioned was the great "Roadmaker," Sir West may well be called the great "Railway-maker," for he has made himself directly responsible for three separate lines—the Northern, on the broad gauge, from Kurunegala through Anuradhapura and Jaffna to the sea, 198 miles, which will be opened throughout by 1905; the Kelani Valley line, 2½-feet gauge, of 48 miles opened this year; and the Nuwara Eliya-Udapussellawa line, also 2½-feet gauge, 19 miles, to be completed in 1904. Then, in Sir West Ridgeway's time, with the consent of Mr. Chamberlain, so much as five million rupees were allotted to "Irrigation," a separate department formed, and, apart from detached works, a whole chain of restored tanks and irrigating channels arranged alongside the Northern Railway from Kurunegala for 150 miles northwards. No wonder, therefore, though anticipations as to a great increase of rice-growing, and to the introduction of industries in cotton, gingelly, fibres, &c., as well as in stock-raising, are entertained for the next decade in North Ceylon. Then, again, the administration just closing has seen vast additions to the Colombo Harbour Works, in north-west and north-east breakwaters; in a graving dock as well as patent slip; coaling depôt reclamations; new jetties, warehouses, &c.; while there is a proposal for a "wet dock" in the Blomendahl swamps capable of taking in 30 of the largest ocean-going steamers. This, however, may be checked by the plans of the South Indian Railway Company to cut a ship canal and establish a dock, coaling and shipping depôt, near Paumben, in connection with their railway. Sir West Ridgeway is a firm believer in railway communication being established between India and Ceylon; and one of his last acts is to provide for a survey and estimates for the last section in Ceylon from Madawachchi to the end of Mannar island. As already mentioned, the author of this book first brought this project of an Indo-Ceylon Railway, before the London Chamber of Commerce in 1897 and before the Imperial Institute in 1898. There can be no doubt that Colombo —bound to be one of the first artificial harbours in the world—is well fitted to be the port for Southern India. Other railway projects favoured by Governor Ridgeway are—an extension to Ratnapura and perhaps Pelmadulla; a light railway from Colombo to Negombo, Chilaw and Puttalam; and later on a line to connect Trincomalee (in which the War Office and Admiralty should help) and Batticaloa with the Ceylon railway system. Then every provincial capital and town of any importance would be connected by railway, just as they are already by telegraph; while the postal system goes everywhere now in the island. Another great work arranged for the Colony by Governor Ridgeway is a Topographical, Trigonometrical and Cadastral Survey, as well as Land Settlement, and investigation into Waste Lands—all measures of the first importance and most successfully carried out. In new roads and bridges, and public buildings, a great advance has also been made. Nearly 300 miles of new roads, 300 new bridges, and a large number of hospitals, police and law court buildings have been made since 1896. A new Victoria Memorial Eye Hospital as suggested by Lady Ridgeway, a new Technical College, and Law Courts are among the additions to Colombo; but a grand central railway station has still to follow. The notable additions to the scientific staff of the Botanic Gardens will always make this *régime* remarkable; for the Colony has now got a thoroughly equipped Advisory Board in respect of all branches and diseases of tropical agriculture. The duplicating of the water supply of Colombo, and a beginning as to a scientific scheme of drainage, are great improvements; while arrangements have also been made in respect of providing a good water supply to several other towns. Much has been done for the improvement of Kandy and Galle; but especially of the Sanatorium, Nuwara Eliya, which ought to attract visitors in the season more freely than ever before. The reorganization of the Civil and Clerical Services, as of several other Public Departments, is among Governor Ridgeway's special successes; but he has failed to suppress serious "crime"—mainly, we think, because of the arrack-renting system and its concomitant evils in prevalent illicit sales; and he has also failed to stop the public indiscriminate sale of opium through licensed shops. Most admirable have been the Governor's plans for regulating cooly immigration so as to keep out plague and cholera, and the result has been a great triumph in perfect immunity. The Geological Survey has yet to come; but the Governor has given us a mineralogist and a gold-prospecting expert; but of far more importance he has set Professor Herdman, F.R.S., and Mr. Hornell, F. Z. S., to investigate our pearl oyster fisheries and to promote oyster culture; and His Excellency has seen the first (March-April 1903) of what we trust will prove a long series of successful pearl fisheries. The Government Archæologist has had every encouragement in his important work at Anurádhapura and Polonnaruwa, our two famous "Buried Cities"— the former of which is sure to be thronged with visitors when the railway next year brings it within a few hours of Colombo. In 1908 we hope to welcome the British Association for the Advancement of Science to Ceylon, an invitation having gone to the Council from Sir West's Government to hold the annual meeting that year in Colombo. Education has made immense strides during the past eight years, and about three-fifths of all the children of a school-going age have been, or are being, taught, leaving only two-fifths to be overtaken. The Volunteer Forces have received special encouragement from Sir West Ridgeway who arranged for, first, a Ceylon Contingent of Mounted Infantry to go to the War in South Africa and afterwards a Contingent of the Planters' Rifle Corps (infantry). One great service rendered by the Governor and Ceylon to the Imperial Government was in the reception and interning of 5,000 Boer prisoners at the Diyatalawa Camp for over two years—the said Camp in the healthiest part of the Uva Highlands, being now available for the annual excercises of the Volunteers (who, of all forces, including cadets, now aggregate nearly 3,000 and do not cost so much as R200,000 to the general revenue—against ten times that amount paid in "Military Contribution"). The Diyatalava Camp will also be used as a Military and Naval convalescent station and for various other useful purposes.

We may now add a few figures to justify the application of "Prosperity Ridgeway" to our latest Governor. In 1896 the General Revenue was R21,974,573, in 1902 it was R27,198,056 and for 1903 it is certain to exceed R28,500,000, including the proceeds of the Pearl Fishery. The Public Debt—notwithstanding an addition of £1,400,000 in 1902 for Railways, Harbour Works and Irrigation—does not much exceed 2½ years' revenue even now, and could be all paid off if the railways belonging to the Colony were sold as going concerns. The Census of 1901—full details of which are given in an appendix—showed a great increase in

Sir West Ridgeway's Administration.

population (so that now the island cannot have much less than 3,700,000 souls)—a sure index of prosperity; while in respect of the staples of our planting enterprise, here are some figures and remarks applicable to the past eight years:—

The progress of the Tea Planting Industry (and its allied products) during the term of Sir West Ridgeway's Government may be readily seen from the following statistical table:—

EXTENT PLANTED IN ACRES:

	Tea.	Cacao.	Cardamoms.	Rubber.
1896	330,000	21,000	4,850	100
1897	350,000	23,000	5,050	300
1898	370,000	25,260	5,153	750
1899	385,000	27,000	6,300	900
1900	392,000	29,000	6,841	1.200
1901	388,000	31,500	7,530	2,500
1902	385,000	33,000	8,621	4,356
1903	386,000*	35,000*	9,746	11,630

EXPORTS OF TEA AND ALLIED PRODUCTS:

	Tea lb.	Cacao cwt.	Cardamoms lb.	Rubber lb.
1896	108,141,112	31,	452 595	17,591
1897	116,054,567	34,503	532,830	8,981
1898	110,769.071	36,982	531,473	2,792
1899	129,894,156	42,475	449,959	7,910
1900	148,431,639	33,476	537,455	8,233
1901	146,299,018†	44,549	559,705	7,392
1902	148,991,241†	60,455	615,922	21,168
1903	154,000,000†a	70,000a	650,000a	22,512 (for ½ yr.)

For several years now, the tea industry has had the great advantage of a watchful and competent scientific staff, under Mr. Willis's direction, at Peradeniya, and various insect and fungoid pests have been kept in check or entirely removed through attention to timely warnings and instructions. There is still, in many districts, great need for watchfulness and care; but it is satisfactory to know that, on the whole, the Governor leaves the tea enterprise in the field as in the market, in a healthy and even vigorous condition—this being testified to by the satisfactory reports recently published on the condition of the very oldest (up to 36 years) and richest tea plantations in the island. The good done

---

* Including native gardens. † Including green teas. a Estimated.

in developing a fresh demand for our teas in America and on the Continent of Europe, through the cess and planting commissioners, must not be overlooked. The outlay on the Paris Exhibition in this department was, for this reason, well bestowed; and greater results may be anticipated for Ceylon tea, from what will be shown and done at St. Louis Exhibition in the coming year.

In 1895, out of a total tea export of 97,939,871 lb. only 12,186,532 lb. were diverted from the London market; in 1902 no less than 45,447,369 lb. went to other countries out of a total export of 148,991,241 lbs. This can be seen more clearly as follows:—

EXPORT TO UNITED KINGDOM & OTHER COUNTRIES.

	To United Kingdom. lb.	To Russia. lb.	To Australia. lb.	To other countries. lb.
1895	85,753,339	333,548	9,379,561	2,473,423
1902	103,543,932	11,599,553	18,718,794	15,128,962

The CACAO planting has been intimately connected with the old coffee industry (now practically defunct) as well as with tea; and its expansion in the 8 years of Sir West Ridgeway's rule, from 21,000 to about 35,000 acres, including native gardens, while the export of the product has nearly doubled in the same time from 31,000 cwt. to over 60,000 cwt.—is very satisfactory.

CARDAMOMS is another product cultivated along with, or alongside of tea, in certain of the planting districts; and it has increased greatly in importance as an industry since 1895. The area under cultivation has just about doubled from 4,850 to 9,746 acres; the export rising from 415,595 lb. to 616,922 lb. Latterly there has been a fear of overproduction here as in tea; but the steps taken to interest new markets, in Australia and America, as well as in Europe, may be hoped to prevent any further lowering of price.

Most satisfactory in every way is the development of the new industry in the growing of trees yielding INDIA-RUBBER in certain of our planting districts. We all agree that there is no risk of overproduction here and Ceylon rubber has already secured a very high character and good price, in the London market. Long may these be maintained Early in 1896 very few Para rubber trees can have been planted out. Now of all kinds, the calculation is that the equivalent of nearly 12,000 acres are planted, and the total export this year is likely to reach to from 50,000 lb. to 60,000 lb. This is the beginning of a trade which may well expand during the next five or six years to annual shipments of from 1½ to 2 million lb. worth perhaps between £300,000 and £400,000 sterling. It is quite evident too that in place of being limited to 10,000 acres as was thought a few years ago, rubber (in its several ready-growing and remunerative species) may yet cover as great an extent as cacao or 35,000 to 40,000 acres in Ceylon and the trees on this and ought, when in full bearing, to yield from 7 to 8 million lbs. a year of the crude product which is so much in demand in Europe and America.

Finally, we need only mention the events of national and imperial importance connected with the Royal Family :—the enthusiastic celebration of the Diamond Jubilee of our beloved Queen-Empress in 1897; the lamented death of the Good Queen in 1901; followed seven months after by the visit to Ceylon of T. R. H. the Duke and Duchess of York (now Prince and Princess of Wales) and then in the Coronation and its enthusiastic celebration in the first of Crown Colonies, while its Governor—Sir West Ridgeway—represented all the Eastern Colonies in Westminster Abbey.

IN CONCLUSION.

A very interesting chapter might be written on "What the British have done for Ceylon"—not only in material improvements, and provision against famine, by roads, railways, irrigation works, etc., but through "the Roman Peace" protection of life and property, strict and impartial administration of justice, the great spread of education, and the promotion of health and alleviation of suffering and disease through the multiplying of hospitals, dispensaries, and doctors, the construction of waterworks and drainage, etc. What would happen if the British left Ceylon might be judged from the standing feud (sometimes issuing in riots) between the Buddhists and Roman Catholics; and between the Sinhalese and Moormen (Muhammadans) in certain districts. The decennial census was the great event of 1901—the main results will be found in Appendix III.

Nowhere in the British Empire are there more loyal or contented subjects of Her Most Gracious Majesty than in "Lanká," "the pearl-drop on the brow of India"

HIS EXCELLENCY THE HON. SIR HENRY ARTHUR BLAKE, G.C.M.G.

CHAPTER XVIII.

CEYLON'S NEW GOVERNOR: H. E. SIR HENRY BLAKE, G.C.M.G.*—Dec., 1903.

(Reprinted from the "Ceylon Observer" Dec. 3rd, 1903.)

GOVERNOR Gregory—who by the way was a warm personal friend of our new Governor—said in 1872 that Sir Hercules Robinson had so thoroughly and successfully administered the affairs of Ceylon up to the very hour of his quitting office, that it seemed to him nothing was left for him to do beyond routine work, save to carry out his predecessor's design for the improvement of Colombo Harbour. Sir William Gregory, as it turned out, was very much mistaken. He had to break his predecessor's spell of "Nawalapitiya and finality" in regard to Railway extension up-country; he began the seaside line to Galle on his own responsibility; he created the North-Central Province; vastly improved Kandy as well as Colombo (giving it for the first time a museum) and Nuwara Eliya (Lake Gregory and Queen's Cottage, among other things)—while doing much in many directions towards social and administrative improvement for the benefit of the community. Active and successful as Sir West Ridgeway has been

---

* His Excellency was appointed Governor of Ceylon on September 1st, and arrived in Ceylon on December 3rd 1903. His career previous to this appointment was as follows:—Born at Limerick, January 18th, 1840 – son of the late Peter Blake, County Inspector of Irish Constabulary. Cadet Irish Constabulary. 1859; Resident Magistrate, 1876; appointed Special Resident Magistrate, 1882; Governor of Bahamas, 1884-87; Newfoundland, 1887-88; appointed to Queensland, 1888, but resigned without entering upon the administration; Captain-General and Governor in-Chief. Jamaica, 1889-97: at request of Legislature and public bodies of the Island his term was extended in 1894, and again in 1896; Governor of Hongkong, 1897-1903.

during his specially prolonged term of administration, it cannot for a moment be said that he has left nothing beyond routine for his successor to take up. It has been Sir West's fortune to set agoing not a few public works, to inaugurate several experiments, and to appoint more than one Commission with the completion, outcome or results of which, his successor must have both official connection and responsibility. Sir Henry Blake will have to gather up the loose strings of not a few important public questions much discussed and even reported on during the past year or two, without final decisions being arrived at. A very big question indeed—one of the most momentous that has been opened up since the days of Sir Emerson Tennent, or the Ceylon League, or the Cobden Club interference with the paddy rents—is that of the local "Incidence of Taxation," on which the Commission presided over by the Hon'ble the Lieut-Governor has yet to make its Report, although it is understood that several Sub-Committees (on Arrack, Education and Medical Cess, Customs, Salt, Railway Rates, &c.) have completed their labours. A few weeks back, Mr. Harold Cox, the Secretary of the Cobden Club, attacked Mr. Chamberlain in a very pointed letter, for decrying the influence and significance of that body, and soundly asserted that its object had ever been at all times and in all countries to promote Free Trade principles and practice. We have not seen Mr. Chamberlain's rejoinder, if indeed he made one; but what a crushing reply might be given from the experience of Ceylon where the Cobden Club was instrumental in moving a Tory Secretary of State (Lord Knutsford) to abolish the immemorial rent (or tax, or levy) on locally-grown rice (or paddy), while agreeing to say nothing against the 10 per cent *ad valorem* Customs duty on the rice imported for the urban population (and estate coolies) including some of the very poorest and most heavily-taxed people in the Island. Eleven years have gone by, and neither the Cobden Club nor Mr. Harold Cox has ever made the slightest movement to promote

Free Trade, to get Protection abolished, or to remove a very considerable, objectionable, nay iniquitous Food Tax in Ceylon! Whatever else may be the outcome of the Incidence Commission, we trust the duty on grain will be abolished, even if export duties on all the staples are imposed, pending the day—after Surveys and Land Settlements are finished,—for a scientific system such as is administered in India. Under this heading of Taxation and Revenue, Sir Henry Blake will also find there is much room for a reform of the Arrack Monopoly and the entire suppression of illicit sales both of arrack and palm "toddy" more or less intoxicating. Not only do we think the revenue may be increased, rather than diminished, by the abolition of renters ; but we think such a reform has a direct bearing on the suppression of serious Crime, a matter which baffled Governor Ridgeway to cope with successfully—through legislation, the headmen or the police—and which almost, more than anything else, has been left for his successor to investigate and, if possible, check and diminish. Where arrack is distilled, illicitly sold or intoxicating toddy vended to coolies and villagers, and where ignorance most prevails, —in such districts, as a rule, crime prevails. With the spread of primary and industrial education,—it used to be an established fact, that no artificer (carpenter, ironworker, mason, &c.) was ever found in gaol—with the strict enforcement of law in regard to the sale of all intoxicating drink, and with the introduction of "penal servitude in the Andamans" as a new and much-dreaded punishment, serious homicidal crime among the Sinhalese ought greatly to decrease. Speaking of arrack —to the use of which, unfortunately, the Sinhalese have been accustomed from time immemorial, though forbidden in their Buddhist teachings—brings us to "opium" which has never been prepared or used by them as a drug, practically, until within the past fifty to sixty years, and only to any appreciable extent since the British Government licensed opium shops in the towns and villages thirty years ago, and more freely within the past ten years. The result is that the annual import of the drug has run up from 800 to 1,000 lbs. fifty years ago, to over 20,000 lbs.—a serious matter as laying the foundation of an "opium habit" among a people already specially effeminate and only too ready to fall into the lazy, helpless, if not worse, state which opium promotes. Sir Henry Blake knows far too much of opium in China and other countries, for us to say more now than refer His Excellency to the debate of last Session in the Legislative Council, and to express the hope that before he leaves Ceylon it may be His Excellency's felicity to meet the views of the Sinhalese, Kandyan, Muhammadan, Burgher and General European representatives as expressed on that occasion. Public Instruction in Ceylon in all its branches,—including technical, industrial and agricultural—is in a state of transition. The same may be said to some extent of the work of the Scientific Department in connection with the Royal Botanic Gardens, from which much good has already come and much more is expected.

The continuance to completion of important Surveys, the promotion of Land Settlement, the construction of much-needed new roads and bridges, and the restoration of irrigation tanks now well in hand, will all mark the period of Sir Henry Blake's administration. It should see the final disposal of the Colombo Harbour Works in Breakwaters, the foundation-stone of the first of which was laid by His present Majesty when Prince of Wales in 1875, Sir William Gregory being Governor. There is also our Graving Dock to be finished, although not so large as one or two Sir Henry Blake has left in process of construction at Hongkong. Then comes the railway which ought to be opened right through the island to Jaffna by Governor Blake, who has also to see the proper completion of the Udapussellawa Hill line; but His Excellency must not be content to open merely what his predecessor started. We hope it will be Sir Henry Blake's happiness to have his name identified with at least two Railway extensions which are certain to be financially prosperous, namely, the branch to Ratnapura and the line from Colombo northwards to Negombo, Chilaw, and Puttalam; while, possibly, there may be an extension of the Southern Seaside line to Tangalla and Hambantota; of a feeding hill line to Badulla and Passara—and if the Admiralty and Home Government do their duty, a line to Trincomalee (and Batticaloa), and the promotion of an Indo-Ceylon Railway *via* Mannar and Rameswaram,—the extension from Madawachchi to Mannar island being as good as guaranteed in connection with the Cooly Immigrant Labour route and supply

It will be seen from this hurried sketch that, apart from every-day matters of Administration, and educational, philanthropic and social calls on his attention, Sir Henry Blake is likely to have as many large and important questions come under his attention as had any of his predecessors. We trust the same experience of a period of prosperity in Agriculture (Tea, Cacao and Palm planting especially), in general Import and Export Trade, and in Revenue returns may be continued in 1904 and onwards as prevailed from 1896 to 1903. Much is rightly expected from a series of successful Pearl Fisheries and from the important investigation and experiments inaugurated by Professor Herdman and Mr. Hornell. To His Excellency the Governor and Lady Blake, personally, we tender the heartiest welcome in the name of the people of all races and classes in Ceylon, and we trust the Divine blessings will rest on their aspirations and labours, and that, when the time comes for retirement, they will have no cause to look back on their stay in Ceylon with any feeling save that of satisfaction and thankfulness.

APPENDICES.

Ceylon in 1903.

APPENDIX I.

GLOSSARY.

[H. = Hindustani ; A. = Aryan ; P. = Pali ; Tel. = Telugu.]

Áchári.—Blacksmiths ; also the name of a Siŋhalese caste.
Áchchila.—A Kandyan form of the word *árachchila, q. v.*
Adappın.—A customs headman in the Northern Province.
Adigár.—(From Skt. *adhikári.*) Superintendent, prime minister, or chief officer of state under the kings of Kandy.
Adikar.—The chief revenue officer of a division in the Mannár District.
Adipalla.—The lower layers of stacked paddy on a threshing-floor, allowed to the watcher as a perquisite.
Adukku.—Dressed provisions supplied to an officer travelling on duty, as distinguished from *pęhidum* raw provisions, *q. v.*
Agáré.—*Deņiya,* low land between hills ; high land attached to a field ; tributary stream.
Agas.—First-fruits of a crop ; offering of first-fruits.
Agata or *Agáwata.*—(From *aga* end, and *ata* direction.) Lower side of a paddy field *or* range of paddy fields.
Agubalanná.—The headman who tasted the food of the Kandyan king.
Ahaskambé.—The tight rope (literally "air-rope") used in rope dancing, which is a service of tenants of the Badulla Déwálé.
Akampaḍiyar.—Those who attend to any business in the *interior* of temples and palaces.
Akyála.—Contribution of rice or paddy on the occasion of a procession at a *déwálé ;* first-fruits offered for the protection of the crops by the *dewiyó.*
Alagu.—A mark to assist the memory ; a tally, *e.g.,* in counting coconuts one is put aside to mark each hundred : those thus put aside are called *alagu.*
Alis-ilis nętuwa.—Without disloyalty or carelessness.
Aliyandure.—The morning music at a temple.
Almirah(Port. *ulmaria.*)—A cabinet,wardrobe,cupboard,chest of drawers.
Amánı (Aumany).—Held in trust or deposit ; applied especially to the collection of revenue direct from cultivators or renters by officers of Government, upon the removal or suspension of an intermediate claimant.

Glossary.

Amarapura Samágama.—(From *Amarapura* the capital of the Burmese Empire, and *samágama* a society.) The Amarapura sect of Buddhists in Ceylon who are in communion with the monks of Burma. This sect was introduced into Ceylon about 1800 A.D. by Ambagahapiṭiye, a monk of the Halágama caste.

Ambalama.—A native resthouse or halting-place. (From the Tamil *ambalam*—v. *madam*.)

Ampaḍḍar.—Barbers; also the name of a Tamil caste.

Amuṇa.—A dam; also a measure of grain, equal in the District of Colombo to six bushels, in the Kandyan-country four bushels. The measure varies in different parts of the Island. It generally consists of four *pélas*; v. *péla*. Also the extent of land sown by the above measure: as a measure of arecanuts = 24,000.

Anaméstaraya.—A shed in which lights are kept at déwálé festivals.

Anda, Andé.—Share, or, more appropriately, half share. *Anda* land is that which is delivered by the proprietor to another to cultivate on condition of delivering to him half the crop as rent. This is the usual condition on which fertile fields are annually let.—(D'Oyly.) The term is now applied to other shares than half given by the cultivator of a field to its proprietor: thus *tunen-anda* is one-third share, *hataren-anda* one-fourth, and so forth. Half share is sometimes called *hari-anda* (from *hari* equal, and *anda* share) to distinguish it from other shares.

Anda-muttettu.—(From *anda* and *muttettu*.) Those *muttettu* lands which are cultivated on the condition of giving half the crop to the proprietor, as distinguished from *ninda-muttettu, q. v.*

Anda-pravéṇi.—(Corruptly *anda-paravéṇi*.) Signifies lands originally the property of Government, abounding with jungle, which have been cleared and cultivated by individuals without permission. One-seventh part of the produce of these lands (in the first place) is given as *wálahan*, and then the seed corn is deducted; after which one-half of the remaining produce is appropriated to Government and the other by the *goyyas*. The cultivators or the persons who converted them into fields are entitled to one-half the soil of this description of land, which they may either sell or mortgage and which is heritable. —(*Ceylon Almanac*, 1819.)

Áṇḍi.—Pilgrim, religious mendicant, fakir.

Aṇga, Aṇge.—The uppermost part of a field; small fields detached from the main tract of fields.

Aṇgama.—A magical ceremony performed to inflict an injury on some one.

Aṅgudalupat.—Small villages dependent on large ones given for the performance of some sort of service, as that of dhoby, tom-tom beater, devil-dancer, or jaggery-caste people.

Anicut.—(From the Tamil.) A dam across a river, to fill and regulate the water in the irrigation channels cut from it.

Aniyam ẹlapaṭa.—The temporary bottom of a field ; *i.e.*, when a portion of land is cleared for cultivation, and when only the upper half of it is asweddumized, the bottom of the asweddumized portion is *aniyam ẹlapaṭa* ; when the remainder is also asweddumized the bottom of it is *pahala ẹlapaṭa*, and *aniyam ẹlapaṭa* no longer exists.

Aniyaṃ Paṇguwa.—(From *aniyam* unfixed, and *paṇguwa* a share or portion.) Portion of land for which there is no fixed service.

Aṇkeḷiya.—Horn-pulling. The ceremony of pulling horns or forked sticks to propitiate the goddess Pattini in times of epidemics.

Anna.—(Skt. *áná.*) The sixteenth part of a rupee.

Anumẹtiráḷa.—A respectful term for a *kapuráḷá*, *q. v.*; one through whom the pleasure of the *deviyó* is known.

Anunáyaka Unnánsé.—Assistant or second chief monk.

Appu.—An honorific. In colloquial use the word "appu" has come to mean "butler" among Europeans.

Appuhámi.—A respectful term applied to one of a higher grade than appu.

Ára.—(From the Tamil *áru.*) A stream.

Árachchila, Árachchi.—An officer over a village or group of villages, and in rank below a *kórála* in the Kandyan and below a *muhandiram* in the low-country.

Arrack, Arakku, or Arukki.—A fermented liquor from the juice of the coconut palm, probably a dialectical modification of the Arabic *árak*. (Siṇ. *arakku.*)

Aráwa.—A portion of land newly asweddumized and lying detached from the range of paddy fields.

Asgiri Viháraya.—The college of Buddhist monks at Asgiriya, Kandy.

Askaṇukumburu.—(From *as* aside, and *kaṇu* or *kon* a corner.) Exterior fields lying towards the boundary of the range, or at a distance from the centre. Border fields which, in remote districts, have certain privileges, light taxation, &c., in consideration of their being subject to danger from wild beasts.

Aswanáta.—(From *as* aside, *wana* jungle, and *ata* direction.) An uncultivated portion of a field bordering a jungle. *v. Wanáta.*

Aswẹdduma.—Land recently converted into a paddy field.

Aswẹddumize.—A verb anglicized from the above, "to convert into a paddy field."

Atapattu Árachchi.—Árachchi of the Atapattu.

Atapattu Lékama.—The lékama (writer or secretary) of the Atapattu.

Atapattu Mudiyansé.—Mudaliyár of the Atapattu.

iv   *Glossary.*

Atapattu Péruwa.—The department of the Atapattu.
Atapattuwa.—The peon or messenger staff of a *disáwa.*
Atikári.—A petty irrigation headman in the Eastern Province.
Aṭmaga.—A portion of jungle outside a field to preserve it from wild animals, sometimes cultivated with fine grain. A common term in the Mátara District.
Attanáyakarála.—Custodian, storekeeper, overseer ; corresponding to *wannakurála* (accountant).
Atukórála, Atukóralayá.—An assistant to a *kórála.*
Aṭuwa.—A granary. *v. Bissa,* the corresponding word used in the Kandyan districts.
Áwatéwakirima.—Ministrations ; daily service at a *déwálé.*

Baḍahęlayó.—Potters ; also the name of a Siŋhalese caste.
Baḍallu.—Gold and silversmiths. Siŋhalese caste.
Baḍawędilla.—Land granted by Government to certain individuals in consideration of offices held or services rendered by them.
Baḍawęṭiya.—A hedge or belt of jungle bordering a field or a garden.
Baḍḍe.—Division when it occurs as the latter part of a compound word *e.g.,* Maggonbadde, Maggona Division.
Baddeminihá.—A respectful term for a tom-tom beater.
Badukaraya.—Deed of lease.
Balana paŋguwa.—The share of the produce of a garden given to the occupant by the owner for taking care of it.
Bálapúwa.—A separate portion of a paddy field of a small extent cultivated for the exclusive benefit of an individual cultivator.
Bála-wi.—(From *Bála* young, and *wi* paddy.) A kind of paddy sown after the expiration of the proper season, as it ripens sooner than other descriptions of paddy.
Bali.—Offerings to propitiate the planets.
Ballam.—A large dug-out canoe.
Bambánęṭima.—A wickerwork frame on which a man walks, carrying it along at Diyakępíma. [*Diyakępíma* is the ceremony of striking the water with a sword at a certain place in the Mahaweli-gaṅga or the Kalu-gaṅga, and putting some water into a pot, which is then considered holy water.]
Bambupídima.—Sprouting of *bambu.* Applied to a paddy disease : a blight which affects the young paddy plants, due to unusually prolonged rains. From want of sun the young plant fails to mature the ear, and a shoot of grass like a *bambu* leaf appears in its stead. *v. Hálpanpidima.*
Baṇa.—The word of Buddha.

Ceylon in 1903.

Baṇḍá.—An honorific title in the Kandyan districts.

Baṇḍárawatu.—(From *Baṇḍára*, or more correctly *bháṇḍágára*, a storeroom, a treasury ; and *wattu* gardens.) Gardens belonging to the royal store or treasury, *i.e.*, gardens belonging to Government. Most of them were planted by the Dutch Government. The whole of their produce was annually rented by Government for its own benefit, but in a few instances some of these gardens were planted by individuals who possess the planting share of the trees only, in such proportion as the nature of the soil will admit ; *i.e.*, those gardens on the coast pay annually to Government two-thirds of the produce of the trees (chiefly coconut trees), and the remaining one-third or planting share is enjoyed by the planter ; and those gardens situated in the interior pay half to Government.—(*Ceylon Almanac*, 1819.)

Baṇḍárawaliya.—Certain noble families in the Kandyan country.

Baṇḍáriya.—The designation by which the one-fifth share paid to Government by the holders of the paddy fields in the *batgam* is known.

Bande, Bunde.—Tel. A fine for trespass by cattle —(Wilson.) (The Siṇhalese word *wandiya* fine, or payment of compensation, is evidently of the same origin.)

Bankshall.—Etymology doubtful : 1, a warehouse ; 2, the office of a harbour master ; 3, name of street in Colombo.

Barapęn.—Remuneration given to copyists ; hire given for important services, as the building of a *vihárè*, making of images, and copying sacred books.

Basnáyaka Nilamé.—Principal or lay incumbent of a *déwálé* or Hindu temple.

Batgam.—Corruptly *bajjam*. (From *bat* rice, and *gama* a village, lit. a "rice village.") There are four villages known as the "four batgam," or "bajjam," in the Gaṅgabaḍa pattuwa of Mátara. They were originally given to certain families on condition of service, but when that service was no longer exacted, the holders or occupants (called *Nayidés*) of these lands were required to give up to the State one-fifth of the produce of their fields, which one-fifth part is designated *baṇḍáriya*, and belongs absolutely to the Crown.—(Cairns.)

Batgamayó.—The name of a Siṇhalese caste, commonly called Paduwó.

Batkawópu-nama.—Name given when a child is first fed with rice.

Baṭta.—Additional allowance. Extra pay or allowances to officers employed on special duties or in distant places.—(Wilson.)

Bazaar.—(In the dialects which have not a *z bájár*.) A market, a daily market, a market place.—(Wilson.)

Bêche-de-mer.—Sea islug or trepang. A species of *Holothuria* much esteemed as a delicacy by the Chinese.

Glossary.

Bęmma.—The bund or earthen dam closing the outlet of the valley in which the water of a tank is retained.

Bere.—A tom-tom. As a measure of capacity equal to 5 kurunies or 20 nęlies.

Berawáyó.—Tom-tom beaters ; also the name of a Siṇhalese caste.

Beri-Beri.—An acute disease of a dropsical nature.

Betma.—A divison, especially of a water-course,into channels or branches

Betmerála.—The officer in charge of a number of villages belonging to a temple, corresponding to a *ridáne*.

Bhang.—An intoxicating preparation of hemp.

Bimpulutu.—Fees levied for the privilege of cremation.

Bindunkaḍa.—A breach in a bund.

Binna.—Corruptly *beena*. That species of marriage among the Kandyans where the husband is received into the house of the bride, and abides therein permanently. *v. Diga.*

Bintęnna.—(Sabaragamuwa.) Term applied to Kolonná kóralé and parts of Aṭakulan and Męda kóralés, where the climate does not permit of el-wí cultivation ; also a division of Uva.

Bisókoṭuwa.—A square shaft or well sunk through the bund of a tank to the bottom of a sluice leading from the inside of the tank to the fields outside. " It is probable that the well served as an entrance to the sluice for the purpose of cleaning it, removing roots, pieces of wood, or other obstructions. It is true that a man might enter the sluice from the outside for that purpose, but without the well he would be in darkness ; and it is only in the embankments of large tanks that the well is found. Besides, in the event of the sluice gates getting out of order, supplementary gates could be put to the sluice in the well while they were being repaired."—(*Ceylon Almanac*, 1857.)

Bissa.—A granary, round, of wickerwork, and plastered with mud. *v. Aṭuwa.*

Bodel Kamer (Dutch).—Testamentary or estate funds deposited with the Loan Board. *v. Budalé.*

Bógaha.—The bó-tree (*Ficus religiosa*). Gautama, the Buddha of the present age, is said to have attained Buddhahood whilst seated at the foot of a bó-tree at Buddha Gaya in India. The tree is believed to exist there still, and is an object of worship to the Buddhists. The bó-tree at Auurádhapura, planted there in the reign of Dévánanpiyatissa, 306-266 B.C., is said to be the right branch of that tree.

Bóla-atta.—A bundle of leaves, generally of *gurulla*, set up at a field to show that it had been appropriated by the party setting it up, and that no one had a right to enter upon it for the purpose of cultivating it. Also a broom made of leaves.

Bombay Duck.—A small fish. *Harpodon nehereus*, eaten fresh, and also in the well-known dried state.

Boutique.—(From the Portuguese *butica* or *boteca*.) A small native shop or booth.

Brahma.—The first deity of the Hindu triad ; the creator of the world.

Brahman, Brahmun.—(Dialectically *bahman* or *bohman*, or in Tamil *parappan* or *piramanan*. Corruptly *braman*, *bramin*, &c. Skt. *Bráhmaṇa*.) A man of the first order or caste of Hindus, properly charged with the duty of expounding the *védas*, and conducting the ceremonies they enjoin. In modern times engaged not only in such duties, but in most of the occupations of secular life.—(Wilson.)

Brinjal.—*Solanum melongena*. Called in the West Indies "the egg plant."

Bubula.—A spring of water, often used for purposes of irrigation.

Búdalé.—Estate of a deceased person. *v. Bodel Kamer.*

Buddha.—(From the root *Budha* to know, to comprehend. P. *Buddho*, Buddha.) The founder of Buddhism ; a being who has attained perfect knowledge ; the enlightened.

Buddha Varshaya.—The Buddhist era. It is reckoned from the death of Gautama Buddha, 543 B.C.

Bulat-hurulla.—A fee of a few *ridís* given by a complainant to the headman. Lit. a bundle of betel leaves, inside which the money is generally placed.

Bund.—A dam or dyke ; a raised bank or mound of earth constructed to confine the waters of a tank

Bungalow.—Probably from *banga*, Beng., a thatched cottage, such as is usually occupied by Europeans in the provinces or in military cantonments.—(Wilson.)

Burgher.—(Dutch *burger* a citizen.) 1, Dutch descendants ; 2, a generic name in Ceylon for Eurasians.

Cabob.—A specific kind of curry of meat in small pieces placed on skewers alternately with onions and green ginger.

Cabook.—Laterite, disintegrated gneiss, used for gravelling roads and for buildings. It hardens on exposure to the air, and is impregnated with iron peroxide.

Cadjan. - A Malay word. The plaited leaf of the cocoanut palm used for thatching houses.

Candy.—A measure of weight used in South India and Ceylon, varying from 500 to 600 lb.

Caravel, Carvel.—Frequent in old Portuguese narratives. A round built vessel, *i.e.*, not long and sharp like a galley. Perhaps connected with the Celtic " coracle."

Glossary.

Cashew, Cadju.—The tree, fruit, or nut of the *Anarcardium occidentale*. Introduced into the East Indies from America. The nuts, containing much oil, are called "promotion nuts" and "coffin nails."

Caṭamaran.—A raft formed of three or four logs of wood lashed together. v. *Teppam.*

Chaityaya.—(Pali *Chetiya,* Eḷu *Séya.*) A depository of the relics of Buddha.

Chakkiliyar.—Tanners and shoemakers. A Tamil caste.

Chánár.—Toddy-drawers. A Tamil caste.

Chardu.—Equivalent to Duráve. The name of a Siṇhalese caste.

Chank.—A large kind of shell found especially in the Gulf of Mannár. The right-handed chank with its spirals opening to the right is highly prized. Chanks are used as horns for blowing at temples, and also for cutting into armlets and other ornaments. Another name is "conch." (Skt. saṅkha).

Charpoy.—A Hindu word meaning "four feet," a common bedstead.

Chattiriyar.—Warriors (*Kshatriya*). A Tamil caste.

Cháyakkárar.—Dyers. A Tamil caste.

Cheḍi.—Low jungle, small bushes.

Chckku.—A mill worked by bullocks for expressing oil from copperah, *q.v.*

Chembu.—A small pot, usually made of brass or copper.

Chempaḍ ɩvar.—A tribe of fishers.

Chena, corruptly for "héna."—Jungle land burnt and cleared at intervals of years and sown with fine grains and vegetables.

Chéniyar.—Weavers. A Tamil caste.

Chetty.—A trader, merchant. A Tamil caste.

Chit.—A note or letter.

Chitpar.—Sculptors, stone-cutters, masons. A Tamil caste.

Chittirakkárar.—Painters. A Tamil caste.

Chiviyár.—Palanquin bearers. A Tamil caste.

Chóḷiya Vellálar.—Vellálas from the Sóḷiya country, about Tanjore and Trichinapalli.

Chóṇakar (*or Tulukkar*).—Moormen.

Chow-chow.—Pigeon-English for mixed preserves imported from China.

Choya root.—A root (*Hedyotis umbellata*) affording a red dye called "Indian madder."

Chule.—A torch of coconut or other leaves.

Chunam.—Prepared lime, chewed with betel leaf, arecanut, and tobacco. Also lime for mortar, and especially fine polished plaster.

Coir.—The fibre of the coconut husk from which rope is made. Thence a synonym for rope itself.

Comboy.—A cloth or skirt worn by the natives of Ceylon.
Conjee.—Rice water or gruel.
Cooly.—A hired labourer or carrier of burdens.
Copra, also Coprah and Copperah.—The dried flesh of the coconut used for the expression of its oil. The refuse is called *poonac*, *q. v.*
Cowle.—Arab. *kaul.* A written agreement. Used in the Northern Province for "conditions of sale."
Coyta.—A Public Works Department tool ; a bill-hook.
Crediet Brieven.—Promissory notes of the Dutch Government in Ceylon.
Cutchery, also Kachchéri, Kaccéri.—In Ceylon the use of this word is entirely confined to the revenue office of a Government Agent or Assistant Agent. In India an office of administration or court-house.

Dágaba, Dágęba, or Dágoba.—(From *dá* relics, and *gaba* or *gęba* a womb, a receptacle.) A bell-shaped structure in which the relics of Buddha or other holy personages are deposited.
Daladá.—The canine tooth-relic of Buddha.
Dalada Máligáwa.—(From *dáladá* the canine tooth-relic, and *máligawa* a palace, a mansion.) The temple of Buddha's tooth-relic at Kandy.
Dalumuré.—The turn of a tenant to supply betel for a temple or proprietor.
Dalupota.—Land lately brought into cultivation as a paddy field, or more recently than an original field.
Dalupotkárayá.—A sub-tenant, garden-tenant ; one who has asweddumized land belonging to a *mulpaṅguhárayá* (original tenant).
Daránḍa.—The upper side of a field.
Dęhęt-ata.—A roll of betel leaves given to a monk.
Dehikępuma.—Cutting of limes : a magical ceremony to avert the evil influence of stars or demons.
Dękum.—Presents.
Demala Gattaru.—(From *Demala* Tamil, and *gattaru* captives.) A Siṅhalese caste so called, supposed to be the descendants of Tamil captives taken by Siṅhalese kings. These people are found chiefly in the villages of Indigastuḍuwa and Bondupiṭiya in the Pasdun kórálé of the Western Province ; Wallambégala and Galkanda in the Bentota-Walalláwiṭi kóralé ; and Galahénkanda and some other villages in the Gaṅgabada pattu of Galle in the Southern Province.
Deṇiya.—A narrow valley running up between the spurs of a range of hills and cultivated with paddy ; high ground, as distinguished from low or marshy ground.
Depá-éla.—A water channel constructed along an embankment ; an ela having two sides or banks, which have to be kept in repair by the cultivators, as distinguished from the majority of elas, which have but one side or bank.

Glossary.

Depá-wélla.—A ridge or bank running through fields, either as a boundary or as a path, and which the cultivators of fields lying on either side of it are bound to keep in repair.

Déwálagama.—(From *déwále* a Hindu temple, and *gama* a village.) A village or land belonging to a *déwále* or temple of some heathen deity.

Déwálé.—A temple dedicated to a god.

Déwa-nágara.—The (divine) Sanskrit characters or Sanskrit alphabet.

Dewata.—A path between two fences or hedges.

Dhal.—(Hindu *dál.*) A kind of pulse resembling split pease.

Dhátu.—Relics.

Dhoby.—(Hindu *dhobi.*) A washerman.

Dhoni.—A nundecked vessel. The word is used generally for a native ship.

Diga (Deega).—That species of Kandyan marriage where the bride leaves her parents and lives permanently with her husband. The opposite of *Binna, q. v.*

Diggé.—Porch of a *déwále*, to which alone worshippers have access.

Disáwa.—Governor of a Province in the Kandyan kingdom.

Disáwané.—The jurisdiction of the above.

Divel.—(From the root *div*, to live.) Lands granted to individuals for their maintenance in consideration of certain services rendered or offices held by them.

Diwa Nilame.—Principal lay officer of the Daladá Máligáwa (palace of, the tooth-relic).

Diyabetma.—See *Batma.*

Diyatara.—Fields which are irrigated by means of tanks and channels and not dependent on rain, as distinguished from *malan kumburu*, which are dependent on rain for irrigation.

Diyawadana Nilame.—Another term for the *Diwa Nilame.*

Diyawáraya.—(From *diya* water, and *wáraya* turn or season.) The turn for water, or time for each range of fields to receive water from an *ela* which irrigates different ranges of fields in rotation.

Dola.—A natural water-course.

Dówa.—A field or place between rising grounds, and into which water flows during rains.

Dubsah.—(From Skt. *dwi-bháshá* of two languages.) An interpreter ship's purveyor.

Dugganna Nilame.—A personal attendant on the king.

Dugganna Péruwa.—The class from which the personal attendants on the king were selected.

Duráwe.—The name of a Sinhalese caste.

Durayá.—A headman of the Wahumpura, Baddé, and Paduwa castes.

Ebittayá.—The juvenile attendant of a Buddhist monk.

Edauḍa.—A small foot-bridge over a stream, usually a single log with (occasionally) a hand rail.

Eḥelagaha.—Tree or post set up at a *déwále* at a lucky hour in the month of Eḥela as a preliminary to perahera.

Ela.—A water-course ; a channel for carrying water from a tank or stream to the fields.

Ela-agata.—Lower end of a water-course.

Ela-amuṇa.—Water-course and its dam.

Ela-mulata.—Upper end of an ela or water-course.

Ela-polla.—Portion of the ela assigned to each cultivator to keep in repair.

Ella.—A rapid ; a water-fall.

Elu.—The old Siṇhalese language.

Eluttukkárar.—Scribes. A Tamil caste.

Etaná.—Applied to a Siṇhalese lady of a Kandyan family of the Vellála caste.

Etani.—Rather lower than the above.

Fanam.—Six cents, from Siṇhalese *panama, q. v.*

Fathom.—Six feet. In the West, a measure of depth of water ; in Ceylon, a measure of distance and of length.

Gabaḍá-gama.—(From *gabadá* a store, and *gama* a village.) A royal village.

Gabaḍá Nilame.—Officer in charge of the royal stores of the Kandyan king.

Gáḍi.—The respectful term for a Roḍiyá. The name used by a Roḍiyá for his caste.

Gahalayo, Gahalagambaḍayo.—Executioners, scavengers.

Gahóni.—Cloth covering of pingo loads of presents.

Gajanáyaka Nilame.—Officer in charge of the elephants of the Kandyan king.

Gal-addo.—Workers in precious stones ; lapidaries.

Galgáná Haṇgiḍiyá.—Chief of stone-cutters.

Gallatgama.—" A species of village much in the nature of a *ninda* village, and sometimes bearing that name."—(D'Oyly.)

Gallnut.—The fruit of *Terminalia chebula,* Siṇ. *aralu.* Plentiful in the Bintenna of Uva, and largely exported under the name of *Myrobolans, q. v.*

Gama.—A village. The Siṇhalese word *gama* properly signifies a village, but in the Kandyan country it is also frequently applied to a single estate or a single field. The latter is often called *paṇguwa* or shares

Gamarála.—A village chief or headman.
Gammahé.—A village headman, a headman of Veddás.
Gan Arachchi.—An árachchi of a village.
Gaṇa-dewiyó.—(Skt. *Ganésha.*) Son of Siva, the god of wisdom and remover of difficulties and obstacles, addressed at the commencement of all undertakings and at the opening of all compositions.
Gangátaya.—Leg of an animal killed in the chase and given to the proprietor of the land whereon it was killed.
Gannile.—The service field in a village held by the *gammahé*, or the village headman, for the time being.

Share under a gam-wasama, the district of a village headman, (gammahé) or (gamarála), who enjoys the paṇgu or share. He must accommodate all the persons who come from the landlord to the village, and carry his messages to the tenants and others. He must also supply provisions in some cases.

Gaṇsabháwa.—Village council or tribunal.
Gamwasama.—The tenement held by the *Gamárálás* of villages from the Crown subject to certain services.
Gasmandá.—A term for a Roḍiyá.
Gattaru.—A low caste, supposed to be descendants of captives, or condemned thieves, &c.
Gautama.—The name of the Buddha of the present *kalpa* or age.
Gawettuwa.—A small box for cash or jewellery.
Gawwa.—A measure of distance, about four English miles.
Gebarála.—Storekeeper, whose duty it is to measure the paddy, rice, oil, &c., received into and issued out of a temple *gabaḍáwa* (store).
Gedaranama ; *Génama.*—House name ; family name.
Gentoo.—(Port. *gentio.*) Heathen generally, not including Mohammedans, found in old books, but now obsolete.
Gewatupaṇama.—Rent paid for possession of houses and gardens.
Ghaut.—A landing place ; steps on the bank of a river ; a quay ; a wharf where customs are commonly levied ; a pass through the mountains ; the mountains themselves, especially applied to the eastern and western ranges of the south of India, &c.
Goḍa-bima.—High land.
Goḍa-kumbura.—The highest land in a tract of fields.
Godown.—(Beng. *gudám*, from the Malay *gadang.*) An outhouse, a warehouse, a place where household implements or goods are kept. The "black hole" was nothing else than a godown.
Gotama,—*v. Gautama.*
Goyan, or more correctly goyam.—Standing corn, paddy plants.
Goyigama.—The name of a Sinhalese caste ; also called Vellálas.

Goyi-gánawá.—Smoothing the bed of a field, being the last process preparatory to sowing.
Goyipola.—High or low ground under cultivation.
Goyiyá.—A cultivator.
Grantha.—A book, a metre or measure; the *grantha* alphabet used in the south of India in writing Sanskrit.
Gravet.—A post or station. *Kadawat-hatara*, the Four Gravets or boundaries of Colombo and other towns.
Gunny bag.—(From Sanskrit *góni* a sack.) The popular and trade name for coarse sacks made of jute.
Gurunnęhé.—A term of respect in addressing a tom-tom beater.
Guruwo.—A mixed race (or caste) or Siŋhalese and Moors who profess the Mohammedan religion.
Gymkhana.—A modern word, of which the derivation is uncertain. Usually applied to a small meeting at which horse-racing is combined with athletic and other sports.

Hackery.—A native cart drawn by a bullock.
Hakdure.—The service of blowing conch-shells in daily service in a *déwálé*.
Hakgediya.—A conch-shell or chank, *q.v.*
Hakuró.—Jaggery makers. Name of a Siŋhalese caste.
Halágama.—The name of a Siŋhalese caste.
Hálpan-piduma.—The sprouting of the rice-rush applied to a paddy disease; a blight which affects the young plants, due to the unusually prolonged rains. *v. Bambu-piduma.*
Halpotu.—The bark of the *hal* tree (*Vateria indica*, Lin.) used by the sweet-toddy drawers to prevent the toddy from fermenting.
Haluwadana Nilame.—Officer in charge of the royal robes at the Kandyan palace.
Hámi.—An honorific suffix of names in Siŋhalese.
Háminé.—A respectful term applied to the wife of a *rálahámi, árachchi,* or *hankánama*.
Hámu.—Honorific title of sons and daughters of Mudaliyárs.
Handiram.—A kind of paddy.
Handuruwó.—Another term for Goyigama caste.
Hangala.—The *piruwata* (or cloth) lent by the dhoby.
Hangarammu.—A respectful term for *Wahumpuraya, q. v.* Hence applied to persons of low caste when employed as domestic servants in the Kandyan country.
Hannáli.—Tailors; also the name of a Siŋhalese caste.

xiv   Glossary.

Héna.—Corruptly *chena, q. v.* High jungle ground cultivated at intervals, generally of from five to fourteen years, but in some cases at longer intervals. The jungle is cut down and burnt for manure, and the land is then sown with hill paddy, fine grain, &c.

Hénayá.—A term for a washer or dhoby, *q. v.*

Hẹndẹ́-duré.—The evening music at a *déwalé.*

Hẹreṇapaṭa or *Hẹruṇpaṭa.*—A field asweddumized subsequent to the formation of the original field, and in another direction from it.

Héwápanné.—Soldiers. The body guard of the Maha Mudaliyár.

Héwáwasam.—Belonging to the military class.

Hẹtẹpma.—More correctly *sẹtẹpma*, corruptly *hẹtẹkma*, resting-place. A distance supposed to be equal to an English mile.

Hiléhammiṭiya.—Register of *ploughed lands* under the Kandyan Government.

Hill paddy.—A kind of paddy grown without irrigation on chenas and high lands.

Hinna.—Hill, hillock.

Hinnáwó.—Washers for people of the Halágama caste. The name of a Siṇhalese caste.

Hopper.—A colloquial term for a cake of rice flour.

Hoo.—Hallo or hi. A loud call, and thence applied to the distance at which a loud cry can be heard.

Hulawáliyà.—A headman of the Rodiyás, *q. v.*

Húniyama.—A magical incantation to injure a human being.

Húniyam kepuma.—A ceremony used to ward off the effects of a *húniyama.*

Huṇkiri Áchchila.—Officer who supplied fresh milk to superiors when travelling.

Hunnó.—Lime burners; also name of a Siṇhalese caste.

Huwandiram.—(All spelt *suwandiram.*) A certain share of the produce of a paddy field given to the irrigation headman. The proportion so given varies in different parts of the Island. In the Southern Province it is 1/48th.

Iḍaiyar.—Shepherds and cowherds. Tamil caste.

Iḍaŋge or *iḍama.*—The principal building where visitors of rank are lodged in a village.

Ihala ẹlapaṭa.—That portion of a field which is nearest to the tank which irrigates it, as distinguished from *pahala ẹlapaṭa, q. v.*

Imprest.—An advance, *c. g.*, of travelling expenses.

Inniyara.—The limitary dam or ridge of a field.

Ismatta.—*v. Anga.*

Iṭṭamkaraṇawá.—To emancipate a slave.

Iṭṭaṇkēré.—(From *iṭṭaṇ* act of emancipating, and *kēré* a deed.) A deed of emancipation.

Jambudvipaya.—The *terra cognita* of the Buddhists; also the Continent of India.

Jât.—Caste, nature, kind. Planters use it of the tea plant as being of good or bad jât or stock.

Játaka-pota.—The book of birth-stories of the life of Gautama Buddha in the various stages of his existence, of which 550 are recorded. Hence the book is sometimes called *Pansiya-panas Jataka-pota*, "The Book of the 550 Birth-stories."

Játaka-urumé.—The right of inheritance by the father's side, from *játaka* birth, and *urumé* right, inheritance.

Jerque.—Examination by Customs officers.

Jinriksha—A light two-wheeled vehicle drawn by a man in the shafts: introduced by Americans into Japan and thence into Ceylon.

Jungle.—(Skt. *jangala*, a forest or thicket.) Any tract overrun with bushes or trees.

Kabab v. Cabob.

Kabook v. Cabook.

Kachchéri v. Cutchery.

Kadaiyar.—Lime burners. Tamil caste.

Kadawata v. Gravet.

Kaduttam.—A marriage certificate or promissory note expressing the amount of dowry among Moors.

Kahadiyara.—The sprinkling of water by a *Kapurála* in religious ceremonies.

Kahawaṇu.—An ancient gold coin. (P. *Kahápaṇa*, Skt. *Karshápana*.)

Kaikkiḷavar.—Weavers. Tamil caste.

Kaḷaireḍḍi.—A threshing-floor.

Kaḷam.—A threshing-floor.

Kalaṇda.—An apothecaries' and jewellers' weight equal to $\frac{1}{8}$ of an oz avoirdupois weight, *Kalañchu*.

Kalañchu.—A weight equal to about 73 grains avoirdupois; 16 make a *palam*.

Kálapokam.—The season of cultivation in Jaffna corresponding with the Siṇhalese *maha* and *munmári* in the Eastern Province.

Kálaveḷḷánamai.—Cultivation of grain at the proper season of the year.

Kaliñgula.—A sluice; a dam or bank of stones.

Kaḷḷar.—Lit. thieves.

Glossary.

Kamata.—Threshing-floor, when cattle are used.
Kanáde.—A measure of arrack equal to two bottles.
Kanakkapillai.—An accountant.
Kanatta.—Land overgrown with low jungle ; scrub.
Kaṇḍiya.—A bank or bund of a water-course.
Kandura.—A mountain stream.
Kaṇgáni.—An inferior officer below the rank of an árachchi ; an overseer of a number of coolies employed in public works or on an estate.
Kaṇṇár.—Brassfounders. The name of a Tamil caste.
Kaṇuispravéṇi.—These were originally forests or jungles of large extent cut down and cleared by individuals, which they sowed once every seven or eight years. These lands were free from all tax under the Dutch Government, but since the present Government took possession they are subjected to pay one-tenth of their produce, and the remaining nine-tenths are divided between the gcyiyás and the person who originally cleared them, or their heirs.
Kapurála.—The officiating priest of a *déwálé* or *kóvila, q. v.*
Kapuwá.—A less respectful form of above.
Káraikháḍḍu Veḷḷáḷar.—Vellálas from the south of Madras.
Karaiyár (called also Mukkuvar, Valaiyar, Nuḷaiyar—The name of a Tamil caste.
Káraka Saṇghayá.—There are two bodies bearing this name, one at the Malwatta and the other at the Asgiriya College in Kandy. The managing body of the above colleges consists of twenty priests.
Karáwe.—The name of a Siṇhalese caste.
Káriyakaranná.—An irrigation headman ; in some parts of the Southern Province *Mayoral ;* lit. " an executive officer."
Kartika-maṇgallé.—A Kandyan festival in honour of the gods, celebrated generally the night of the full moon in the month of *Kartika* (December).
Kasakára Lékama.—Officer in charge of the whip-crackers, or persons appointed to walk with whips in front of the *adigárs.*
Katamaran v. Katamaran.
Kataragama Dewiyó.—The Indian god of war. The deity presiding at Kataragama Déwálé.
Kuṭawaha.—Evil mouth, corresponding to evil eye.
Kaṭṭáḍiyá.—A devil-dancer ; an inferior officer in the Kandyan country.
Ketta.—A billhook.
Káṭubullé or *Kaṭupullé.*—The messenger or police staff of an Adigár under the Kandyan Government.
Kaṭusarabóga.—Dry grain.

Kédagaṇ.—Palanquins, fitted up (with sticks) for the occasion, to take up the insignia of the *Dewiyo* in procession.
Kędapan.—Correspondence between the Kandyan and the English Governments.
Redgeree.—A preparation of fish with rice, a common breakfast dish.
Kęlę Kórála.—Officer in charge of forests; Conservator of Forests.
Kehulama.—A kind of fields cultivated without irrigation.
Kéṇi.—A tank or reservoir.
Kęṇmura.—The regular services of a *déwálé* held on Wednesdays and Saturdays.
Képumkaḍa.—An opening made in a tank for the purpose of irrigating fields.
Kęrė.—A document or deed.
Kęṭapęgima.—Treading down the clods in a field.
Khaki.—A kind of yellowish cotton cloth much used by soldiers in the field and by sportsmen.
Kinnaru.—Mat weavers; also the name of a Siṇhalese caste.
Kist.—(Vernacularly modified as *Kisti*, Beng.; *Khist*, Mar.; *Kisti*, Tel.; *Kisti* or *Kistu*, Karn.) Instalment, portion; the amount paid as instalment; the period fixed for its payments; as a revenue term, it denotes the portion of the annual assessment to be paid at specified periods in the course of the year.
Kochchiyar.—Emigrants from Cochin.
Koḍituwakku Lékama.—Officer in charge of the gingals (artillery) in the Kandyan kingdom.
Koḍituwakku Muhandirama.—The Muhandiram of the Gingal Department.
Kolakęṭiya.—Stack of reaped corn.
Kollar.—Ironsmiths. Tamil caste.
Komaḍḍi.—A class of Chetties. Tamil caste.
Kompaññawidiya.—The Siṇhalese name of *Slave Island* in Colombo.
Koṇḍé.—A chignon; the bunch or knot in which the Siṇhalese (both men and women) tie up their hair.
Konsėjuwa, Konsėduwa.—The Siṇhalese forms of the Dutch word for court of justice.
Kórála.—A revenue officer under a Raṭémahatmayá in the Kandyan country corresponding to a Muhandiram in the low country.
Kóraḷé.—A division or district in a Province.
Koraṭuwa.—A separate enclosure in a large garden or estate planted with coconuts, betel, or vegetables. Much used in the Mátara District.
Koṭṭalbaddé Muláchāriyá.—Head of the artificers or smiths.
Koṭṭalbaddé-Vidáné.—The headman of smith villages.

Kottu.—An enclosure [for storing salt by the manufacturers in the Puttalam District.
Koviyar.—Slaves and descendants of slaves.
Kówil.—A Hindu temple.
Kuḷám.—A tank.
Kumárihámi.—A lady of rank.
Kumbaha.—A wooden pipe placed underground through which water is conveyed from one division of a field to another. *v. Kumbussa.*
Kumballu.—Potters. Siṇhalese caste.
Kumbura.—A paddy field. *v. Wela* S., and *Vayal* T.
Kúnammaḍuwa.—The establishment of palanquin bearers of the kings of Kandy.
Kuppáyama.—A Roḍiyá village; habitation of a Roḍiyá.
Kurahhan.—*Eleusine coracana.* A small grain, of pungent flavour, much eaten by the poorer classes in the form of cakes. It is grown on chenas.
Kuṛavar.—Fowlers, snake catchers, and basket makers; also the name of a Tamil caste.
Kurumpar.—Blanket weavers; also the name of a Tamil caste.
Kurukkaḷ.—Non-Bráhman priests from Vethárniam, near Point Calymere.
Kuruṇiya.—A measure of grain, about one-eighth of a bushel; the extent of land that can be sown with the above measure.
Kúruwe.—The Elephant Department of the Kings of Kandy.
Kúruwé Lékama.—A headman of the Kúruwé, or Elephant Department.
Kusavar.—Potters. Tamil caste.
Kshatriya.—Skt., the name of the second or military and regal caste, or a member of it; the warrior, the king.—(Wilson). According to the Buddhist Páli authorities, the Kshatriyas form the first order or caste, and the Bráhmans the second.

Lac.—(Skt., but current in all dialects; sometimes modified as *Lak*, or more commonly *Lákh*, or in compounds *Lakh*). A hundred thousand, or *Lac* or *Lákh*, commonly, though not exclusively, applied to coin, as a *Lákh* of rupees 100,000 rupees; or at 2*s.* the rupee £10,000.— (Wilson).
Lachcham.—A measure of capacity and of sowing extent used in Jaffna. It is about one-fifth of a bushel. Twenty-four lachams go to the acre in paddy and eighteen in varaku culture.
Láduru.—Leprosy.
Láha.—A measure of capacity containing about 4 *ṇeli* or quarts.
Lamá-etaná; *Lamá-etani.*—Honorific terms of address to females.
Landa.—Low jungle land.

L nd wind.—An unwholesome wind which blows seawards. It prevails in Colombo during the north-east monsoon.

Laṇká.—A name of Ceylon. The oldest name of Ceylon in the literature connected with the religion of Gotama Buddha, and derived from its beauty and perfection.—(Turnour.)

Lascoreen.—Derived from the Persian *lashkar*, a native soldier. Survives now in Ceylon as a guard of honour only.

Leaguer.—A measure of arrack equal to 150 gallons.

Lebbe.—A Mohammedan priest ; also an honorary affix of Mohammedan names.

Legumgé.—Dormitory ; monk's cell.

Lékama.—Writer, secretary, registrar.

Lékam Mahatmayá.—The above, with the addition of the honorific affix *mahatmayá.*

Lena.—A cave ; a cave temple.

Léwáya.—Salt pan.

Liyadda.—The bed of a paddy field.

Liyana Appu.—A writer ; a clerk.

Liyana Árachchi.—A writer holding the rank of árachchi.

Liyana Muhandirama.—A writer holding the rank of muhandiram.

Liyana Rála.—Another term for a clerk, with the honorific *rála.*

Lókuruwó.—Brassfounders. The name of a Siṅhalese caste.

Madaku.—A sluice. *v. Bisókoṭuwa.*

Madam.—A shed or *ambalam, q. v.*

Madaméminihá.—A respectful term for *guruwo, q. v.*

Madaran.—A fine paid by a cultivator to a proprietor of land for cultivation.—(Armour) = ground rent. Also applied to grain commutation tax.

Madappali Vellálar.—A class of *Vellálas*, supposed to be descended from the ancient Tamil kings of Jaffna.

Madappulirála.—Officer in the Náta Déwálé, who sweeps out the sanctuary, cleanses and trims its lamps.

Má-del.—A large fishing net or *seine* made of coir yarn. *v. Núl-del.*

Madigé.—The Bullock or Carriage Department of the kings of Kandy.

Madihungaṇ.—Taxes, tolls, &c., levied at the *kadawata* (gravets) or *murapola* (stations for guards) on travellers or traders crossing it.

Maduwa.—An open shed or verandah.

Magulpóruwa.—(From *magul* auspicious, and *póruwa* a board.) A board or platform on which the bride and bridegroom are made to stand while the marriage ceremony is being performed.

Glossary.

Mahabaddé.—Another term for Halágama caste.

Mahá Brahma.—The highest of the gods ; the first person in the Hindu triad (Brahma Vishṇu, and Ṣiva).

Maha harvest.—The paddy crop sown in August-September and reaped in February-March.

Maha Lékama.—The principal writer or secretary.

Maha Mudiyansé.—Maha Mudaliyár.

Maha-naḍuwa.—The great court under the Kandyan Government.

Maha Náyaka Unnánsé.—Principal Buddhist High Priest.

Maha Nilame.—Another term for *Adigar ;* lit. "the great officer."

Mahaṇunnánsé.—A term for a Buddhist monk.

Mahátmayá.—Sir, Mr.

Maha Vidáné.—A rank above an árachchi and below a muhandiram.

Maha Vidána Muhandirama.—A rank higher than the above.

Maha Vidáné Mudiyansé.—A rank still higher.

Mahékada.—Pingo of raw provisions given regularly once a month to a temple or chief by the tenants of the *mulpaṇguwa* in a village.

Maḷa-ęla.—(From *maḷa* dead, and *ęla* a water-course.) An artificial water-course which dries up at some seasons of the year. *Maladola* is a natural water-course which does the same.

* *Maḷapalá divel* are *maḷapalá* lands, wholly belonging to and remaining in the possession of Government, but conditionally and temporarily granted for cultivation to certain classes of petty headmen, as a remuneration for their services in connection with the husbandry of their district, and occasionally for other services. One-fourth of the produce of lands of this tenure is given to Government, but its right over the whole soil, and to provide for its occupation, in undoubted and absolute. As regards *gardens* of this tenure, the Government is entitled to one-fourth or one-fifth of the produce.— (Cairns.)

---

* All the Governments—both European and native—which preceded the British in Ceylon generally paid all native office-holders, not in money, but by a grant of land to be cultivated by the office-holder by way of remuneration for his services, and to be held by him so long as he continued in office. When compulsory services were abolished, and the Government ceased to exact the services formerly rendered by the holders, *virtute offici*, of *maḷapalá divel* and other lands, the right of the Crown to the absolute ownership of these lands appears to have been overlooked, and they consequently are now held free of service, on the favourable terms originally granted in consideration of certain services to be rendered without other payment by the holders.

Maḷapalá; Maḷapáḷu.—(From *maḷa* dead, and *páḷu* deserted, or voided by death.) Lands originally held by private persons which have reverted to the Crown through failure of other heirs. In the District of Mátara all produce grown on such lands pay half to Government. Previous to division between the cultivators and Government as lord of the soil, one-seventh is invariably deducted as compensation to the reapers and threshers under the designation of *walahan*, the cultivator being put to the additional expense of providing at his sole cost the seed corn, on which he is charged interest in kind at the rate of 50 per cent. It sometimes happens that the Government abates its claim to the half where the soil is poor and difficult to work. In such cases one-third or one-fifth is levied, and the residue left to the cultivator.—(Cairns.)

Maleyyálikal.—Emigrants from Travancore.

Malwatté Viharé.—The Buddhist College or establishment of Malwatta in Kandy.

Mammoty.—A hoe.

Manchádi.—A seed weighing four grains, used by jewellers.

Maṇḍapaya.—A shed or hall erected on festival occasions and adorned with flowers, &c.; an open temple.

Maṇḍappaya.—Covered court or verandah attached to a *déwálé*.

Maniyagar.—The chief revenue officer of a division in Jaffna.

Mantra.—A prayer, a prayer of the Véda, a mystical or magical formula, the prayers or incantations of the Tantras, counsel, advice.— (Wilson.)

Marakhál.—A land measure in the Northern Province—about one-fifth of an acre.

Maráḷa.—A mortuary belonging to the king, which amounted to one-third part of the movables of the deceased.

Maravar.—A class of Tamils, mostly residents of the country ruled by the Rája of Ramnad.

Márayá.—A god, the enemy of Buddha; death personified.

Mariweḷla.—Custom-house.

Máruwenakumbura.—(From *máruwenawá* to change.) A field, the tenure of which is subject to change.

Máruwena panguwa.—(From *maruwena* changing, and *paṅguwa* a share.) A land held by a tenant-at-will, as distinguished from *pravéṇi paṅguwa, q. v.*

Mataka dáné.—Alms given for the benefit of the soul of the deceased.

Mauláná.—H. and A. The title of a person of learning or respectability; teacher; doctor; in the Maratha countries the usual designation of the Mohammedan village schoolmaster.—(Wilson.)

Maund.—H., &c., *mana,* from the A. *manu* (Hebrew, *manh*); *mahana,* Uriya ; *manugu,* Tel. A measure of weight of general use in India, but varying in value in different places. Four principal varieties are specified by Mr. Princep :—(1) The Bengal *maund*, containing 40 *sers*; (2) the *maund* of Central India, consisting of half of this quantity, or 20 *sers* ; (3) the *maund* of Guzerat, consisting of 40 *sers,* but of lesser value, making the Bombay *maund* 28 lb. avoirdupois ; and (4) the *maund* of Southern India, fixed by the Madras Government at 25 lb.—(Wilson).

Maw-urume.—Inheritance by right of the mother.

Miyá.—An [ancient division of Ceylon between the Deduru-oya and Kalu-gaṇga. *v. Pihiṭi* and *Ruhunu.*

Mayoral.—*See* Káriyakarannā. An irrigation headman in parts of the Northern and Southern Provinces.

Medakanna.—A middle crop or harvest between the *yala* and *maha* seasons. *v. Muttes.*

Meniké.—An honorific term applied to females.

Menikgerima.—Gemming.

Minindóru tena or mahatmayá.—Surveyor.

Miniranpatalaya.—Plumbago pit (mine).

Mohoṭṭála.—A clerk or secretary.

Mohoṭṭiyár.—A rank in the low-country below a Mudaliyár and above a Muhandiram.

Mohoṭṭi Mudiyansé.—A rank in the low-country higher than a Mohoṭṭiyar, but below an effective Mudaliyár.

Mohurrum.—Sacred, unlawful, prohibited ; the first month of the Mohammedan year, in which it was held unlawful to make war. Among the Shias this month is held in peculiar veneration, as being the month in which *Hasan* and *Hasain,* the sons of Ali, were killed : their deaths are the subject of public mourning during the first ten days, when fasting and self-denial are also enjoined.—(Wilson).

Mohur.—Corruptly *Mohur,* H. and P. A seal, a seal ring ; a gold coin of the value, in accounts, of 16 rupees.—(Wilson.)

Mudali.—A rank or title conferred by the kings of Kandy.

Mudalipéruwa.—A title class. The class of persons holding the rank of *mudali.*

Muḍḍiyar.—Jugglers ; itinerant beggars. The name of a Tamil caste.

Mudiyansé.—Mudaliyár.

Muhandiram.—A rank so called, below a Mudaliyár and above an árachchi.

Mulata.—Upper side of a range of fields.

Milaku-tannir.—Pepper broth or pungent soup.

Mulpaṭa.—A field orginally asweddumized, as distinguished from *hereṇa-paṭa,* or *herunpaṭa, q. v.*

Multen; Muluten.—Food offered to a god or king.

Mulutenmewediṃa.—The carrying of the *mulutenkada* (pingo-load of food) from the kitchen into the sanctuary.

Munmári.—The Tamil paddy crop, which corresponds to the Siṇhalese *maha* harvest.

Muruten.—v. Muluten.

Mutalikal.—A class of Vellálas. Tamil caste.

Muttes.—A kind of paddy; a middle crop between the two regular seasons of the *yala* and the *maha* harvests, *q. v.*

Muttettu.—A field which is sown on account of the king or other proprietor, temporary grantee, or chief of a village, as distinguished from the fields of the other inhabitants of the village who are liable to perform services or render dues.—(D'Oyly.) Cf. *anda muttettu* and *ninda mutettu.*

Mutukimidima.—Pearl fishery.

Nachohereen or Natchirry.—Kurakkan, q. v. (Indo-Portuguese.)

Náohohiré.—An honorific term applied to females of the smiths, potters &c.

Nadduvar.—Dancers, trumpeters, tom-tom beaters. Tamil caste.

Nágári.—H., &c. (fem. of *Nágara*). Relating to a town or city; applied especially to the alphabet of the Sanskrit language, sometimes with *Déwa*, divine, prefixed, as *Dévawnágiri.*—(Wilson.)

Naide.—A term of respect to a man of an inferior caste; *e.g.*, smiths, fishers, potters.

Naḷavar.—A low-caste, peculiar to the north of Ceylon.

Nambirála, Namburálz.—A headman corresponding to an overseer; a term in use in Moorish villages.

Nampúri.—Brahmins from Travancore.

Nanshey.—Wet or mud cultivation; paddy cultivation.

Nawandanná.—Gold or silversmith; also the name of a Siṇhalese caste.

Náyaka.—A leader in general, and particularly a Buddhist chief monk.

Nayuda.—(Commonly written *Naidu* or *Naidoo*, Telugu.) A title added to the names of respectable persons among the low or Sudra caste.—(Wilson.) This is probably the origin of the Siṇhalese term *Náyidé* applied as a term of respect to a man of inferior caste.

Nekata.—A star; a constellation.

Nekatiyá.—A term for a tom-tom beater; an astrologer.

Neli.—A measure of capacity, about one quart.

Nétra pinkama.—The festival of painting the eyes of an image of Buddha when first made.

Nilakáraya.—A tenant; a tenant-at-will, as distinguished from *paŋgukáraya.*

Nilame.—An officer, or office.

Nilapálu; Nilapalá.—(From *nila* and *pálu.*) Are lands formerly held *ex officio* under Government, but which from failure of male heirs, or because the office itself may have been discontinued, are again in direct possession of the Crown. There is no other distinction than the name and its origin between these and *malapala* lands —(Cairns.)

Nilapaŋguwa.—(From *nila* and *paŋguwa.*) It is the land possessed on condition of cultivating the *muttettu,* or performing other menia. service, or both, for the proprietor, grantee, or chief of a village. The possessor of such land is called *Nilakáraya*. In some instances he is the proprietor, and cannot be displaced so long as he performs the service; in others, a tenant-at-will, and removable at pleasure! —(D'Oyly.)

Nilé.—An office: service.

Nindagama.—(From *ninda* exclusive possession, and *gama* a village). A village which, for the time being, is the entire property of the grantee or temporary chief; if definitively granted by the king, with *sannas,* it becomes *paravéni.*—(D'Oyly.)

Ninda muttettu.—Is a *muttettu* land sown entirely gratuitously for the benefit of the proprietor, grantee, or chief by other persons, in consideration of the lands which they possess (as distinguished from *anda-muttettu, q. v.*).—(D'Oyly.)

Nischaladé.—Immovable property.

Niyara.—The narrow ridge separating the beds of a paddy field.

Núl-dẹl—A large fishing net or *seine* made of cotton twine.

Odávi (called also Tachchaŋ).—Carpenters; also the name of a Tamil caste.

Oddiyár.—Those who sink wells or make tanks; men employed generally at earthwork.

Ola.—The leaf of any kind of palm, especially, though not exclusively, applied to the leaf as used for writing upon.—(Wilson.)

Oli.—Dancers; also the name of a Siŋhalese caste.

Oli Vidáné.—Vidáné over the Oliya caste, or dancers.

Oppam.—A license; *kai yoppam,* a signature.

Orchilla weed.—A lichen. Tamil *mara pási,* from which a kind of dye is obtained; one of the exports from Ceylon.

Otu.—Tithe; one-tenth of the produce. Sir John D'Oyly gives the following explanation of the term. " *Otu* is of three kinds: (1) A portion of the crop equal to the extent sown, or to one and a half or double the extent sown in some *paddy fields* or *chenas*. It is the usual share paid to the proprietor by the cultivator from fields which are barren or difficult of protection from wild animals, particularly in the Seven Kóralés, Sabaragamuwa, Héwáhẹṭa, and some chenas in Hárispattu. In many royal villages in the Seven Kóralés are lands paying *otu* to the Crown. (2) The share of one-third paid from a field of tolerable fertility, or from a good *chena* sown with paddy. (3) The share which the proprietor of a chena, sown by another with fine grain, cut first from the ripe crop, being one large basket full, or a man's burden."—(Sir J. D'Oyly, Transactions of the Royal Asiatic Society, vol. III., 1831.)

Owita.—Low land, which may be used for the cultivation of yams or fine grain.

Oya.—A river or stream smaller than a *gaṇga* and larger than an *ẹla*.

Páda (boat).—A large flat-bottomed boat.

Paḍḍaṇam.—A seaport town.

Paḍḍáni.—Descendants of Patans, class of Mohammedans.

Paḍḍunúṭhárar.—Silk cloth makers.

Paduwó.—Palanquin bearers; also the name of a Siṇhalese caste.

Pahạla ẹlapạṭa.—v. *Ihạla Ẹlapạṭa,* of which it is the opposite.

Paisá.—(Corruptly *Pysa, Pyce, Pice,* H., &c.; Mar. *Paisá.*) A copper coin which, under the native Goveram ent, varied considerably in weight and value. The Company's *Paisá* is fixed at the weight of 100 grains, and rated at 4 to the *anná* or 64 to a rupee. In common parlance, it is sometimes used for money in general.

Pákkuḍam.—Curiosities, valuable presents.

Palam.—A weight, one-sixth of a pound avoirdupois.

Paḷáta.—A division of a country. A district.

Pali.—Fines. Compensation or satisfaction.

Pạli.—The language in which the Scriptures of Buddhism are written in Ceylon, Burmah, Siam, and other countries. The language of *Magadha, q. v.*

Palí.—Washers for low castes.

Pallịr.—The name of a low and servile Tamil caste, or of an individual of the caste, most commonly the slaves of the *Vellálas* or agricultural tribes; they are much upon the same footing as the *Pareyan,* but hold themselves superior to him, as they abstain from eating the flesh of the cow.

Glossary.

Pallaru.—A subdivision of the *Pali* caste.

Palli.—A small town, a village ; in Tamil, a school or mosque. It is no doubt the same word as the H. and Beng. terms, but is in more general use, especially in combination, when it is corruptly written *poly*, as in *Trichinopoly*, properly, *Trisirá-palli*, the city of the Giant *Trisirá.* It is also the name of a servile tribe of Hindus in the south, similar to the *Pallar*, but who are more especially the bondsmen or slaves of the Brahman proprietors of land.

Pámmaḍuwa.—(From *pán* lamps, and *maḍuwa* a temporary building.) A ceremony in honour of the goddess *Pattini*, in which a number of small torches are lighted up by the *kapuwá*, *q. v.*

Paṇam.—Money. In Siṇhalese, *panama*, equal to 6 cents. *v. Fanam.*

Pandal.—A temporary shed or booth ; structure of cloth or basketwork supported on posts for giving shelter to persons assembled on any festive occasion, as at the marriage ; also any shed.

Paṇḍáraṇkal.—Non-Brahman priests and devotees.

Paṇḍári.—A class of agriculturists.

Paṇḍita.—Vernacularly *Pandit* or *Pundit.* A learned man ; a scholar.

Paṇḍurumila.—A Kandyan term for a fine.

Paṇguwa.—A share ; an estate, a field.

Paṇgukárayá.—The holder of a *paṇguwa.* This term is confined to pravéṇi holders. *See* also *Pravéṇi Nilakárayá.*

Panikkila.—A term applied to a tom-tom beater.

Panikkiyá.—A headman of low caste. An elephant catcher, elephant trainer ; a barber as used in the low-country.

Paṇiwiḍakárayá, Payḍakárayá.—A Kandyan term for a headman of inferior rank ; petty headman.

Paṇiwiḍakaraṇa Nilame.—An attendant on the king, corresponding to lord in waiting.

Pansala.— Páli. (From *paṇṇa* leaf, *sálá* a hall.) The hut of an ascetic made of branches and leaves ; a hermitage ; the residence of a Buddhist monk.

Páppár or *Pirámaṇar.*—Brahmans.

Paraiyar.—Pariah.

Parama.—Weight equal to 560 lb.

Paraṇgi.—*Feringhee*, European or Portuguese. An obstinate chronic disease endemic in Ceylon, superficially resembling syphillis.

Paravar.—Those who live on the seashore ; now applied exclusively to *Paravas* who are immigrants from Tuticorin.

Parrah.—A measure equal to 5 kurunies.

Páruwa.—A large flat-bottomed boat.

Pasaloswaka.—Full moon ; fifteenth day of a lunar month ; last day of the *first* lunar fortnight.

Pasé Budu.—(Skt. *Pratyéka Budáha, Pachcheka Buddha.*) An order of Buddhas inferior to the supreme Buddha.

Pata.—A measure, one-fourth of a *seer.*

Paṭabęndá.—A headman of the Karáwé caste.

Paṭabęndi Árachchi.—A rank generally held by people of Karáwé caste.

Paṭabęndinama.—A title conferred by the kings of Kandy by tying on the forehead a metal plate or a piece of embroidered silk.

Patana.—Undulating country covered with *máná* grass or brushwood and destitute of trees, resembling the English downs.

Patkaḍa.—Priest's kneeling cloth or leathern rug.

Pàtra.—Alms-bowl of a Buddhist monk.

Pattini Deviyó.—The goddess *Pattini*, the patroness of chastity.

Pattirippuwa.—An elevated place or a raised platform in the *vidiya* (street) of a *déwálé.*

Pattuwa.—A subdivision of a Province.

Páwara.—Threshing floor when men tread out the corn. *v. Kamata.*

Paychchal.—Water for irrigation.

Payiṇḍapaṇguwa.—Office lands, the appurtenance of the office, but belonging to the Crown.

Pé.—Tree, occurs as a suffix to names of certain villages ; as Halpé, Nikapé.

Pęhidum.—Raw provisions supplied by the people to an officer travelling on duty. *v. Aḍukku.*

Pęla.—A watch-hut.

Péla.—An extent of paddy land which can be sown by the contents of a measure containing about 1½ bushel ; 4 pélas equal to 1 amuna, *q.v.*

Pęlęssa.—Lair or kennel of an animal, bed of a hare, &c.; a grove of trees of the same kind by which certain villages take their names, *e.g.,* Bógahapęlęssa, Demaṭagahapęlęssa.

Pęmiṇitęṇ, Peminitęnwahansé.—Your honour ; a term of address to officials or superiors.

Peon.—A messenger of a Public Department or office. From the Portuguese ; lit. "a footman."

Perahankaḍa.—Water strainer of a monk or devotee, used to obviate destruction of animal life by swallowing insects.

xxviii *Glossary.*

Perahęra.—A procession, a festival. The Perahęra takes place in Esaḷa (July–August), commencing with the new moon in that month and continuing till the full moon.

The most celebrated of these processions is held at Kandy. It is a Hindu festival in honour of the four deities, Nátha, Vishṇu, Kataragama, and Pattini; but in the reign of King Kírtisirí (1747 - 1780 A.D.) a body of monks who came over from Siam for the purpose of restoring the Upasampadá ordination objected to the observance of this Hindu ceremony in a Buddhist country. To remove their scruples the king ordered the daḷadá relic of Buddha to be carried thenceforth in procession with the insignia of the four deities; neverthelss the Perahęra is not regarded as a Buddhist ceremony.

Pérudan.—Food given to monks according to turns arranged among the tenants.

Péruwa.—District of a petty headman; family descent.

Petmaṇ.—Footpaths.

Pettah.—The town attached to a fortress. Siṇ. *Piṭakoṭuwa;* Tam *Porakóṭṭa.*

Pęya.—A measure of time, equal to 24 minutes, measured by an hour glass.

Pice, Pie.—*v.* Paisa.

Picottah.—A well sweep or long lever bearing a line and bucket on the long arm for raising well water.

Pidawilla.—Land offered by individuals to temples, private dedications or endowments.

Pidénna.—An offering to a demon.

Pihanarála.—A Kandyan term for a cook.

Pihiṭi.—An ancient division of Ceylon to the north of the Dęduru-oya, *v. Maya* and *Ruhuṇu.*

Pila—Verandah or porch of a native house.

Pillęwa.—High land appurtenant to and adjoining a paddy field, used often as a threshing floor.

Pinattu.—The pulp of the palmirah fruit.

Piṇḍapáta.—Food received into the alms-bowl of a Buddhist monk; a term specifying that particular sort of alms which consists in the food being placed in or thrown into the bowl of a monk while on his rounds.

Pingo.—A load suspended from the two ends of a pole carried on the shoulder.

Pinkama.—A meritorious act or religious festival.

Pinmári.—The paddy crop sown during the earlier months of the year. *v. Yala* and *Munmári.*

Pinpaḍi.—Charitable allowance.

Pinpára.—Used in the North-Central Province for village paths constructed by the inhabitants under Gaṇsabaháwa rules.

Pintáliya.—(From *pin* charity, and *táliya* a pot or vessel.) A pot or vessel of water placed on the roadside for the use of travellers.

Pirit.—Protection ; protectionary formula ; a collection of short hymns and sermons publicly read on certain occasions with a view to warding off the influence of evil spirits.

Piriwena.—A college attached to a Buddhist monastery.

Pisáchi.—A ghost or goblin of malevolent character.

Pissankoṭuwa.—Lunatic asylum.

Piṭaka.—A division of the sacred writings of Buddha ; lit. a " basket."

Pitakaṭṭalé.—The exterior of a *déwálé*, outside the sanctuary ; the tenants who serve outside the sanctuary.

Piṭ wana.—(And simply *wana*.) A spill water, generally blasted out of rock or along a natural rocky channel.

Piyadi.—A tax of three-eighths of a pice for every ten coconut trees, and the same for three jak trees bearing fruit, levied by the Dutch Government from gardens of a certain description.—(*Ceylon Almanac*, 1819.)

Piya-wurume.—Paternal inheritance. *v. Maw-urume*.

Piyavilla.—The carpet or cloth spread on the ground by the dhoby on duty for the *kapurala* to walk upon, or at the entry of a distinguished visitor.

Plantain.—This word in Ceylon corresponds with *banana* in the West Indies ; *Musa sativa*.

Polwákara.—Arrack of the first distillation.

Pommelo.—The gigantic species of orange (*Abrus decumana*) called shad dock in the West Indies ; also pummelo and pampelmoose.

Pongal.—Incorrectly *Pongol* from the verb *ponhgu kiratu* to boil or bubble (to boil rice). A boiling or bubbling up ; the boiling of rice, whence it becomes the name of a popular festival held by the Hindus in the Madras Provinces on the entrance of the sun into the sign of Capricorn, or on the 12th January, the beginning of the Tamil year, when rice is boiled and distributed. The festival lasts several days, but the chief celebration is confined to the first three days.

Poonac.—*Pinnákku*. The residue after expression of the oil from cocoanuts, rape seed, &c. ; oil cake, used for feeding cattle.

Póruwa.—A flat board used for levelling the mud of a paddy field.

Potána.—High land subject to inundation ; the upper portion of an abandoned tank or field.

Póṭáwa.—A spill water, usually in the earth bank of an ęla ; a collection of water from a bank, retained by a bund, for use below after it has passed over the upper fields.

Glossary.

Pó.—The days on which the moon changes, held sacred by the Buddhists.

Póyagé.—A building in which certain priestly rites are practised on *póya* days.

Pravéni.—(Corruptly *paraveni.*) Paraveni land is that which is the private property of an individual proprietor, land long possessed by his family, but so-called also, if recently acquired in fee simple.—(D'Oyly.)

Pravéni andé.—*Anda pravéni.*

Pravéni divel.—(From *pravéni* and *divel.*) Divel lands which have become private property. One-fifth of the produce of these lands is given to Government.

Pravéni nilakáraya.—The proprietor of a heritable *pangu* in a *ninda* village, who cannot be displaced by the superior lord so long as he performs the service in consideration of which the *pangu* is held. The same as *Pangukáraya.*

Pravéni panguwa.—The *pangu* held by a *pravéni nilakárayá, q. v.*

Pudgalika.—Belonging to an individual. *Pudgalika wastuwa* is property belonging to *individual* priests, as distinguished from *Sánghika wastuwa,* property belonging to the body of priests *in common.*

Pújá.—An offering, a festival. Curruptly *Poojá. v. Póya.*

Pulam.—A rice field in Mannar and the Wanni; cultivation of the bed of a tank.

Pullimal.—Earrings.

Puluk-atta (Mátalé), *Puluk-goba* (Sabaragamuwa).—Tender cocoanut branch used for decoration. *Goh-atu,* commonly used in maritime districts.

Punchey.—Dry grain cultivation. *v. Nanchey.*

Purai.—A watch-hut.

Purana.—A field lying fallow.

Purána.—Lit. "old," the especial designation of a class of work of which eighteen principles are enumerated, in which the ancient traditions of the Hindus, and legends and doctrines belonging to the chief sects as Saivas and Vaishnavás, are embodied.

Puranketuma.—First turning over the ground in large clods with the *mamoty* in paddy cultivation.

Purappádu.—Vacant, or without owner. A land becomes *purappádu* either in failure of heirs or by abandonment.

Puruk-goba.—*v. Puluk-goba.*

Quintany.—A Public Works Department tool; a jumper.

Radaw.—Washers ; also the name of a Sinhalese caste.

Rahat (Skt. *Arhat*).—A *rahat* ; one who has attained the last of the four paths or stages of sanctification leading to *Nirwâna* ; a being entirely free from evil desire, and possessing supernatural power.

Ráhu.—An asura, to whom the eclipses are ascribed ; the ascending node

Rahubadda.—Small temples or dependencies of the Kandyan Pattin. Déwálé ; also a kind of dance of the *nawabadda* or nine trades.

Raja, Rájá.—A prince, a king.

Rajadekma.—Levée.

Rajcgedara.—King's House.

Rájakáriya.—Royal, or Government compulsory service.

Rákshayá.—A demon, a monster.

Ráḷa, Ráḷahámi.—Honorific title.

Ramaññanikáya.—(*Rámañña* a term for lower Burmah, and *nikáya* society or sect = *samágama.*) A sect of Buddhists introduced into Ceylon about 1870 A.D. by Indásabha Terunnánse of Ambagahawatta. Monks of this sect lead a very self-denying life, and profess to observe Buddha's precepts more strictly than monks of the two sects Amarapura and Siam.

Ran-hivigé.—The royal howdah in which the insignia of certain deities are taken on the back of an elephant.

Ratémahatmayá.—Chief revenue officer of a Kandyan Province.

Ratéminihá.—A term for a Vellála.

Ratmahera, Ratnahera.—Signifies what of right belongs to the Crown. It is a term used to describe all waste and uncultivated lands to which no private title can be shown, and includes all Government forests, hénas, &c. It never applies to paddy fields, except in cases where by unauthorized appropriation of such Government lands portions may have been worked or *improved* into a condition suitable for grain cultivation. The tax on such fields and gardens, where the claim of the appropriator is admitted on the ground of long possession, is one-tenth of the produce (in the case of the gardens, it it asserted by some authorities and denied by others, that Governmens can claim one-tenth of the *soil* as well as the *produce*). There are, however, in the maritime districts *ratmáhera* lands granted by the Dutch to private individuals, on condition of their conversion into fields and gardens, the produce to be taxed at one-tenth.—(Cairns.)

Ratninda.—Lands cultivated by Government, whose sole property they are.

Retti.—A class of Telugu-speaking Tamils.

Réguwa.—Warehouse, custom-house.

Relapáṇa.—Stone revetment on inner slope of the bund of a tank to prevent scour by waves.

Glossary.

Ridi.—A Kandyan silver coin, about eightpence in value.

Riṭṭá.—The fourth, ninth, or fourteenth days of the lunar fortnight They are considered as unlucky days.

Riyana.—A cubit.

Roḍiyá.—An outcast.

Ruhuṇuraṭa.—An ancient division of Ceylon to the south of the Kalugaṇga. *v. Máyá* and *Pihiṭi*.

Rupee.—(From Skt. *rúpya* silver.) A silver coin, the general denomination of the silver currency of India, and the standard measure of value.........The weight, intrinsic purity, and value in shillings of the present " Company's rupees " is as follows : —

Weight	Pure Contents.	s.	d.
Tr. *grs.* 180	165	2	0½

As, however, silver is subject in the London mint to a seigniorage of nearly 6 per cent., the London mint produce of the Company's rupee, if of full weight and standard value (11 dwts. fine), should be 1*s.* 11*d.*—(Wilson.)

Now much depreciated.—H. W.

Sabé.—An assembly, a council. Skt. *Sabhá. v. Gansabháwa.*

Sabháwa.—Another form of the same word. *v. Gansabháwa.*

Sádhu.—An expression of joy. Well done ! good !

Saivar.—Followers of the rules of Saivam, the religion that owns Siva as the godhead.

Sakawarshaya.—An era in general, but the terms is applied especially to that which is reckoned from the reign of a prince of the South of India named *Sáliváhana*, commencing in the 79th year of the Christian era, and to be identified with the latter by adding 78¼.—(Wilson.)

Sakrayá.—The Chief Diety of the six lower heavens ; god Indra.

Sakwala.—A system of worlds, the Universe.

Sákyawaṇsa.—The royal race to which Gautama Buddha belonged.

Salágama.—Another form of Halágama.

Samanala.—The mountain Samanala (Adam's Peak), on the top of which Buddhists believe that there is the impression of Buddha's left foot.

Saman Dewiyó.—The tutelar deity of Samanala (Adam's Peak).

Sámaṇera.—A novice ; a monk who has not received the rite of *Upasampadá* ordination.

Saṇgha.—The associated brotherhood of Buddhist monks.

Sáṅghika.—Belonging in common to the above. *v. Pudgalika.*

Sannasa.—A royal grant, usually on copper, but sometimes on silver or stone. Pl. *sannas.*

Sanné.—A translation, a paraphrase.

Sannyási.—A Hindu of the fourth order, who has renounced the world and lives by mendicancy. The term is now applied to a variety of religious mendicants, some of whom wander singly about the country subsisting on alms. The *Sannyási* is most usually a worshipper of Śiva.

Sáramárugam.—Lands held in rotation, so that each proprietor may in turn enjoy the fertile and unfertile parts.

Sarong.—A Malay word. A body cloth or kilt. It differs from the ordinary cloth in being stitched together at the ends.

Seer.—A measure of capacity about equal to a quart.

Shaddock.—*v. Pommelo.*

Shroff.- (*Saraf, Saravh, Sarapé, Sarápu, Sarábu,* corruptly *Saraff Sharáf, Shroff,* H.) A money changer, banker, or cashier.

Shuck.—In planting slang, sick, seedy, ill.

Sihinbóga.—Fine grain.

Sikh.—(H. Śikha, from *Sishya,* Skt.) A scholar, a disciple; the name of the people of the Punjáb, as the disciples or followers of Nanak Shah.—(*Wilson.*)

Sil.—Religious precept or observance.

Siláléḱhanaya.—Inscription on a stone.

Símá.—Boundary; a consecrated place having certain limits, in which monks are ordained and other religious rites performed.

Sinnakkaraya.—Deed of transfer.

Sipiriyá-gé.—Jail.

Sirupokam.—The season of cultivation in Jaffna, corresponding to *yala* in Siṉhalese and *pinmári* in the Eastern Province.

Śishyánuśishya Paramparáwa.—Succession from pupil to pupil of a monk of Buddha; pupilary succession.

Siṭṭuwa.—A document, generally applied to a document or order written on a palmirah or talipot leaf. *v Chit.*

Śiva.—The third person of the Hindu triad—the Destroyer.

Siyam Samágama.—(From *Siyam* Siam, and *Samágama* society.) The Siamese sect of Buddhists in Ceylon introduced by King Kírtiṣrí, Rajasiṉha, 1750 A.D.

Slóka.—A Sanskrit stanza.

Sokaḍé.—Clappers of bamboo tied around the necks of cattle.

Soḷosmasthánæ—Sixteen sacred places in Ceylon, viz., Mahiyangaṇa, Nágadípa, Kęlaniya, Dígahavápi, Śrí Pádaya, Mutiyaṅgaṇa, Tissa-mahárāma, Abhayagiri, Ruwanwęli, Lówámahapáya, Mirisawęṭi, Śiláchaitya, Diváguhá, Kataragama Kiriwehera, Jétawanárámaya, Srímahábódhiya, and Thúpáráma.

Śramaṇa—A Buddhist monk.

Glossary.

Śri—Prosperity ; signature of the kings of Ceylon.
Sucanny—A coxswain (in the Master Attendant's Departments) ; Anglo-Indian *Seacunny ;* Arab *Sukkan,* a helm.
Sútra—A discourse or sermon of Buddha.
Sweet potato—The yam or root of *Batatas edulis* grown in chenas, and yielding heavy crops.

Taprobane—*v. Támraparṇi.*
Taḍapapu-redda—Country-made cloth of coarse texture ; the annual *peṇuma,* or present, *q. v.*
Taṭṭár—Goldsmiths ; also the name of a Tamil caste. A goldsmith is familiarly known as " Taṭṭán " up-country.
Tahanchi-kada, Tahandikad ı—Penum-kada given to a Disáwa (Kégalla)
Taiyaṭhárar, Paṇar—Tailors ; also the name of a Tamil caste.
Talwákara—Arrack of the second distillation.
Talagaha—The talipot tree.
Talaikhárar—Mahouts, elephant-keepers. Tamil caste.
Talapata—Leaf of the talipot tree.
Taláwa—An open glade, or meadow.
Tali—The marriage necklace of Tamil and Moor women.
Tambákka—A composite metal, copper mixed with gold. *Pinchbeck.*
Tamby—Younger brother ; a term of respect used by an elder to a younger person implying kindness ; a term used in addressing a Moorman.
Tampiráṇ.—A class of devotees.
Támraparṇi.—An ancient name of Ceylon—*Tambapanni* in Páli. Hence the *Taprobane* of the ancient Greeks and Romans.
Tanahál.—A kind of fine grain.
Tánáyama.—A resthouse ; a division of country attached to a resthouse.
Taṇḍal.—The master of a dhoni. *Tindal.*
Taṇgama.—Fourpence.
Tappal.—(Tel. and Karn. *Tappalu;* Mar. *Tapál;* Guz. *Tapál.*) The post ; the carriage and delivery of letters.
Tát.—(H., &c., *Tát* ; Mar. *Tat.*) Canvas, sackcloth. *Taṭi,* more usually *Taṭṭi* and *Tati.* A matted screen, a frame of wickerwork.
Tátar.—Slaves ; itinerant beggars.
Taṭṭumáruwa.—A field, héna, or other land cultivated by the joint owners in turns : thus, if a field belongs to three families in *taṭṭumáru* possession, each family will cultivate the whole field every third year ; if it were held in common, each family would take one-third of the produce every year. The rotation of the members of the family among themselves is called *karamáruwá.*

Távádi.—A tank which has no village attached to it. Common in the Northern Province.

Távalám.—A number of oxen laden with merchandise ; pack cattle.

Tawalla.—The upper part of the bed of a tank cultivated when the water is low.

Teapoy—A small tripod table, from the Hindu *Tipai*. The first part of the word has no connection with *tea*, as is popularly supposed.

Tee—The metallic decoration on the top of a dágaba representing the *chatra*, or umbrella, emblematic of royalty.

Tégipatraya—Deed of gift.

Teppam.—A raft. *v. Katamaram.*

Terunnánsé.—A Buddhist monk of a superior order.

Théro.—The Páli form of the above.

Tómbuwa.—A register (Dutch).

Timba.—A measure of capacity equal to four kurunies. A *timba* is rather larger than a *laha, q. v.*

Timilar.—Ferrymen ; also those who dwell on the seashore.

Tiruwa.—Duty on goods.

Tisaraṇa.—The three helps, viz., Buddha, his doctrines, and the associated brotherhood of monks.

Tompar.—Jugglers and pole-dancers. Tamil caste.

Tom-tom.—A small drum, especially one beaten to bespeak notice to a public proclamation ; it is laxly applied to any kind of drum.— (Wilson.)

Toraṇa.—A triumphal arch.

Totamuna.—Originally a seaport. Now applied to certain divisions on the sea-borde, *e.g.*, Kalutara totamuna.

Tóṭṭam.—An estate or garden.

Tripiṭaka.—(From *tri* three, and *piṭaka* a basket, a receptacle.) The three divisions of the sacred writings of Buddhism, namely, the *Abhidharma, Vinaya,* and *Sútra Piṭakas.*

Tuḍapata.—An order or grant given by word of mouth and recorded on an ola.

Tukkuwa.—A weight of 50 lb.

Tuláṇa.—A division of country, a district. The term is peculiar to the District of Nuwarakalawiya.

Tun-bó.—The three Bohodis, *i.e.*, the dágeb, which are the receptacles of Buddha's relics, bó-trees used by Buddhas, and image-houses erected in commemoration of Buddha.

Tunkawul lands.—This term is applied to waste lands which during the Dutch occupation of Ceylon were given to be cultivated on the following condition: One-third of the land to be planted with cinnamon for the exclusive use of the Dutch East India Company, the remaining two-thirds to be planted with cocoanut, jak, and other fruit trees for the use of the grantee. If the plantation was not made the whole land reverted to the Company.

Tuppoṭṭiya.—Cloth of ten yards worn round the waist of Kandyans.

Turumpar.—Those who wash the clothes of outcasts.

Uḍaiyár.—The chief revenue officer of a subdivision in the Northern and Eastern Provinces.

Uḍękkiya.—A Kandyan musical instrument; a small kind of drum.

Ukas.—Mortgage.

Uḷiyam.—Corruptly *velian.* Service due to a deity, a guru, a superior by birth; a natural obligation; the obligation of a slave to his master.

Uḷuvár.—A class of Vellalas from Koṇkaṇ or Travancore.

Ulpęngé.—The bathing establishment of the kings of Kandy.

Uṇḍiyal.—Draft; a bill of exchange.

Uparája.—A sub-king.

Upásaka.—A lay devotee.

Upasampadá.—Ordination to the order of *Upasampadá* or that of superior monk.

Upásiká.—A female lay devotee.

Upayanapaṭa.—Is a field orginally asweddumized, as distinguished from *hęrenapaṭa, q. v.*

Uppida.—Sheaf of corn.

Vaḍḍai Vitánai.—Superintendent over a small tract of fields.

Vaṭṭi.—Interest.

Vaishṇavar.—Followers of Vishnu.

Vaisya Vaḷḷur.—The priests of Pariahs. They are generally learned in Tamil literature, and pursue the occupation of astrologers.

Váṇiyar.—Merchants, traders. There are different classes, according to the merchandise they deal in. This word corresponds to *banian* in Northern India.

Vaṇṇár.—Washers; also the name of a Tamil caste.

Vanni.—Skt. *wanya* wild forest. Parts of the Northern and North-Western Provinces.

Vánni Unnęhé.—A chieftain of Wanni district.

Vanniyá.—An oil man; one who keeps a chekku, *q. v.*

Vanniyar.—Chief revenue officer of a division in the Eastern Province.
Várakkudi.—A cultivator of the soil, *goyiya, ryot.*
Váram.—Rent of land ; the share due to the cultivator of a field.
Varampu.—A low ridge in a tilled piece of ground ; a boundary.
Vayál.—A rice field ; ground fit for rice cultivation ; any open field or place.
Váykkál.—Water-course.
Véda.—Skt. The general name of the chief scriptural authorities of the Hindus ; it is most correctly applied to the four canonical works entitled severally the Ṛig-Véda, Yajur-Véda, Sáma-Véda, and Atharva-Véda, but it is extended to other works of supposed inspired origin in the sense of a science or system, as Áyur-Véda, the science of life, *i.e.*, medicine ; Dhanur-Véda, the science of the bow, or archery ; Gándharva-Véda, the science of music, so named from the heavenly musicians or Gándharvas.—(Wilson.)
Veḍḍá.—A Veḍḍá ; a hunter. Supposed to be the descendants of the aborigines of Ceylon.
Veḍḍuráy.—Corresponds to the Siṅhalese term *wakkaḍa, q. v.*
Veli.—A field.
Véli.—A fence.
Vibhíshaṇa.—A god, brother of Rávaṇa, the tutelar deity at Kẹlaṇi.
Vidána Árachchi.—A revenue officer in the low-country in charge of a village or number of villages. Corruptly *vidahn áratchy.*
Vidána Muhandirama.—A rank higher than the above.
Vidáné Durayá.—A headman of the Paduwá caste.
Vidáné Hénayá.—A headman of the Washer caste in the Kandyan country.
Vidáné—(From *vidhána karanawá* to order, to manage.) An inferior officer so named. Corruptly *vidahn.*
Viháraya.—A Buddhist temple or monastery.
Villu.—A pond or tank.
Vishnu.—The second person of the Hindu triad—the Preserver ; the tutelary deity of Laṅká.

Wáhanse.—An affix to names as a term of respect.
Wakunpurayó.—Another term for jaggery-makers, signifying *cooks*, cooking being one of the occupations of this caste. Also the name of a Siṅhalese caste.
Wajjankárayo.—Tom-tom beaters ; also the name of a Siṅhalese caste.
Wakaturé.—A field of circular shape.
Wakkaḍa.—A gap made in a bund to let water into the fields.

Wálahan.—One-seventh of the produce of a paddy field given to those who are employed in reaping and threshing the corn.

Walawwa.—A house ; a term applied to the house of a chief or a man of high rank.

Walawwé-Mahatmayá.—The lady of the house.

Wali-dẹl.—Nets for night fishing.

Wána.—Spill of a tank.

Wanáta.—Reservation round a field.

Wannakurála.—Accountant.

Wansé.—Caste, race.

Warágama.—Coin varying from 6s. to 7s. 6d.

Was.—The four months of the rainy season from the full moon of July to the full moon of November, during which period Buddhist priests are permitted and enjoined to abstain from alms pilgrimage, and to devote themselves to stationary religious observances.—(Turnour.)

Wásala.—Palace gate.

Wasama.—Service-holding ; family name ; branch of service as Héwáwasama (military service) ; a district or division of a petty headman.

Waṭṭórurála.—Tenant whose duty is to open and close the doors of the sanctuary in a *déwàlé*, to sweep it out, to clean and trim the lamps.

Waṭṭóruwa.—A list, an inventory. Particularly a list of lands and of the share of produce due to the Government. A doctor's prescription is *behet waṭṭóruwa*.

Waturáwa.—Swampy ground which cannot be drained.

Wedarála—A term for a native doctor.

Wẹḍawasan.—Service pravéṇi lands.

Wẹikkiya.—A district or division of a petty headman.

Wela.—A field ; a common ending of place names.

Weldévayá, Weldurayá.—An irrigation headman of a low caste.

Wel-vidáné, Wel-vidáné Árachchi.—An irrigation headman.

Wélla.—A dam, an embankment. A common suffix of place names, *e.g.* Avisáwélla.

Wẹlla.—A sandy place. A common suffix of place names, *e.g.*, Hanwẹlla.

Wesamuṇi.—The deity presiding over demons.

Wewumkaraya.—Planting voucher, *i.e.*, an agreement between the owner of a garden with the planter as to the terms on which the latter will plant fruit trees, &c.

Wibadu Lékama.—A writer of the paddy waṭṭóru. *v. Waṭṭóruwa*.

Wibadu Árachchi.—An árachchi attached to the Paddy Tax Department.

Wiharagama.—(From *wihara* and *gama*, a village.) A village or land belonging to a Buddhist temple.

Wila.—A swamp or field, the higher parts only of which can be cultivated; a small pond.

Winna.—Grove. Used as a suffix denoting certain villages, as Dambawinna, Náwinna.

Wiyakolamila.—Hire of buffaloes for threshing paddy.

Yaká.—A demon. The term is also applied to the aborigines of Laṇká, who were expelled by Wijaya, the first Siṇhalese king.

Yakunneṭima.—A devil ceremony; dancing to propitiate the demons.

Yala.—The *yala* harvest, sown in March-April and reaped in August-September.

Yala.—A score, 20 *amunams*' extent, or 20 *amunams* of grain, or 20 head of cattle.—(Armour.)

Yámánna, Yapammu.—Smelters of iron. Their service consisted in giving a certain number of lumps of iron yearly; in burning charcoal for the forge, carrying baggage, assisting in field work and at devil ceremonies. They pull the tálimána (pair of bellows) for the smith and smelt iron.

Yantra.—A magical diagram. A machine.

Yava.—Barley.

Yáya.—A tract of paddy fields.

Yelamuṇa.—One and a half *amuṇams* or six *pélas*.

Yoduna.—Páli and Skt. *yójana*, equal to 4 *gaw*, or 16 miles.

Yoná.—A Moorman (disrespectful).

Yotta.—Wooden trough with a long handle for baling water.

Zebu.—A whimsical word applied in zoological books to the humped domestic cattle of the East.

APPENDIX II.

DERIVATIONS AND MEANINGS.

OF THE NAMES OF SOME OF THE PRINCIPAL TOWNS VILLAGES, DISTRICTS, RIVERS, AND MOUNTAINS IN CEYLON.

(As corrected and revised by the late B. Gunasekara, Esq., Mudaliyar, Chief Sinhalese Translator to Government; the late K. C. B. Kumarakulasingam, Esq., Mudaliyar, Tamil Interpreter to H. E. the Governor and Chief Tamil Translator, Colonial Secretary's Office; W. P. Ranasinha, Esq., Proctor, Supreme . Court, M.C.B.R.A.S.; A. M. Gunasekara Esq., Mudaliyar of the Registrar-General's Office; and others.)

[It must be borne in mind that each word admits of so many interpretations that it is impossible in most cases to give the correct meaning or derivation of words without studying the history connected with the objects indicated by them.]

Agarapatana	—Plain of pits	Aranayaka	—Jungle
Akkaraipattu	—Division at further bank or shore	Asgiriya	—Horse mountain
		Atakalankorale	—Eight-*Kalan* Korale
Akmimana	—Forest of *Akmi* trees	Atulugamkorale	--Korale in which Atulugama is
Akuramboda	—Bordering Akuram, a temple	Awissawella	—Unreliable dam··
Akuressa	- Gravel heap (?)		
Alagalla	—Yam rock	Badalgama	—Silversmiths' village
Alakola-ella	Yam leaf rapid or waterfall	Badulla	- *Badulla-tree* village
		Balangoda	- View mound
Alawatugoda	—Yam-garden village	Balapitimodara	--Embouchure of the *bala*-fish plain (or of warriors, being inhabited by the "Hewapanne" people of the " Salagama " caste)
Alawwa	—(Ghost village ?)		
Alutgama	—New village		
Alutkurukorale	---Newly apportioned korale		
Alutnuwara	—New city		
Aluwihara	—Illuminated or bright wihara		
		Balapitiya	—*Bala*-fish plain (or do.)
Ambagamuwa	-Mango village	Balane	—The view
Ambalangoda	—Resthouse village	Bambalapitiya	.--C o n t r a c t e d from *B a m buwalapitiya*, plain of the *bambu* forest
Ambalantota	—Resthouse ferry		
Ambawela	—Mango field		
Ambepussa	- Mango bush		
Ampitiya	—Horn-plain	Bambarabotuwa	---Bee-gullet or swarm [tree
Anamaduwa	—Shed of the forest	B a m b i g a h a totupala	Ferry of the *Bambi*
Andiambalama	Resting place of the mendicants (Andiyas)	Bandaragama	- Treasury village
		Bandarawela	—Royal field
Angulana	—Forest of *Angulu* trees*	Batalgala	—Sweet-potato rock
		Batgala	--- Rice rock
Anuradhapura	—City of Anuradha	Batagalla	— Bamboo rock

* Forest of canoes.—W.P.R.

Place Names and their Derivations. xli

Batawatta	—Bamboo garden	Dumbara	—(A contraction of *Ud-umbara*), the fig country
Batticaloa	—*Madakalapu*, the muddy lake		
Batticotta	—Round fort		
Battuluoya	—Rice-grain river	Elbedda	—Cold jungle†
Beliatta	—*Hibiscus* garden (from Beliwatta)*	Elkaduwa	—Cold brook†
		Elpitiya	—Cold plain ‡
Beligalkorale	—Beli rock korale	Eravur	—Place which one cannot reach.
Belihuloya	—River of the *Beli* stakes or slimy river	Erukkalampiddi	—*Calotropis gigantea* hillock
Bentota	—Dreaded or terrific ferry	Eruvil	—Cowdung tank
Beruwala	—Beru-forest(forest of a kind of water plants)	Elalai	—
		Etapola	— Tusker's place
Bibile	—Bubble	Etugala	— Elephant rock
Bingiriya	—Subterranean rock		
Bintenna	—Level surface plain	Galagedara	— Stone house
Bogawantalawa	—Happy or prosperous plain	Galawela	—Rock field
		Galboda	—Rocky bank
Bogawatta	—Bo-tree garden or garden of minor cultivation	Galkandewatta	— Rock hill garden
		Galkissa	—Rocky inlet of the sea
		Galle	—Rocky place
Bolgoda	—Chaff or barren village	Gallena-kandura-oya	[stream —Rock cave mountain
Bopatalawa	—Bo-tree plain	Gammaduwa	—Village shed
Bulatgama	— Betel village	Gampaha	—Five villages
Bulatkohopitiya	-Betel store plain	Gampola	—River city.
Buttala	—Buddha's hall	Gandara	—River mouth (?)
Chammanturai	—Small vessel port	Gangabodapattu	-River bank pattu
Chavakachcheri	—Malay village [water	Gaura-Eliya	—White or beautiful plain § [jungle
Chilaw	—*Salapam*, diving in		
Chinnachcheddikulam	—Small Cheddi tank	Gaurakele	— White or beautiful [took fire
Colombo	From *Kolamba*,seaport	Gingaranoya	--
Copay	— [valley	Ginigathena	—Hena (c h e n a) which
		Gintota	—*Gin* ferry, (mouth of *Gin* river)
Dambadeniya	— *Damba* tree plain or [trees	Giriulla	---Rocky village
Dambagastalawa	— Open glade of *Damba*	Giruwapattu	---Rocky pattu [swam
Dambulla	— *Damba* cave	Gonapinuwela	---Field where the elk
Dandagamuwa	— Timber village		
Darawella	—Firewood bank	Habarana	—Habarala forest
Dehigampal-korale	— Korale in which Dehigampola is	Hakgala	—Conch rock ‖
		Hakmana	---Walk
Dehiowita	—Lime-tree meadow	Haldummulla	—Corner where *Hal* (va-teria) was given
Dehiwala	—Lime-tree forest		
Dekande	—Double rock	Hapitigam	— Hare plain village
Deltota	—Breadfruit ferry	Haputale	—*Sapu* plain
Demodara	—Doubleriver mouth	Hambantota	—Sampan ferry
DemalaHatpattu	-Seven pattus of the Tamils	Hangranoya	—Stream where the fighting occurred
		Hanguranketa	—Field of hidden gold ¶
Dewamedi Hatpattu	Temple Hatpattu	Hantane	—Slaughter place or place of signs
Dikoya	—Long river	Hanwella	— Coarse sand village
Dikwella	—Long beach	Harispattuwa	—*H a r a s i y a-pattuwa* (pattuwa of the 400.)
Dimbula	—*Dimbul* trees village		
Diyatalawa	—Water plain	Hatarakorale	---Four korales
Dodanduwa	— Orange island	Hatkorale	— Seven korales
Dodangaslanda	-Orange trees grove	Hatton	—From *Hatton* estate
Dolosbage	- Twelve divisions	Heneratgoda	—Senerat's mound
Dondra	— From Dewundara,city of the gods	Hettimulla	— Chetties' corner
		Hettipola	---Chetties' place
Dullewa	—Fibrous plant tanks	Hewa Eliya	---Soldiers' plain

¶ " Hibiscus Branch" is the literal meaning of the word, but there is a word "Beliat" which means a notice of sale. Perhaps a place where such notices are affixed—W.P.R. † Hill paddy jungle.—W P.R. ‡ Hill paddy plain.—W.P.R. § Plain of the Gawaras (Bubelus baffelus)?—D.W.F. ‖ Far more in appearance like "jaw" mountain—and does not "Hakka" mean "jaw"?---COMPILER. ¶ Field devoted to the Sangharatna or Priesthood.—W.P.R.

6

xlii Ceylon in 1903.

Hewagamkorale	—Korale of the soldiers' villages	Katana	—Firewood forest
Hewaheta	—Sixty soldiers	Katubedda	—Thorny jungle
Hikbaduwa	—From *Sippikaduwa*, oyster creek *	Katugampola	—Thorny village
		Katugastota	—Thorn-tree ferry
Hiniduma	—Hill vapours †	Katukenda	—From a tree of the same name
Horana'	—Hora forest		
Hor. gasmulla	—Nook of hora trees	Katukurunda	—*Katukurundu* tree village
Horekele	—Forest of *hora* trees	Katunayaka	—Chief thorny bush
Horetuduwe	—Headland of the hora-tree	Kawataru-oya	—
Hunasgiriya	—mountain which looks like a lying-down h rse	hayts	—Dutch name for *Urkavatturai*, port guarding the country
		Kegalla	—Paddy field rock §
Hunugaloya	—Lime-stone rock river	Kehelwatte	—Plantain garden
Hunukatugala	—Coral stone rock	Kekirawa	—Cucumber village
Hunupitiya	—Chunam plain	Kelaniganga	—River of Kelaniya
Idama	—Land property	Kelaniya	—Happy or fortunate place
Ilukkumbura	—*Iluk* field	Kelewatte	—Jungle garden
Imaduwa	—Arrow shed or boundary hut	Kelebokka	—Jungle recess
		Kendangamuwa	—Village of the Kenda forest
Imbulpitiya	—Cotton tree plain		
Indibedda	—Date palm forest	Kesbewa	—Turtle village
		Kiklimana	— [nook
Ja-ela	—Malays' canal	Kilakkumulai	—Eastern corner or
Jaffna	—From *Yalppanan*, a lute-player (the land of the lute player).	Kimbulapitiya	—Plain of the crocodile
		Kinigoda	—
		Kirigalpotta	—Milk-stone slab
		Kirindiwela	—Fields of tares
Kadawata	—Gravet	Kitulgala	—Kitul-palm rock
Kadawela	—Corner field	Kochchikade	—Chillie boutique
Kadugannawa	—Battle field	Kollupitiya	—Gram plain
Kaduwela	—Sword field	Kolonna	— [Korale
Kaikawala	—Strongly-guarded place	Koralawella	—Sandy beach of the
		Kosgoda	—Jak village
Kakkapalliya	—Crow church or Moorish church	Koslanda	—Jak grove
		Kotadeniyawa	—Timber meadow
Kalmunai	—Rock point	Kotagala	—Short rock
Kalpitiya	—*kal*, stone ; p i d d i, hillock	Kotahena	—Timber chena
		Kotapola	—Timber village
Kaluganga	—Black river	Kotmale	—Tower mountain
Kalupahana	—Black stone	Kotiyagala	—Tiger rock
Kalutara	—Black river ferry	Kotte	—Fort
Kamburupitiya	—Smiths' village	Kudaoya	—Small river
Kandabadapattu	—Pattu bordering the mountain	Kuduhugala	—Bent or crooked mountain
Kantalai	—Tamil for Gangatala, country along the bank of the river	Kukulkorale	—Fowl korale
		Kumbalgama	—Potter's village
		Kumbalwela	—Potter's field
Kandana	—Hill forest	Kumbukan-oya	—*Kumbuk* forest river
Kandapola	—Hill city	K u r a n a-	
Kandy	—Hill town ‡	Katunayeka	—
Kankesanturai	—Port of Gangesan, god of Ganges	Kurunegala	—Small elephant rock
		Kuruwiti Korale	—Round korale
Kappittawatta	—Captain's Garden		
Karikkaddu-mulai	—Charcoal bund corner	Labugama	—Gourd village
		Lindula	—Place of the well-spring or well-bordering village
Karunkodditivu	—*Karunkoddi* (black kind of *Aponogeton monostachyon*)island		
		Lunawa	—Salt village
Karawanella	—Dark coloured rapid	Lunugala	—Salt rock

---

* From *Siŋ* and *Kaduwa*, Sword of Arts.—W.P.R † Small tree forest.—W.P.R. ‡ From *Khanda* in the old name *Senkhanda saila nagara*—W.P.R. § "I am not at all convinced of the correctness of this rendering, but as I cannot give a better one leave it alone."—W.P.R.—A correspondent gives the meaning a "Rock on which a meal was partaken."—COMPILER.

Place Names and their Derivations. xliii

Lunupokuna	— (Tanque Salgad) Salt tank
Madampe	—Tope of *Mahadam*(big berry) trees
Madampitiya	—Plain of the big berry trees
Madawalatenna	—Mire (slough) plain.
Madampela	—Resting huts row
Madulkele	—*Madol* forest
Madulsima	—*Madol* boundary
Magampattu	—Great village pattu
Maggona	—Furious village
Maha Eliya	—Great plain
Mahahunupitiya	—Great chunam plain
Mahaiyawa	— [tain
Mahakudugala	—Great crooked moun-
Mahamodera	—Great ferry
Mahanuwara	—(Kandy) Great city.
Mahaoya	—Great river
Mahara	—Country yielding a great tax
Mahawela	—Great field
Mahaweliganga	—Great sandy river
Malabe	—Great gain
Malimboda	—Bank of the great well
Mallakam	—Wrestling village
Manippay	—
Mankulam	—Deer tank
Manmunai	—Earth point
Mannar	—" They tucked up their clothes."
Mantai	—
Mapalagama	—Great fruit village
Maradana	—*Maradan* grove or forest
Maradankadawela	—*Maradan* boutique field
Marawila	—*Mara* lake (*Mara*, a kind of trees)
Maskinawattaganga	
Maskeliya	—Fish gamboling place
Matale	—Great plain
Matara	—Great ferry
Matugama	—Higher village
Maturata	—Higher country
Mawanella	—Great forest rapid
Medakumbura	—Centre field
Medakorale	—Centre korale
Medamahanuwara	—Centre great city
Meenagalla or Miyanagala(?)	—(Fern rock?)
Melpattu	—Western division
Mihintale	—Mahinda's mound
Minuwangoda	—*Minuwan* mound
Mipitikanda	—Mi-tree plain hill
Mirigama	—Village of sweetness
Miriswatte	—Chilly garden
Modera	—(Mutwal) from Muwadora, mouth of the (Kelani) river
Monaragala	—Peacock rock
Moragala	—*Mora* tree rock
Moratumulla	—Moratuwa corner
Moratuwa	—*Mora* loft *
Morawaka	—From *Monarawaka*, Peacock's bend
Mullaittivu	—Jasmine island or sylvan tract island
Muturajawela	—King's pearl field
Nadukadu	—Country and jungle
Nainamadama	—Naina's resting place
Namunukulakanda	—Hill of the nine peaks (Hill of the peak of worship—D.W.F.]
Nanuoya	—Ointment-stream [ner
Naranmulla	—Mandarin orange cor-
Nawadunkorale	—Nine-given Korale †
Nawalapitiya	—Iron-wood forest plain
Neboda	—*Na*-tree village
Negombo	—Honey village (Migamuwa)
Nikaweratiya	—*Nika* fire-wood village
Nilambe	—Green mango
Nildandahena	—Green-timber chena
Nintavur	—Solely-owned country
Nuwara Eliya	—Light of city. [Plain of the Royal city?—D W.F.]
Nuwarakalawiya	—Kala tank of the city [According to Knox from *Nuwara* a city, *kaha* turmeric and *lava*, put into the river—But is it not from the three great tanks within its boundaries, Nuwarawewa, Kalawewa & Padawiya?—D.W.F.]
Ohiya	—Head of the stream from Oya-iha
Palai	—Den
Pallegama	—Lower village
Palolpitiya	—Plain of the *Palol* tree
Palugama	—(Wilson's Bungalow) Deserted village
Pamunugama	—Granted village
Panadure	—Rocky ferry
Panankanam	—Palmyra village
Panawalkorale	—Jak-forest korale
Pandiruppu	—The abode of Pandu
Pannala	—Grass village
Panwila	—Bulrush pond
Paranagama	—(Fort MacDonald)—Old village
Paranakurukorale	—Old division korale
Pasbage	—Five divisions
Pasdumkorale	—Korale which supplied earth, or the korale which was given afterwards ‡
Passara	—Five arrows
Pasyala	—Five yalas (of paddy sowing extent)

* From "Moratugaha," a shrub which is largely found growing wild in the Cinnamon Gardens near Moratuwa.—C. D. D. Silva, Muhandiram. † "Korale of the nine yojanas" (a *yojana*=12 English miles).—A.M.G. ‡ "Korale of the five yojanas."—A.M.G. & W.R.P.

Pattipola	—Cattle fold	Sripadaya	---Holy foot [Adam's Peak]
Payiyagala	—Purse ditch *	Suduganga	—White river
Pelmadulla	---Huts district		
Peradeniya	—Guava plain	Talankanda	—Flat mountain [river
Pesalai	---Beautiful [rock	Talatu-oya	---Talipot palm-leaf
Pidurutalagala	—Stack-of-straw-like	Talawakele	—Jungle of the plain
Pilana	---*Pila* forest	Talpepattu	—Palmyra grove division
Pitigalkorale	- Sandy rock korale		
Polgahawela	—Coconut tree field		
Polonnaruwa	—Sinhalese form of the Pali word Pulasthinagara or city dedicated to Pulasthi.	Tampalakamam	--Mudland farm
		Tanamalwila	---Grass flower lake
		Tangalla	--Resting place
		Teldeniya	--Oil plain
Potuhera	--From *potwehera*, inferior dagoba in which books were enshrined	Tellippalai	—Probably for Tellup-palai, a stage where palanquin-bearers change [place
Pugoda	---Flower village	Tempola	—From *Panpola*, water
Puhulpitiya	--Ash-pumpkin plain	Tihagoda	--Thirty mounds
Pundaluoya	—*Pundalu* tree river or the river of leeches	Tispane	--Thirty plains [Tissa
		Tissamaharama	--Great monastery of
Pussellawa	--Village of the *Puswela* creepers	Totapola	--Ferry; fording place
		Trincomalee	—Three-cornered [rock or sacred unbending
Puttalam	---*Puttu* (new), *alam* (salt pan).	Tumpane	--- [rock
Puttur	---New country	Tunmodara	- Three river mouths
Puwakpitiya	—Arecanut plain	Tunukkai	---(A piece?)
Radella	—From *Radá-ella*, Dhoby's stream or rapid	Udagama	---Upper village
		Udagoda	---Upper village
Ragalla	—Toddy hill	Udapalata	---Upper province
Rajakadaluwa	---	Udugahapattu	---Upperside division
Rakwana	---Demon forest †	Udugampola	---Upper village
Ramboda	—(Golden Bank?) Border of the forest	Udukinda	—Upper Kinda
		Udunuwara	---Upper city
Rambukkana	—*Rambuk* (cane ‡) thicket	Udupihilla	---Upper spout
		Udupila	---Upper match or upper side party
Rangala	—Gold rock		
Ratgama	- Royal village	Ukuwala	—Sugarcane forest
Ratmalana	—Forest of red blossoms	Ulapane	---
Ratnapura	—City of gems	Umaoya	—Uma's oya
Rattota	---Washers' ferry §	Urakanda	—Hog rock
Rayigamkorale	--Rayigama's korale	Urugala	—Pig rock
Ritigala	—Treacherous mountain	Utuwankanda	--Camel rock
Ruwanwella	—Gem sand	U v a	—Grape country b
Sabaragamuwa	--Mountaineers' village ¶	Valluvettiturai	---*Velluveddi* shrub port
		Vavuniyavilankulam	Woodapple tank of Vavuniyan
Salpitikorale	---Korale of the *sal* flour or plains ‖	Veyangoda	--White ant hill c
Siduwa	---Lion's islet	Wadduwa	—Resting-place
Sinigama	---Sugar village [Chinese village ?---D.W.F.]	Walaha	—Bear village
		Walallawitikorale	---
Sita Ella	—Sita's (or cold) stream		
Sita Kanda	- Sita's (or cold) mountain	Walapane	---
		Walasmulla	--Bears' corner
Situlaganga	---Cold river	Wangie oya	—Winding river
Siyanekorale	—Hundred relations korale *a*	Wanni	---Wild *d*
		Wariapola	—Watering-place

---

* Mr. Ranasinha does not agree with this rendering.—COMPILER. [Has it any reference to *lingum* stones?—Cor.] † "Protection rock."—B. G. ‡ *Saccharum Procerum*—W.P.R. § "Royal ferry."—W. P. R. ¶ "Village of the Veddas."—A.M.G. & W.P.R. ‖ "Korale in which Salpitiya is."—A.M.G. *a* "Hundred chieftain korale—A.M.G. *b* The late Wm. Hall ascribed the origin of the word to "Uvah!"—an exclamation of sudden surprise or joy.—COMPILER [From *Huwa*, which is known from the *Mahavansa* to have existed long before Lusitanians set foot in Ceylon.—D.W.F. *c* "Land of the *Ratan* forest."—W P. R. *d* "Trading place"—A, M. G. Colony of the Wanniyas.—*Cor*.

Place Names and their Derivations. xlv

Watagoda	—Round village	Weragoda	—Wihara village
Watawela	—Round field [plain	Weraketiya	---Group of wiharas
Wattala	—From Waltala, jungle	Werellagama	—*Werella* tree village
Wattegama	---Garden village	We-uda	---Village above the
Waturugama	---Water village	Weweltalawa	—Cane plain [tank
Weligama	---Sandy village	Wiyaluwa	---Dry land
Weligatta	--Sand pit		
Welimada	--Sandy mud	Yakdessa	—Village of the devil-
Wellabodapattu	--Pattu near the shore		dancer
Wellassa	---One hundred thousand fields	Yakdessagala	---Demon-priests rock
		Yatawatta	---Lower garden
Wellawatta	—Beach garden	Yatiyantota	—Yatiyana ferry
Wellawaya	---	Yatinuwara	--Lower city

APPENDIX III.
THE CEYLON CENSUS OF 1901.

FROM the valuable Report on the Census issued by the energetic Superintendent (Mr. P. Arunachalam, C.C.S.) we gather the following. The fourth decennial Census of Ceylon was taken on the night of 1st March, 1901, and employed 591 Supervisors and 10,919 Enumerators.

The total population of Ceylon exclusive of the Military, Shipping, and Prisoners of War is 3,565,954 (1,896,212 males and 1,669,742 females) which for 25,332 square miles gives 141 to the square mile, the greatest density being 643 in the Western and the lowest 20 per square mile in the North-Central Province. Colombo is now a capital city and a central steamer port with 155,000 people. (For 1903 it may be reckoned to have close on 160,000). The rates of increase of the Island's population in the decade since 1891 is so large as 18·6 per cent., a sure sign of prosperity though allowance must be made for continuous and increasing Cooly Immigration from Southern India. There are 598,076 occupied houses in the Island. The table of nationality gives the following result :—

Europeans	6,300
Burghers and Eurasians	23,482
Low-country Sinhalese	1,458,320
Kandyan Sinhalese	872,487
Tamils	951,740
Moors (Mohammedan)	228,034
Malays do.	11,902
Veddahs (Aborigines ?)	3,971
Others	9,718

[One practical deduction from the above is that the Low-country Sinhalese at once deserve a second representative in the Legislative Council.

The "others" include some 70 nationalities or races from Abyssinians to Kaffirs, Armenians and Jews to Chinese. Among "Europeans," English come first, then Scotch and Irish; while, curiously enough, we have more French (198) than German (163) residents.—As regards "religions," here is a summary for the Island :—

Christians	349,239
Buddhists	2,141,404
Hindus	826,826
Mohammedans	246,118
Others	2,367

The total number of "Christians" given in the census for 1891 was 302,127, so that the increase of 47,112 in the decade is not quite equal to the increase in total population; but allowance must be made for the

The Ceylon Census of 1901. xlvii

large immigration of Hindus from Southern India in the interval. Then of the Christians, 287,419 are Roman Catholic, leaving 61,820 for all "Protestant" denominations (including 1,718 "Independent Catholics" who repudiate the Pope). In 1891 the Roman Catholics numbered 246,214 and other Christians 55,913—so that the former have increased in a greater ratio than the latter.—A very serious revelation as regards the work of the Government is made in the tables of "Education by Nationality and Religion," the total number of persons able to read and write any language being only 773,196 ; while no fewer than 2,790,235 are unable to read and write, and of this so large a number as 1,553,078 are females. Making allowance for the very young and old, this shows a most unsatisfactory state of affairs ; and if the mass of Sinhalese and Tamils are to be advanced materially as well as morally, there can be no doubt that Government should add greatly to its elementary Vernacular Schools, including industrial teaching and inculcating habits of thought such as Sir Antony Macdonell desiderates for the people of India. If proper advantage is to be taken of the Northern Railway and Irrigation works in Ceylon, the stimulus afforded by education must be applied to the people, and the lesson that would thus be taught in little Ceylon might prove a most valuable one for its big neighbour—India. With reference to immigrants from India, it is interesting to learn that the India-born population was 10 per cent. of the total population in 1881, 8·8 per cent. in 1891, and 12·2 per cent. in 1901. The total Tamil population increased by 5·3 per cent. in 1881-1891, and by 31·5 per cent. in 1891-1901. Nearly the whole of this increase was by immigration.

The total number of Towns and Villages in Ceylon is 12,898 ; Chief Headmen's Divisions 112 ; Districts 20 ; Provinces 9.

CHRISTIAN BY SECT.—CEYLON.

TOTAL—			BAPTIST—		
Males	...	182,632	Males	...	1,733
Females	...	166,607	Females	...	1,576
ROMAN CATHOLIC—			CONGREGATIONALIST*—		
Males	...	149,685	Males	...	1,188
Females	...	137,734	Females	...	1,258
CHURCH OF ENGLAND—			SALVATIONIST—		
Males	...	17,740	Males	..	518
Females	...	14,774	Females	...	493
PRESBYTERIAN—			INDEPENDENT CATHOLIC—		
Males	...	1,688	Males	...	914
Females	...	1,649	Females	...	804
WESLEYAN METHODIST—			OTHER CHRISTIANS†—		
Males	...	7,673	Males	...	1,493
Females	...	7,318	Females	...	1,001

(See Review of Christian Mission in Ceylon for the years 1891-1901 ; further.)

---

* Chiefly belonging to American Mission, Jaffna. † Including Members of Society of Friends.

xlviii   *Ceylon in* 1903.

Population, 1901, by Nationality and Religion.
(EXCLUSIVE OF THE MILITARY, THE SHIPPING, AND THE PRISONERS-OF-WAR.)

CEYLON.	Total.	Population. M.	F.	Christians. M.	F.	Buddhists. M.	F.	Hindus. M.	F.	Mohammedans. M.	F.	Others. M.	F.
Europeans	6300	3852	2448	3794	2432	8	11	1	1	1	1	49	3
Burghers & Eurasians	23482	11681	11801	11589	11717	66	74	6	...	...	3	19	6
Lowcountry Sinhalese	1458320	759834	698486	104142	99645	655501	598799	71	56	95	74	25	12
Kandyan Sinhalese	872487	458179	414308	2763	2888	455199	411689	158	174	53	51	6	6
Tamils	951740	520409	431331	59252	49978	11994	6054	447966	374629	1116	634	81	36
Moors	228034	126798	101236	7	6	17	10	16	4	126753	101208	5	8
Malays	11902	6418	5484	18	8	7	12	...	...	6392	5463	1	1
Veddahs	3971	2028	1943	43	33	228	235	707	732	...	...	1050	943
Others	9718	7013	2705	1024	500	1285	215	1741	563	2892	1382	71	45
Total	3665954	1896212	1669742	182632	166607	1124305	1017099	450666	376160	137302	108816	1307	1060
Colombo Municipality.				349239		2141404		826826		246118		2367	
Europeans	2039	1259	780	1232	776	1	...	...	...	1	1	26	3
Burghers & Eurasians	11851	5823	6028	5803	6007	8	15	...	...	1	3	11	3
Lowcountry Sinhalese	67207	35521	31686	13078	12292	22415	19364	8	3	7	17	13	10
Kandyan Sinhalese	1388	836	547	149	120	682	421	1	...	1	2	3	3
Tamils	34640	24600	10040	6247	3206	3103	1405	15044	5390	172	29	34	10
Moors	28898	17937	10961	3	4	1	...	6	...	17927	10957	...	...
Malays	4493	2435	2058	4	1	...	1	...	...	2430	2056	...	...
Veddahs	...	...	...	...	...	...	...	...	...	...	...	...	...
Others	4180	3227	953	308	122	859	136	772	68	1225	584	63	43
Total	154691	91638	63053	26824	22528	27070	21342	15831	5462	21763	13649	150	72

PROPORTION OF EACH RELIGION TO 10,000 OF THE TOTAL POPULATION, 1901.

Ceylon ...   Buddhist. 6005   Hindus. 2319   Christians. 979   Mohammedans. 690   Others. 7

EDUCATION BY NATIONALITY AND RELIGION, 1901.

NATIONALITY.	Total.	UNABLE TO READ AND WRITE ANY LANGUAGE.										
				Christians.		Buddhists.		Hindus.		Mohammedans.		Others.
		Males.	Females.	Males.	Females.	Males.	Females.	Males.	Females.	Males.	Females.	Males. Females.
CEYLON :—												
Europeans	737	379	358	376	350	3	7	4	1	1	1	13 3
Burghers & Eurasians	7495	3466	4029	3415	3972	34	52	—	—	—	—	7 11
Lowcountry Sinhalese	1070170	449497	620673	44378	68523	405005	552013	45	56	62	70	4 6
Kandyan Sinhalese	724090	316868	407222	1284	1699	315411	405294	125	172	44	51	51 32
Tamils	786819	373459	413360	31851	41571	5853	9266	331543	365282	748	622	2 8
Moors	193325	84676	98649	2	5	9	10	13	4	84650	98622	— 1
Malays	7569	2977	4592	4	6	3	12	—	—	2970	4573	— —
Veddahs	3889	1951	1938	32	32	201	235	680	730	—	—	1038 941
Others	6141	3884	2257	422	313	846	174	1083	491	1526	1238	7 11
Total	...2790235	1237157	1553078	81764	116501	730778	963650	333493	366736	90000	105178	1122 1013
			198,265		1,694,428		700,229		195,178			2,135

		UNSPECIFIED.								
			Christians.		Buddhists.		Hindus.		Mohammedans.	Others.
	Total.	Males.	Females.	Males.	Females.	Males.	Females.	Males. Females.	Males. Females.
Europeans	10	9	3	7	3	—	—	—	—	— —
Burghers & Eurasians	21	12	9	12	—	—	—	—	—	— —
Lowcountry Sinhalese	1006	578	428	56	42	521	386	1	—	— —
Kandyan Sinhalese	818	462	356	3	2	455	353	1	1	— —
Tamils	507	285	222	37	33	21	11	227	175	1 3
Moors	121	73	48	—	—	—	—	—	—	73 48
Malays	19	11	8	—	—	—	—	—	—	11 8
Veddahs	6	4	2	—	—	—	—	—	—	— —
Others	15	11	4	1	1	4	1	3	1	4 2 3
Total	2523	1440	1083	113	93	1001	751	282	177	86 57
			206		1,752		409		143	13

EDUCATION BY NATIONALITY AND RELIGION, 1901.

Ceylon in 1903.

NATIONALITY.	Total Population of Ceylon.			Males.	Females.	ABLE TO READ AND WRITE ANY LANGUAGE.								
						Christians.		Buddhists.		Hindus.		Mohammedans.		Others.
CEYLON :—	Males.	Females.	Total.			Males.	Females.	Males.	Females.	Males.	Females.	Males.	Females.	Males. Females.
Europeans	3852	2448	5553	3466	2087	3411	2079	5	4	1	1	—	—	49 3
Burghers & Eurasians	11681	11801	15966	8206	7760	8165	7733	52	22	2	—	1	2	6 3
Lowcountry Sinhalese	759834	698486	387144	309759	77385	59708	30980	249975	46400	25	—	33	4	18 1
Kandyan Sinhalese	458179	414308	147579	140849	6730	1476	687	139333	6042	32	1	7	—	1 —
Tamils	520409	431331	164414	146665	17749	27364	8374	2707	190	116196	9172	368	12	30 1
Moors	126798	101236	44588	42049	2539	5	1	8	—	3	—	42030	2538	3 —
Malays	6418	5484	4314	3430	884	14	2	4	—	—	—	3411	882	1 —
Veddahs	2028	1943	76	73	3	11	1	27	—	27	2	—	—	8 —
Others	7013	2705	3562	3118	444	601	156	435	40	655	71	1366	143	61 34
Total	1896212	1669742	773196	657615	115581	100755	50013	392526	52698	116941	9247	47216	3581	177 42
						150,768		445,224		126,188		50,797		219

	Total.	Males.	Females.	ABLE TO READ AND WRITE ENGLISH.								
				Christians.		Buddhists.		Hindus.		Mohammedans.		Others.
				Males.	Females.	Males.	Females.	Males.	Females.	Males.	Females.	Males. Females.
Europeans	5473	3423	2050	3370	2043	3	3	1	1	—	—	49 3
Burghers & Eurasians	14949	7677	7272	7651	7267	18	12	2	2	—	—	6 3
Lowcountry Sinhalese	32205	25603	6602	11464	4440	14122	2161	5	—	1	1	11 —
Kandyan Sinhalese	2831	2470	361	483	189	1985	172	2	—	—	—	— —
Tamils	16131	13909	2222	6254	1820	241	7	7379	395	26	40	9 —
Moors	1755	1715	40	—	—	—	—	—	—	1715	40	— —
Malays	2235	2151	84	7	—	1	—	—	—	2142	83	1 —
Veddahs	1	1	—	1	—	—	—	—	—	—	—	— —
Others	916	789	127	379	91	39	3	53	2	263	7	55 24
Total	76496	57738	18758	29609	15841	16409	2358	7442	398	4147	130	131 31
				45,450		18,767		7,840		4,277		162

The Ceylon Census of 1901.

Races in Ceylon.

STATEMENT SHOWING ALL THE RACES OF THE POPULATION OF CEYLON, 1901.

(Exclusive of the Military, the Shipping, and the Prisoners of War.)

	Males.	Females.		Males.	Females.
Abyssinian	—	1	Jew	4	2
Afghan	193	77	Kaffir	166	152
African	10	2	Maharati	72	47
American	32	27	Malagasy	2	4
Arab	306	139	Malay	6,418	5,484
Armenian	1	—	Malayali	668	164
Australian	13	13	Maldivian	12	1
Austrian	6	3	Manx	2	2
Baluchi	1	1	Mappillai	1	—
Batavian	2	—	Moor	126,798	101,236
Belgian	20	11	Negro	24	29
Bengali	1,320	704	North Indian	4	—
Brazilian	—	—	Norwegian	2	—
British	13	4	Parsi	96	43
Burgher and Eurasian	11,681	11,801	Pattani	444	357
			Persian	5	—
Burmese	124	101	Portuguese	13	5
Canadian	6	5	Punjabi	24	5
Canarese	340	298	Rajput	23	2
Cape Colonist	—	2	Roumanian	—	1
Chinese	26	13	Russian	31	20
Circassian	—	1	Scotch	627	299
Cochinese	2,388	278	Siamese	5	3
Dane	2	1	Sinhalese (Low-country)	759,834	698,486
Dekhani	3	1			
Dutch	10	3	Sinhalese (Kandyan)	458,179	414,308
East Indian	28	2			
Egyptian	15	5	Soudanese	—	2
English	2,469	1,643	Sikh	46	7
European (otherwise unspecified)	62	29	Spanish	1	3
			Swede	11	9
French	132	66	Swiss	6	4
German	81	82	Syrian	9	2
Goanese	33	9	Tamil	520,409	431,331
Greek	2	2	Tasmanian	—	3
Gujerati	2	—	Telugu	113	72
Hindustani	133	37	Turk	2	1
Hungarian	1	1	Veddah	2,028	1,943
Indian	191	22	Welsh	44	12
Irish	283	237	West Indian	1	—
Italian	32	10	Unspecified	121	72
Japanese	6	—			

Ceylon in 1903.

OCCUPATIONS BY NATIONALITY AND SEX, 1901.

EXCLUSIVE OF THE MILITARY, THE SHIPPING, AND THE PRISONERS OF WAR.

Occupation or Means of Livelihood. CEYLON.	All Races. EARNERS. Males. Females.		DEPENDENTS. Males. Females.	
A—GOVERNMENT.				
Administration.				
Civil Service of the State—				
In the employ of the Government	18723	676	14055	23987
Service of Local or Municipal Bodies—				
Municipal or Local Board service	681	73	439	921
Defence.				
Army—				
Military service	429	—	168	522
Volunteer service	25	—	22	39
	454	—	190	561
Navy and Marine—				
Naval service	49	—	26	48
B—PASTURE AND AGRICULTURE.				
Provisions and care of Animals.				
Stock breeding and dealing—				
Cattle breeders, dealers	1571	101	816	1239
Cowherds, shepherds	4081	323	502	762
Elephant dealers	6	—	2	6
Horse breeders, dealers	4	—	4	4
Pig breeders, dealers	6	3	—	—
Sheep and goat breeders, dealers	153	3	44	57
	5821	430	1368	2068
Training and care of animals—				
Cattle shoers	73	—	51	80
Elephant trainers, keepers	156	—	45	99
Mule drivers	4	—	—	—
Veterinary surgeons, farriers	249	1	257	392
	482	1	353	571
Agriculture.				
Landowners, tenants, and labourers—				
Cocoa plantations : owners, managers, superior staff	1660	724	1575	2288
Cocoa plantations : labourers and other subordinates	4338	2894	1226	1663
Cinnamon plantations : owners, managers, superior staff	559	68	497	768
Cinnamon plantations : labourers, and other subordinates	5907	1731	3922	5260

The Ceylon Census of 1901.

Occupation or Means of Livelihood.	All Races.			
	EARNERS.		DEPENDENTS.	
	Males.	Females.	Males.	Females.
CEYLON.				
Cocoanut plantations: owners, managers, superior staff	33282	14825	40654	59964
Cocoanut plantations: labourers, and other subordinates	20706	4390	13875	19984
Coffee plantations: owners, managers, superior staff	97	30	55	64
Coffee plantations: labourers and other subordinates	368	86	115	270
Cotton plantations: owners, managers, superior staff	1	—	—	—
Cotton plantations: labourers and other subordinates	195	177	155	275
Citronella plantations: owners, managers, superior staff	459	101	513	686
Citronella plantations: labourers and other subordinates	1641	2965	1531	1822
Landed proprietors (otherwise unspecified)	23636	12078	28651	41955
Paddy land owners	126745	47553	136696	205292
Paddy land cultivators	169438	48209	134013	209958
Cultivators (otherwise unspecified)	66002	9503	54236	87669
Sugarcane plantations: owners, managers, and superior staff	88	10	43	96
Sugarcane plantations: labourers and other subordinates	161	99	144	217
Tea plantations: owners, managers, superior staff	3838	197	2149	3957
Tea plantations: labourers and other subordinates	173224	135392	32184	36729
Tobacco plantations: owners, managers, superior staff	22957	4776	15473	27143
Tobacco plantations: labourers and other subordinates	1671	256	966	1663
Planters (otherwise unspecified)	632	64	414	701
Vegetable and fruit growers	6985	1029	5216	8068
Labourers (otherwise unspecified)	74658	30952	37533	62529
	739248	318109	511786	779021
Agriculture training, and supervision and forests—				
Estate agents	98	1	75	138
C—PERSONAL SERVICES.				
Personal, Household, and Sanitary Services.				
Personal and domestic services—				
Barbers	2732	31	1404	2888
Dhobies	12625	8224	9162	13024
Domestic servants	31289	25584	4462	8682
Gardeners	803	45	245	446

Ceylon in 1903.

Occupation or Means of Livelihood. CEYLON.	EARNERS. Males.	EARNERS. Females.	DEPENDENTS. Males.	DEPENDENTS. Females.
Governesses	...	36	1	2
Grooms	2438	...	766	1529
Talipot bearers	5	...	1	3
Watchers	1451	21	584	1132
	51343	33941	16625	27706
Personal non-domestic services—				
Bar-keepers	219	1	96	193
Club, lodge, bungalow-keepers	142	4	95	136
Hotel managers, keepers, eating-house keepers, resthouse keepers	924	401	841	1291
	1285	406	1032	1620
Sanitation—				
Scavengers	372	62	107	207

D.—PREPARATION AND SUPPLY OF MATERIAL SUBSTANCES.

Food, Drink, and Stimulants.

	Males	Females	Males	Females
Provision of animal food—				
Butchers and meat-sellers	737	1	455	829
Collectors of birds' nests	6	...	1	8
Fishermen	24086	616	17692	32243
Fishmongers	5123	2729	4727	6862
Milk, butter, ghee sellers	652	249	417	580
Oyster dealers	364	14	37	80
Poultry, egg sellers	412	24	280	445
Miscellaneous	318	16	205	308
	31698	3649	23814	41355
Provision of vegetable food—				
Bakers	1082	4138	1723	2506
Bread, rice-cake sellers	2496	10043	3368	5383
Confectioners	643	486	334	605
Coconut sellers	1224	544	1220	1855
Copperah sellers	310	16	211	329
Curry stuff sellers	2865	462	1793	2480
Greengrocers	1448	904	1206	2128
Jaggery manufacturers	191	255	298	232
Jaggery dealers	142	182	129	192
Oil millers	121	6	103	152
Oil sellers	1741	966	1477	2271
Poonac sellers	88	4	15	14
Sugar manufacturers	8	31	23	30
Sugar sellers	23	1	13	9
Rice, paddy, gram sellers	4034	3282	3385	4940
Rice pounders and huskers	60	4074	1650	1813
Vegetable sellers	191	109	142	208
	16617	25503	17090	25147

The Ceylon Census of 1901. lv

Occupation or Means of Livelihood. CEYLON.	EARNERS. Males.	EARNERS. Females.	DEPENDENTS. Males.	DEPENDENTS. Females.
Provision of drink, condiments, and stimulants—				
Aerated water manufacturers	19	1	19	34
Aerated water dealers	5	...	2	9
Arrack distillers	196	6	235	255
Arrack sellers, tavern keepers	1542	19	865	1329
Betel, arecanut sellers	2081	2649	2320	3414
Brewers	22	24	9	8
Cacao sellers	109	8	78	89
Cinnamon dealers	204	12	184	277
Coffee and tea sellers	353	256	205	370
Grocers	126	11	53	96
Liquor-shop keepers	234	1	126	198
Opium sellers	90	2	37	78
Salt makers	79	255	87	122
Salt sellers	311	87	298	533
Tobacco, cigars, snuff makers	2012	17	556	1444
Tobacco, cigars, snuff sellers	3851	333	2325	4066
Toddy drawers	8512	...	6778	10645
Vinegar sellers	7	...	5	14
Water sellers	162	36	65	104
Waterworks service	36	36	42	39
	19953	3753	14289	23124
Light, Firing, and Forage.				
Lighting—				
Candle makers	12	...	8	12
Candle sellers	6	1	5	5
Electric light service	1	...	1	1
Gasworks services	172	2	64	125
	191	3	78	143
Fuel and Forage—				
Coal contractors	21	...	16	18
Coal labourers	908	15	266	618
Coal owners	49	...	38	66
Charcoal burners	79	24	87	102
Firewood sellers	1225	1207	1160	1646
Grass sellers	600	542	374	570
Straw sellers	209	58	175	269
	3091	1846	2116	3289
Buildings.				
Building materials—				
Brick, tile makers	2777	64	1738	2947
Brick, tile sellers	276	6	303	481
Limestone pickers	106	2	55	87
Limestone sellers	23	—	37	55
Lime burners	370	47	304	432
Lime sellers	443	405	372	574
Stone workers	1338	112	931	1485
	5333	636	3740	6061

Ceylon in 1903.

Occupation or Means of Livelihood. CEYLON.	All Races.			
	EARNERS.		DEPENDENTS.	
	Males.	Females.	Males.	Females.
Artificers in building—				
Building contractors	126	1	122	209
Masons	9069	11	5648	10125
Thatchers	18	2	7	11
Whitewashers	49	4	49	86
	9262	18	5326	10431
Tramway plant—				
Tramway factories, operatives, and other subordinates	198	—	72	162
Vehicles and Vessels.				
Carts, carriages, &c.—				
Carriage builders	65	...	53	105
Carriage sellers	7	...	7	4
	72	...	60	109
Ships and boats—				
Shipbuilders, boatbuilders	29	...	15	81
Ship chandlers & marine store dealers	29	...	28	69
	58	...	43	100
Supplementary Requirements.				
Paper—				
Palm-leaf binders	3	...	...	...
Stationers	15	...	7	18
	18	...	7	18
Books and prints—				
Bookbinders	224	3	142	264
Booksellers	257	2	144	216
Printers, compositors	807	4	423	870
	1288	9	709	1350
Watches, clocks, and scientific instruments—				
Watch and clock makers, repairers	222	21	157	301
Watch and clock sellers	11	...	1	2
Other scientific instrument makers, menders	8	...	6	12
Other scientific instrument sellers	3	...	2	10
	244	21	166	325
Carving and engraving—				
Engravers	23	...	12	22
Ivory carvers	3	...	1	1
Rubber stamp makers	...	...	...	5
Typefounders	5	...	3	3
Wood and ebony carvers	13	...	8	16
	44	...	24	47

The Ceylon Census of 1901.

Occupation or Means of Livelihood-CEYLON.	EARNERS. Males.	EARNERS. Females.	DEPENDENTS. Males.	DEPENDENTS. Females.
Toys and curiosities—				
Curiosity dealers	40	...	32	55
Tortoise-shell workers	39	...	34	78
Toy makers and sellers	21	...	20	24
	100	...	86	157
Music and musical instruments—				
Musical instrument makers and repairers	8	...	7	3
Musical instrument sellers	1	...	...	...
	9	...	7	3
Bangles, necklaces, beads, & sacred threads—				
Beads, bangles sellers	20	...	8	14
Flower garland makers and sellers	127	10	67	146
Glass bangle makers and sellers	5	...	5	4
	152	10	80	164
Furniture—				
Furniture dealers	154	3	151	231
Do. makers	50	...	24	31
	204	3	175	262
Harness—				
Harness makers and sellers	17	...	7	27
Saddlers	54	...	35	89
Whip makers	1	...	...	1
	72	—	42	117
Tools and machinery—				
Bicycle repairers	1	...	...	...
Knife and tool grinders	6	...	...	...
Do. makers	...	...	1	...
Do. sellers	...	...	3	...
Mechanics	1239	62	618	1292
	1246	62	622	1292
Arms and ammunition—				
Firework sellers	1	...	2	2
Gun makers, menders	7	...	1	9
	8	...	3	11
Textile Fabrics and Dress.				
Cotton—				
Cotton spinners	313	3741	721	1649
Do. traders	...	4	3	4
Do. weavers	146	50	67	125
Weavers (otherwise unspecified)	607	49	321	803
	1066	3844	1112	2581

Ceylon in 1903.

Occupation or Means of Livelihood. CEYLON.	EARNERS. Males	EARNERS. Females.	DEPENDENTS. Males.	DEPENDENTS. Females.
Jute, hemp, flax, coir, &c.—				
Broom makers	9	4	14	10
Coir manufacturers	1688	28295	5794	6224
Coir dealers	1031	1491	1143	1815
Fibre sellers	62	44	68	99
Hemp manufacturers	55	1291	250	810
Net makers	88	368	142	177
Rope makers	145	218	121	198
	3078	31711	7532	9333
Dress—				
Drapers, cloth dealers	4319	39	2583	3415
Dress hirers	7	32	9	15
Dress sellers	41	42	26	51
Hat makers, repairers, sellers	8	68	7	10
Lace makers	69	5952	534	867
Tailors, milliners, dressmakers & darners	2564	3561	2009	3482
Umbrella sellers	30	—	26	44
	7038	9694	5194	7684
Metals and Precious Stones.				
Gold, silver, and precious stones—				
Gem diggers	378	...	113	183
Goldsmiths	7267	54	4683	9857
Gilders and platers	5	...	2	7
Gem dealers	135	4	50	96
Jewellers	397	13	314	597
Lapidaries	408	3	292	541
	8590	74	5454	11281
Brass, copper, and bell-metal—				
Brass, copper, and bell-metal workers	773	18	583	1089
Do. do. sellers	101	1	80	140
	874	19	663	1229
Tin, zinc, quicksilver, lead, and plumbago—				
Plumbago mine workers	15055	2139	4615	7430
Do. dealers	1180	110	1068	1640
Do. factory labourers	272	365	202	375
Do. mine owners	39	1	38	45
Workers in tin, zinc, quicksilver, and lead	420	4	211	448
	16966	2619	6134	9938
Iron and steel—				
Sellers of iron and hardware	209	19	157	258
Workers in iron and hardware	5148	34	3390	6242
	5357	53	3547	6500

The Ceylon Census of 1901.

Occupation or Means of Livelihood. CEYLON.	EARNERS. Males.	All Races. Females.	DEPENDENTS. Males.	Females.
Glass, Earthen, and Stone Wares—				
Glass and china ware—				
Glass and china ware dealers	50	1	31	50
Earthen and stone ware—				
Grindstone makers, menders, and sellers	35	6	30	38
Makers of pottery	2863	2592	2506	3235
Sellers of pottery	174	129	132	150
	3072	2727	2699	3423
Wood, Cane, and Leaves, &c.				
Wood and bamboos—				
Carpenters	21902	45	14988	27420
Coopers	176	...	102	212
Sawyers	5869	1	3801	5979
Timber dealers	915	44	859	1412
Wood-cutters	568	27	430	698
	29430	117	20180	35721
Cane work, matting, and leaves—				
Basket makers	450	1907	505	758
Cadjan makers and sellers	159	1810	420	704
Cane workers	268	60	159	260
Comb makers and sellers	355	13	284	478
Fan makers	51	44	44	90
Mat weavers	1070	15848	3278	4649
Tat makers	46	54	33	52
	2399	19736	4723	6991
Drugs, Gums, Dyes, &c.				
Gum, wax, resins, and similar forest produce—				
Wax, honey, and forest produce collectors	5	12	15	9
Drugs, dyes, pigments, &c.—				
Chemist and druggists	269	41	117	165
Cinnamon, citronella, oil manufacturers	9	...	9	7
Do. do.	72	10	56	79
Dyers	300	11	167	457
Dye root diggers	26	54	28	45
Do. sellers	1	13	5	9
Ink makers and sellers	2	...	1	2
Perfume, incense sellers	10	...	4	8
Soap manufacturers	1	...	1	1
Soap sellers	11	...	7	5
	701	129	395	778

Ceylon in 1903.

Occupation or Means of Livelihood. CEYLON.	All Races.			
	EARNERS.		DEPENDENTS.	
	Males.	Females.	Males.	Females.
Leather, &c.				
Leather, horn, and bones—				
Bone pickers	1	...	2	1
Bone dealers	13	1	3	8
Hides, horn sellers	41	...	34	75
Shoemakers, sandlemakers	895	10	616	1222
Tanners	32	2	19	60
Taxidermists	11	...	10	18
	993	13	684	1384
E—COMMERCE, TRANSPORT, AND STORAGE.				
Commerce.				
Money and securities—				
Bankers, money lenders	586	173	247	393
Money changers	51	...	5	6
	637	173	252	399
General Merchandise—				
Accountants, managers, shroffs, cashiers, &c.	507	5	412	465
Merchants	5310	754	3121	5844
Mercantile clerks	3428	13	1617	2720
Do. peons	329	1	136	312
	9574	773	5586	9341
Dealing unspecified—				
Basket women and pingo carriers	121	3530	1072	1325
Hawkers, pedlars, &c	295	21	145	253
Salesmen	3482	8	428	601
Shopkeepers and other tradesmen	30649	5693	17458	27711
Do , clerks, &c.	500	7	135	242
	35047	9259	19238	30132
Middlemen, brokers, and agents—				
Auctioneers	26	...	37	65
Brokers	237	...	178	350
Clerks employed by middlemen	458	2	131	244
Contractors for labourers, emigration agents, &c.	106	...	76	163
Contractors (otherwise unspecified)	958	43	772	1297
Farmers of arrack, other liquor, opium, &c.	123	4	151	218
Do tolls, ferries, &c.	254	3	126	198
Renters (otherwise unspecified)	29	6	40	41
	2191	58	1511	2576

The Ceylon Census of 1901.

Occupation or Means of Livelihood. CEYLON.	All Races. EARNERS.		DEPENDENTS.	
	Males.	Females.	Males.	Females.
Transport and Storage.				
Road—				
Cart drivers	15045	...	7263	12567
Cart owners	1182	56	940	1405
Coach proprietors	20	1	4	16
Coachmen	151	...	86	177
Pulanquin bearers	12	..	5	10
Rickshaw drawers	1488	...	316	581
Tavalam men	382	2	273	448
Transport contractors	4	...	3	6
Do. coolies	3	...	4	5
	18287	59	8894	15215
Water :—				
Boatmen	3542	12	2257	4249
Boat owners	419	7	257	508
Divers	49	...	42	54
Dubashes	51	...	48	81
Harbour works service	407	10	102	294
Ship owners	12	1	11	31
Shipping agents	30	1	14	27
Steam boat service	25	3	23	56
Stevedores, ship coolies	545	1	122	322
	5080	35	2876	5622
Storage and weighing :—				
Warehouse owners, managers, and superior staff	249	1	193	306
Warehouse workmen and other subordinates	1070	22	374	731
	1319	23	567	1037
F—PROFESSIONS.*				
Learn and Artistic Professions.				
Religion—				
Astrologers	276	...	264	386
Buddhist priests	7331	...	...	...
Catechists, bible women	244	84	266	394
Church, chapel service	137	18	124	290
Devil dancers	1751	2	1562	2196
Hindu priests	737	1	427	947
Hindu temple service	696	30	356	810
Missionaries, clergymen, ministers	398	60	553	654
Monks, nuns, lay brothers	23	51	2	100
Mohammedan priests	507	...	394	622
Mosque service	186	1	160	288
Salvationists	25	29	12	10
Seminarists	85	5	86	...
Upasakes, sannasis, fakirs, devotees	35	14	11	20
Vihara, Buddhist temple, service	4359	3	291	54
	16740	298	4508	6771

* Does not include those in the service of the Government.

Ceylon in 1903.

Occupation or Means of Livelihood. CEYLON.	All Races.			
	EARNERS		DEPENDENTS.	
	Males.	Females.	Males.	Females.
Education—				
Pundits	7	...	3	11
Teachers	3126	1507	2110	3525
	3133	1507	2113	3536
Literature—				
Authors, editors, journalists ...	111	...	96	146
Bana book or ola book writers	94	4	49	76
Reporters, shorthand writers ...	18	...	10	21
Service in libraries and literary institutions ...	51	1	26	67
	274	5	181	310
Law—				
Barristers, advocates, proctors ...	366	...	464	825
Lawyers' clerks and articled clerks	1011	7	699	1272
Notaries public ...	268	...	351	555
Petition, pleading, drawers, and translators ...	155	1	161	312
Stamp vendors ...	74	1	64	130
	1874	9	1739	3094
Medicine—				
Apothecaries	235	6	95	165
Compounders	104	15	52	77
Dentists	13	...	6	12
Midwives	...	893	171	253
Nurses	...	18	...	...
Oculists	31	9	31	55
Physicians, surgeons, medical practitioners	340	13	319	522
Vaccinators	7	...	5	11
Vedaralas	3350	74	3098	5136
	4080	1028	3777	6231
Engineering and survey—				
Civil engineers	108	...	35	83
Draughtsmen	46	...	32	54
Land surveyors	170	...	149	278
Mining engineers ...	8	...	3	4
	332	...	219	419
Natural science—				
Astronomers	17	...	15	27
Botanists	2	...	...	1
Persons engaged in scientific pursuits	13	...	7	17
	32	...	22	45

The Ceylon Census of 1901.

Occupation or Means of Livelihood. CEYLON.	EARNERS. Males.	EARNERS. Females.	DEPENDENTS. Males.	DEPENDENTS. Females.
Pictorial, art, and sculpture—				
Artists	66	4	45	93
Painters*	702	4	517	866
Photographers	69	2	34	64
Sculptors	30	1	11	38
Tattooers	2	...	2	2
	869	11	609	1063
Music, acting, dancing, &c.—				
Actors, dancers, singers	196	20	105	175
Bandmasters and players	138	4	50	94
Music teachers	131	12	56	157
Nautch girls	...	9	4	9
Piano tuners	2	...	1	3
Tom-tom beaters	1319	6	1047	1583
	1786	51	1263	2021
Sport.				
Sport—				
Bird catchers	4	...	1	3
Book-makers	3	...	2	3
Huntsmen	150	39	136	235
Jockeys	10	...	...	4
	167	39	139	245
Games and exhibitions—				
Acrobats	10	...	3	1
Exhibitors of trained animals	107	14	71	115
Fortune tellers and conjurors	210	14	126	220
	327	28	200	336
G—UNSKILLED LABOUR NOT AGRICULTURAL.				
Earthwork and General Labour.				
Earthwork, &c.—				
Archæological Department coolies, &c.	114	18	14	27
Forest Department coolies	93	8	30	61
Irrigation Dept. coolies, overseers, &c.	422	65	110	176
Miners	45	9	26	37
Road coolies, overseers	10465	3078	3252	5405
Survey Department coolies	606	19	117	215
Well sinkers	26	...	20	41
	11771	3197	3569	5962
General labour—				
General labourers	37493	10753	18079	32502

* Mechanic-painters, clearly.—*Compiler.*

Ceylon in 1903.

Occupation or Means of Livelihood. CEYLON.	EARNERS. Males.	EARNERS. Females.	DEPENDENTS. Males	DEPENDENTS. Females
Indefinite and Disreputable Occupations.				
Indefinite—				
Uncertain or not returned	723	401	392	703
Disreputable—				
Gamblers	4	...	...	...
Prostitutes	...	46	4	7
	4	46	4	7
H.—MEANS OF SUBSISTENCE INDEPENDENT OF OCCUPATION.				
Independent.				
Property and alms—				
Beggars	3338	2508	1240	1846
House rent, shares, and other property not being land	130	139	133	264
Mendicants	42	11	12	20
	3510	2658	1385	2130
At the State expense—				
Exiles	5	...	...	...
Inmates of asylums	41	42	64	62
Juvenile offenders	7	1	128	11
Pensioners	1248	393	863	1736
Prisoners whose previous occupations have not been specified	9	6	4	5
	1310	442	1059	1814
Grand Total	1144593	490814	751619	1178928

The Provinces of Ceylon.

THEIR AREA, DENSITY OF POPULATION, AND PERCENTAGE OF TOTAL AREA AND TOTAL POPULATION.

Province.	Area in Square Miles.	Persons.	Persons per Square Mile.	Percentage of Total Area	Percentage of Total Population.
CEYLON	25332	3565954	141	...	...
Western Province	1432	920683	643	5·65	25·82
Central Province	2299½	622832	271	9·08	17·47
Northern Province	3363¼	340936	101	13·28	9·56
Southern Province	2146¼	566786	264	8·47	15·89
Eastern Province	4036½	173602	43	15·93	4·87
North-Western Province	2996¾	353626	118	11·83	9·92
North-Central Province	4002¼	79110	20	15·8	2·22
Province of Uva	3154½	186674	59	12·46	5·23
Province of Sabaragamuwa	1901½	321755	169	7·5	9·02

The Ceylon Census of 1901.

PROVINCES, DISTRICTS, TOWNS, VILLAGES, HOUSES, FAMILIES, AND MALES AND FEMALES.

Province, District, and Chief Headman's Division.	Number of				Population.		
	Towns.	Villages.	Occupied Houses.	Families.	Persons.	Males.	Females.
CEYLON.							
CEYLON (Including the Military, the Shipping, and Prisoners of War)	28	12870	598076	664311	3578332	1908272	1670060
CEYLON (Excluding the Military, the Shipping, and Prisoners of War)	28	12870	598076	664311	3565954	1896212	1669742
The Military	...	...	...	...	3360	3136	224
The Shipping	...	...	...	...	4105	4011	94
Prisoners of War	...	...	...	...	4913	4913	...
Western Province	5	1533	161157	176083	920683	489350	431333
The Military	...	...	...	...	1599	1470	129
The Shipping	...	...	...	...	2556	2486	70
Prisoners of War	...	...	...	...	504	504	...
Central Province	5	1635	67498	75667	622832	339219	283613
The Military	...	...	...	...	171	161	10
Prisoners of War	...	...	...	...	8	8	...
Northern Province	4	739	63959	76544	340936	171724	169212
The Shipping	...	...	...	...	1047	1026	21
Prisoners of War	...	...	...	...	2	2	...
Southern Province	5	1531	105625	112464	566736	288715	278021
The Shipping	...	...	...	...	189	189	...
Eastern Province	2	452	33467	41343	173602	90516	83086
The Military	...	...	...	...	592	512	80
The Shipping	...	...	...	...	94	94	...
North-Western Province	3	3573	72696	80325	353626	195711	157915
The Shipping	...	...	...	...	219	216	3
North-Central Province	1	1093	19471	19615	79110	43273	35837
Province of Uva	1	888	25755	30394	186674	100936	85738
The Military	...	...	...	...	998	993	5
Prisoners of War	...	...	...	...	4899	4899	...
Province of Sabaragamuwa	...	2	1426	48448	51876	321755	176768	144987

Ceylon in 1903.

Province, District, and Chief Headman's Division.	Towns.	Villages.	Occupied Houses.	Families.	Persons.	Males.	Females.
Western Province.							
Colombo Municipality	1	...	27268	30113	154691	91638	63053
The Military	...	...	...	...	1178	1049	129
The Shipping	...	...	...	...	2203	2136	67
Prisoners of War	...	...	...	...	156	156	...
Colombo District (exclusive of Municipality)	...	1	693	67524	76212	387886	200574	187312
The Military	...	...	...	...	421	421	...
The Shipping	...	...	...	...	110	110	...
Prisoners of War	...	...	...	...	348	348	...
Negombo District	...	1	350	27893	28234	148249	77384	70865
The Shipping	...	...	...	...	127	124	3
Kalutara District	...	2	490	38472	41524	229857	119754	110103
The Shipping	...	...	...	...	116	116	...
Central Province.							
Kandy District	...	3	864	41866	48152	277591	204318	173273
The Military	...	...	...	...	125	115	10
Prisoners of War	...	...	—	...	...	8	8	...
Matale District	...	1	430	15136	16255	92203	50056	42147
Nuwara Eliya District	1	341	10496	11260	153038	84845	68193
The Military	...	...	...	...	46	46	...
Northern Province.							
Jaffna District	...	1	262	55051	67284	300851	149185	151666
The Shipping	...	...	...	...	910	898	12
Prisoners of War	...	...	...	...	2	2	...
Mannar District	...	1	220	5262	5318	24926	14123	10803
The Shipping	...	...	...	...	137	128	9
Mullaittivu District	...	2	257	3646	3942	15159	8416	6743
Southern Province.							
Galle District	...	1	735	48389	51062	258116	129869	128247
The Shipping	...	...	...	...	176	176	...
Matara District	...	2	381	37542	41543	203750	104007	99743
Hambantota District	2	415	19694	19859	104870	54839	50031
The Shipping	...	...	...	...	13	13	...
Eastern Province.							
Batticaloa District	...	1	346	27893	34581	145161	74835	70326
The Shipping	...	...	...	...	68	68	...
Trincomalee District	1	106	5574	6762	28441	15681	12760
The Military	...	...	...	...	592	512	80
The Shipping	...	...	...	...	26	26	...
North-Western Province.							
Kurunegala District	...	1	3002	52219	57299	249429	137564	111865
Puttalam District	...	1	287	6324	7378	29779	17091	12688
The Shipping	...	...	...	...	219	216	3
Chilaw District	...	1	284	14153	15648	74418	41056	33362

The Ceylon Census of 1901.

lxvii

Province., District, and Chief Headman's Division.	Number of				Population.		
	Towns.	Villages.	Occupied Houses.	Families.	Persons.	Males.	Females.
North-Central Province.							
Anuradhapura District	1	1093	19471	19615	79110	43273	35837
Province of Uva.							
Badulla District	1	888	25755	30394	186674	100936	85738
The Military	...	...	...	...	998	993	5
Prisoners of War	...	...	...	...	4399	4399	...
Prov. of Sabaragamuwa.							
Ratnapura District	1	526	21838	23578	132964	73603	59361
Kegalla District	1	900	26610	28298	188791	103165	85626
Western Province.							
Colombo Municipality.							
Fort Ward	...	...	...	126	126	1279	1164	115
Pettah Ward	...	...	...	1367	1375	7561	6271	1290
St. Paul's Ward	...	...	...	3039	4180	20260	12614	7646
St. Sebastian Ward	...	...	...	1782	1783	9349	5640	3709
Kotahena Ward	...	...	...	5702	6370	33350	18277	15073
New Bazaar Ward	...	...	...	3554	3836	17470	9785	7685
Maradana Ward	...	...	...	5421	5805	30377	17318	13059
Slave Island Ward	...	...	...	3482	3713	16764	9854	6910
Kollupitiya Ward	...	...	...	2795	2925	18281	10715	7566
The Military	...	...	...	...	...	1178	1049	129
The Shipping	...	...	...	...	...	2203	2136	67
Prisoners of War	...	...	...	...	...	156	156	...
Colombo District (exclusive of the Municipality).							
Alutkuru Korale South	...	115	13179	14334	69599	34793	34806
Estates	...	...	...	...	233	143	90
The Military	...	...	...	...	337	337	...
Prisoners of War	...	...	...	...	283	283	...
Hewagam Korale	...	120	11623	13223	68995	37151	31844
Estates	...	...	...	...	4348	2458	1890
Salpiti Korale	1	99	16940	20829	99966	50692	49274
Estates	...	...	...	...	1003	601	402
The Military	...	...	...	...	84	84	...
The Shipping	...	...	...	...	110	110	...
Prisoners of War	...	...	...	...	65	65	...
Siyane Korale East	...	155	9165	10127	51527	27446	24081
Estates	...	...	...	...	92	53	39
Siyane Korale West	...	204	16617	17699	91799	47035	44764
Estates	...	...	...	...	324	202	122

lxviii   Ceylon in 1903.

Province, District, and Chief Headman's Division.	Number of				Population.		
	Towns.	Villages.	Occupied Houses.	Families.	Persons.	Males.	Females
Negombo District.							
Negombo Local Board	1	...	3770	3770	19819	10020	9799
The Shipping	...	...	...	...	127	124	3
Alutkuru Korale North	...	205	18333	18486	95252	48986	46266
Estates	...	...	...	...	1363	874	489
Hapitigam Korale	...	...	145	5790	5978	31638	17392	14246
Estates	...	...	...	...	177	112	65
Kalutara District.							
Kalutara Local Board	1	...	1993	2416	11500	5821	5679
Kalutara Totamune	1	208	18713	20904	104218	51555	52663
Estates	...	...	...	...	95	61	34
The Shipping	...	...	...	...	116	116	...
Pasdun Korale East	...	78	4308	4393	24059	13700	10359
Estates	...	...	...	...	2557	1501	1056
Pasdun Korale West	...	65	4513	4790	23294	12564	10730
Estates	...	...	...	...	9632	5603	4029
Rayigam Korale	...	139	8945	9021	49821	26345	23476
Estates	...	...	...	...	4681	2604	2077
Central Province.							
Kandy District.							
Kandy Municipality	1	...	4615	5270	26386	15049	11337
The Military	...	...	...	...	125	115	10
Prisoners of War	...	...	...	...	8	8	...
Harispattu	...	129	6369	8166	33431	16954	16477
Estates	...	...	...	...	2768	1617	1151
Pata Dumbara	...	138	7427	8798	40131	21024	19107
Estates	...	...	...	...	14605	8201	6404
Pata Hewaheta	...	33	2834	3241	13917	7375	6542
Estates	...	...	...	...	13040	7286	5754
Tumpane	...	110	2255	2358	11734	6139	5595
Estates	...	...	...	...	101	63	38
Uda Bulatgama	1	59	2978	3123	16367	9873	6494
Estates	...	...	...	...	84663	46440	38223
Uda Dumbara	...	143	4184	4978	20398	10565	9833
Estates	...	...	...	...	7439	4094	3345
Udu Nuwara	...	92	2965	3127	15647	8037	7610
Estates	...	...	...	...	1163	663	500
Uda Palata	1	84	4863	5551	25663	13729	11934
Estates	...	...	...	...	24919	13789	11130
Yati Nuwara	...	76	3376	3540	18473	9629	844
Estates	...	...	...	...	6746	3791	2955
Matale District.							
Matale Local Board	1	...	966	1021	4951	2981	1970
Matale South	...	173	6155	6857	28324	14831	13493
Estates	...	...	...	...	17666	9931	7735
Matale East	...	121	3462	3719	14550	7787	6763
Estates	...	...	...	...	8300	4654	3646
Matale North	...	136	4553	4658	18242	9767	8475
Estates	...	...	...	...	170	105	65

The Ceylon Census of 1901.

Province, District, and Chief Headman's Division.	Number of				Population.		
	Towns.	Villages.	Occupied Houses.	Families.	Persons.	Males.	Females.
Nuwara Eliya District.							
Nuwara Eliya Local Board	1	...	617	716	4106	2609	1497
Estates	...	...	...	...	920	475	445
The Military	...	...	...	...	46	46	...
Kotmale	...	125	3311	3321	16213	9629	6584
Estates	...	...	...	...	78252	43586	34666
Uda Hewaheta	...	118	3773	4346	16973	8798	8175
Estates	...	...	...	...	14997	8158	6839
Walapane	...	98	2795	2877	12182	6425	5757
Estates	...	...	...	...	9395	5165	4230
Northern Province.							
Jaffna District.							
Jaffna Division	1	9	8046	10753	45659	23073	22586
Estates	...	...	...	...	18	10	8
Prisoners of War	...	...	...	...	2	2	...
Valikamam East	...	18	4377	4960	24408	12236	12172
Valikamam North	...	28	7723	9077	44319	22004	22315
The Shipping	...	...	...	...	82	82	...
Valikamam West	...	21	8559	10911	45860	21994	23866
Vadamaradchi East	...	9	1055	1065	4240	2176	2064
Estates	...	...	...	...	7	4	3
Vadamaradchi West	...	27	8142	9361	48301	22658	25643
The Shipping	...	...	...	...	247	247	...
Tenmaradchi	...	34	7520	9587	37444	18850	18594
Estates	...	...	...	...	204	109	95
Pachchilaippalli	...	21	1062	1333	5510	3069	2441
Estates	...	...	...	...	566	347	219
Karaichchi	...	25	468	551	2879	2147	732
Punakari	...	23	937	1212	4715	2695	2020
Estates	...	...	...	...	102	80	22
The Islands	...	18	6339	7366	32075	15370	16705
The Shipping	...	...	...	...	581	569	12
Delft Division	...	3	690	934	3906	1965	1941
Tunukkai	...	26	133	174	638	398	240
Mannar District.							
Mannar Island Division	1	44	2237	2266	9936	5232	4704
The Shipping	...	...	...	...	64	64	...
Mantai Division	...	90	1288	1293	7582	4758	2824
Nanaddan Division	...	86	1737	1759	7408	4133	3275
The Shipping	...	...	...	...	73	64	9
Mullaittivu District.							
Maritime Pattus	1	27	1592	1666	6663	3560	3103
Vavuniya North	...	72	567	631	2500	1477	1023
Vavuniya South	1	158	1487	1645	5996	3379	2617

lxx   Ceylon in 1903.

Province, District, and Chief Headman's Division.	Towns.	Villages.	Occupied Houses.	Families.	Persons.	Males.	Females.
Southern Province.							
Galle District.							
Galle Municipality	1	...	6550	6842	37165	18773	18392
The Shipping	...	...	...	...	151	151	...
Galle Four Gravets (beyond Municipal limits) and Akmimana	...	41	3892	4121	20606	10429	10177
Estates	...	...	...	...	551	345	206
Gangaboda Pattuwa	...	45	5873	6054	29749	15319	14430
Estates	...	...	...	...	2702	1596	1106
Wellaboda Pattuwa	...	272	12829	13580	64891	32010	32881
Estates	...	...	...	...	1385	905	480
The Shipping	...	...	...	...	25	25	...
Talpe Pattuwa	...	159	9773	10239	51332	25310	26022
Estates	...	...	...	...	60	35	25
Walallawiti Korale	...	165	8307	9002	43161	21621	21540
Estates	...	...	...	...	403	228	175
Hinidum Pattuwa	...	53	1165	1224	6111	3298	2813
Matara District.							
Matara Local Board	1	...	2003	2391	11848	6007	5841
Matara Four Gravets (beyond Local Board limits)	...	34	2734	2914	15087	7446	7641
Wellaboda Pattuwa	...	30	7583	8883	42571	21194	21377
Weligam Korale	1	96	10250	11454	54411	27459	26952
Morawak Korale	...	67	3410	3650	15852	8646	7206
Estates	...	...	...	...	3072	1755	1317
Kandaboda Pattuwa	...	58	4777	5343	25545	13211	12334
Gangaboda Pattuwa	...	96	6785	6908	35031	18095	16939
Estates	...	...	...	...	333	194	139
Hambantota District.							
Hambantota Four Gravets	1	...	495	565	2843	1534	1309
The Shipping	...	...	...	...	13	13	...
Magam Pattu (exclusive of Hambantota Four Gravets)	...	60	1500	1592	7636	4494	3142
Giruwa Pattu East	...	66	2147	2150	11646	6113	5533
Giruwa Pattu West	1	289	15552	15552	82745	42698	40047
Eastern Province.							
Batticaloa District.							
Batticaloa Local Board	1	...	1827	2408	9969	5159	4810
The Shipping	...	...	...	...	68	68	...
ManmunaiPattuNorth	...	60	4899	6242	24862	12485	12377
Estates	...	...	...	...	20	20	...
ManmunaiPattuSouth	...	25	1227	1516	8173	4249	3924
Bintenna Pattu	...	44	819	819	4380	2426	1954

The Ceylon Census of 1901. lxxi

Province, District, and Chief Headman's Division.	Number of			Population.		
	Towns.	Villages.	Occupied Houses.	Families.	Persons.	Males.	Females.
Chammanturai	...	...	34	1598	1903	9123	4728	4395
Eravur and Rukam Pattus	...	...	26	2999	3583	14382	7687	6695
Estates	...	...	...	...	...	187	129	58
Koralai Pattu	...	...	42	2373	2557	10835	5943	4892
Estates	...	...	...	...	...	85	59	26
Eruvil and Porativu Pattus	...	...	39	2364	2949	13814	7270	6544
Estates	...	...	...	...	...	35	33	2
Karaivaku and Nintavur Pattus	...	...	20	6380	8227	31188	15273	15915
Estates	...	...	...	...	...	52	43	9
Akkarai Pattu	...	...	34	2651	3593	14396	7311	7085
Estates	...	...	...	...	...	163	129	34
Panawa Pattu	...	...	22	756	784	3477	1872	160$_5$
Estates	...	...	...	...	...	20	19	1
Trincomalee District.								
Trincomalee Local Board	1	...	2085	2892	11295	6125	5170
The Military	...	...	...	...	592	512	80
The Shipping	...	...	...	...	26	26	...
Kaddukkulam Pattu	...	...	30	702	765	3452	1990	1462
Estates	...	...	...	...	...	29	29	...
Koddiyar Pattu	...	...	34	1580	1613	7145	3917	3228
Tampalakamam Pattu	...	...	42	1207	1492	6520	3620	2900
North-Western Province.								
Kurunegala District								
Kurunegala Local Board	1	...	1222	1342	6483	4013	2470
Hiriyala Hatpattu	...	...	367	5962	6383	30022	17294	12728
Estates	...	...	...	...	...	264	172	92
Weudawili Hatpattu	...	...	480	8288	12082	42941	23433	19508
Estates	...	...	...	...	...	3121	1904	1217
Dambadeniya Hatpattu	...	...	409	8402	8727	41584	22483	19101
Estates	...	...	...	...	...	1102	708	394
Dewamedi Hatpattu...	...	...	584	7453	7817	32059	17380	14679
Estates	...	...	...	...	...	595	415	180
Katugampola Hatpattu	...	...	615	11637	11662	53312	29377	23935
Estates	...	...	...	...	...	763	485	278
Wanni Hatpattu	...	...	547	9255	9286	37183	19900	17283
Puttalam District.								
Puttalam Local Board	1	...	1219	1320	5115	2786	2329
The Shipping	...	...	...	...	70	68	2
Demala Hatpattu	...	...	131	1177	1735	7256	3944	3312
Kalpitiya Division	...	...	70	2070	2267	8497	4992	3505
Estates	...	...	...	...	...	56	43	13
The Shipping	...	...	...	...	149	148	1
Puttalam Division	...	...	86	1858	2056	8428	5015	3413
Estates	...	...	...	...	...	427	311	116

Ceylon in 1903.

Province, District, and Chief Headman's Division.	Towns.	Villages.	Occupied Houses.	Families.	Persons	Males.	Females.
Chilaw District.							
Chilaw Local Board	1	...	750	845	4168	2280	1888
Pitigal Korale North	...	109	2319	2607	11034	6312	4722
Estates	...	...	...	...	709	480	229
Pitigal Korale Central	...	110	5697	6243	28308	15523	12785
Estates	...	...	...	...	2391	1583	808
Pitigal Korale South	...	65	5387	5953	27509	14670	12839
Estates	...	...	...	...	299	208	91
North-Central Province.							
Anuradhapura District.							
Anuradhapura Town	1	...	852	878	3672	2351	1321
Nuwaragam Palata	...	446	7491	7492	30262	16541	13721
Hurulu Palata	...	358	5561	5579	22514	12122	10392
Kalagam Palata	...	221	4209	4264	16854	9011	7843
Tamankaduwa Palata	...	68	1358	1402	5808	3248	2560
Province of Uva.							
Badulla District.							
Badulla Local Board	1	...	1126	1255	5924	3293	2631
Yatikinda Division	..	111	5202	5353	22263	11832	10431
Estates	...	..	...	...	26288	14299	11989
Bintenna Division	...	64	1866	2248	10551	5509	5042
Buttala Division	...	130	2816	3541	15694	8689	7005
Estates	...	...	...	...	1180	676	504
Wellawaya Division	...	152	1532	1890	8558	4882	3676
Estates	...	...	...	...	9707	5744	3963
Udukinda Division	...	222	5519	7194	31763	16707	15056
Estates	...	...	...	...	10825	5986	4839
The Military	...	...	...	...	998	993	5
Prisoners of War	...	...	...	...	4399	4399	...
Wellassa Division	...	136	3695	3	23114	12409	10705
Estates	...	...	...	...	335	196	139
Wiyaluwa Division	...	73	3900	4200	17019	8858	8161
Estates	...	...	...	..	3453	1856	1597
Prov. of Sabaragamuwa.							
Ratnapura District.							
Ratnapura Local Board	1	...	692	767	4084	2440	164$_4$
Kuruwiti Korale	...	104	4928	5063	29427	16484	1294$_3$
Estates	...	...	...	...	1597	932	66$_2$
Nawadun Korale	...	100	4593	4671	23814	13042	1077$_9$
Estates	...	...	...	...	3447	2008	143$_8$
Atakalan Korale	...	72	3504	3962	17877	9859	801$_9$
Estates	...	...	...	...	2742	1460	128^2
Kadwata Korale	...	65	1945	2349	9696	5146	455^0
Estates	...	...	...	...	3572	1955	161^7
Kolonna Korale	...	42	1992	2136	10293	5542	4751
Estates	...	...	...	...	2023	1154	869
Kukulu Korale	...	40	1515	1520	7613	4409	3204
Estates	...	...	...	...	1390	781	609
Meda Korale	...	103	2669	3110	13518	7831	6187
Estates	...	...	...	...	1871	1060	811

The Ceylon Census of 1901.

Province, District, and Chief Headman's Division.	Towns.	Villages.	Number of Occupied Houses.	Families.	Population. Persons.	Males.	Females.
Kegalla District.							
Kegalla Local Board	1	...	405	479	2340	1312	1028
Paranakuru Korale	...	166	4782	4782	26114	13945	12169
Estates	...	...	...	...	5298	3041	2257
Beligal Korale	...	239	6407	7523	37933	20466	17467
Estates	...	...	...	...	725	437	288
Galboda Korale	...	143	4120	4428	21350	11257	10093
Estates	...	...	...	...	466	281	185
Kinigoda Korale	...	120	3036	3036	16248	8800	7448
Estates	...	...	...	...	65	43	22
Atulugam Korale	...	78	2061	2062	11716	6548	5168
Estates	...	...	...	...	6128	3324	2804
Dehigampal Korale	...	81	3159	3208	17202	9895	7307
Estates	...	...	...	...	8650	4735	3915
Panawal Korale	...	26	1132	1156	6362	3570	2792
Estates	...	...	...	...	3701	2027	1674
Lower Bulatgama	...	47	1508	1624	8027	4465	3562
Estates	...	...	...	...	16466	9019	7447

Population of Ceylon by Religion, 1901.

CEYLON:	PERSONS.	MALES.	FEMALES.
Christians	349239	182632	166607
Buddhists	2141404	1124305	1017099
Hindus	826826	450666	376160
Mohammedans	246118	137302	108816
Others	2367	1307	1060
Total	3,565,954	1,896,212	1,669,742

Population of Ceylon by Race, 1901.

CEYLON:	PERSONS.	MALES.	FEMALES.
Europeans	6300	3852	2448
Burghers	23482	11681	11801
Lowcountry Sinhalese	1458320	759834	698486
Kandyan Sinhalese	872487	458179	414308
Tamils	951740	520409	431331
Moors	228034	126798	101236
Malays	11902	6418	5484
Veddahs	3971	2028	1943
Others	9718	7013	2705
Total	3,565,954	1,896,212	1,669,742

Ceylon in 1903.

Districts of Ceylon.

Their Population, Area, and Density, 1901.

District.	Population.	Area in Square Miles.	Number of Persons per Square Mile.
Western Province.			
Colombo Municipality	154,691	10	15,469
Colombo District (exclusive of the Municipality)	387,886	$550\tfrac{3}{4}$	704
Negombo District	148,249	$247\tfrac{1}{2}$	599
Kalutara District	229,857	$623\tfrac{3}{4}$	369
Central Province.			
Kandy District	377,591	911	414
Matale District	92,203	$925\tfrac{5}{8}$	100
Nuwara Eliya District	153,038	$462\tfrac{1}{8}$	331
Northern Province.			
Jaffna District	300,851	1,265	238
Mannar District	24,926	$943\tfrac{1}{4}$	26
Mullaittivu District	15,159	$1,154\tfrac{3}{4}$	13
Southern Province.			
Galle District	258,116	$652\tfrac{1}{4}$	396
Matara District	203,750	$481\tfrac{1}{4}$	423
Hambantota District	104,870	$1,012\tfrac{3}{4}$	104
Eastern Province.			
Batticaloa District	145,161	$2,871\tfrac{1}{2}$	51
Trincomalee District	28,441	1,165	24
North-Western Province.			
Kurunegala District	249,429	$1,844\tfrac{7}{8}$	135
Puttalam District	29,779	$889\tfrac{3}{4}$	33
Chilaw District	74,418	$262\tfrac{1}{4}$	284
North-Central Province.			
Anuradhapura District	79,110	$4,002\tfrac{1}{4}$	20
Province of Uva.			
Badulla District	186,674	$3,154\tfrac{5}{8}$	59
Province of Sabaragamuwa.			
Ratnapura District	132,964	1,259	106
Kegalla District	188,791	642	294

Towns in Ceylon.

Their Population, Area, and Density.

Name of Town.		Population.		Area in Square Miles.		Number of Persons per Square Mile.
Western Province.						
Colombo	...	154,691	...	10	...	15,469
Moratuwa	...	29,600	...	$8\frac{1}{5}$	...	3,610
Negombo	...	19,819	...	$7\frac{1}{4}$	...	2,734
Kalutara	...	11,500	...	$1\frac{2}{3}$	...	6,900
Panadure	...	3,845	...	1	...	3,845
Central Province.						
Kandy	...	26,386	...	11	...	2,399
Matale	...	4,951	...	$\frac{1}{4}$	...	19,804
Nuwara Eliya	...	5,026	...	$4\frac{7}{8}$	...	1,031
Gampola	...	3,791	...	$\frac{2}{3}$	...	5,686
Nawalapitiya	...	3,454	...	$\frac{1}{3}$	...	8,502
Northern Province.						
Jaffna	...	33,879	...	$7\frac{1}{2}$	...	4,517
Mannar	...	5,332	...	1	...	5,332
Mullaittivu	...	1,308	...	3	...	436
Vavuniya	...	566	...	$2\frac{1}{4}$	...	252
Southern Province.						
Galle	...	37,165	...	$6\frac{1}{2}$	...	5,718
Matara	...	11,848	...	$1\frac{1}{2}$	...	7,899
Weligama	...	7,583	...	$2\frac{1}{2}$	...	3,033
Hambantota	...	2,843	...	$1\frac{1}{2}$	...	1,895
Tangalla	...	2,333	...	$\frac{1}{2}$	...	13,998
Eastern Province.						
Batticaloa	...	9,969	...	$1\frac{1}{4}$	...	7,975
Trincomalee	...	11,295	...	1	...	11,295
North-Western Province.						
Kurunegala	...	6,483	...	$1\frac{1}{2}$	...	4,322
Puttalam	...	5,115	...	$8\frac{5}{8}$	...	593
Chilaw ...	...	4,168	...	$\frac{3}{4}$	...	5,557
North-Central Province.						
Anuradhapura	...	3,672	...	$5\frac{3}{8}$	...	683
Province of Uva.						
Badulla ...	...	5,924	...	$3\frac{1}{32}$	...	1,954
Province of Sabaragamuwa.						
Ratnapura	...	4,084	..	$2\frac{1}{4}$	...	1,815
Kegalla ...	...	2,340	...	$\frac{7}{8}$	...	2,674

Ceylon.

VILLAGES, HOUSES, FAMILIES, PERSONS, AND DENSITY, 1871—1901 (EXCLUSIVE OF ESTATES).

Year.	No. of Villages and Towns.	No. of Houses.	No. of Families.	No. of Persons.	Village per Square Mile.	Persons. Per Village.	Persons. Per House.	Persons. Per Family.	Houses per Square Mile.	Area per House in Acres.	Average Distance between adjoining two Houses in Yards.
1871	12,069	389,018	494,175	2,277,828	·48	189	5·9	4·6	15	41·7	488
1881	12,438	477,917	532,193	2,553,243	·49	205	5·3	4·8	19	34·0	436
1891	13,088	535,621	559,886	2,745,527	·52	210	5·1	4·9	21·0	30·3	411
1901	12,898	598,076	664,311	3,124,353	·51	242	5·2	4·7	23·6	27·1	389

Colombo.

AREA, HOUSES, PERSONS, DENSITY OF HOUSES AND PERSONS, AND INCREASE PER CENT. OF HOUSES AND PERSONS IN THE TOWN OF COLOMBO AND ITS WARDS, 1881—1901.

Name of Ward.	Area in Acres.			Houses.			Persons.		
	1881	1891	1901	1881	1891	1901	1881	1891	1901
Fort	220	220	228	81	95	126	1,008	1,530	1,279
Pettah	92	92	118	1,203	1,141	1,367	6,955	7,961	7,561
St. Paul's	143	143	157	3,295	3,419	3,039	15,465	16,322	20,260
St. Sebastian	116	116	116	1,433	1,575	1,782	7,851	7,943	9,349
Kotahena	1,649	1,649	1,684	5,063	5,142	5,702	26,692	27,935	33,350
New Bazaar	289	289	289	2,866	3,119	3,554	14,064	14,506	17,470
Maradana	1,297	1,297	1,297	3,454	4,611	5,421	17,201	23,562	30,377
Slave Island	313	313	313	2,321	2,903	3,482	11,426	13,622	16,764
Kollupitiya	1,928	1,928	1,990	1,953	2,330	2,795	10,340	13,449	18,281
Total	6,047	6,047	6,192	21,669	24,345	27,268	110,502	126,825	154,691

Name of Ward.	No. of Houses per Acre			No. of Persons per Acre.			No. of Persons per House.			Increase per Cent. of Houses.		Increase per Cent. of Persons.	
	1881	1891	1901	1881	1891	1901	1881	1891	1901	1881-1891	1891-1901	1881-1891	1891-1901
Fort	·4	·4	·6	5	7	6	12·4	16·1	10·1	17·3	32·6	51·8	—16·4
Pettah	13·1	12·4	11·6	76	86	64	5·8	7·0	5·5	—5·2	19·8	14·5	— 5·0
St. Paul's	23·0	23·9	19·4	108	114	129	4·7	4·8	6·7	3·8	—11·1	5·6	24·1
St. Sebastian	12·4	13·5	15·4	63	68	81	5·1	5·0	5·2	9·9	13·1	8·1	17·7
Kotahena	3·1	3·1	3·4	16	17	20	5·3	5·4	5·8	1·6	10·9	4·7	10·4
New Bazaar	9·9	10·7	12·2	48	50	60	4·9	4·6	4·0	8·8	13·9	3·1	20·5
Maradana	2·7	3·5	4·2	13	18	23	5·0	5·1	5·6	33·5	17·6	37·0	28·9
Slave Island	7·4	9·2	11·1	26	43	54	4·9	4·7	4·8	25·1	19·9	19·2	23·1
Kollupitiya	1·0	1·2	1·4	5	7	9	5·3	5·8	6·5	19·3	20·0	30·1	35·9
Total	3·6	4	4·4	18	21	25	5·1	5·2	5·7	12·3	12·0	14·8	22·6

The Ceylon Census of 1901.

Chief Towns and Villages in Ceylon.

[The following is a list of all the towns and villages in the Island containing a population of 1,000 and upwards according to the Census of 1901, *arrnged by population for each district.*]

WESTERN PROVINCE.
Colombo District.

	Population		Population
Colombo Municipality	154691	Dematagoda	1546
Wellawatta	4253	Erawwala	1516
Moratumulla	3631	Bokolagama	1513
Koralawella	3390	Gangodawila	1513
Moratuwella	3116	Nawagamuwa	1510
Rawatawatta	3080	Heiyantuduwa	1505
Galkissa	2895	Hinatiyana	1500
Sea street (Negombo)	2887	Krillapone East	1499
Egoda Uyana	2691	Makola North	1455
Welikada	2682	Udammita	1447
Horampella	2225	Katukurunda	1442
Kendaliyaddapaluwa	2092	Kurana Katuneke	1430
Ratmalana North	2053	Weboda	1428
Ratmalana South	2033	Kandana	1416
Kalubowila West	2030	Hiripitiya	1400
Ragama	2018	Hanwella Ihala	1374
Wattala	1959	Koratota	1367
Kurana	1952	Biyagama	1351
Pitipana	1924	Kimbulapitiya	1350
Pitipana	1903	Dedigomuwa	1323
Boralesgomuwa	1902	Biyanwila Ihala	1309
Avisawella	1840	Mampe	1301
Kottawa	1791	Gonawela	1298
Laksapatiya	1783	Gonahena	1290
Dehiwala	1747	Angulana	1268
Talangama South	1706	Gampaha Medagama	1267
Walgama	1695	Kandawala	1265
Idama	1686	Lunugama	1263
Weligampitiya	1681	Peliyagoda Pattiya	1257
Pita Kotte	1659	Etgala	1252
Talangama North	1654	Bomiriya Pahala	1238
Etul Kotte	1642	Maha Hunupitiya	1236
Egoda Kolonnawa	1636	Niwandama	1232
Udugampola	1629	Karagampitiya	1230
Dandugama	1596	Panagoda	1224
Peliyagoda Gangaboda	1585	Bolawalana	1215
Doranagoda	1578	Kochchikada	1210
Embaraluwa	1567	Indibedda	1197
Uyana (Lunawa)	1566	Nawala	1191
Dagonna	1557	Katuneke	1188
Botale	1547	Narahenpita	1184

xxviii   Ceylon in 1903.

	Population.		Population.
Homagama	1180	Dalupota	1070
Tihariya	1176	Kossinna	1069
Hunupitiya 2nd Division	1174	Assanawatta	1067
Nagoda	1157	Hunupitiya 1st Division	1064
Grand street (Negombo)	1153	Kehelella	1064
Batagama South	1152	Asgiriya	1058
Puwakpitiya	1143	Kelanimulla	1050
Kalubowila East	1142	Yatiyana	1047
Raddoluwa	1140	Mobadale	1046
Kanuwana	1123	Kumbaloluwa	1043
Welisara	1117	Pallansena North	1041
Hunupitiya	1116	Hokandara North	1038
Welihena	1101	Mirihana	1038
Padukka	1097	Batagama North	1036
Mitotamulla	1092	Tumbowila	1032
Rahatuduwa	1091	Makewita	1029
Weliweriya East	1079	Katubedda	1014
Madelgamuwa	1076	Petiyagoda	1012
Radawana	1076	Siduwa	1011
Battaramulla	1075	Tudella	1009
Periyamulla	1072	Willorawatta	1004
Biyanwila Pahala	1070	Asgiriwalpola	1002

Kalutara District.

	Population.		Population
Desastra Kalutara (within Local Board Limits)	4299	Migahatenna	1315
		Malamulla	1313
Panadure	3845	Diyalagoda	1290
Welapura Kalutara	3736	Maradana	1276
Talpitiya	2795	Kaluwamodara	1275
Pattiya North	2380	Horana	1256
Potupitiya	2137	Kuda Paiyagala	1249
Katukurunda	2091	Alutgama	1228
Wekada	2031	Rayigama	1224
Kuda Waskaduwa	2004	Kalamulla East	1223
Molligoda	1745	Pohaddaramulla	1207
Mahagama	1668	Kuda Wadduwa	1191
Maha Paiyagala	1569	Bombuwala	1180
Maggona East	1491	Pinwatta	1179
Alutgama East	1467	Etagama	1178
Nalluruwa	1466	Kalamulla West	1175
Horetuduwa	1463	Millewa	1111
Alutgamwidiya	1431	Kumbuke	1087
Kehelwatte	1424	Uduwa	1086
Dodangoda	1424	Godigomuwa	1039
Walane	1398	Udahamullapattiya	1023
Maha Waskaduwa	1382	Ittapana	1023
Pattiya South	1373	Alubomulle	1020
Dinagoda	1372	Miwananpalana	1009
Maha Wadduwa East	1349	Moragalla	1001
Kuda Hinatiyangala	1340		

The Ceylon Census of 1901. lxxix

CENTRAL PROVINCE.

	Population.		Population.
Kandy Municipality	26386	Hatton	1440
Nuwara Eliya Local Board	5026	Halloluwa Udagama, Kandy District	1193
Matale Local Board	4951		
Gampola Local Board	3791	Uduwela, Kandy District	1190
Nawalapitiya Local Board	3454	Kadugannawa	1066
Atabage Udagama, Kandy District	1579	Kahatapitiya, Kandy District	1002

NORTHERN PROVINCE.

Jaffna District.

	Population.		Population.
Jaffna Town	33861	Koppay South	2303
Chankanai	5942	Chandiruppay	2260
Karaitivu West	4450	Thumpalai	2246
Karaitivu East	4400	Puloli East	2223
Alaveddi	4234	Tholpuram	2181
Tellippalai West	4126	Alvay North	1999
Vaddukkoddai West	3955	Madduvil South	1964
Karaveddi West	3902	Palali	1960
Chavakachcheri	3813	Surasalai	1936
Chullipuram	3809	Muntuvil	1934
Elalai	3464	Alvay South	1928
Tellippalai East	3388	Koppay North	1918
Vaddukkoddai East	3289	Chunnakam North	1911
Kondavil	3225	Kokkuvil West	1909
Misalai	3219	Madduvil North	1898
Manippay	3183	Puttur East	1892
Thanakkarakkurichchi	3098	Thunnalai South	1799
Neerveli	3046	Mallakam	1770
Point Pedro	2999	Imaiyanam	1742
Uduvil	2981	Achchuveli South	1709
Mathakal	2896	Siruvilam	1708
Valvedditurai	2856	Narantanai	1659
Navali	2812	Puttur West	1614
Kokkuvil East	2750	Nunavil	1613
Puloli West	2734	Mandaitivu	1690
Karampan	2688	Inuvil	1600
Punkuditivu East	2615	Kidavidditoppu	1590
Karaveddi North	2610	Arali South	1570
Kaitadi	2602	Chiruppiddi	1566
Punkuditivu West	2588	Thunnalai North	1557
Karaveddi East	2483	Analaitivu	1543
Urumparay	2474	Thavadi	1506
Velanai East	2473	Navatkuli	1494
Chutumalai	2460	Mayiliddi North	1487
Puloli South	2429	Saravnaai	1443
Karonavay South	2358	Delft East	1412
Anaikkodai	2349	Vimankamam	1398
Karonavay North	2321	Tirunelval East	1384
Mayiddapuram	2313	Velanai West	1378

Ceylon in 1903.

	Population.		Population.
Delft West	... 1333	Kadduvan	... 1218
Vasavilam	... 1325	Vidattaltivu	.. 1214
Mulay	... 1323	Irupalai	.. 1193
Naiynativu	... 1318	Delft Middle	.. 1161
Chunnakam South	... 1313	Kudattanai	.. 1142
Avaraukal	... 1293	Periyavilan	... 1121
Alvay West	... 1292	Thavalai Iyathalai	... 1119
Pattaimeni	... 1267	Mirrusuvil	.. 1063
Punnalaikkaduvan	... 1251	Varani North	... 1054
Palai	... 1246	Valluveddi	... 1047
Polikandi	... 1239	Karampai kurichchi	... 1021

Mulliattivu District.

			Population.
Mullaittivu	...	...	... 1308

SOUTHERN PROVINCE.

Galle District.

	Population.		Population.
Galle Municipality	... 37165	Ginimellagaha	... 1197
Talpe	... 2007	Gammeddegodde	... 1173
Gintota Welipiti-modara	... 1831	Ihala Kimbiya	... 1147
Malalagama	... 1750	Koggala	... 1123
Kitnlampitiya	... 1442	Pitiwala	... 1086
Walpita	... 1407	Pahala Kimbiya	... 1075
Ganegama South	... 1351	Narawala	.. 1061
Brahmanawatugoda	... 1334	Metaramba	.. 1050
Patabendemulla	... 1326	Ihalagoda	... 1012
Baddegama North	... 1307	Modarapatuwata	... 1009
Patuwata	... 1302	Baddegama East	... 1007
Bussa	... 1297	Balapitiya	.. 1000

Matara District.

	Population.		Population.
Matara Local Board	... 11848	Kongala	... 1594
Dewundara South	... 3606	Muratamura	... 1564
Dikwella, Sinhalese	... 3418	Urulamuwa East	... 1527
Denepitiya, Sinhalese	... 2949	Narawelpita	.. 1520
Gandara	... 2598	Kadawidiya	.. 1518
Dodampahala	... 2538	Kotapola	... 1428
Pategama	... 2529	Urugamuwa West	... 1411
Bambarenda North	... 2357	Wattegama	... 1390
Kottagoda	... 2326	Malimmiada I	... 1389
Kirindamagin Ihala	... 2235	Wepotaira	.. 1341
Kamburugamuwa	... 2184	Parahera	.. 1331
Midigama East	... 2040	Naotunna	.. 1313
Walgama	... 1983	Kekanadure	... 1312
Mirissa North	... 1981	Witiyala Pahala	... 1306
Denegama	... 1722	Kapugama East	... 1296
Bambarenda South	... 1653	Tallalla South	... 1264
Mirissa South	... 1639	Talaramba	.. 1254

The Ceylon Census of 1901.

	Population.		Population.
Uduwa East	1218	Madiha	1086
Batigama	1211	Walliwila	1063
Poramba Kananka	1208	Kadaweddwa	1062
Karagoda Uyangoda I	1184	Uda Aparekka	1059
Paraduwe	1139	Polwatta	1055
Kotawila	1119	l'elena	1053
Hittettiya	1117	Palle Aparekka	1047
Midigama West	1092	Pilatuduwa	1030
Witiyala Ihala	1087		

Hambantota District.

	Population.		Population.
Getamanna	2733	Puwakdandawa	1431
Hambantota	2686	Sitinamaluwa	1388
Medaketiya	2215	Kahawatta	1380
Tangalla	2137	Nakalugamuwa East	1329
Galagama	1738	Tissamaharama	1286
Kudawellakela	1728	Kudahilla	1236
Kammuldeniya North	1696	Mahahilla	1228
Pallattara	1562	Ambala	1175
Taraperiya	1556	Nakalugamuwa West	1089
Kadurupokuna	1541	Ranakeliya	1081

EASTERN PROVINCE.

Batticaloa District.

	Population.		Population.
Batticaloa Local Board	9969	Pottuvil	1835
Kattankudi	9420	Oddamavadi	1786
Eravur	6487	Naippaddimunai	1738
Karunkodittivu	6289	Palukamam	1710
Chantamarupu	5886	Periyakallaru	1683
Chammanturai (Moorish)	4483	Valichchenai	1428
Nintavur	4394	Talankuda	1355
Kalmunaikkudi	4161	Miravodai	1355
Arappattai	2869	Tampiluoil	1335
Karativu	2610	Vantarumulai	1317
Marutamunai	2476	Mandur	1272
Turainilavanai	2326	Panduruppu	1197
Kalmunai	2290	Oluvil	1191
Kalutaval	2284	Koddaikkallar	1118
Addalaichenai	2134	Tettattivu	1092
Chittandikudi	1896	Ampilanturai	1028

Trincomalee District.

	Population.		Population.
Trincomalee	10614	Muttur (Moor)	1725
Periyakiniyai	2180	Chinnakiniyai	1186

Ceylon in 1903.

NORTH-WESTERN PROVINCE.

Kurunegala District.	Population.	Puttalam District.	Population.
Kurunegala	... 6483	Puttalam	... 5115

Chilaw District.

	Population.		Population.
Chilaw ...	... 4168	Nainamadama West	... 1198
Ulhitiyawa	... 2073	Ihala Walahapitiya	... 1102
Pahalakatuneriya	... 1999	Marawila	.. 1087
Wennappuwa	... 1853	Boralessa	.. 1086
Mudukatuwa	... 1490	Haldanduwana	... 1060
Uddappuwa	... 1486	Etiyawala	.. 1017
Kirimetiyana	... 1277		

NORTH-CENTRAL PROVINCE.

Anuradhapura District.			Population.
Anuradhapura ...	..	...	... 3672

PROVINCE OF UVA.

Badulla District.			Population.
Badulla ...	...	...	... 5924

PROVINCE OF SABARAGAMUWA.

Ratnapura District.

	Population		Population.
Ratnapura	... 4084	Niyangama	... 1161
Balangoda	... 1848	Morahela	... 1144
Kendangama Ihalagama ...	1434	Bambarabotuwa Kuda-	
Nivitigala	... 1338	bage	... 1096
Gilimale North	... 1303	Eratna	.. 1076
Bibilegama	... 1276	Marapona	. 1074
Gilimale South	... 1226	Ellawala	.. 1061
Kumburugamuwa	... 1200	Madampe	.. 1020

Kegalla District.

	Population.		Population.
Kegalla ...	... 2340	Dehiowita	... 1217
Dedigama	... 1652	Maniyangama	... 1153
Diwela ...	... 1271	Talduwa	... 1070

[The total number of towns and villages in Ceylon is given as 12,898, in 3,762 of which there is a population between 1 and 50 ; in 2,686 between 50 and 100 ; in 5,202 between 100 and 500 ; in 829 between 500 and 1,000 ; in 310 between 1,000 and 2.000 ; in 88 between 2,000 and 5,000 ; in 12 between 5,000 and 10,000 ; in 4 between 10,000 and 20,000 ; in 4 between 20,000 and 50,000 ; and in 1 over 100,000.]

CHRISTIAN MISSIONS IN CEYLON.

REVIEW OF THE DECADE: 1892-1902.

(*By J. Ferguson.*)

INTRODUCTION.

Ceylon has an area of 25,332 square miles and the population by the Census of 1901 was 3,565,954. Allowing 1·8 per cent. per annum increase and for cooly immigrants, the population of 1902 is probably 3,619,443. The races embraced in the 1901 Census were : (See page 259.)

The Island is divided into nine Provinces, of which the Tamils occupy chiefly the Northern and Eastern, with a considerable number of Mohammedans in the latter; the Tamil cooly immigrants are chiefly in the hill country of the Central, Uva, and Sabaragamuwa Provinces, with a certain proportion in Colombo where also is a large portion of the Mohammedans. The Sinhalese are strongest in the Western and Southern Provinces and on the coast of the North-Western Province ; while the Kandyan Sinhalese are in the Central, North-Western, and North-Central, the Uva, and Sabaragamuwa Provinces.

INTRODUCTION OF CHRISTIANITY.

Christianity first reached Ceylon with the arrival of the Portuguese in 1505. The Dutch concurred the Maritime Provinces and ousted the Portuguese authorities in 1656. The British took possession in 1796, and in 1815 sent away the Kandyan King as a prisoner and assumed the government of the whole Island. The Portuguese Government favoured the baptism and conversion of all its subject population. The Dutch gave no appointment and no favour to a native who did not profess to be a Protestant. The British Government told the people it was neutral as regards religion. Keshub Chunder Sen has protested against " the denationalization so general among native converts to Christianity, who abandon the manners and customs of their country, and so are estranged from their countrymen, forgetting that Christ was an Asiatic." The great laxity of the companions and successors of Xavier upon the Malabar and Ceylon coasts, in the matter of caste, signs, and customs, is supposed to explain much of their wonderful success among the natives of Southern India and Ceylon. As Emerson Tennent in his "History of Ceylon" says : "The fanatical propagandism of the Portuguese reared for itself a monument in the abiding and expanding influence of the Roman Catholic faith. This flourished in every province and hamlet where it was implanted by the Franciscans, whilst the doctrines of the Reformed Church of Holland, never preached beyond the walls of the fortresses, are now extinct throughout the Island,

Ceylon in 1903.

with the exception of an expiring community at Colombo." This latter statement is both an exaggeration and a false prophecy. The Wolfendahl Dutch Reformed Church, now free of State aid and control, is a flourishing community with branch Presbyterian Churches, albiet its services are all in English and its ministers Scotch or Irish Presbyterians.

Of the Evangelical Missions in Ceylon, the Baptist Mission agents came first, arriving in 1812 ; the Wesleyans in 1814 ; the agents of the American Board of Foreign Missions in 1816 ; and the Church Mission in 1818 ; while a number of agents of General Booth's Salvation Army under "Major" Tucker (formerly Commissioner in the Indian Civil Service) arrived in 1885-6. The Society for the Propagation of the Gospel has had agents since 1840 ; but their activity chiefly dates from the appointment of a Bishop of Colombo in 1845. The Society of Friends commenced a Mission in 1896 ; and there are also several members of Faith Missions.

The Roman Catholic agents are to be found in nearly every town and district of the island ; but they are strongest along the coast among the fishermen, especially the North-west Coast from Colombo northwards and in the North and East of the island. The Baptist Mission has its stations chiefly North and East of Colombo ; near Chilaw ; in Kandy and Matale and Sabaragamuwa. The Wesleyan is the largest of the Protestant Missions with stations in every Province save in the North-Central and Sabaragamuwa, and it works amongst the Sinhalese, Tamils, Mohammedans, and Portuguese. The American Mission (Independents) is confined to the Northern Province among the Tamils, and is closely allied with the American Madura Mission. The Church Mission stations are also extended to the Tamil as well as Sinhalese Provinces and are in all save the Eastern Province.

RESULT OF WITHDRAWAL OF STATE AID FROM ANGLICAN AND PRESBYTERIAN CHURCHES.

It should be mentioned that, in 1881, the connection of the British Government with the endowment of religion by ecclesiastical votes from the general revenue to the Bishop of Colombo and a number of Episcopal and Presbyterian Chaplains was discontinued by Ordinance, provision being made for existing incumbents. There remain now only two chaplains drawing State salaries and the transfer of Bishop Copleston to Calcutta ends the vote for a Bishop. The result has been very cheering in bringing new life and Christian liberality into the Churches affected, which are now in a much more satisfactory condition than when connected with the State. The Synod of the Anglican Church and the Presbytery of the other meet regularly ; provision has been made for a Bishopric Endowment Fund as well as for clergy funds, and Mission work is by no means forgotten.

EDUCATION : ANALYSIS OF 1901 CENSUS.

I think it well to begin with an analysis of the results of last year's Census so far as it bears on Religion and Missions ; and I take up Education first; for ability to read and write at least one's own language, though not indispensable to the planting and development of Christianity, must be acknowledged to be a very important aid to the work of the Christian Missionary. The total numbers able to read and write any one language in all Ceylon in the three decades were thus given :—

	Total.
Census of 1881	404,441
Do. 1891	603,047
Do. 1901	773,196

The proportions of the above (in which males and females are included to the whole population) are :—

	1881.	1891.	1901.
Percentage of males	24·6	30·0	34·70
Do. females	2·5	4·3	6·92

Considering the greater attention given to education by the Government as well as by Churches and Missionaries, and the revival of Buddhism with special attention to schools, which, as well as Hindu schools, get grants-in-aid for secular results from Government, the figures representing the progress made in the last decade are disappointing. The percentage proportions are affected by the large immigration into Ceylon year by year of ignorant Tamil coolies; but nothing can get over the fact that, while nearly 200,000 were added to the number able to read and write between 1881 and 1891, only 170,000 were so added between 1891 and 1901. To show how greatly the Government educational work had increased in these intervals we may extract the following from the report of the Director of Public Instruction :—

	1881. Rs.	1891. Rs.	1901. Rs.
Expenditure of Public Revenue on Education	482,841	508,361	907,596
Total Pupils in Government and Aided Schools	84,757	116,601	183,261

The total of scholars in Ceylon is given for 1901 at 218,479 in 3,972 schools and about 118,000 of those pupils are in Vernacular schools. But a great lead of attention has been given by Churches and Missions, too, to higher education through English schools and colleges during the past decade, and that may be one explanation of the total added to the number of those who can read and write being less in the past than in the previous decade.

THE ILLITERATE AMONG THE CHRISTIAN COMMUNITY.

But of most interest to us is to contrast the progress and state of education among the different religions; and it may make the matter more expressive if we give figures this time representing those "*unable to read or write any language.*" Here are the proportions according to the Census of 1901 out of the whole population :—

Unable to read or write :—	Males. Per cent.	Females. Per cent.	
Christians	45	70	nearly
Buddhists	65	95	,,
Hindus	74	97	over
Mohammedans	65 (over)	96	,

It is rather startling to find 81,764 male and 116,501 female Christians returned as unable to read and write their language even if we make allowance for infants. There is good reason to suppose that the vast proportion of these illiterate "Christians" belong to the Roman Catholics, who, while very active of recent years about higher education in Colleges, Convents, &c., cannot be doing much for their poorer native adherents in the villages, seeing that in the Archdiocese of Colombo with "a total Catholic population of 204,769," the "total number of school children is 29,784"; while the Wesleyan Mission alone against a total Christian (Wesleyan) community of about 15,000 has 29,918 children in school. I have not got the total of children attending Roman Catholic Schools throughout the island (the diocese of Jaffna has 6,798), but at a liberal calculation it cannot exceed 43,000 to 45,000 against a total of adherents of 287,419 ; whereas Protestant Missions numbering little over 60,000 adherents, count at least 75,000 children in school. If it be the case that Roman Catholics do not care to receive the children of heathen parents into their schools, whereas Protestant Missionaries welcome all, some of the difference may be explained ; but it would seem as if the Roman Catholic do not do their full duty towards their own people by providing vernacular teaching in the villages. The progress made with education among the Buddhists and Hindus may be still further seen from the following figures showing the progressive decrease in the number of illiterate :—

Unable to read or write :—	1881. Per cent.	1891. Per cent.	1901. Per cent.	
Christian—Males	58·6	50·0	45	
,, Females	86·4	78·3	70	nearly
Buddhist—Males	76·5	71·3	65	
,, Females	98·6	97·4	95	nearly
Hindus—Males	80·2	76·7	74	
,, Females	99·0	98·2	97	over
Mohammedans—Males	73·1	69·5	65	,,
,, Females	98·5	98·5	69	,,

Female education is very slowly advancing among the heathen ; and still more slowly among Mohammedans. Hindu figures are affected by cooly immigrants. Among Christians the female rate of progress is better than that for males. And, indeed, the Buddhist male percentage exceeds the latter, no doubt owing to a multiplying of vernacular schools.

The Ceylon Census of 1901.

It may be worth noting that only 76,137, are returned as able to read and write English, or 2·13 per cent. of the whole population ; and that a large number of Tamil males professing Hinduism (7,379) than of Tamil males professing Christianity (6,255) can read and write English, but the Tamil females with this qualification number 1,820 Christians and only 395 Hindus.

In the same way there are more male Sinhalese Buddhist (15,836) than male Sinhalese Christians (11,879) able to read and write English; but fewer females (4,614 Christians to 2,324 Buddhists).

RELIGIONS IN CEYLON.

Of the total population last year :—

Buddhists (largely demon-worshippers)	...	2,141,404 and represent	60 per cent.
Sivaites (Hindus)	...	826,826 ,,	23 ,,
Mohammedans	...	246,118 ,, nearly	8 ,,
Christians	...	349,239—Roman Catholics 8·03	
		Independent (1,718) ·05	9·8 ,,
		Protestant 60,102 1·70	
Others	...	2,494 ...	... 0·2

The progress of CHRISTIANITY is thus given :—

	1881.	1891.	1901.
Total No. of Christians ...	267,977	302,127	349,239
Percentage to total population	9·71	10·04	9·80
Roman Catholics ...	208,000	246,214	287,419
Other Christians ...	60,000	55,913	61,820*

It is worth mentioning that 7 male and 6 female Moors and 18 male and 8 female Malays were returned as Christians ; also 43 male and 33 female Veddahs. On the other hand, 8 male and 11 female Europeans were returned as Buddhists in last Census, against 1 of each in 1891. There were 66 male and 74 female Burgher or Eurasian Buddhists ; 17 male and 10 female Moor Buddhists ; 7 male and 12 female Malay Buddhists ; and 11,994 male and 6,054 Tamil Buddhists—very probably ignorant Tamil servants so returned. There are also one male and one female European Hindu, and one female European Mohammedan returned.

The above return shows a very poor rate of progress for Protestant Christianity : the number for 1901, being properly 6,002 shows an increase of only 4,189 on 1891, or about 7½ per cent.; while the whole population has increased by 18½ per cent. (due partly to cooly immigration) and Roman Catholics (who took special pains through bishops and priests to get all their people counted) increased by 16·73 per cent. The Roman Catholics

---

* This includes 1,718 Independent Catholics (who have broken with the Pope's adherent over the Goanese Settlement) ; these were counted as Roman Catholics in 1891.

lxxxviii   *Ceylon in* 1903.

include only 787 Europeans and 10,464 Burghers, leaving 276,168 native adherents; while the Protestant Christians include 5,427 Europeans and 12,842 Burghers; which numbers, if deducted from their total of 61,102, leave only 42,833 for all native adherents.

CHRISTIAN CHURCH AND MISSION REVIEW.

We may now give the total of adherents of the different denominations in 1901, and the total of natives, apart from Europeans and Burghers, thus:—

Denomination.	Total.	Natives.
Church of England	32,514	21,244
Presbyterian	3,337	283
Wesleyan	14,991	12,629
Baptist	3,309	2,922
Congregationalist	2,446	2,411
Salvationist	1,011	957
Independent Catholics	1,718	1,613
Other Christians	2,494	1,580

In connection with the above it is interesting to note how the different races in our Island population are represented among the Christian community, thus:—

Races.	Roman Catholics.	Other Christians.
Low-country Sinhalese	178,405	25,282
Kandyan ,,	2,921	2,230
Tamils	93,646	15,584
Malays	10	3
Moors	23	3
Veddahs	23	53
Others ,,	1,140	384

That is as far as the Census enables us to go. There were no returns for Christian denominations, apart from Roman Catholics, in the Census of 1891, and therefore no means of comparison. We have to depend on the various Mission Reports and the resident Missionaries for information to enable anything like a review to be made.

ROMAN CATHOLICS.

Our appeal for latest information to the Secretary of the Roman Catholic Archbishop has not met with a response. Ceylon has now, besides the "Archdiocese of Colombo" with its Archbishop, five Roman Catholic Bishops—one of Colombo as Coadjutor to the Archbishop, one each of Jaffna, Galle, Kandy, and Trincomalee, which are separate dioceses; but these four divisions do not include more than 84,000 of Roman Catholic community against 205,000 in the Colombo Archdiocese. There has been great activity not only in multiplying dignitaries, but in promoting high education among the Roman Catholics during the past decade; and this has been stimulated by the arrival in Ceylon and location at Kandy of a

Delegate Apostolic to the East Indies from the Pope, His Excellency Monseigneur L. M. Zaleski, Archbishop of Thebes. A great deal of money, much of it, it is believed, lent from the papal treasury, has been invested in valuable property in Colombo and Kandy, and in the latter town as "General Seminary for India" has been established in a large new block of buildings specially erected, for which, besides the Rector, there is a staff of about a dozen Reverend Ministerial and Scholastic Fathers and Brothers There are, at present, about 70 students drawn from all parts of India and Ceylon to be trained as Priests. St Joseph's College, Colombo, with over 700 pupils, is about the best equipped in the Island, and a large property has been acquired and new buildings erected for the College and School, St. Benedict's Institute is an older institution, with close on 800 pupil, and nearly every Ceylon town now has its college, high school, seminarys monastery or convent school. As already shown not so much is done for the mass of the poor people's children ; and there must be a large propoition of Roman adherents who are illiterate, unable to read and write. Altogether there must be about 200 Roman Catholic Priests of many races and nationalities in Ceylon, besides lay professors and a large number of Reverend Mothers and Sisters. Clearly a great start has been made in higher education, in acquiring property, multiplying colleges, convents, and schools and press offices. But we should like to see more attention given to enlightening the ignorant of the professing Roman Catholic community as well as some of the Muhammedans and Heathen. Some years ago a leading Roman Catholic assured a pro-Buddhist Government official that the Roman Catholic policy was not one of aggression on Buddhism, but was directed chiefly to the care and teaching of their own people. This was afterwards denied, or rather it was denied that the statement had been made, although published by the late Sir John F. Dickson.

It is not easy to give a proper idea of the work of Roman Catholic presse in Ceylon ; but they have become increasingly active of late. Two news papers are published in English—one at Colombo and one at Jaffna—the former being conducted with considerable enterprise and having a circulation of 1,000 (bi-weekly) and the Jaffna weekly paper printing 800 copies.

BAPTIST MISSION.

We next take the Baptist Mission in Ceylon as the oldest among Protestant Missions, dating from 1814. It was strongly manned at one time and had an active press in Kandy ; but for many years there have been only two European Missionaries and sometimes only one in the field; with the veteran Mr. Waldock's return, three are now on the list, and there is a prospect of the Home Committee sending another Missionary shortly. In the Rev. C. Carter, now retired to new Zealand, the Mission had perhaps the most competent European student of the Sinhalese language, and his Sinhalese Bible, English-Sinhalese Dictionary, Grammar and other works are much prized. During the decade, the most notable work has been the development

Ceylon in 1903.

of self-support among the native Churches, 19 of which are now altogether or nearly, independent of aid from England. The formation of a Native "Baptist Union" and "Lanka Mission" has fostered a laudable spirit of co-operation and brotherliness, as well as of evangelisation, which should bear good fruit in the early future. In education the Girls' Boarding School has been a continuous success for well-nigh 50 years. A monthly little paper in English and Sinhalese, the *Baptist Intelligencer*, is conducted with much zeal. For the decade, the statistics show no increase, save in respect of the English-speaking, self-supporting Cinnamon Gardens Church, which is flourishing and in Sunday School work. Here is a summary of "approximate statistics" extracted from the annual Reports of the Baptist Missionary Society (London), for 1892 and 1902 :—

	1891-2	1901-2
European Missionaries	2	3
Missionaries' Wives and Lady Helpers	—	2
Superannuated Missionaries	—	1
Pastors of Self-supporting Churches	1	7
Evangelists and Colporteurs	24	19
Evangelist Pensioners	—	1
Stations and Sub-stations	99	80
Baptisms	45	24
No. of Christian Members	1,055	1,033
Day School Teachers	68	63
Sabbath School Teachers	95	113
Day Scholars	3,297	3,196
Sabbath Scholars	1,201	1,493

In the Sabaragamuwa and North-Central district, only occupied of recent years, a great deal of preliminary work has had to be done amongst an extremely backward and ignorant people; while in the districts long occupied, the Buddhist revival and the small number of Agents have operated against progress.

WESLEYAN MISSION.

We come next to the Wesleyan Mission, one of the most widely extended, best manned and most prosperous in its evangelistic, pastoral, educational and press work in Ceylon. There are two distinct branches : (1) to the Sinhalese in the South and West of the Island, which, however, includes work among the Tamils, in Colombo especially, and a limited Portuguese-speaking class; and (2) to the Tamils in the North and East. There are three "districts" with separate Chairmen (Colombo, Galle, Kandy) in the former; and one (Jaffna) for the latter; but all meet in one Synod. The Statistics and Reports show progress all along the line and much good work through ladies in medical, hospital, nursing as well as educational and evangelistic work; and in successful industrial schools; while Wesley College has become a power for good in Colombo. The Statistics given opposite are extracted from the minutes of a Synod held early in 1893 as compared with results published in January, 1902.

The Ceylon Census of 1901.

In the early days some of the greatest masters of Sinhalese, Páli, and Buddhistical lore—Clough, Gogerly, and Spence Hardly—belonged to the Sinhalese Mission ; but the distraction of multiplied work in English and Schools allowed their successors, within the decade, far less time to master the vernacular. It may be a question whether the work in the two languages should not be done by different agents. The Missionaries in the North and East have nearly always become masters of Tamil because they have little English work to district them. A great deal has been done—more than the finance figures show—towards the self-support of native churches in the Wesleyan Mission.

Much progress has been made in the Southern Province—one of the darkest and most ignorant parts of the island ; and from a letter of the acting Chairman (Mr. Prince) I quote as follows :—

"The most remarkable as well as most hopeful figures are the increase of 31 preaching places (all in heathen villages where we have no Christians, and almost entirely supplied by lay preachers) and the increase of over 100 per cent. in Sabbath Schools, and of 82 per cent. in the number of scholars attending. This is *Foundation* work, and is full of hope for the future. In the Southern Province, where Buddhism is strong, and the people greatly prejudiced, where Spence Hardy declared that "to win a convert was like taking the prey from the jaws of the lion," an increase of 22 per cent. in the decade in the Church membership may be considered full of encouragement. This is increased to 33 per cent. if the "Members on trial" are included, and the great bulk of these are converts from heathenism. It may be added that we lose annually at the rate of one-fifth of our membership by removals out of the District. Most of these go into the Western Province, particularly to Colombo.

WESLEYAN MISSION, CEYLON : 1892-1902.

Year.	Chapels & preaching places.	Ministers, European and Native.	Evangelists.	Local Preachers.	Members.	Christian Community.	Sunday School Teachers.	Sunday Schools.	Sunday Scholars.	Day School Teachers.	Day Schools.	Day Scholars.	Total attending School.		
													Girls.	Boys.	Total.
1892	249	64*	50	152	4,652	11,699	722	241	13,120	623	280	20,132	6,830	14,456	21,295
1902	306	64	58	199†	5,969	15,339	977	337	17,777	877	373	29,918	9,515	21,490	31,005
Increase	57	..	..	47	1,317	3,640	255	96	14,657	254	93	9,788‡	2,676	7,034	9,710

* 18 European and 46 Native Ministers,
† Besides 223 Class Leaders.
‡ Or 48 per cent.

FINANCIAL	Rs.
Support of Ministry, 1892	19,051
Do. 1902	23,115
Increase	4,064

Grand Total including Extension, Auxiliary Fund, Chapel Income, School Fees, Government Grants, &c. :—

	Rs.
In 1892	99,702
In 1902	195,846
Increase	96,144

"We have added to our agency two Bible-women—one at Matara, one at Tangalla—and the work of the latter, who has a large number of women meeting weekly for religious instruction, is yielding much fruit. A large number of boys' schools have been made into mixed schools providing some Christian instruction for the girls. We need, however, a much more aggressive policy in regard to "Women's work for women," and ought to have three European ladies for the training of Bible-women, the management of a Boarding School, and Medical Mission work. There is ample scope among the thousands of heathen women in the backward district of this Province."

The increase is also very remarkable in the Kandy District during the decade—more so than the statistical returns indicate; for, as the Chairman, Mr. Rigby, writes—and this is true of all Protestant Missions:—

"The tendency during the decade has been to apply our rules of membership more stringently. This is true of the whole Mission. As to the Day Schools the increase is considerable, and it should be borne in mind that through the decade there has been a great outbreak of Buddhist educational activity, which we do not deplore, except that it sometimes takes the form of a deliberate attack on our schools. Our progress has been steady and uneventful except so far as the 'Happey Valley' goes. The most remarkable development has been in the direction of self-support. That seemed a wild dream of the future in 1891. It has now been achieved in some of our churches and is within sight for others. We have really done on a small scale the thing Missionaries are here to do—we have created self-supporting and self-governing churches."

As already remarked the Colombo District has seen the varied work of the Missions greatly advanced in its many departments. Of late a spirit of active evangelisation has revived all over South Ceylon. Sunday services in the vernacular are held in nearly every school as well as chapel of the Mission. (Mr. Spence Hardy's "Jubilee Memorials" of the South Ceylon Mission published in 1863 is one of the most interesting books ever written of any Mission and people).

In respect of the important work in the North and East—the Tamil Provinces—I have an interesting report from the Acting Chairman,

The Ceylon Census of 1901.

Mr. Restarick, who expects to be at the Conference, and from this a few questions are made :—

"In the ten years under review the most prominent features of our work have been—(1) A Revival in the Churches (1892-3-4) concurrent with increased evangelistic success, (2) Progress in the organization of the churches; (3) Increase of numbers in Schools, but especially in English Schools; (4) Development of Female Education especially in English.

"*Problems of the Future.*—(1) Evangelism is slow, and though the pace of progress has been accelerated, it is not yet sufficiently rapid. We have no large depressed classes who gain socially by becoming Christians. There are no homogenous masses who are likely to come over in communities. Intelligence and education are commoner than in India, and a man needs individual treatment, and clear and reasonable presentment of truth. This subject has occupied our attention during the whole decade, and by the assistance of our Committee in England we are going to detach a Missionary as Evangelist, who will be also a Commissioner to report upon the prospects of the most important branch of our work. (2) The increase of school work is interesting, but enlarges our burden of semi-secular engagements. It is true that we estimate that more than 60 per cent. of our converts came to us in connection with educational work, but the requirements of the Department of Public Instruction are yearly growing greater, and there is too much to do. We shall have to clearly understand our own requirements and our limitations in this matter. (3) Race misunderstandings have been an obstacle which appears no smaller as the peoples of the island advance in prosperity and education. They are partly unavoidable, as the gulf which separates race from race is to be bridged over only by a sympathy and knowledge which are uncommon. Christ can fill it up, and I suppose that only the forebearance, charity, and understanding of Christian brotherhood will solve a problem which has hurt many and grieved more.

"The total number of adult baptisms during the ten years has been :—

	No.		No.
1892	60	1899	53
1893	86	1900	80
1894	105	1901	103
1895	82		
1896	86		
1897	92		820
1898	73		

—or an average of 82 a year. A. E. RESTARICK."

The Wesleyan Mission Press is always at work and is a power for good. In 1901 the outturn was represented by 457,807 copies or 10,285,086 pages.

CHURCH MISSION.

We now come to the Church Missionary Society's work which dates from 1818 and which enters every Province, save the Eastern, including the special Tamil Cooly Mission. Progress is reported in all departments,

Ceylon in 1903.

and Ladies and Lay-workers have come freely to the aid of the regular Missionaries during the decade. Zenana work among the Muhammedans of Colombo is a new feature, and schools for the daughters of Kandyan Chiefs and others of the better classes of Ceylon, are doing great good in up-country and in Colombo. The veteran Missionary, Mr. J. Ireland Jones, who wrote the "Jubilee Memorials" of the Church Mission in Ceylon in 1868, and who has now given over 40 years to Mission work, is still in the field, and is as earnest after the Evangelisation of the Sinhalese as ever he was. From the local Secretary of the Church Mission (the Rev. A. E. Dibben) we have received a very clear and concise Statistical Review for the decade, accompanied by explanatory remarks as follows :—

COMPARATIVE STATISTICS OF CEYLON MISSION, 1891-1901.

	1891.	1901.	Increase Decrease.
Native Adherents (viz., Christians and Catechumens)	8,056	10,175	+ 2,119
Communicants	2,666	3,525	+ 859
Native Pastors and Assistant Missionaries	15	19	+ 4
Parent Committee's Grants to Native Churches	Rs. 2,456	Rs. 1,575	— Rs. 831
Contributions from Native Christians	Rs. 13,939	Rs. 22,618	+ Rs. 8,679
Number of Missionaries { Men	17	18	+ 1
{ Women*	4	17	+ 13

EDUCATIONAL.

Higher Schools and Colleges	4	6	+	2
Students in Schools and Colleges	500	852	+	352
Vernacular and Anglo-Vernacular Schools	265	277	+	12
Scholars	13,500	17,061	+	3,561†

Among the features noticeable are :—

1. A decrease in the number of conversions from Buddhism.
2. Increased demand for Education.
3. The success of Girls' Boarding Schools (in connection with which I might name the Clarence Memorial School at Kandy for the daughters of Kandyan Chiefs, now full to overflowing with over 50 girls. This, however, is C. E. Z. M. S., not C. M. S.).
4. Marked and steady progress towards self-support (financially) of Native Churches.
5. Growing restlessness and discontent among Native Pastors.
6. Satisfactory results from Evangelistic work on Tea Estates, but growing difficulty of conducting educational work, on account of the early age at which children begin to work in the field.

---

* Missionaries wifes not included.   † Or 26 per cent. increase.

The Ceylon Census of 1901.

We may take it that most of the 1,132 Kandyan Sinhalese returned as 'Church of England' in the Census belong to the interesting Kandy Itinerating Mission of the Church Mission, begun by the late Mr. Higgens and Mr. Ireland Jones, and continued under the supervision of Mr. Garrett and Mr. Sydney Symons. The Tamil Cooly Mission has had a very encouraging measure of success during the past few years, and the way in which many of the Christians among the Tamil coolies appreciate their privileges (scanty enough) is an example to all other Christians in the Island, as is also their liberality in respect of giving in proportion to their means.

AMERICAN CEYLON MISSION.

We come next to the American (Congregational) Mission in North Ceylon for which an interesting Report by the Rev. R. C. Hastings has been received on the decade's work, well deserving to be given in full; but which we tabulate to some extent to meet the exigencies of space :—

	1891.	1901.
Foreign Missionaries, Wives and Lady Missionaries	7	12*
Professors in Colleges and Wives	2	4
Native Pastors	13	15
" Catechists and Evangelists (same number in both years.)		
Bible-women	"	"
Native Churches	15	18
" Members (Communicants)	1,521	2,100
" Contributions	Rs. 7,064	Rs. 10,214
" Support of Pastorate partly out of above	Rs. 5,000	Rs. 7,641†
Village Schools	130	138
" Scholars	8,800	10,500
College, High Training, and Boarding Schools	4	6
Pupils	250 (about)	377

But these figures give a very inadequate idea of the work, and if Mr. Hastings' Report cannot be reproduced, at least the following quotations should be given :—

"AMERICAN CEYLON MISSION.
Established, Oct. 1816, in the Jaffna Peninsula.
Ten years : 1892-1901.

"I.—Missionaries.—The number of Missionaries is nearly twice as large as that at the close of 1891. At the close of the decade (December 31, 1901) we have four ordained men with their wives, and four single ladies. One of the ordained men, his wife, and two of the single ladies are physicians. There are also, in addition to the above, two American Professors (one ordained) and their wives, teaching in Jaffna College. During the decade

---

* Including one Missionary and wife and two single ladies, qualified Medical Practitioners.
† Besides Rs. 1,000 for tw new societies started ;—Students and Womens Foreign Missionary Society,

13 new Missionaries. men and women, have joined the Mission, and 7 have left. Two only have been removed by death, —one after 46 years of service, and the other after 28 years. Of the 7 who have severed their connection with the Mission, 3 had served for 25 years each. Another worked here for between 5 and 6 years, but is now connected with one of the Missions in China. Three left the Mission owing to ill-health or other causes after only a few months' service. Two others, who were formerly connected with the Mission, after 6 years' absence from the field, returned and spent two years and then went back to America. Of the present staff of 12, only 3 were connected with the Mission ten years ago. The one who has been here the longest, counts 28 years of service.

"II. Native force.—Two years ago we had 13 Tamil pastors. Two of these have died during the decade, and one has left for the Straits Settlements where he is pastor of a flourishing Tamil congregation under the M. E. Mission. Four have been inducted into this sacred office, and one other, after several years' absence in Singapore, has returned and taken up work again in our Mission. This makes a total of 15. The number of catechists or preachers is slightly less than ten years ago, while the number of teachers is slightly larger. The number of Bible-women employed is about the same. Two of our 15 pastors are in higher educational work, and two others are working as catechists without charge of an organised church.

"III. Native church.—(1) We had 15 organized churches a decade ago, 13 of which were presided over by pastors. Since then 3 new churches have been organized making 18 in all, but only 11 of these have pastors. One-third of our churches are without ordained pastors. In other words while native congregations have increased, the number of ordained men ready and willing to take charge of these small churches has not increased proportionately, a state of affairs which is causing no little anxiety to the Mission.

"(2) Substantial progress has been made in the erection of new buildings for the worship of God, and in the re-modelling and repairing of old churches. In one village a large fine building is being put up at a cost of Rs. 10,000. Another congregation is repairing their house of worship at a cost of Rs. 2,000. Another practically rebuilt their church a few years ago at a cost of Rs. 5,000. Five new chapels have been built and dedicated at an average cost of Rs. 1,000 each.

"(3) The membership has increased by 38 per cent. In 1901 we had 1,521 communicants; at the close of last year we had 2,100. Nine hundred and thirty have been received into full membership on confession of their faith, a large proportion of them from Sivaite families. Most of our converts come from our boarding schools for girls and boys. The number of adherents has increased but slightly.

"(4) The contributions from purely native sources in 1891 were Rs. 7,063·97; in 1901 Rs. 10,213·73, or a gain of 44 per cent. This does not include about Rs. 1,000 raised for the Students' Foreign Missionary Society and the Women's Foreign Missionary Society, which would raise the percentage considerably. The position of the pastor is better financially than 10 years ago. At that time only about Rs. 5,000 went to to the support of the pastorate; last year Rs. 7,641 was contributed for this purpose. The amount raised for the Native Evangelical Society (Home Missionary) has increased, but not so much proportionately.

"(5) Two new Societies have been started in the past three years. One is called the 'Students Foreign Missionary Society' and has for its field of operation the Tondi District in South India. The other is the 'Women's Foreign Missionary Society' and for the present they are working in connection with the Student Mission. The raising of funds for these two infant organizations has not in the least lessened the contributions for the home work.

"IV. Educational Work.—(1) The number of our village schools remain about the same, though the number of pupils has increased by 20 per cent We have 135 schools with 10,500 pupils. Of these six are English with over 800 pupils, the remaining being purely vernacular. Of the 324 teachers in the 135 village schools, over three-fourths are Christian. In all the higher institutions the teachers are all Christian, and only boarders are taken as pupils. The College gets no Government grant nor does the Girls' English School. The two Girls' Boarding and the two Training Schools earned Rs. 5,417 of Government grant in 1901. The tuition fees collected from all these schools amounted to about Rs. 9,800.

"The Industrial School earned Rs. 1,779 during the year, mainly from carpentry and printing.

"Our schools are becoming more and more a force for good. A large proportion of our annual gain of church membership comes from our Boarding Schools for boys and girls.

"(2) Divinity School.—No new class in Theology has been taken since the one started in 1891 for a three years' course, but arrangements are being made to start one in 1902, and we hope that a few candidates may be enrolled every other year, at least during the next decade. Perhaps the most discouraging feature of our whole work lies in the fact that so few are coming forward for the work of the Ministry.

"V. Medical Work.—Great progress has been made in the past ten years. In 1891 we were just reviving our medical work after having been without a Medical Missionary for 18 years. A commodious building was put up at Manipay as a General Hospital at a cost of nearly Rs. 20,000. A Medical Missionary (his wife also an M.D.) was sent out from America, and an efficient staff of native helpers employed. A few nurses were also trained. The receipts the last year from fees were Rs. 1,160 and from sales of medicines, dressings, &c., Rs. 3,750. A hospital for women and children was started two or three miles distant, and buildings put up at a cost of overs Rs. 60,000 including the land. Two Lady Doctors, one from Scotland and one from America, took charge in 1899, and it has been well patronised ever since. The past year the receipts from fees were Rs. 1,675 and from medicines, &c.. Rs. 3,175. A nurses' class was started, and it is hoped that every year from now on some may be sent out qualified to do nursing in the homes of the people. Two branch dispensaries are maintained at the extremes of our field, and are doing good work."

One important matter is that Mr. Hastings shows "communicants" 2,100, very nearly equal to the total number of adherents—2446—given in the Census. It is quite evident from this that in the case of the American Missions and probably in that of other Protestant Missions in Ceylon—many non-communicating adherents or attendants in public worship did not return themselves as such.

S. P. G. MISSION.

We next come to the Anglican Society for the Propagation of the Gospel whose agents first came to Ceylon in 1840, though not till 1845, when the first Bishop of Colombo arrived was the Mission specially fostered. It has been the peculiar care of the four successive Bishops, and especially of Dr. Copleston (now Metropolitan of Calcutta), who, notwithstanding a reduction in the grants from England in the ten years from £1,600 to £700, has nevertheless maintained the work of the various stations, at some of which much good has been done. On the whole Mission, however, there is no evidence of an advance against heathenism; but rather of fewer adherents. To account for this, the Rev. M. J. Burrows, Hony. Secretary S. P. G., Ceylon, reporting from Buona Vista Mission in the Southern Province in November, 1900, makes remarks which are more or less applicable to the whole of Buddhist Ceylon, comprising three-fifths of the population :—

"The Congregation at Buona Vista is but very small. Some of the members have gone away and are doing well as Christians elsewhere. Some have fallen back into Buddhism. But the few there are, are, on the whole, exemplary in their lives, and keen in their interest in their church. Considering how poor they are, they subscribe, I think, liberally for church purposes, and some of those who have left the station continue to send help from time to time.

"It would naturally be expected that new converts would be regularly added to our number. But this is the case to a very small extent. The whole character of Buddhism has changed during the last few years. Whereas some time ago the mass of the people knew nothing of Buddhism and had for their religion little more than devil-worship, Buddhism is now a *popular force* opposed to Christianity. It is taught in schools which vie with our own, and are like them supported by Government Grants. It takes care to familiarize its adherents with all the stock objections to Christianity. By its institution of 'pan-sil' it continually presents to its disciples an elevated morality, requiring them to observe these five precepts—not to kill, not to steal, not to lie, not to be impure, not to drink

The Ceylon Census of 1901.

strong drinks. It upholds outward acts of benevolence and easy religious duties as so many ways of acquiring merit. It appeals to men's pride representing man's own efforts as sufficient without any help from God. And finally it is supported by the tradition of the past and the strong feeling of conservatism and attachment to ancient customs by which the Sinhalese are peculiarly animated: they are now from a kind of patriotism setting themselves in many ways against Western fashions, and reverting in dress and manners to ancient usages.

"Such in brief outline is popular Buddhism among the intelligent people of these thriving and populous districts. It is not to be expected that under such circumstances conversions would be many, particularly when the example set by Christians, both European and Natives, often is so little better (and not seldom worse) than that of the Buddhists themselves."

Mr. Burrows then adds what is certainly not correct for other districts—some close by—considering the advance made by the Wesleyan and Church Missions:—

"The scriptural phrase 'a door is opened' cannot in my opinion be applied to this part of the Island: rather having been opened in the past, it is now shut. But I imagine that it is none the less needful to maintain at its highest efficiency all that can be done for the strengthening of those already within the fold, and gathering others one by one as opportunity offers, although it may be a question whether this is the district in which it is wise to spend money on schools for heathen children."

We now give the Statistics of the Missions whose seven stations are confined to the Eastern (Batticaloa), the Western (Dandugama, Kurana, and Galkissa), and the Southern (Matara, Tangalla, Buona Vista, and Galle) Provinces—presuming that the figures for 1891 not being available we give those for 1896:—

	1896.	1901.
Stations	7	7
Villages	17	17
European Clergy (some Pastors of English Churches)	5	5
Native Clergy	7	4
Churches and Chapels	—	12
Catechists and Readers	—	10
Baptised Persons	2,205	2,094
Communicants and Catechumens	682	429
Native Contributions	—	Rs. 1,565
Schools of all kinds	29	29
Masters and Mistresses	96	78
Pupils—Boys and Girls	2,798	2,612

MINOR MISSIONS.

We now come to certain Minor Missions. The Presbyterians have no regular Mission in Ceylon, but Wolfendahl Dutch Reformed Church has begun some good work in this direction through Catechists, and counts 283 native adherents.

Ceylon in 1903.

The Friends commenced an interesting Mission in the Matale District—largely industrial—in 1896 under Mr. and Mrs. Malcomson, whose hands have lately been strengthened by three more Missionaries, Mr. Long and Mr. & Mrs. Annet.

The following Statistics have been placed at our disposal :—

FRIENDS' MISSION IN CEYLON.

Statistics for 1901.

Native Helpers.

Preachers, male	4
Teachers, „	10
„ female	6
Other native helpers	3
Voluntary helpers	6
Total	29

CHURCH STATISTICS.

Regular indoor meetings	12
Adherents about	78
Average attendance	225
Sunday Schools	13
„ membership	324

EDUCATIONAL STATISTICS.

Schools	15
Total pupils under instruction	569

MEDICAL STATISTICS.

Dispensaries	1
Out-patients	1,764
Visits to patients	2,320

The Mission was begun in 1896. It now has three male and one female European Missionaries, and one female European Missionary in England.

SALVATION ARMY.

The Salvation Army began work in Ceylon with a great flourish of trumpets in 1883; and Commissioner Tucker and his wife paid several visits during which he promised us faithfully, there should be no interference with other Protestant Missions—a promise by no means kept by his followers. Latterly, however, the Mission has been much more quietly carried on, and some good work has been done in Colombo by a Prison and Rescue Brigade. For such work the Army's Agents are, as a rule, much better fitted than for evangelistic or teaching work in the vernacular. Strangely enough, although Colombo is the headquarters, the Census shows but a small number of professing " Salvationists " in town :—13 men and 8 females, European, are doubtless nearly all Agents. The adherents include 33 Burghers or Eurasians ; 44 Tamils ; 1 Moorman ; and 212 Low-country Sinhalese, against 697 Kandyan Sinhalese and 3 others—in all 518 males and 493 females—so that the large majority are Kandyans, we fear in villages first occupied by the Church Mission near the foot of the hills. The Army figures, in their latest report, differ a good deal from the Census, as may be seen from the following extract :—" The present strength of the Ceylon territory is about 2,000, of whom about 125 are officers (men and women) with 40 stations. There are also 30 village schools and two village banks."

The Ceylon Census of 1901.

HENARATGODA MISSION.

The Henaratgoda (Faith) Mission, 18 miles from Colombo, was established by the Rev. J. Gelson Gregson and his daughter, the late Mrs. Liesching, about eight or nine years ago ; and a second agency has been opened at Katugastota near Kandy. There are five or six European Lady-workers and they are assisted by one or two Eurasian helpers.

INDEPENDENT CATHOLICS.

We cannot make any account of the 1,718 "Independent Catholics reported in the Ceylon Census ; for, save in rebelling against the Pope's authority, on the old Goa cause of quarrel, they do not differ from other Roman Catholics, and are destined, we should say, to re-enter the Pope's body of adherents.

BIBLE AND CHRISTIAN LITERATURE SOCIETIES.

Finally we come to the two great literary Auxiliaries of Missions, the Bible Society and the Christian Literature Society. They are both doing a most important and widespread work in Ceylon, and from the indefatigable Secretary, Mr. Gracie, we have the following brief summary of Statistics :—

"During the last 10 years the *Ceylon Christian Literature and Religious Tract Society* has *printed 3,738,235* copies of publications, and it has effected a *circulation* of *3,775,549* copies."

"It has eight depôts throughout the Island and employs five Colporteurs."

BIBLE SOCIETY.

Circulation of Scriptures in South Ceylon during last ten years.

	Bibles.	New Tests.	Portions.
English	10,330	3,574	19,590
Sinhalese	5,037	6,991	91,762
Tamil	2,809	2,012	38,062
Portuguese	—	165	—
Other European and Indian languages	245	404	1,046
Total	18,421	13,146	150,460

Total circulation : 182,027 copies.

The Colombo Auxiliary of the Bible Society at present employs 19 Bible-women and 3 Colporteurs.

The above figures do not include those for Jaffna and Kandy Auxiliaries which we quote from the latest Home Report as follows :—

Kandy Auxiliary Bible Society : Circulation 1901-02 :—English, 596 ; Sinhalese, 2,856 ; Tamil, 1,056.

Jaffna Auxiliary Bible Society :—English, 861 ; Tamil, 12,176.

Conclusion.

In conclusion we have to say that the course of our present inquiry has convinced us that the number of nominal adherents to the Protestant division of Christianity is inadequately given in the Ceylon Census of 1901, owing to the indifference and ignorance of many of the natives, and to omission of the Missionaries and Ministers to warn or advise their people beforehand, as the Roman Catholic Bishops and priests did very zealously. The inadequacy of the Census is clearly demonstrated by the case of the Congregationalists (American Mission) in the Jaffna Peninsula who, counting nominal adherents, must number a total considerably above the Census figures. But at best the total of Protestant Christians is comparatively poor, and does not indicate much gain from heathenism (always excepting one or two leading Missions) during the decade. Much preparatory work in sowing the seed, by evangelical preaching and opening schools, has been done in some of the most densely ignorant and darkest districts in the Island. Where Buddhism is strongest, there is invariably found the largest population of illiterate people, although it was the special duty of the Buddhist monks to teach the boys of every village at a "temple" school. Where their temples are endowed with land, they have utterly neglected this duty, as a rule, for generations, and otherwise offered a bad example in many cases to the people.

Several interesting and successful experiments with Industrial Schools have been made in Ceylon, and flourishing institutions of this kind now exist.

Much has been done in promoting self-support and a spirit of co-operation and love of evangelical work among the existing native churches. Education has made great strides; but more has to be done in elementary vernacular teaching to get at the masses. The ladies have taken a more prominent part than in any previous decade in medical, hospital, nursing, as well as educational, zenana, and direct evangelistic work.

Perhaps the most unfailingly satisfactory and successful branch of Mission work has been found in the Boarding Schools for girls as well as for boys; but especially for the girls. If a Christian philanthrophist were to stipulate that his wealth had to be devoted solely to that branch of Mission operations which had been found to give the most uniformly satisfactory results, we fancy the vote of the Missionaries, as of Christian laymen, in Ceylon, would go by a large majority in favour of Girls Boarding Schools.

APPENDIX IV.

OLD AND NEW COLOMBO.

(*By J. Ferguson.*)

Thursday, November 23, 1899; SIR THOMAS SUTHERLAND, G.C.M.G., LL.D., M.P., in the chair.

INTRODUCTORY.

THE following paper was suggested by one on "Calcutta," read before this Society on 1st June last, by Sir Charles Cecil Stevens, K.C.S.I.; but on that occasion it was especially the Port and Trade of Calcutta, with reference to successive improvements in the navigation of the Hugli that was dealt with; while, in the case of Ceylon, my object is to present you with a rapid sketch of the founding of Colombo on the sea-coast, and of its history under the Sinhalese, the Portuguese, and Dutch, and then to treat more in detail its rise under the British Government to be the commercial and political capital of the island, and, later still, its claim to be the great steamer calling and coaling port between Asia and Australasia, with one of the most convenient and commodious of artificial harbours in the world. Incidentally, I will endeavour, however, poorly, to present you with a word-picture of one of the most beautiful and interesting of tropical cities, with its people—their social life, industries, and trade—representative of nearly every Eastern land, and offering in the native bazaars an ever-varying scene of marvellous kaleidoscopic effect.

"Old Colombo"—with the history of the town from its foundation to its occupation by the British in 1796—might well form the subject of a paper in itself. But I must content myself with a very brief outline, and first of all would mention that the rocky headland, forming a small shallow harbour, was the *Jovis Extremum*, or Cape of Jupiter, of Ptolemy. According to old Sinhalese authorities *Kolamba* means a port of call for vessels, and there we have the origin of the name, and not in fanciful modern derivations, one of which actually connected this far Eastern port with the name of the great Genoese navigator and discoverer of America, Columbus. The first authentic notice of the town seems to be by the Mohammedan traveller, Ibn Batuta, who visited the island about 1346. He writes:—" We started for the city of Ķolambú, one of the finest and largest cities of the island of Serendib. It is the residence of the Wazir, Lord of the Sea, Jâlasti, who has with him about 500 Habshis (Abyssinians)." By an old Chinese writer the port is spoken of as Kao-lang-wu or Ko-ling-lo.

THE PORTUGUESE ERA.

Strangely enough, in view of what we are told of the town as described in 1346, when the Portuguese arrived in 1505 or 1506 they seem to have found at Colombo no more than a few huts covered with cadjans or dry plaited cocoanut leaves, the Sinhalese King at the time having his residence at Cotta, some miles inland. In occupying Colombo, with its natural advantages for the shelter, during a great part of the year, of the small vessels of those days, the Portuguese at first erected a few buildings for trading purposes, a store for cinnamon, a residence for their factor, &c.; and it was not till 1518 that they constructed a fort which, however, was dismantled, for some reason unknown, a few years later, and then the Portuguese made their headquarters at Cotta, the Sinhalese monarch having formed an alliance and come under their protection. This alliance was very displeasing to the majority of the native chiefs and people, and war broke out, forcing the Portuguese once more to fortify Colombo. One story told is that from the scarcity of lime, shiploads of shells of pearl oysters were transferred from Aripo, to be made into mortar for the fort walls. The warlike Sinhalese king—Raja Sinha or Lion King—besieged Colombo in 1563-4, and fortifications must then have existed; but these were greatly extended later on, for the account of the long but ineffectual siege of 1585-7, by the same monarch, with 50,000 men and 2,000 elephants, shows that the walls (mounting upwards of 200 guns) extended as far as they did when the Dutch besieged the town 70 years later. Several churches, convents, and monasteries had been built, and there was a Chamber with aldermen, and names were given to various suburbs now included in the town. Building outside the fort commenced some years later, and by 1613, we are told by one writer that the houses were getting near to the Kelani river, the present northern boundary of the city. I will attempt no further description of Colombo in Portuguese times; but will allow you to gather some idea from the plans which will be shown you on the screen later on. But I may mention that the trade of Colombo, in the time of the Portuguese, scarcely repaid them for the expenditure required for its protection in the almost continuous wars with the Sinhalese and their allies, the Moormen—or Arab descendants—who bitterly resented the advent of Europeans to take away viâ the Cape of Good Hope, the trade they had so long controlled

Old and New Colombo.

by way of the Red Sea and Persian Gulf, with overland caravans. Conquering and administering the maritime provinces, the Portuguese Captain-General of Colombo, took the title of King of Malwane, and strictly prohibited trade to every other nation, even to the Sinhalese. Royal monopolies were formed of cinnamon, pepper, and musk, while cardamoms, sugar, and ebony, arecanuts, elephants, ivory, gems, pearls, and some silk, tree cotton, and tobacco were included in the exports. Vessels came for these commodities from Persia, Arabia Bengal, and China, as well as from Europe or the Cape.

THE DUTCH ERA.

Meantime, towards the end of the 16th century the Dutch had formed a trading " company for distant lands," and soon after the first flee started round the Cape for the East. On 30th May, 1602, the first Dutch ship seen in Ceylon anchored off Batticaloa on the east coast, and the admiral in command entered into an alliance with the Kandyan King and this had momentous consequences for the Portuguese, eventually leading to their expulsion from the island which their monarch had said he "would rather lose all India than imperil." The conflict between the two European powers for supremacy in Ceylon commenced in 1638, and culminated with the great siege of Colombo nineteen years later. Very elaborate accounts of this siege, lasting from October, 1655, till 12th May, 1656, are extant ; but I must only mention that the Portuguese offered a most determined, strenuous defence, and although assisted by the Kandyan king with an army of 40,000 men, the Dutch lost their General, 3,000 men killed, besides the wounded, and were reduced to the last strait before victory was attained. Of the Portuguese and native soldiers in the Fort, numbering perhaps 1,500, only a small percentage survived to surrender. Upwards of 900 noble Portuguese families were, at the time of the siege, residing within the town, besides 1,500 families of those connected with the Courts of Justice, merchants and traders—some of these left with the remnant of the garrison for India ; many settled in Kandyan territory, especially at Ruanwella, under the auspices of the Sinhalese king, while the rest are represented by mixed descendants who use a *patois* of Portuguese in Colombo to the present day.

Refusing to give up their conquests, the Dutch found themselves in turn attacked by the native king, whom, however, they defeated and very soon became masters of the seaports and lowlands of Ceylon, doing their very utmost to develop trade and avoid war. Among other improvements due to the Dutch and which benefited Colombo, was the system of canals to the north and south of the capital ; while cultivation in cinnamon, pepper, coffee, and cocoanuts was encouraged. A new fort was built at the capital after a substantial and scientific plan by Cohorn, and the Dutch were determined to retain what they deemed the gem of their Eastern possessions. Just as the Portuguese burnt all the cinnamon for which there was no sale at the end of each season, the Dutch made it a crime punishable by death for any native to harvest bark or cut down a cinnamon bush even in his own garden, so strict was their monopoly, and they esteemed the cinnamon growing between Colombo and Negombo as the best in the world; while they encouraged trade from the Government stores—no private trading being allowed—with all parts of the East as well as Holland. If time and space permitted, an interesting picture might be sketched of the settlement and life of the Hollanders—the officials and citizens or burghers—in Colombo for the last 100 years of their occupation; of their public spirit in respect of canals and in founding churches and some schools; but also of their harsh treatment of the natives, thousands of whom they kept as slaves, and of their selfishness and extortion in respect of trade. Notwithstanding the great value which they attached to their possessions, it is amusing to read in the account of a Belgian physician, who resided 18 months in Ceylon in 1687-89, that in his estimation the whole island (save for its cinnamon) was not worth as much as an ordinary village in Brabant or Flanders; the fruits not worth describing; the cattle so thin as scarcely to be eatable; while the harvest of fish for a year was not worth as much as the fish, that came into the market of Antwerp on a single Friday. The Kelani River, north of Colombo, he regarded as about half as broad as the Scheldt at Antwerp. He described Colombo as divided between an old town and a new one or castle or fort. The old town was an oblong quadrangle 1,000 by 700 spaces, divided by three streets both ways, so the city was made up of 12 squares or cubes. But I must content myself with showing you, later on, plans of Colombo in the times of the Dutch, by the help of the lantern.

COLOMBO IN 1796.

On 16th February, 1796, the Dutch Governor surrendered Colombo to the British, who took possession in the name of William of Orange Holland being at the time in the hands of the French.

In "Walsh's Military Reminiscences" there is a description worth quoting of the town at the time of its capitulation to the British :—

Colombo, the capital of the Dutch in Ceylon, is a place of considerable consequence and strength from its natural position, as well as from its works, which were numerous and in good condition. The fort, which is extensive, contained many capital dwelling-houses, including the Governor's palace, which is a most superb building. The Pettah had also several good houses, churches, &c., in it; and in the place, altogether, were many respectable inhabitants. Without a chance of relief it would have been madness to have [held out; and by an early capitulation private property was preserved. Colombo is also a place of great traffic by sea, the roadstead being extremely safe and commodious, particularly during the north-eastern monsoons.

On the surrender of Colombo, many of the principal Dutch inhabitants left for Batavia; but the clergy, judicial officers, and the bulk of subordinates employed in the different departments continued at their posts; and their descendants are found in Colombo to this day in the majority of our lawyers, physicians and teachers, and of the Government clerks, a most worthy body of public servants. The dominion of the Dutch had lasted about the same time as that of the Portuguese, namely, 140 years: the latter left their mark in the very considerable number of Roman Catholics among the natives, to whom high-sounding names were given in Baptism; while the chief inheritance from Holland was the code of Roman Dutch law.

EARLY BRITISH RULE.

For some years the change to British rule made little difference to Colombo; indeed, up to 1815, when the Kandyan kingdom was formally annexed, the island was expected to be given back to Holland; but in that year it was finally decided to retain Ceylon and to give the much larger and richer Java in exchange to the Dutch. With the advent of Sir Edward Barnes as Governor in 1824 a new era of activity began, through the opening of the island by military roads, the construction of a bridge of boats over the Kelani River and the starting of the first mail coach in Asia between Colombo and Kandy. Sir Edward also built at a cost of £30,000, a palatial residence for himself at Mount Lavinia, on an eminence jutting into the sea, seven miles from Colombo, and here and in the neighbourhood some strange episode occurred in those early days when Ceylon was a mere military dependency. On one occasion, in the adjacent cinnamon gardens, the Chief Justice and Major-General commanding in the island exchanged pistol shots in a duel about a trifling difference of opinion; and many other stirring experiences are related in the autobiography of the late Major Skinner, the great road-maker of Ceylon, who served the colony in the most admirable way for over 40 years. In the time of Governor Sir Robert Wilmot Horton, 1832-37, Moormen and Tamils were allowed for the first time to own house property in the Pettah and Fort of Colombo, a privilege which the Dutch would never grant. The first Savings' Bank, Royal Academy or College, and the Legislative Council with unofficial members date from the same time, as also the establishment of the Press and of the Indian rupee currency. Steps were taken by Governor Stewart Mackenzie for the complete abolition of slavery, and this was finally consummated in 1845; although the name of "Slave Island" still adheres to the peninsular division of Colombo in the midst of the lake, because there the Dutch kept their slaves—an arrangement due to the fact that one night the slaves of a certain Dutch household in the Fort rose and murdered the whole family. After that, all the slaves in the Fort, after the day's work was done, were collected in punts and rowed out into what was nearly an island and there kept under guard until the time came to return and engage in their daily toil. A description of Colombo in the Thirties comes to us in verse from the pen of a military officer, Captain Anderson, who wrote "Wanderings in Ceylon":—

> "Hence, let the eye a circuit take,
> Where gently sloping to the lake,
> A smiling, lively scene appears,
> A verdant isle, its bosom rears,
> With many a lovely villa grac'd,
> Amid embow'ring cocos plac'd!
> Here once, to all but int'rest blind,
> The Colonists their slaves confin'd ;
> But now the name alone remains.
> Gone are the scourges, racks, and chains!
> When Britain sought the eastern world,
> And her victorious flag unfurl'd,
> She came to heal, and not to bruise,
> The captive's fetters to unloose ;
> And 'tis her brightest boast and fame,
> That nought is left beyond the name
> Yet here the African remains,
> Though broken are his slavish chains,
> Prepar'd to conquer or to die
> For her who made his fetters fly.
> As soldier of a free-born state,
> He feels his dignity and weight;
> And with alacrity and zeal,
> The sable warrior learns to wheel,
> But view him at the set of sun,
> His military duties done,
> His native glee will then be seen
> In antic frolics on the green!

Old and New Colombo.

> See him with sparkling eyes advance
> To tread his own Mandingo dance,
> And view his smiling jetty bride,
> In cadence moving by his side;
> Then own no joys the soul can move,
> Like those of liberty and love!"

The "Africans" referred to were Kaffirs inported to work as pioneers on the roads, which the Sinhalese were too lazy to do, after the *rajakariya*, or forced labour, imposed on them by their own rulers, and by the two preceding European Powers, was abolished under the more civilized and benign administration of the British. Kaffir descendants are still to be noted among the many races and nationalities—some 70 in all—comprised in the population of Colombo.

I have said that the colony was a mere military dependency for many years: five or six infantry regiments,, with artillery, Royal Engineers, and even a troop of cavalry being maintained at the expense of the Imperial Government up to the Forties—so that Colombo, as the headquarters of a Lieut.-General and Staff and of most of the troops, was a lively place from a military point of view. When such regiments as the 90th (Perthshire) Light Infantry, with its band playing reminiscences of "The Lass o' Gowrie"—

> "'Twas on a simmer's afternoon,
> A wee before the sun gaed doon
> My lassie wi' her braw new gown
> Cam' o'er the hills to Gowrie"—

were paraded with the 18th Royal Irish, its music reiterating this inquiry—

> "Oh, say were you ever at Donnybrook fair?
> An Irishman all in his glory was there,
> With his sprig of shillelagh and shamrock so green!"—

and the 95th, or Ceylon Rifles, band giving "British Grenadiers,"—Colombo had a large and lively garrison. But from a commercial and trading point of view the town was then very insignificant. We date the practical beginning of the coffee planting enterprise in Ceylon from 1837, although Governor Barnes and Geo. Bird had started plantations 13 years earlier; and I have often heard my relative and predecessor in the *Ceylon Observer*—the late A. M. Ferguson—say how depressing was the sight of Colombo. roadstead when he entered it with Governor Stewart Mackenzie in November, 1837, with only one or two of Messrs. Tindall's barques of 400 to 500 tons representing the tonnage for imports from and exports to Europe, the wharves silent and almost lifeless, and a general appearance of do-nothingness about the place. The planting industry wrought a wondrous change, for in 40 years the coffee exports rose from 30,000 to 1,000,000 cwt. per annum, and steamers as well as sailing ships were required to carry the trade even before the opening of the Suez Canal introduced so complete a revolution in our Eastern shipping experience. I may mention here that the export of tea has now attained a heavier net weight, in 125 million pounds, than ever coffee reached ; while Ceylon products exported, which represented a shipping tonnage of 120,431 in 1888, had risen by 1897 to 245,830 tons, and must altogether require a freight of about 280,000 tons. Of this, tea makes up about 46 per cent. and the produce of the coconut palm about 41 per cent.

COLOMBO FORTY YEARS AGO.

But now, having touched on Colombo as seen in the Thirties and Forties, the years of a big garrison, small trade, and the start of a planting, I must show what it was like in the Fifties after our great Governor Sir Henry Ward gave so great an impetus to roads, bridges, and irrigation works through Major Skinner's department, and through Captain (afterwards General) Gosset, R. E., multiplied land surveys and sales, while he further started the great railway between Colombo and Kandy. I have had two pictures presented to me in writing, one by an official, the present Master Attendant of Colombo (Capt. Donnan), who has lived to see the breakwater which he first advocated for that port in 1864 completed ; and the other from a planting friend, Mr. Wade Jenkins. Both landed in Colombo over 40 years ago. Capt. Donnan says he found in 1858 about a dozen sailing vessels from 300 to 1,000 tons at anchor in the outer roads, and perhaps a dozen or more native craft in the inner roadstead, and it seemed to him shipping operations were carried on safely and with some expedition ; but he changed his mind when the monsoon set in. To Mr. Jenkins, in 1857, Colombo seemed a busy but truly oriental city, the Europeans few and far between ; while coaches and sailing ships were in evidence where railways and steamers now prevail. There was but one hotel and one boarding-house (and those insignificant) in the place ; but mercantile hospitality made up for this deficiency, and indeed the whole of the little European civil community seemed to regard each other very much as one family, and newcomers—generally arriving round the Cape, which was the almost invariable route for ladies and children, with a voyage of 85 to 105 days—were heartily welcomed as dear friends from the homeland. Such was my own experience on landing in Ceylon in November, 1861 ; but it was my good fortune to voyage

Old and New Colombo.

out, not by the Cape, but by the P. and O. steamer *Pera*, under Commodore Jameson, from Southampton to Alexandria, to spend some days in Cairo before the European era, when that town truly represented the "Arabian Nights;" and to voyage from Suez to Point de Galle in the same Company's *Simla*, which often gave us a London mail even in those far-off days in 18 or 19 days. I found the mail coach journey from Galle to Colombo one of special and continuous interest, being never out of sight of a wayside hut or coconut palm for the whole lengeth of 72 miles; while the naked native children, sitting on mother earth and clapping their sides as we galloped by, seemed the perfection of contentment with little, nay with absolutely nothing, save the banana they longed to pluck from the plant overshadowing them. I found the road near Colombo crowded with native pedestrians, with hackeries—tiny gigs drawn by small Sinhalese bullocks with deer-like legs and feet—or with the larger bandies drawn each by a pair of large Indian bullocks. There were a few carriages as we got to the city, many being of the old palankin shape, but seldom occupied by any save pale-faced Europeans, and the respectful attitude of the natives as these passed by was remarkable. Here, again, the last thirty years has wrought a marked change; there are as many horses and carriages used in Colombo now by wealthy natives as by colonists, and the rule of "Jack is as good as his master" is almost too freely illustrated as the hackeries of Sinhalese dash by and race, and even pass, the equipages of Europeans, of the respectable Dutch descendants, and of their own wealthy brethren. In 1861 we drove through Colpetty, the fashionable southern suburb, and across Galle Face, the maidan of Colombo, where all Society of an afternoon "eat the air," and ride on soft turf, drive on the smooth gravelled road, or promenade on the unequalled seaside walk constructed by order of Sir Henry Ward in the interests of the ladies and children of Colombo. Driving over a drawbridge across the moat, and passing through a heavy gateway with ponderous iron-studded doors guarded by a military sentry, the coach entered the old Dutch fort, built nearly 200 years earlier, and drove along a street shaded by rows of light green hibiscus trees with tulip-like flowers, merchants' offices and military quarters facing each other, while right in front was the campanile tower, built by Governor Ward to serve the double object of a clock-tower and lighthouse and still advantageously used for the same purpose, although nearly everything else is much changed in the Fort Ward of Colombo. On the other hand the Pettah, or native town, with its rows of one-storey shops and bazaars, stands much the same, with certain exceptions to be noted hereafter while, in 1861, the principal bungalows lay along the Colpetty, Slave Island, and Mutwal roads the Cinnamon Gardens, or New Colombo, being as yet unbuilt on.

Modern Colombo.

The first great change in modern Colombo took place in 1869 when Governor Sir Hercules Robinson got authority to demolish Cohorn's fortifications, obsolete as they were for purposes of defence, and requiring 6,000 men properly to man them. The levelling of the walls and filling up of the moat made the Fort much more accessible and healthy, an important matter since here all the banks and nearly all the mercantile offices, big retail stores, and Government offices, as well as some of the principal hotels, are found. Facing the sea, on the site of the old wall, military barracks were erected, and this handsome range of buildings, in an unequalled position for fresh air, is among the finest barracks for British troops in all the east. The military married quarters and hospital were at the same time erected on the side of Galle Face, and altogether these buildings added much to the appearance of the western side of the city. The disbandment of the local rifle regiment followed, most of the Malays and Sepoys being, however, drafted with their consent into a newly-constituted police force, and very much under their old officers. New banks and mercantile offices of two stories now became the rule in the Fort, the landlords and builders being chiefly wealthy natives, only too ready to invest their capital in big houses when assured of adequate rent. The old Oriental Bank, under its able and veteran manager, Mr. George Smyttan Duff (still alive and I suppose the *doyen*, as well as about the most successful of eastern bankers), first led the way with a massive block of buildings. This is now occupied by the Hongkong and Shanghai and Chartered Banks; while we have besides in the Fort suitable and handsomely located branches of the Mercantile Bank and Bank of Madras, and more lately, though it has become almost our leading office, of the National Bank of India. This brings me to the later building developments within the Fort in the rise and expansion of the Grand Oriental Hotel and Wharf and Warehouse Company, of the Bristol Hotel, of a number of fine mercantile and public offices— notably our new General Post Office—and last of all the Victoria Arcade erected under the auspices of the Fort Land Company, which the present Governor has happily called the Fort Improvement Company, and in whose block, among others, the agency of the Peninsular and Oriental Company finds a fitting office. The lower portion (as in the case of the Grand Oriental Hotel) is fitted up for shops, principally dealers in the gems and curios for which Ceylon is famous,

Old and New Colombo.

and the Victoria Arcade affords a nice place of rest and shelter to passengers or other visitors, while the first floor is occupied by offices, and above are residential flats, a new feature in Colombo. This modern block of building is a great improvement on the old godowns, and offers a pleasing indication of enterprise to fresh arrivals, as do also the new offices of the National Bank of India, to be followed by handsome stores and offices for our greatest importing house (Cargills, Limited), and further on the handsome block now being erected for Mr. Davis of Melbourne.

But I must also refer to the rise of "a new Colombo" in that portion of the city known as Cinnamon Gardens, and which was all covered with cinnamon bushes from Turret road eastwards within my time. With wise prescience the Government first laid out an extensive park and flower gardens, and then sold the surrounding land for building purposes. Here, then within the past thirty years has sprung up a large number of residential bungalows in what is a favourite division of the town, intersected by delightful gravelled roads called after successive British governors. The most prominent building, and perhaps the most stately, with the finest site in the island, is the Colombo Museum, which we owe to the æsthetic taste and progressive spirit of Governor Sir Wm. Gregory, Mr. J. G. Smither being the very competent architect ; just as Mr. Tomalin designed the new General Post Office, perhaps our next most imposing public edifice. At the farther end of the Cinnamon Gardens division, a Lunatic Asylum has been erected on a somewhat cumbrous plan ; and in another direction will be found the group of buildings comprising the extensive Civil Hospital of Colombo in all its divisions, and the Medical Schools, much being due to private munificence, more particularly of the philanthropic Sinhalese De Soyza family, whose head first came into prominence through his splendid entertainment to H.R.H. the Duke of Edinburgh in 1870 at his Bambalapitiya residence, since known as Alfred House. Time would fail me to remark on all the noteworthy edifices and institutions in the capital of Ceylon ; but mention must be made of the grand old Wolfendalh Church, crowning an eminence overlooking the native town, and erected in 1746 for the Reformed Dutch Presbyterians. It is a massive building, and contains the graves of many of the Dutch Governors, whose names and arms are carved on the stone floor, or hung on the walls. Governor Gregory took a special interest in this structure, and presented some artistic windows to it. Then there is the Anglican Cathedral and College at Mutwal ; St. Lucia's Roman Catholic Cathedral, and the several churches and chaples, mosques and temples, educational colleges and high schools in different parts of the town, belonging to the different religious bodies, as well as the colleges and schools of the Government. Then the town hall and market buildings should not be forgotten, any more than the public hall, with its fittings for concerts or theatricals. The law courts and several departmental offices are worthy of attention.

I have alluded to the Victoria Park, and it is satisfactory to know that in other parts of the town provision has been made for open spaces and recreation grounds,—the Campbell Gardens, the extensive Havelock racecourse, the golfing, hockey, and cricket grounds, the racquet court and Galle Face esplanade being prominent. The successful hold which the English game of cricket has taken on all classes of Ceylonese is sure to strike the visitor, who may see brown-skinned, bare-backed, and bare-headed Sinhalese urchins playing the game as well as they can under their cocoanut palms with a branch of the tree, stripped and cut to make a bat, while the ball is of coir fibre, and the wickets, &c., are equally improvised after the simplest fashion. On the other hand, the Colombo Colts Cricket Club, composed of burghers and native young men, have achieved a name for themselves right over the island and beyond its limits, by defeating teams of young Englishmen, many of them fresh from leading public schools. Another sight worth mentioning as showing the great advance of the people of Colombo, apart from the colonists, is thus referred to in a contribution before me:—

Only the other day an immense throng was gathered on the Galle Face, behind the modern club house, to witness the Colombo inter-Collegiate Cricket Match, hundreds of fine equipages clustered about the enclosure, gaily and fashionably-dressed ladies and their husbands, brothers and sons filled the seats, and a big crowd encircled the ground all round.—*with not a single European amongst them all.*"

LOCAL INDUSTRIES.

I must now refer to some of the industries specially associated with Colombo, and more particularly to those in native hands as of most general interest. But first let me say that in the height of the coffee-growing enterprise, 20,000 men, women, and children (chiefly Sinhalese and Tamils) found employment in the large factories and stores of the merchants scattered over the town, where the coffee was cleaned, prepared, sorted, and packed for shipment. Tea, on the contrary, is prepared and packed on the estates; but there is a considerable amount of work still done in the Colombo stores, in sorting, blending, and repacking such teas as are sold at the local public sales; also in dealing with cacao, cardamoms, cinchona bark, and the remnant still

COFFEE STORES AND "BURBACUES" (DRYING GROUNDS).

A COCONUT CLIMBER.

Old and New Colombo.

left of coffee. Of greater interest will be found a visit in the proper season to a cinnamon store (such as that of Lady de Soyza) where the ingenious scraping, peeling, drying, and quilling of the bark can be witnessed, all done very cleverly, though simply, by the special Chalia caste of cinnamon peelers. Cinnamon may be said to be the oldest of all exports from Ceylon ; for no doubt it was included in the spices traded for by the Arabs, who brought gold, silver, ivory, peacocks, and apes (all found in Ceylon) to Solomon ; while in the time of Augustus, Ceylon cinnamon was sold in Rome at the equivalent of £8 a pound weight, and so down through the centuries when Venice and Genoa commanded Eastern trade, followed by Portugal, Holland, and Britain, until now the finest of our cinnamon can be got for less than 2s. a lb. Then we have in Colombo, some very extensive cocoanut oil mills, with hydraulic power, and fibre machinery, and mills for desiccated cocoanut—all well worth a visit.

PLUMBAGO.

Next in interest, perhaps, are our Gems ; but first I will take the one mineral of commercial importance, namely, graphite or Plumbago. It may not be generally known that Ceylon is the chief source of supply for this form of crystallised carbon, allied not simply to petroleum, peat, and coal, but also to amber and the diamond. It is so largely used in these modern days for the manufacture of metal-melting crucibles, especially in England and the United States, that the supply has not been equal to the demand, and the price has lately trebled, although our export is enormously increasing, so bringing wealth to a large number of Sinhalese, and exciting much interest as to the best means of extending the mining industry. One Ceylon estate proprietor, recently deceased (Mr. C. Tottenham) brought out a Cornish mining engineer to develop a mine on his land, and this has been done with success, both in an engineering and financial point of view, and now several large capitalists are beginning to turn their attention to Ceylon plumbago mines. One leading Sinhalese owner of mines (Mr. de Mel) confessed some 15 years ago that one plumbago mine had given him a net return of £2,000 a year for 11 years. The export is at present steadily increasing ; and a very interesting sight in Colombo is to visit plumbago stores, where large numbers of women and children are employed picking out all foreign substances—such as pieces of ironstone—from the plumbago, and grading it according to quality before it is packed for shipment. The Ceylon trade in plumbago was first opened about 70 years ago, but by 1860 the total export was under 50,000 cwt., while last year (1898) it was 473,075 cwt.; and up to

October 31st of the current year, 528,986 cwt. had been shipped—indicating an export of over 600,000 cwt. for 1899, while the value has risen from £25 to £75 per ton for the best quality. 1,692 plumbago mines and pits were reported in the island in 1898, and 412 "gem-quarries." The most complete account of the plumbago industry is contained in a monograph by my relative, the late A. M. Ferguson ; but it is impossible to do justice to the mineral resources of the Island in this and other respects until we have a Geological and Mineralogical Survey of Ceylon—an undertaking I have long been pressing for—and which I am glad to think is, at last, about to be secured by our present energetic Governor. I believe it is no secret that the geological staff at present employed by Lord Cromer in Egypt is, in a few months, to be transferred to Ceylon ; and so we may look forward not only to the wealth of the island in plumbago being approximately defined, but also to the settlement of long-vexed questions in reference to the existence of gold in paying quantities, of ironstone of a wonderfully pure character, and of the various precious stones so long associated with the island.

GEMS.

Ceylon rubies, sapphires, catseyes, and other precious gems which, with all their brilliancy, are simply crystallised clays), have been famous from time immemorial, and an industry is maintained in digging for the same up to the present time, in which some thousands of natives find a more or less precarious means of existence. The result of their labours cannot be tested, for most of the gems found, are privately sold and either transmitted by Colombo dealers to jewellers in London or Paris, or sold to the agents of Indian rajas and other purchasers. Almost the first experience of passengers and visitors as steamers anchor in Colombo, or on the boats, wharves, or if not, on each side of the first avenue entered, is to be accosted with " Buy one ring," or " one very fine saffire, sar," or it may be a ruby or other stone :

> " And as engirdled figures crave
> Heed to thy bosom's glittering store,
> We see Aladdin in his cave,
> We follow Sinbad on the shore."

The shops of numerous native dealers are full of such gems, as well as of jewellery, carved ivory, tortoiseshell, and other work ; but the origin of a good many of the stones and rings may be traced to Birmingham ; and in Governor Gregory's "Autobiography," several experiences are specifically related which may be taken as fairly illustrating a not uncommon experience ; indeed, few residents in, or visitors to Ceylon, do not know of the ring with "stone" offered at £50, £20, £10, or £5, and eventually sold as a bargain (because a piece of glass) at a rupee or less! Still there can be no doubt that valuable gems have been found in Ceylon from time immemorial. Many Eastern nations knew Lanka of old to be the land of the hyacinth and ruby. The name "Ratnapura" (the capital of the gemming country) means the "town of gems ;" and not unfrequently now an exceptionally fine ruby, sapphire, emerald, topaz, catseye, or large piece of Alexandrite fresh from the Ratnapura or Matara district, is placed on show in Colombo by its native owner. Europeans have tried to develop this industry ; experts like Mr. Barrington Brown have reported favourably of the hidden riches ; but the difficulty has always been to prevent the clever appropriation of gems when found in the clay by the native workmen, who can pick them up with their toes, conceal them in their hair or swallow them. To check this, an ingenious machine working on the principle of the specific gravity of precious stones and metals has been invented by Mr. W. S. Lockhart, M. Inst. C.E. (who had experience to guide him in the Burma ruby mines), and a "Ceylon Prospecting Syndicate" sent out a set of this machinery capable of dealing with 50 tons of gravel a day. The patent machine worked admirably, and many gems were the result ; but owing to the pits not being sunk deep enough to get to the gem-clay, the return so far has not proved a financial success, although I am glad to learn that with increased capital the company is likely to go to work on a larger scale, and develop what I feel sure ought to be a very profitable industry. Good gems such as are found in Ceylon are at this moment in great demand in London and Paris, and I cannot see why with such reliable and advantageous machinery financial success should not be achieved so soon as the lower beds are struck Mr. Lockhart will exhibit a diagram of his patent on the screen later on, and although I have no personal connection with the enterprise, I feel it right to refer to an invention that may have important result, for Ceylon (and other countries), not only as regards precious stones, but also precious metals, especially gold where found in the alluvial.

Whether the geologists will be able to widen the gem-yielding area— at present confined to two districts, Ratnapura, or Rakwana and Matara—remains to be seen. Sir Samuel Baker some years before his death paid a visit to Ceylon—with which his name as sportsman, agriculturist, and author was closely related 50 years ago—in connection, I believe, with gem or gold exploration ; but nothing came of it.

Gem-digging, like gambling, has great attractions for the Sinhales and probably 50,000 of them altogether find employment in connection with plumbago mining and gem-digging ; while the old industry of smelting with charcoal the iron ore found in many parts of the country has almost entirely died out. It is possible, however, that if any large quantities of this ore (with from 70 per cent. upwards of pure metal) were found on the banks of a navigable stream, it would pay, with cheap freight, to transport it to Europe, so adding to the trade of Colombo. No coal, not even in the form of anthracite—long supposed to be present—has been found in Ceylon.

Pearls.

Before passing away from Ceylon gems, familar to the ancient Greeks and Romans, as well as to the Hindus and Chinese, I must refer to another allied precious product derived from the pearl oyster fisheries of the Gulf of Mannar. Known and famous from very early times, the native kings had for one of their titles, "Master of the Fisheries of Pearl." When titles were being sought for the sons of H. R. H. the Prince of Wales (some 25 years ago) I remember suggesting that Eastern cities should not be forgotten, that the then second son, now the Duke of York, might well be made Duke of Bombay, Colombo, or Calcutta, or Prince of Kandy. My suggestion was copied into the London *Times* ; but in the following week *Punch* improved on it by showing that Prince George at his then age would probably prefer to be " Prince of Sugar-candy ! " The existence of pearl fisheries for generations off the coast, and the absence of limestone in the low-lying country of Ceylon, was evidenced, as already mentioned by the Portuguese when they built the first Fort of Colombo early in the 16th century, carrying many shiploads of pearl shells from Arippu to burn them for lime to use as mortar. There are no records of results in Portuguese times ; but the Dutch frequently had good fisheries for several successive years, alternating with as many annual blanks. Thus in the four years, 1747-50, the Dutch netted pearls to the value of £130,000. Then in the first four years of our occupation, 1796-00 the British got a revenue of no less than £342,000. After that, fisheries fell off grievously till 1814, which gave £105,000, and then a comparative blank till 1828, when four years yielded £120,000 ; the years, 1833 to 1837, gave £108,000 ; but then came a long interval with no fishery till 1855, since when the richest returns were £51,000 in 1863, £60,000 in 1881, £80,000 in 1888, and over £96,000 in 1891. For eight years now there has been no fishery.° Altogether the British Government has secured from this welcome source of revenue, this "harvest of the seas," no less than the equivalent of £1,000,000 sterling after deducting all expenses. The accounts have been kept very carefully for 60 years during which 345,000,000 of oysters were fished, two-thirds of which were sold by auction for Government, the rest going to the divers, the average price being £2. 10s. per 1,000 ; one year, in 1860, the price rose to nearly £13 (again, in 1857, falling to 16s.) according to the size of the pearls found, a perfectly round pearl of large size and silky white lustre being greatly valued by Indian rajas, who would pay up to £200 for such a one. Pearl oysters are of mature age in the sixth year ; but they often die off then, so that fisheries have to be fixed for the fourth or fifth year to make sure of the harvest, the information being obtained by annual inspections with native divers on the banks where the oysters locate and breed. Several Governors of Ceylon have taken a special interest in trying to guard against the many enemies to which the pearl oyster is liable ; and Sir Hercules Robinson (afterwards Lord Rosmead) had out a trained naturalist who during several years wrote interesting reports on the results of his investigation, but failed to suggest anything practicable by which we might guard against adverse currents sweeping of the oyster beds, or shoals of voracious skates which sometimes devour the young oysters by millions ; and to such or similar causes, the present veteran inspector of our pearl banks (Capt. Donnan) attributes the fact that there has been no pearl fishery since 1891, and that there is no prospect at present of one for some years to come. But considering all that science and practical skill have done in the breeding of the edible oyster off the British, French, and Italian coasts, and of the increased knowledge of ocean currents and marine zoology generally within the past twenty years, I think the time has come for a fresh scientific inquiry into the Pearl Oyster Fisheries of the Gulf of Mannar, by calling in the most competent naturalists and experts available. In this inquiry the Indian might well join with the Ceylon Government, because the former owns certain banks in the proximity of Tuticorin which occasionally yield a fishery.

SILVERSMITHS.

Pearls, like gems, give occupation to a separate caste of the Sinhalese—the silversmiths, after whom a special street in the native town is called—and a large number continue to manufacture jewellery,

---

* Since then, there has been a fishery in March, 1903, yielding a total of 44,000,000 oysters, the Government share of which realised £55,152 at Rs. 15 to the £.

there being some 500 "silversmiths' workshops" in the Western Province. Operations are carried on in a very simple way, so far as tools are concerned, and generally as they were 1,500 or 2,000 years ago. Tamils or Moormen, as well as Sinhalese now engage in the occupation. Gems are often badly cut by the natives, and their mounting is also not secure. A great deal of tortoise-shell work is found in the bazaars, as also carvings in ivory, ebony, &c., and there is a widespread trade in local pottery; while the shops with locally-made furniture should be visited, and Mr. Don Carolis especially has made a name not only in Ceylon, but in India, Australia, and even in London, for some of his cabinet work An annual Art Exhibition in Colombo affords some encouragement to local talent, not only in painting, but in photographing, designing, and in art metal work. The native lace of the Sinhalese women should be mentioned; it is freely offered for sale to passengers and visitors, and some is both good and cheap; while purchasers have the satisfaction of encouraging many industrious villagers, most of whom owe their training to mission schools.

POPULATION.

Before dealing with industries, I should have specified the details of the population of Colombo. At the beginning of the century the estimate was that the town held 30,000 to 50,000 people. The first regular census, that of 1871, gave a total of 95,000 including 2,500 for the military and the stations in the harbour; 1881 gave 112,000; 1891 made it 128,000; and it is with good reason supposed that the population now equals 150,000, including Tamil immigrants from Southern India Every Eastern race will be found represented, and the native streets and bazaars present a most striking picture as the effeminate Sinhalese men with their long black hair tied in a knot surrounded by a comb—the women of the human race—are contrasted with the darker, sturdier Tamils, all the fat Nattucotta Chetties, or still more with the big stalwart Moormen—many of them veritable father Abrahams or Ishmaelites; while one or two Chinese, some Kaffirs, Afghans, Bengalis, and a sprinkling of the paler and richer Parsees of Bombay, add further variety.

SANITATION, &C.

As regards the amenities of the city, it cannot yet be said to be altogether well lighted, although gas introduced 20 years ago (chiefly through the efforts of Sir John Grinlinton) with incandescent lamps, and even electric lighting of recent times in the Fort hotels, clubs, &c. have made a great improvement. Colombo is a town of magnificent distances, and it difficult to overtake its requirements fully in light.

COLOMBO: PETTAH ACROSS LAKE.

RAILWAY TERMINUS APPROACH, COLOMBO.

ing. More important is a good supply of pure water, and this was brought to us by Mr. Bateman and his lieutenant, Mr. Burnett, by a scheme which tapped a hilly region, specially reserved, some 30 miles off. The piping is now being duplicated so as to make the supply adequate for all requirements; but Bombay in its experience of plague, the germs of which revel in a damp soil, has taught us the danger of an Eastern town becoming water-logged through provision by means of adequate drainage, not being made to take away the waste or surplus water supply. Colombo—in the flat portion of its Pettah, or native town, especially—stands much in need of systematic drainage, and the present Governor has had a survey, report, and estimate from a leading London sanitary authority, Mr. James Mansergh, M.Inst.C.E., on which, we trust, action may ere long be taken. The disposal of sewage by burning and burying is effectually carried out, and sanitation is as well attended to as it can be in a tropical town without systematic drainage, and with a people, many of whom do not understand that "cleanliness is next to godliness."

Time would fail me to speak of social progress among the people, of what the different Christian Missions with their schools have done to educate and uplift them—English being freely spoken and read by the natives in Colombo—or, again, of the drawbacks in the multiplied sale of arrack and other intoxicating drinks, and of opium which; so far as Ceylon is concerned, ought to be confined as in England to icensed apothecaries. Steps are being taken to mitigate these evils.

RAILWAYS AND TRAMWAYS.

I now come to what the railway has done for Colombo. The grand mountain line to the interior, to Kandy, Matale, Nawalapitiya, Dimbula, and Uva, has concentrated the vast bulk of the planting traffic on the capital; and the new line about to be made to the north of Jaffna must still most centralize trade, especially in imports and exports. Sir Wm. Gregory carried a seaside line (extended by Sir Arthur Gordon to Galle and Matara), so as to traverse a considerable portion of the city, and in seven to nine stations from Maradana, through Pettah, Slave Island, and Kollupitiya, to serve a teeming town and suburban population as effectually as do the metropolitan underground lines. This is now to be supplemented by a line through Cotta (a district that feeds Colombo with working people, fruit, &c.), to the Kelani Valley tea district, and I maintain that the Government should lose no time in carrying this new 2½-ft. line through the city to the north and on to Negombo (if not to Chilaw and Puttalam), so as to serve a dense population, a large number of whom is continually on the move between the Pettah, Mattakkuliya, Ja-ela, Negombo, &c.

Through the enterprise of Messrs. Boustead Bros., their home supporters and engineers, Colombo has had for sometime now a system of electric tramways at work on certain roads in the town, and so far they have done well and in every way given satisfaction. Altogether the double line of tramways laid in Colombo cover two routes of 3¼ miles each on the 3½-feet gauge. The cars are neat and convenient and are well patronized, the people taking readily to this mode of locomotion, stimulated by the low fares charged. Considering that only two routes in the city are so far served, it is remarkable that a maximum of 25,000 passengers a day has been attained out of a total population of 150,000. [*]

COLOMBO HARBOUR WORKS.

I have now to deal with the most important public undertaking in connection with Colombo, namely, the breakwater and other works, which are going to make it one of the most commodious and convenient artifical harbours in the world. I need not refer to the steps or

---

[*] The following more explicit facts respecting the Colombo Electric Tramways and Lighting may be given :—(1) Two routes, each 3¼ miles of double line, out of a proposed five routes converging from all parts of the town to a point within the Fort of Colombo, are already in operation. (2) The traffic is quite abnormal, and the present rolling stock has proved quite insufficient to carry the passengers wishing to ride. About 15,000 a day are now travelling in ten to twelve cars, which ply from 6 A.M. to 10 P.M. The rolling stock will shortly be doubled. (3) The gauge is 3 ft. 6 in. (4) The power-house contains three units, one of 225 and two of 150 kilometres: a fourth unit of 300 kilometres is now being added. (5) A large and rapidly-increasing lighting business is being worked from the power-house through a small sub-station within the Fort of Colombo. A feature of this business is a considerable day load caused by the use of slow speed oar-bladed fans, which have entirely superseded the punkah. Arc lamps are now being erected along the main tramway routes, and alternating plant is being put down at the Power Station to serve the Galle Face Hotel, the Club, and the various residential portions of Colombo. When the remaining routes are opened to traffic a possible goods business developed along the tramway routes, and the lighting mains extended throughout Colombo, the undertaking will be far the largest and most complete thing of its kind in the East.

Old and New Colombo.

reports which led Governor Sir Hercules Robinson finally to determine on, and Sir William Gregory to carry out, a breakwater at Colombo on the designs of the late Sir John Coode and executed under his direction by Mr. John Kyle. The foundation stone was very auspiciously laid by H. R. H. The Prince of Wales during his visit to the East in 1875. This grand wall, 4,212 feet long, took ten years, and an outlay of £705,000 to complete. It changed an open roadstead into a harbour completely sheltered on the most exposed or south-west side; but there was still liability in certain months to storms from the north-west and north-east, and after much local discussion the Government at length decided to go on, and with Mr. J. H. Bostock, resident engineer, Messrs. Coode, Son, and Matthews are now carrying out two additional arms : (1) a north-east breakwater from the Mutwal shore to be 1,000 feet long ; and (2) an intermediate or north-west breakwater, 2,200 feet long, leaving two openings—800 feet between it and the south-east arm and another of 700 feet between the central and the north-east arms. These two additional arms, with lighthouses and connected works of land reclamation, coaling depôts, and other conveniences, are estimated to cost £527,000, the value of the work executed to the end of last year being £166,000. These works were commenced in April, 1894, and the firm estimated for completion in eight years, so that if nothing unforeseen occurs this extended harbour should be available for use in 1902.

Still more—apart from a patent slip, costing £33,000, now being made—a first class graving dock has been sanctioned by Mr. Chamberlain for Colombo, half the cost (of £318,000) being borne by the Admiralty, on condition of Her Majesty's ships of war having a special claim to attention. Governor Sir West Ridgeway cut the first sod of this work on the 1st of March last with some ceremony, and the engineer, Mr. Matthews, as representing his firm, stated on that occasion : " The dock will be the largest of its kind in the Eastern Seas. It will be 600 feet in length on the floor, 113 feet in width between copings, and 63 feet at the bottom. Its entrance will be 85 feet in width, while it will have a depth of 32 feet over the sill at high water and 30 feet at low water of ordinary tides. To facilitate ingress and egress, a guide pier 700 feet in length will be formed on the north side of the entrance channel. It is estimated that this work will occupy about five years."

By 1903 or the beginning of 1904 the Colombo Harbour Works, costing from first to last not much less than £2,000,000, may be expected to be complete ; and with the convenience of a first class graving dock, as well as safe and commodious harbour, it is possible that the Admiralty may consider the prudence of removing the naval headquarters from Trincomalee to Colombo. Be that as it may, there will be no want of steamers to occupy the harbour. Already as many as 15 to 20 large ocean-going steamers (five or six of them being often Peninsular and Oriental Company's mail steamers) have been counted at anchor in one day, and the tendency is steadily to increase as the central position of Colombo as a calling and coaling port—apart from local trade—is more and more realized. When the breakwaters are completed the harbour will have an area of about 640 acres or one square mile, and will thus exceed the great National Harbour at Dover (now being made from designs by the same eminent firm of engineers), if the area of the " commercial harbour " already made be excluded. The depth of water inside the Colombo harbour will range to as much as 40 feet, and provision will be made for mooring to buoys quite 30 large ocean-going steamers.

The entrance to the dock will be made specially convenient, and there are to be separate coaling depôts for the Admiralty and for commercial purposes, while all the chief steamer companies or their agents will have their own coal stores. The justification for all this outlay on the part of Colombo is found, first, in the determination of the great British mail steamer company represented by our Chairman to shift its place of call from Point de Galle to Colombo ; nearly all other steamer companies—mail or commercial—trading with Eastern or Australasia doing the same. Then there is the splendidly-central position of Colombo, with reference not only to India and Australasia, but also in regard to the Southern and Eastern Africa, the Straits, Eastern Archipelago, and China. Then there is the marvellous exemption of the port (and indeed the whole island) from the hurricanes which periodically devastate Mauritius ; from the destructive cyclones which sometimes range in the Bay of Bengal, but have never come farther south than the north of Ceylon ; and thirdly, from the earthquakes and volcanic eruptions which disturb Java and and other islands of the Eastern Archipelago. Verily there was some reason for the first Mohammedan voyagers deciding that Ceylon must have been the home of Adam and Eve, and they accordingly proceeded to name the most prominent mountain Adam's Peak, and the coral reef between the island and India, Adam's Bridge ! So heartily did Arabi and his fellow Egyptian exiles share this belief, that they at first treated their banishment to Ceylon with great satisfaction, and have certainly been as well off there as they would have been anywhere else in the world.

Old and New Colombo.

I have a few figures here to show the advance of the Port of Colombo, beginning with the period 1835 to 1861 when steamers were practically unknown in its waters :—

SHIPPING ARRIVALS AT COLOMBO.

Year.	Ships.	Barks.	Brigs or Schooners.
1835	25	17	9
1845	25	32	13
1857	56	127	75
1861	82	90	131

The tonnage of the 303 vessels in 1861 could not exceed 100,000, against a return now of some 3,000 vessels arriving, representing over 3,000,000 tons. The total tonnage for the port of Colombo in and out was 500,000 in 1870 just after the opening of the Suez Canal ; it reached 1,400,000 tons in 1880, was over 4,000,000 tons for 1890, and is now in excess of 6,000,000 tons a year. Apart from the ready and economical freight thus provided to nearly all parts of the world for the exports of this island, as many as 25,000 passengers call at Colombo in the year, some for a few hours, others for a day or two, while the practice of spending a week or two or a month in the island is becoming common, and the day is approaching when Ceylon should rival Egypt as a place of winter resort. Already it is becoming a place of holiday resort for residents in many Indian towns and stations at Rangoon and Singapore. In this connection it may be mentioned that Colombo has three first-class hotels, the finest in the East, besides that at Mount Lavinia, seven miles out, where there is a favourite marine hotel with good sea bathing. Then, if Colombo is thought too hot to stay in long, Kandy 1,650 feet above sea-level (where the nights are comparatively cool) has two good hotels, besides boarding-houses. Hatton at 4,000 feet has an Adam's Peak Hotel, and the sanatarium, Nuwara Eliya, at 6,200 feet, has also first class hotel accommodation.

COLOMBO THE PORT FOR SOUTHERN INDIA.

Returning to the harbour it is evident to anyone who will study the map [not reproduced] and note the absence of any good harbour on the Indian Malabar Coast up to Bombay and on the Coromandel side, save what is afforded at Madras, that Colombo is destined to become the chief port for Southern India. Already passengers find it convenient to come there, assured they can find large steamers for the West, East, or South, and when railway communication—now extending to Paumben in India, and shortly, no doubt, to Mannar in Ceylon (as well as

North of Jaffna) is united—as united it must be one day—across Adam's Bridge, and by the islands of Mannar and Rameswaram, we may expect produce and imports, as well as passengers, to pass to and from Colombo. I have already dealt with this subject in a paper read a few years ago before the London Chamber of Commerce, and afterwards at the Imperial Institute, and so need say no more now, than that two eminent engineers, having examined the route, have pronounced it feasible ; and that if the military and strategic, as well as commercial, interests of the Indian and Imperial, as well as the Ceylon, Governments are fairly considered, the financial problem ought not to be insoluble. As a preparation for that day, I hold that the Ceylon authorities, as guided by the Colonial Office, ought to aim at a less restricted and more liberal policy in regard to Custom's tariff and dues at Colombo. The free port of Singapore, with its marvellous prosperity, is the example that should be aimed at, and when the cadastral survey of Ceylon begun by Governor Ridgeway is complete, fiscal changes leading to a notable reform in the interests of the port of Colombo and of an Indo-Ceylon railway, ought to be practicable.

IRONWORKS AND FOUNDRIES.

In connection with the harbour I must not omit to notice the prominent and useful part taken by the Colombo Ironworks, covering three acres and located close to the inner harbour, and the great service rendered there in the past, in cases of disabled steamers, broken screw shafts or blades, or other casualties. The spirited proprietors, Messrs. Walker, Sons & Co., Limited, have provided a complete set of salvage gear ; but steamers are so well built now and so well engineered, that there are seldom serious breakdowns, and the heavy work of the firm is connected with the planting enterprises, not only of Ceylon but Southern India, the Straits, Java, and even more distant parts of the world for tea, coffee, cacao and coconut oil machinery. Altogether about 1,000 Ceylonese find employment in these works, supervised by some 30 European engineers ; and no fewer than 200 steamers a year are served, the majority only requiring attention in light jobs. The same firm manages a steamer service round the island, which gives the outposts of Ceylon communication every week with Colombo. It has also promoted a Ceylon Brick and Tile Company which is now manufacturing bricks in the neighbourhood of Colombo of special excellence. There are other foundries and factories doing useful work in Colombo and employing larger numbers of natives, notably those of the Railway and Public Works, Messrs. Cave's, Hutson's, Colombo Commercial, and Eastern Produce and Estates'

Old and New Colombo.

Companies, &c.; but the Colombo Ironworks established the first foundry and is by far the largest. A solitary Cotton Spinning and Weaving Mill has not been a success so far, though in the hands of enterprising Parsees, it has now entered on a new career, I trust of prosperity of in every way. Colombo is the scene of great activity in printing, publishing, and newspaper offices, chiefly in English, but also in the vernacular, an indication of the rapid spread of education. It is generally credited with publishing the most complete statistical handbook and directory of any Colony of the British Empire; while five daily English journals indicate greater enterprise than is found, even in Bombay, Calcutta, or any other town in the East. In this connection our Buddhist fellow-subjects show considerable emulation, both in educating and publishing, and it is a great pity that the people were not some years ago given a voice in regard to the disposal of Buddhist temporalities or endowments, which might do much to promote the vernacular, industrial, and technical instruction of the masses. I ought to say something about the Military Defences of Colombo, but that is a thorny subject. There are several batteries, and there can be no doubt of the importance of adequately protecting this great coaling and trading station; but although much money has been spent, a good deal has gone on what are now admitted to be blunders, such as the fortifications which broke up the amenities of the Galle Face esplanade to no useful end. We can only trust that the latest batteries designed will meet with the full approval of our best military authorities. Here I should mention how useful the battalion of infantry stationed in Ceylon has proved in reference to military necessities elsewhere. The 37th regiment was sent from Ceylon at short notice to Calcutta for the Indian Mutiny; the Ceylon Rifles to Labuan, Hongkong, and the Straits; the 50th to New Zealand for the Maori War in 1863; the 57th and Dublin Fusiliers to South Africa; and Sir West Ridgeway has offered Mr. Chamberlain the Highland Light Infantry, now in Ceylon, to go to Durban from Colombo at any time,—our native poulation being most peaceable.

Visitors arriving in Colombo.

It only remains to indicate in a few words what is most likely to impress a stranger arriving in Colombo. First, I never tire of quoting the pithy sentence with which Sir Emerson Tennent, the great historian of Ceylon, opens the first volume of his fascinating work. "Ceylon," he says most truly, "from whatever direction it is approached, unfolds a scene of loveliness and grandeur unsurpassed, if

Ceylon in 1903.

it be rivalled, by any land in the universe." Under favourable circumstances the towering and majestic cone of Adam's Peak, over 7,000 feet above sea level and the subsidiary range of purple hills, should be noted as the coast is approached at break of day. The coral reef encircling a great part of the island is indicated by the snowy foam as the swell of the Indian Ocean breaks upon it. Anon, Colombo harbour is entered, and the rows of palms belting the shore to north and south divide attention with the evidences—in tower and spire rising above dense vegetation—of a considerable city, still more emphasised by the abundant shipping and lively scenes within the breakwater. Acquaintance is made with the curious outrigger canoes of Ceylon—so often confounded by writers with the catamarans of India—as safe as many lifeboats and manned by almost nude humanity. Ashore, a kaleidoscopic scene of the many races already indicated as constituting the population, with every possible variety of skin and dress, arrests the traveller; nor are modes of conveyance less varied from the jinricksha (man-power carriage of the Japanese) introduced some 15 years ago and multiplied in thousands to the old-fashioned gharry or light American wagon with its ample cover from the sun. A visit to the Pettah and fruit market may be followed by a drive along the most delightful carriage roads in the world in the Cinnamon Gardens division of the city, while the wealth of vegetation in every direction makes one feel he is entering one vast botanic garden. The headquarters and boarding schools of several of the Christian Missions, and even a Buddhist College and Schools, deserve a visit ; also the Technical and Agricultural Colleges. Wherever the visitor travels over the ten square miles included in the municipality—for Colombo has its Mayor and Council board—there is novelty and variety in man and Nature awaiting him. In some parts he may find himself in a perfect labyrinth of shady avenues, or lanes and flowery dells, or lagoons. In another his conveyance will be climbing a steep street lined by old-world buildings of Portuguese or Dutch design, or again by the shutters and dead walls which indicate the seclusion of Hindus and Mohammedans in their family life. The seven miles drive through Colombo and beyond to Mount Lavinia, on the other hand, show the Sinhalese living almost in the open air, and their work and domestic duties may be watched in the open huts under their palms or plantains or jak fruit trees ; while frequently there is a mingling of fowls, pigs, pretty little hump-backed bullocks, and little brown-skinned children, which is bewildering. No one, I think, has ever seen Colombo (indeed, Ceylon) and said he was disappointed and unstirred in interest and curiosity.

THE BRITISH ASSOCIATION AND COLOMBO.

May I be permitted before I close to allude to a suggestion made during the recent session of the British Association at Dover, and received with a fair measure of approval by some of the *savants* and members assembled there? It is that the meeting of this body for 1903 or 1904 should take place at Colombo, Ceylon. At first sight "impossible" seems to be the word to apply to this proposal; but the more it is considered, the more possible I feel sure it will be considered to be. In the first place the British Association has been twice to Canada, and it is quite time some other division of the Empire was favoured with a visit. Cape Colony is out of the question for a few years to come; any of the Australian capitals is too far away; and Colombo, though not so important in some respects, is far more central than Bombay or Calcutta. Visitors to meet the Association might well be expected from all parts of India, from Burma, the Straits, and even China, as well as Australasia; and we may feel sure that the novelty and interest of a meeting in a tropical town, in the most beautiful island in the world, would attract a considerable gathering.

The town, and especially the island, would in themselves be full of interest to a large proportion of the *savants* of the Association. Ceylon, the pearl of the British Crown Colonies among the most beautiful of tropical islands, is a little less in size than Ireland, with a varied population of over 3,000,000 (some 70 races being in all represented). It has been described as a vast and most interesting botanical garden. The presence of a certain number of aborigines in the Veddahs at once makes it of special importance to the Anthropologist and Ethnologist; while our Sinhalese people in their history, their language, customs, and religion—Ceylon being the sacred land of Buddhism, and so regarded by Burmese and Siamese, as well as to some extent by Chinese—are full of interest to scientific men in many departments.

The island has been wonderfully opened up by first class roads and railways, including a mountain line rising 6,200 feet above sea level, which is among the finest in the world, and which saves much time in reaching the jungle homes (if such they may be called) of the Veddahs, who live by hunting. Then the railway, projected by our present Governor Sir West Ridgeway and sanctioned by Mr. Chamberlain, and which will be finished by 1903, will be of special interest to learned visitors inasmuch as it will connect Anuradhapura—the ancient capital of the Sinhalese—with Colombo, involving but a few hours' journey, and so make the far-famed "Buried Cities" of Ceylon with their dagobas, temples, and palaces easily accessible. Not only Anuradhapura, but Mihintale, the rock fortress of Sigiri, and the second ancient capital Pollonnaruwa, could be visited, and the results of the Archæological Survey, liberally promoted by the present Government of Ceylon, could be inspected and judged on the spot. For the Geologist, Ceylon, with its primary rocks and absence of fossils, may be less interesting: but as the scene of successful gem-digging for rubies, sapphires, &c · from time immemorial, and as the great source in these modern days, of graphite and plumbago—its one mineral of commercial importance—the island has an interest of its own ; and a geological survey about to be commenced under Governor Ridgeway's auspices ought to have some important and interesting results by 1903. . The fauna of the island are well worth attention, and the coral reefs around the island as well as the Maldives, are even now the subject of elaborate investigations at the competent hands of Mr. Stanley Gardiner ; while the pearl fishery of the Gulf of Mannar, in its history and successful operation, as well as enforced suspension for many years at a time, ought to furnish a subject for Zoological discussion of peculiar interest and practical value. For the Economist there is much to be noted in connection with native life and history, the system of public instruction in all its grades, the hospitals and asylums, as well as in the ancient and modern cultivation of cinnamon and palms, especially the coconut and palmirah ; and in the rise within British times of great flourishing industries in coffee, cinchona, tea, cacao, and rubber growing, maintained on a system of free labour and giving employment to some hundreds of thousands of Tamils from Southern India. Extensive operations in railway extension (including certain feeding lines on a very narrow gauge) just sanctioned by Mr. Chamberlain, and the grand breakwaters and graving dock now under construction at Colombo, should afford much of interest to the Mechanical Engineer, who could not also fail to appreciate the good work shown in many of our river bridges and roads. Competent authorities from India and other surrounding countries might be expected to attend with papers of much interest in several departments ; while there should be no lack of visitors from India and the Colonies, if not from Europe. Ceylon has now some of the finest hotels in the East, not simply in Colombo, but in Kandy, Hatton, Nuwara Eliya, and Galle. There would, I am sure, be abounding hospitality for the Association officials and other *savants* if a visit were arranged. The Government, which commands the railways and many other means of making a visit profitable and interesting, would, I am sure, feel any aid required to be a good investment, inasmuch as a Session of the British Association in Colombo would be a very valuable advertisement for the Colony, its attractions, industries, and resources. A large body of educated, intelligent, and loyal natives, both in Ceylon and India, could not fail to be specially interested in a visit of the British Association, and many would be ready to take a useful part in the proceedings, while all would rejoice in the means afforded by special lectures, papers, discussions, and excursions of adding to their knowledge and of meeting the leaders of the scientific world. Of course, there are difficulties, chiefly : (1) in the length and cost of the voyage to and from Europe ; and (2) in arranging for a suitable time of year. The best time for visiting Ceylon is between February and May, but it is not easy for British Association leaders, especially University workers, to leave at that time. For such August-September would be more suitable, and these are by no means unfavourable months in Colombo. The Red Sea passage in August is very hot, but with modern swift steamers the ordeal is a brief one and seldom trying on a first experience. There would be no chance of steamers being overcrowded at that season, and if a meeting of the British Association to Colombo were decided on, we have no doubt that the public-spirited Chairman of the Peninsular and Oriental Company and his fellow directors would offer every facility possible to make the meeting a success. In any case I must hope that many of my hearers may be able to visit the island that has been described as an Eden of the Eastern wave, and its capital, Colombo, among the most beautiful and most healthful of tropical and oriental cities.

We may now take the slides, and I would wish to acknowledge the courtesy and help given in respect of representations of the Harbour Works by Mr. W. Matthews, the Drainage area by Mr. Mansergh, and the Gemming operations by Mr. Lockhart, who each will explain these slides in a few words. I am also indebted for information to Mr. Donald Ferguson, Mr. Edmund Walker, and Mr. Boustead, while for the slides about to be shown I have to thank Mr. Martin Leake and the Ceylon Association, Mr. W. S. Bennett, and Mr. Jordan.

[The illustration of the City of Colombo is reduced from a plan lent by Mr. James Mansergh, V.P. Inst.C.E., and that of Colombo Harbour from one lent by Mr. W. Matthews, M.Inst.C.E.]

BIBLIOGRAPHY OF CEYLON AND COLOMBO.
Principal Writings on Ceylon at present (or shortly) available.

" Ceylon," by Sir J. Emerson Tennent, Kt., two volumes, illustrated (Longmans)—five editions—out of print—copies procured occasionally. (Apply A. M. & J. Ferguson, Colombo.)

" Ceylon : its attractions to Visitors and Settlers," by John Ferguson. ("Journal of the Royal Colonial Institute," No. 5, Session 1891-92—April, 1892.)

"One Hundred Years of British Rule in Ceylon," by L. B. Clarence, retired Judge of the Supreme Court of Ceylon. ("Journal of the Royal Colonial Institute," No. 5, April, 1896.)

"Murray's Handbook for India and Ceylon."

"Fifty Years in Ceylon : an autobiography of the late Major Skinner, C.M.G." (A. M. & J. Ferguson, "Observer" Office Colombo.)

"Two Happy Years in Ceylon" (illustrated), by Miss Gordon-Cumming. (Blackwood ; 1891.)

"Palms and Pearls, or Scenes in Ceylon" (illustrated), by Alan Walker. (R. Bentley & Son ; 1892.)

"Picturesque Ceylon." A series of volumes, profusely illustrated, by H. W. Cave, M.A. (H. W. Cave & Co., Colombo.)

"India, Ceylon, Straits Settlements, &c.," with two maps. (Kegan Paul, Trench, Trubner & Co., Ltd , London, 1899.)

"The International Geography," by 70 authors, with 488 illustrations ("Ceylon," by J. Ferguson). Edited by Hugh Robt. Mill, D.Sc. (London : Geo. Newnes, Limited, 1899.)

"Ceylon Handbook and Directory for 1898-99," by J Ferguson (A. M. & J. Ferguson, Colombo.)

"Guide to Colombo," by George Skeen, 1899, illustrated. (A. M. & J. Ferguson, Colombo).

"Guide to Kandy and Nuwara Eliya," also "Guide to the Buried Cities" (illustrated), by S. M. Burrows, M.A. (A. M. & J. Ferguson, Colombo).

"Manuals on the Cultivation and Preparation of Coffee, Tea, Cacao, Rubber-yielding Trees, Spices, Fibres, &c.," edited by J. Ferguson. (A. M. & J. Ferguson, Colombo)

"The Tropical Agriculturist for Planters" (published monthly), edited by J. Ferguson. (A. M. & J. Ferguson, Colombo.)

"Ceylon in 1900" (illustrated), by John Ferguson. Being a fifth edition of a popular history and guide to the island. (In the press.) (A. M. & J. Ferguson.)

Mr. W. MATTHEWS, M.Inst.C.E., remarked that after the very clear reference to the Harbour Works at Colombo given by Mr. Ferguson in his admirable paper, it would not be necessary for him to refer at any length to the works in question. He might, however, be permitted to point out that the necessity for extended harbour accommodation at Colombo was brought about by the following causes : (1) By the necessity for increasing the area of sheltered water, due to the great expansion of trade ; (2 the desirability of affording shelter during the north-east monsoon when choppy seas prevail, which were inconvenient to passengers in landing and embarking, and also in the conveyance of goods to and from ships and the shore; the crowded condition of the margin of the harbour and of the shore fringe thereof, at the southern end of the existing sheltered area, where traffic was only carried on amidst considerable congestion at the Custom-house premises. The necessity for increased warehouse accommodation in connection with the Custom-house departments entailed the removal of the existing coal depôts further north, and this could only be done by increasing the shelter. On these grounds, therefore, the additional sheltering works were authorized. The necessity for the Graving Dock arose from the fact that at present there is no dock suitable for berthing a warship of any magnitude between Malta and Hongkong and Malta and Australia respectively. Mr. Matthews showed some slides of the harbour works in progress, and explained the special features of each. He pointed out that during the south-west monsoon heavy ocean rollers strike the existing breakwater and throw up immense masses of spray, rising sometimes to a height of 100 feet. For six months in the year the sea beats continuously on this work, namely, from May to October when the south-west monsoon prevails. From October to May, the period of the north-east monsoon, smooth water is predominant at sea, but as above intimated, occasionally a wind wave is generated during the daytime which proves inconvenient to the carrying on of the business of the port. Mr. Matthews referred to the labour which is available for the carrying on of the works, which consists generally of Tamils imported from Southern India, who do most of the work corresponding with navy operations in England. The skilled work is generally performed by the Sinhalese who are good artisans. About 700 convicts are employed generally in quarry operations. A considerable proportion of these have been incarcerated for the use of the knife. With regard to diving operations, although sharks undoubtedly exist in these waters, no case has occurred during the twenty-five years since the commencement of the works, of a diver having been attacked.

Mr. WILLIAM S. LOCKHART, M.Inst.C.E., in explaining the series of views illustrating mining and washing for precious stones, said Mr. Ferguson had mentioned the various stones found in Ceylon. The most important of them, however, were the sapphires. There were sapphires of all colours, but the most beautiful—the cornflower blue—came from Ceylon. There were a great many other stones, all of value, and, next to the sapphires, rubies and cat's-eyes were the most important. They occurred in alluvial beds on the surface, from which the stones were obtained by open workings. Some also came from deeper-seated beds, consisting of the *débris* of decomposed rocks, but the workings might all be classed under the head of soft earth mining. The upper beds were worked open cast, and the deeper beds, none of which were more than 200 feet in depth, by timbered pits and stopes. The gravel was brought up to the surface, and there the question of theft, which had ever been a bar to the development of this industry, came in. After having been washed the gravel had to come to the picking table, and as picking and stealing seemed even more inseparable in Ceylon than elsewhere it was from these picking tables, when the mines were conducted under European management, that the best gems always disappeared. To illustrate how clever the workmen were in this direction, he must narrate an incident which occurred to a friend of his whom he met on a P. & O. Steamer. His friend had been to Ceylon ostensibly to shoot big game, but incidentally to pick up sapphires, and in the course of his wanderings had come across a mine worked by natives iunder European management. Having been shown round he fell nto conversation with the manager as to the skill of the native pickers, he raising the further question, as to whether they did not occasionally pass stones over. The manager took half-a-dozen small sapphires, put them into a basket with some gravel, and then called one of the men and told him to pick it over. He did so and his friend stood over him the whole time. In a quarter of an hour his task was completed, and the result was that no sapphires were found. The visitor turned round to the manager, with a suspicion of triumph in his eye, but the manager quietly said to the miner : " Now where are those stones ?" and he took them all six out of his mouth, so that he not only had not missed them, but had conveyed them into his mouth under the spectator's very eye. There were no serious difficulties in connection with the work, except theft. [A map of Ceylon having been thrown on the screen, he pointed out the position of what is known as the gem-district, and also others where gems and alluvial gold are found]. The next view was a photograph taken in an open cast gem mine worked under European management. The last slide showed a diagram of the machinery that had now been introduced to wash the gravel and secure the precious stones, or gold, without having recourse to the picking tables at all. The plant shown was the one Mr. Ferguson had mentioned. It was capable of washing about 50 tons of gravel per day, and was driven by a small 6 horse-power engine. The gravel was shot (as the diagram showed) into the first machine, which was called a "grizzley;" here the clay was scrubbed down and the large stones and rubbish ejected, and the portion containing the sapphires then passed on to a puddling machine, which washed out what was left of the clay and the fine sand. The remainder was gravel between 1-8th inch and 1 inch mesh, and this was carried up by an elevator to a classifier, which screened it into eight sizes, each of which then passed to one of eight separators. These separators were the essential part of the plant, and took the place of the picking tables. Their action was simple, and, by taking advantage of the slightly greater specific gravity of precious stones, these separators were able to select them from the valueless quartz and other materials of which the gravel was composed. The mine manager alone had access to the receivers into which the precious stones found their way, and as the total deposit was not greater than could be dealt with by the European staff, the services of the native picker were not required at all. The entire cost of treatment by this machinery was under 6d. per ton, and it was believed that it solved the problem of dealing successfully with alluvial deposits containing precious stones and gold. When more plants of this character were set to work it was to be hoped that gemming in Ceylon would become the important and profitable industry the well known extent of the gem-beds would seem to warrant.

DISCUSSION.

The CHAIRMAN said there was really very little time for discussion of this paper, but fortunately for him he was not called upon to discuss it. His simple duty was to propose a vote of thanks to Mr. Ferguson for the trouble he had taken. They would all agree, especially those who had been in Ceylon, that he had brought before them a picture, not of Colombo only, but of the beautiful Island of Ceylon, such as they had hardly realised. Some years ago a dramatic author wrote a letter to a newspaper saying his object in a certain play was to bring the scent of the hay-fields across the footlights, and those who had been in Ceylon must feel that Mr. Ferguson had been successful in bringing the scent of the cinnamon gardens into a lecture room in London. The story had so admirably told was a story of which Englishmen were thoroughly proud, a story of progress and prosperity—not by any means unalloyed prosperity—but prosperity on the whole, such as could be obtained by hard work and by employing those natural advantages which most of our colonies possessed in a greater or less degree. In reflecting on the subject it was gratifying to know that the progress which Mr. Ferguson had described in connection with Colombo and Ceylon was by no means confined to that Colony. From the Mediterranean to the furthest point of the East, including Egypt, which must almost be considered a Colony of Great Britian, India, Singapore, Hongkong, in every direction they found the same progress and prosperity as had been described in connection with Colombo, and they found also that. English spirit of loyalty prevailing throughout which made our Empire homogeneous, both in time of peace and in a time of war. He had intended to make a speech about Ceylon himself, but after listening to Mr. Ferguson he thought discretion would be the better part of valour. He had intended to go back much further than Mr. Ferguson, whose history belonged to a somewhat modern era, and to tell them something about the voyages of the Phœnicians to Ceylon in old times, because there he should have been on ground where no one could contradict him, because the history was not written. They were all familiar with the fact that gems were very numerous in Ceylon, and they would not doubt his statement when he assured them that, when the Queen of Sheba visited Solomon, she had a necklace made of cat's-eyes, and that Solomon amongst his numerous domestic circle had a very large collection of Ceylon sapphires. Whatsoever the facts of that history might be, of one thing they were confident, that the trade in gems and spices was about the most ancient in the world. The trade in spices was one in which ancient Egypt was peculiarly interested, while the trade in gems was one in which the whole world, male and female, but especially female, was interested. They knew that that admirable ancient character, the Emperor Nero, burned more cinnamon and cassia at his wife's funeral than had been imported into Rome throughout the whole year, but he was not sure whether that was a testimony to the virtues of the wife or to the satisfaction he felt in assisting at that ceromony. Turning to the graver matters which Mr. Ferguson had been discussing, he might concur unquestionably in the view he had expressed that the Colony of Ceylon had the greatest possible reason to be proud of that great work, the creation of the harbour of Colombo, and equally proud of her success in the wonderful trade in connection with tea. Those who visited Ceylon in the days before the break water was made could have no idea of what the appearance of a place like Colombo or Point de Galle was during the prevalence of the south-west monsoon. He himself was more familiar with Point de Galle at the time when the whole of the transhipment work in connection with the P. & O. steamers had to be carried on under circumstances of such extraordinary difficulty, owing to the weather which prevailed during the south-west monsoon, that he even now was filled with astonishment and wonder that it was carried on at all.

In connection with this point Mr. Ferguson had told them how unfortunately there had hitherto been no coal discovered in Ceylon, but he could assure him that if he would employ the engineer who made the breakwater to drain the harbour at Point de Galle, he would find there were a few million tons of coal which had been lost from the P. & O. steamers. If the work which had been explored was creditable, the history of the tea trade in connection with India and Ceylon partook almost of the nature of the marvellous. It was hardly more than 40 years since Robert Fortune was travelling in China collecting the plants to make the first beginning of tea cultivation in India, and now between India and Ceylon the actual development of the tea trade amounted to upwards of 260,000,000 lb., and very curiously he read only the other day in a letter that during the last year 1,000,000 lb. of Indian or Ceylon tea had actually been exported to China. Another point which he thoroughly appreciated was the desire that Colombo should become as far as possible a free port, because there was nothing more mischievous in the world than to lay taxes on shipping. He regretted to say that this broad statesmanlike principle was not so well recognised as it ought to be. If Governments were wise they would look at such great examples as Mr. Ferguson had alluded to in Singapore, and to the still greater example in Hongkong, where commerce in shipping was of gigantic proportions, and had been achieved wholly and solely byt he fact that the port was free from taxes and dues of every possible kind. He must also endorse the view which had been expressed as to the desirability, almost the necessity, that an Island so interesting as Ceylon should be much more widely known to the public than it was. The means of transit were safe, speedy, and economical, and if people would take into consideration how much profit the great section of the public which now spent its time and wasted its money on the Riviera every winter, more particularly at Monte Carlo, would derive from passing a similar length of time in Ceylon—that they could economize by travelling on anyone of the numerous lines of steamers that connected this country with that island, and there was no way of living so economical as on a steamship—if the public would only realise and carry out that idea as widely as possible they would benefit themselves to an enormous extent, and they would benefit Ceylon. Incidentally they might even do a little good to the P. & O. Company, but that was the last thing he thought of in connection with a great public interest of this kind. He desired to thoroughly endorse Mr. Ferguson's wish that the British public should be brought more into contact with that marvellous spirit of the East, which was so splendidly shown in Ceylon and which was at the same time so fascinating and so impossible to describe.

Sir JOHN GRINLINTON, in seconding the vote of thanks, said Mr. Ferguson had given them the result of more than thirty years' experience of Ceylon, and though he was there even before Mr. Ferguson it was impossible for him to add anything to what he had said. Mr. Ferguson had referred to the lighting of Colombo, and he must admit it had not been perfect, inasmuch as the municipal revenues had not, in the past, been large enough to admit of a greater number of lamps, but within the last ten days a telegram had been received saying that the municipality had arranged to increase the number of lamps, and they were to be of the incandescent type, so that the town would soon be lit much better than many large English cities. The great prosperity of Ceylon was attributable to the advent of the planter, to the work which had been done in coffee and tea, and to the effect of the admirable laws which existed under which everybody lived, European and native. The secret of the success of the British Empire throughout the world was the equity of its laws, and he was quite certain there was not a single native in Ceylon who would not as soon, or sooner, be tried by an English judge than by one of his own people.

The vote of thanks having been passed unanimously,

Mr. FERGUSON, in reply, expressed his gratification at the meeting being presided over by the Chairman and representative of a company whose name was a household word in England. The P. & O. Company, which started as the Oriental Company in the Mediterranean, had developed and enlarged its borders to an enormous extent, and, though there were other companies of a similar character, it still represented the British commerce and home life to those in the East in a way no other company could do.

Sir CHARLES KENNEDY, K.C.M.G., C.B., expressed on behalf of the Society his great satisfaction at the success of that inaugural meeting of the section. They had begun the meetings of that section in the most auspicious manner. They were pleased to have as a Chairman one who both personally and also as representative of that great company which it would be found when the history of these latter years came to be fully written had done very much to promote British im_ perial and commercial interests, and to promote the welfare and com_ fort of the large number of passengers who travelled by its steamers.

Sir HENRY TRUEMAN WOOD writes :—

" I was sorry that the length of the discussion on his paper prevented me from keeping my promise to Mr. Ferguson to say something

PART OF GALLE HARBOUR.

THE FALLS OF THE HOOLOOGANGA: KNUCKLES ROAD.

Old and New Colombo.

about his proposal that the British Association should be invited to meet in Ceylon. The suggestion is an important one and ought to be carefully considered, not only with reference to a meeting in Ceylon but with regard to the larger question of meetings of the Association outside the limits of the United Kingdom. Up to the present only two such meetings have been held—one at Montreal in 1884 and the other at Toronto in 1897. But there is, I think, no real reason why the work of the Association should not be extended over the whole of the Empire. Of course there are difficulties, but these will disappear. When it was proposed to hold a meeting in Canada, the idea was scouted as impracticable. It has since been found to be perfectly easy. No doubt the difficulties increase with the distance, but as they were overcome in the first instance as regards Canada, so they ought to be overcome with regard to the more distant portions of the Empire.

"The most important point is to secure a fit representation of British Science. It must be remembered that the Association consists largely of two classes—men of science who do the work, and the more numerous members who, taking an interest in scientific matters, have joined at the different towns where the meetings have been held. This numerous and important class supplies the funds which the Association is enabled to devote to research purposes; but those who compose it cannot in any sense be regarded as representative men of science. No meeting can be successfully held unless a sufficient attendance of the former class is secured. As a rule, men of science are not men of wealth or men of leisure. It is only those who have retired from the active pursuit of their professions who can ever expect to get a three months' holiday in any year, and that amount of time would certainly be required for a visit to Colombo, not to say, to Sydney or to Melbourne. A very large proportion of the workers of the Association belong to the professorial class. It is, of course, hopeless for them to think of getting away for months at a time, especially in the winter, the only suitable time for meetings in many of our colonies, nor as a rule can they afford so costly a trip.

"But if there is evidence of a desire among colonial men of science that they should have meetings of the Association in their own countries, and the Council of the Association can have sufficient evidence of this disire, they ought, I think, to consider the matter carefully and try if they cannot elaborate a scheme by means of which the operations of the Association should be extended through the whole of the Empire. If it seems likely that a sufficient number of well-known scientific men would be willing to go to the Antipodes for a meeting, then let a meeting be organised at the Antipodes. If but a small number of scientific missionaries could be relied upon, then a solution might be found in the organisation of simultaneous or supplementary meetings of the Association which could be held without interfering with the regular sequence of the meetings in England. It is a grievance which is felt by many, especially of the older members of the Association, who are unable or disinclined to undertake foreign expeditions, that the regular sequence of meetings in England should be broken by holding meetings in distant parts of the Empire.

"I would venture, therefore, to express the hope that if invitations are received from Ceylon and from other portions of the Empire, the Council of the Association will appoint a Committee with a view to the preparation of a scheme by which the limits of the Association's regular work should be enlarged, and arrangements should be made for holding meetings in Colonial as well as in British cities. It would, in most cases, I imagine, be possible to get together a sufficient number of representatives of the different sections of the Association to enable such meetings to be organised, and they could not fail to do good by bringing Colonial scientific men and scientific institutions more closely into touch with the institutions and the men of the mother-country. In the meantime I hope that Mr. Ferguson will continue his efforts, and that the result of his labours may, at all events, be that the Association will receive a formal invitation to hold a meeting at such an extremely attractive centre as Colombo would appear to be."

APPENDIX V.

CEYLON IN 1899.

BY JOHN FERGUSON, ESQ. (of Colombo).

Read at a Meeting of the Royal Colonial Institute held at the Whitehall Rooms, Hôtel Métropole, on Tuesday, November 7, at 8 P.M.,

Sir CECIL CLEMENTI SMITH, G.C.M.G., in the Chair.

IN the spring of 1892 I had the honour of lecturing before the Royal Colonial Institute on "Ceylon : Its Attractions to Visitors and Settlers,"* and in April, 1896, Mr. Justice Clarence, in connection with the celebration of the centenary of British rule, read a Paper on "One Hundred Years of British Rule in Ceylon."† It may be asked what has occurred during the interval to justify a third Paper, even on the first and most progressive of Crown Colonies. And, in reply, I can only say that a few years often make a marked difference either for good or evil in the condition of a tropical Colony ; that, in the case of Ceylon, the latter part of the decade now closing has witnessed special progress in nearly every branch of Administration connected with the island. It has seen a great spread of education (almost the beginning of technical instruction) ; of social and sanitary improvement and of material prosperity among the native population ; an increase of irrigation and other public works ; a re-organization of the Civil Service ; a new start in regard to surveys – topographical, cadastral, trigonometrical, and archæological ; with the prospect at an early date of an Agricultural Board, with a scientific staff and experimental stations. We have had, in the closing years of the century, a rapid extension of cultivation under the coconut and other palms, both by natives and Europeans ; the full establishment of a great planting enterprise, chiefly in the hands of Colonists, in tea, and subordinately in cacao and cardamoms, with experiments in rubber-yielding trees and other minor products. A new interest and much additional activity in mining, especially in plumbago, our one mineral, so far of commercial importance; and, consequent on all this, but especially on the rise in tea-planting, a marked advance in the trade and revenue of the island. Then, again, great progress has been made in the harbour works (with the addition of a first class graving dock) which are to make Colombo one of the best

* *Proceedings, Royal Colonial Institute*, Vol. XXIII., p. 209.
† *Ibid*, Vol. XXVII., p. 314.

equipped and most convenient, as it is already the most central, port in eastern waters between Asia and Australasia, and between China and East or South Africa. Still further, there has been a revival of activity in respect of railway extension, so that after witnessing the completion of one of the grandest and most profitable mountain railways in the world, we are now on the eve of extensive works—both on the existing broad and on a very narrow gauge— which, whatever may be thought of them in design and detail, cannot fail to exercise much influence on the future of the Colony, more especially in regard to districts as yet untouched by European enterprise, and, unfortunately, very little occupied by the natives.

We have here, then, a considerable catalogue of topics that may fairly be brought before you this evening. But, before doing so, I think it well to refer, in the briefest possible manner, to a few of the salient facts connected with the development of the island.

THE PLANTING ENTERPRISE.

Following the pioneer, Mr. Geo. Bird, General Sir Edward Barnes distinguished himself by encouraging systematic coffee cultivation, by opening a plantation of his own near Peradeniya. That was in 1825; but it was not till 1837 that a considerable impetus was given to the industry through the introduction of the West Indian mode of cultivation by a young Aberdonian, Robert Boyd Tytler, who had learned in Jamaica, and who, many years after, became the pioneer in cacao cultivation. I am not going to dwell on the wealth and trade which the great coffee industry brought to the island. Doubtless Ceylon proved the grave of many British sovereigns; but the money spent so freely benefited vast numbers of the native Sinhalese and Tamils, and the numbers of roads and bridges, villages, and even towns, which sprung up where all had been waste land and jungle, and the way in which native cultivation followed that of the European planter, attested to the great change wrought through the influence of "coffee" throughout the mountain zone of Ceylon. With the energetic administration of Governors Sir Henry Ward, Sir Hercules Robinson, and Sir William Gregory, the export of coffee by 1877 rose to a million cwt., worth, in the markets of Europe, between four and five millions sterling. I need not give more than a sentence to the decline and fall of this great industry, or to the ten years' conflict of the planters with the leaf fungus, which wrought such widespread ruin, and drove away 400 to 500 of the European planters to seek new scenes of labour. From 800 to 900, however, remained at their posts, and, by the strictest economy, with the aid of cinchona cultivation as a bridge, they carried on until the day came that tea, a much hardier plant, was found to grow where coffee had failed, and indeed to have a sphere so wide that from sea-level to close on 7,000 feet, it is found to flourish, where soil and rainfall are favourable, and, if allowed, would no doubt "flush" or crop well on the top of Adam's Peak or Pidurutalagala. In respect of tea, again, I am not going into

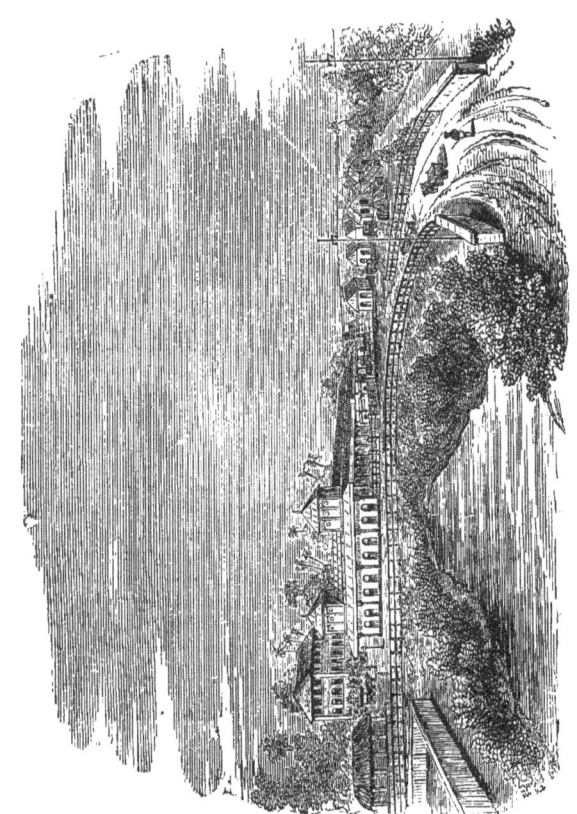

RAILWAY TERMINUS: COLOMBO.

VIEW OF THE SATINWOOD BRIDGE AT PERADENIYA.

Ceylon in 1899.

detail; but I must mention that among the pioneers of the cinchona and tea era, the Colony cannot forget the names of G. D. B. Harrison and W. Martin Leake (and their manager, the late James Taylor), the late A. M. Ferguson, and Sir Graeme Elphinstone. Nor should the special aid given from the Royal Botanic Gardens at Peradeniya and Kew, through the late Drs. Thwaites and Trimen, be overlooked. The former first sounded the alarm about the coffee fungus, while he urged attention to cinchona and tea; and Dr. Trimen did more than any other to encourage the cultivation of cacao. now an important subsidiary industry, just as *his* successor, Mr. Willis, is doing so much for the planting of rubber-yielding trees.

The rise of Ceylon from a mere military dependency to be the first of Crown Colonies is demonstrably due to the enterprise which, Sir Henry Ward and Sir Wm. Gregory acknowledged, gave them the surplus revenue which they were enabled to devote to Hospitals, Schools, Public Works, including irrigation tanks all over the island. As a present member of the Civil Service has well put it: —"The well-being of the native, the success of the civilian, the efficiency of the Government, are bound closely up with the good fortune of the planting industry. For the sinews of Ceylon are represented by her customs and railways, the two sources of revenue which are most closely affected by the ruin or success of the planter." Between 1837 and 1877 the general revenue of Ceylon increased from 4 to 17 millions of rupees, and then it fell, by 1883, with the decline of coffee, to 12 millions, and no Colonial Governor had ever a harder task—discharged most manfully and with marvellous success—than fell to Sir Arthur Gordon, during his six years of office, in keeping up a progressive administration, and the credit of the Colony, so as to secure railway extension and irrigation works, in spite of extremely limited means. His successor reaped a splendid harvest of revenue from the rapid spread of "tea," so that Sir Arthur Havelock saw the revenue rise to 21 millions of rupees; while our present ruler, Sir West Ridgeway, has already 25 millions to deal with, or considerably more than *double* the maximum controlled by Sir Hercules Robinson when he administered Ceylon.

I may as well here indicate a few of the statistics bearing on the above revenual development. The export trade in Ceylon tea began in 1873 with 23 lb. By 1879 it rose to 100,000 lb.; in 1889 to 34,000,000 lb.; and 1899 will probably show a total export of 125,000,000 lb. There are now of all ages about 380,000 acres, including native gardens, cultivated with tea; and were it not for the check given by fixing the value of the rupee at 1*s.* 4*d.* (a blessing in disguise to planters, as discouraging over-production) we should ere now have seen 400,000 or more acres covered with our staple product. Many of us hoped that the Indian Currency Commission would have compromised by selecting 1*s.* 3*d.* as the value of the rupee, and in the interests of the general development of India and Ceylon this would have been better. But, considering how very gradually, though surely, Indian and Ceylon tea is getting into consumption in the United States, Russia, and the rest of the Continent of Europe, it may, as I have said, be just as well that for sometime to come we should be content with having attained practically our maximum production of tea in Ceylon.

When the very commendable efforts of the planters, by means of a self-imposed cess, to advertise their teas in the United States, and, more recently, throughout the Continent of Europe, take fuller effect, there will be room for a greater outturn from Ceylon. A good deal of progress has been made in North America, and there are promising openings, I am glad to learn from a City friend, in several parts of South America, where Ceylon begins to take the place of Maté tea. Much is expected from the Paris exhibition next year, where the Ceylon Court and Tea, as well as other products, will be greatly in evidence; and you, Sir (addressing the Chairman), will preside over a Commission having the interests of the Colony at heart. Altogether no effort is being spared by the producers and by many merchants to bring their pure, wholesome teas, carefully prepared in factories equipped with the latest and best machinery and other appliances, under the notice of likely consumers in all parts of the world. The direct trade to countries other than the United Kingdom fostered by Public Sales in Colombo was represented last year by a total of 23½ million pounds against 96 million pounds to London, and the proportion has been well maintained—indeed, improved—during the present year.

It goes without saying that the tea plant has enemies, and much has lately been heard of fungoid blights which have for many years damaged tea in Assam. It must never be forgotten, however, that tea is a far hardier plant than coffee, and its crop is one of leaf, not of fruit, with chances extending over nine out of twelve months in the year, in place of only one or two gatherings of coffee cherries. Tea can be pruned down, and all affected portions burnt in a very complete way, without much loss of time in cropping. So far as I can judge, therefore, with the attention henceforward to be given to pests and to judicious liberal cultivation, the tea industry of Ceylon in the large majority of districts and estates is a stable, reliable enterprise for many years to come.

Minor Products.

Turning to some of the other estate products there is cacao cultivation which, begun, practically, some twenty years ago, now covers 23,000 acres in Ceylon, the export rising from 10 cwt. in 1878 to 37,000 in 1898, while it promises to exceed 40,000 cwt. in the present year. There is no prospect of this product being overdone in Ceylon, the area of rich sheltered land suited to its cultivation being very limited.

We have next Cardamoms—a spice for which there is a special demand in the Indian Presidency towns as well as in Europe. Some 6,000 acres are planted with cardamoms on Ceylon plantations, the export rising from 16,000 lb. in 1880 to 531,473 lb. last year.

For poor old coffee there is little or no hope of revival in Ceylon, and from the million cwt. of the "seventies" the export fell to a little over 13,000 cwt.

last year; but in 1899 there appears to be an increase, though it can only be temporary; for the Liberian variety does not seem to succeed any more than the Arabian.

The brief record of cinchona planting in Ceylon is a thing by itself, full even of romantic interest. Dr. Thwaites did all in his power to make Sir Clement Markham's historic expedition to the Andes a practical success, so far as Ceylon was concerned; but at first our planters scorned the idea of cultivating a medicinal plant! A few, however, listened to the good old botanist, and gave his *Succirubras* and *Officinalis* a trial as avenue trees, or in corners as shelter belts. When these were successfully tested and coffee had failed, there commenced a rush into cinchona all over the hill country, and with continuous groves in many cases proprietors thought they were on the road to fortune; but, alas! an export of little more than a million lb. in 1880, when quinine was 12s. the ounce, was followed in 1884, and following years by 12, 13, and 15 million lb., and the quinine value came tumbling down to 1s. 3d. an ounce, at which rate it did not pay to harvest the bark in Ceylon. Lately there has been some revival in price, and the export being very low, less than a million pounds last year, it is thought cultivation may prove profitable if judiciously carried out in favourite districts.

There has, of course, been an element of romance running right through the history of planting in Ceylon—from the early days when young men went out on a four or five months' voyage round the Cape to supervise the clearing of jungle in the hill country. They lived often far remote from neighbours, while district roads and bridges were as yet unknown, and food supplies scarce and often difficult to get. But the time came when prosperous plantations were dotted over successive districts, and cosy bungalows invited consorts from the old country, and brothers began to get out their sisters who eventually got exchanged! In the dark days of depression the ladies took their full share in the brave struggle, and the reward came with the success of tea in a country thoroughly opened up with roads and railways, doctors and hospitals, churches and clergymen tennis, golf, and cricket grounds, and a most enjoyable climate over a large portion of the highlands of Ceylon. Many of the coffee planters who had left us [returned, and now we number nearly 1,600 on tea and cacao plantations.

NATIVE AGRICULTURAL INDUSTRY.

But I must now turn to native agricultural industry, and first as to rice, which has been grown as far back as history extends in Ceylon, and there is no doubt that the destruction of tanks by the Tamils led to a woeful contraction of cultivation. But so far back as trading records exist, Ceylon has been dependent on India for part of its supply. There was no attempt to restore irrigation works by the Portuguese or Dutch, or until "coffee" gave a surplus revenue, and then Governor Ward, followed by Sir Hercules Robinson, Sir William Gregory, and Sir Arthur Gordon, did much to promote an extended industry in rice growing by restoring large tanks and reviving village communities, so that the maintenance of channels and even the repair of the smaller tanks could be done by the people interested, the Government providing sluices and engineering supervision. A check on this commendable work took place when the paddy rents were abolished in 1892, it being vainly thought by some that freedom from this immemorial levy, together with the "protection" of a ten per cent. import duty on Indian rice, would lead to greater industry on the part of the natives and to increased production ; but there is no sign of this (save in one interesting experiment under European direction), and the importation of Indian rice, in place of falling off, has steadily increased during the past seven years. Our present Governor, Sir West Ridgeway, however. took in hand the reorganization of the Irrigation Department last year, and with a free hand given to an able and experienced officer, Mr. Henry Parker, we may expect to see some notable results in which, perhaps. other cultivation besides rice may share.

I may next refer to the second great branch of planting in Ceylon, and the one more particularly in the hands of the Ceylonese of all races and classes, namely, that of palms, and notably of the coconut, palmyra, areca and betel palms, and with this I may couple the cultivation of cinnamon and of certain fruits and vegetables. It is a singular fact that so little is made of the coconut and of cinnamon in the old native annals—of the latter especially because there can be no doubt of the spice being indigenous to Ceylon, as evidenced by the wild cinnamon trees in the central jungles. With very few exceptions, Sinhalese own all the cinnamon gardens; and the same is true of the larger proportion of the coconut palm estates and gardens in Ceylon, though Tamils, Moormen, Eurasians, and Europeans are all found among the proprietors of this favourite branch of cultivation. The coconut must have originally floated to the shores of Ceylon from its native habitat in the Eastern Archipelago, and its first growth in the Southern Province is associated with the legend of the Kusta Rajah, or leprous king, who benefited by drinking the milk of this new tree. Gradually the cultivation extended round the coast. The Dutch, by a system of forced labour, compelled the villagers between Colombo and Kalutara to plant up certain tracts of country with this valuable palm. In British times not much was added to cultivation before the middle of the century ; but when the new enterprise in coffee brought money into the hands of a host of native cart contractors, artificers, renters, and traders of all the native races, the planting of coconut gardens became a favourite mode of investment; and since 1861 I have watched the occupation, in this way, of the Maha-oya valley for 30 to 40 miles inland from Negombo, and also the opening of new districts at Madampe, Chilaw, and Puttalam in Kurunegala to the south of Batticaloa, and in different parts of the Western, Central, and Southern Provinces. When coffee fell the extension of coconuts nearly stopped, but, with the return of general prosperity under tea, renewed activity has been observed in opening coconut land,

Ceylon in 1899.

wisely encouraged by the sale of suitable Crown land in several new districts of late years ; even now if the food of the mass of the population as well as the export trade is considered, it may be a question whether the coconut palm is not the most important tree in Ceylon. During the past 40 years, I reckon, the cultivation has extended from 250,000 to about 600,000 acres with 50,000,000 of palms, yielding an annual crop of about a thousand million of nuts, of which not more than one-third is exported in the shape of coconut oil, coir fibre, copra or poonac, desiccated coconut for confectionery, etc., and nuts—the whole of this export being worth, in a good year, about 1,000,000*l.* sterling. The rest of the crop is utilised for the food of the people, apart from a certain number devoted to the intoxicating spirit arrack and to sweet as well as fermented toddy. What the coconut is to the south, the palmyra is to the dry north of Ceylon, to the Tamils of the Jaffna Peninsula and of Mannar, etc., and there can be no good reason why this cultivation should not be greatly extended in the drier portions of the island.

I must dismiss the other palms, fruit and vegetable cultivation, of the island in a word. Betel-nuts are exported to a value of £60,000 to £70,000. No doubt the day will come when a trade in preserved fruit will spring up between Ceylon (as it has already done between Singapore) and Europe. It is the custom now-a-days to despise Oriental fruits as wanting in flavour. Macaulay, writing from Calcutta, said he had seen no fruit on his table he would not readily exchange for a pottle of strawberries in Covent Garden; but those who have enjoyed a really good "rupee" mango in Ceylon or India (or a feast of mangosteens) will scarcely condemn all Eastern fruit, but may rather believe the story of the Duke of Wellington feasting on the first mangoes sent from Bombay to the Queen's table, he being the only gentleman present acquainted with a fruit which he had often enjoyed thirty years earlier when in India !

Altogether we reckon that 3½ million acres are cultivated or utilised as pasture land out of a total of 15,800,000 acres in the island. There is, therefore, plenty of room for expansion with some at least of the existing and with new products. Many of the intelligent natives are full of enterprise in extending palm, banana, and other favourite products when land is made available, and they often only want a lead in regard to trying new plants. Still, in most cases—in regard to growing rice, fruit, and vegetables—moral (or may I say official) pressure, to say the least, has to be put on Sinhalese and even indigenous Tamils to get them to utilise advantages within their reach. The influence of the headmen on the ordinary villagers is great, and that of the civil servants—as the medium of natives honours—is paramount. But some continuous system of agricultural improvement is required, and this, I am glad to think, is likely to be established as the result of a Commission appointed by the present Governor. An Agricultural Board, including representative members of all races and classes, is likely to be the outcome, and this, under the direct eye of the Governor, may be expected to do much for the improvement of old, and the development of new, industries, such, for instance, as pepper growing, which, under the Dutch, was an important industry in several native districts. I should like to see cadets for the revenue service get a training at an Agricultural College in England for a year or two, as is done, I believe, with civil servants intended for Java ; because it often happens now that a district officer, who has taken a warm interest in native agriculture and live stock, is succeeded by a man who never rides about, cares nothing about agricultural improvement, and does not know anything whatever about live stock, in which the property of many of the rural Sinhalese and Tamils largely consists ; and so he neglects or abandons experiments set agoing by his predecessor.

As an adjunct to the Agricultural Board, the Scientific Staff at the Peradeniya Botanic Gardens is, I believe, to be enlarged, so that, besides the present capable Director, Mr. Willis, and his practical assistants (Messrs. Nock and Macmillan) there will be a thoroughly trained entomologist (Mr. E. E. Green already appointed) ; a mycologist, cryptogamist, or fungologist—I do not know which term is preferable—to be sent out shortly from England ; and an analytical chemist, at present represented by Mr. Kelway Bamber, who is in a fair way to remain for a number of years in Ceylon. It may be thought that such a staff will be chiefly available for industries in European hands, but that would be a great mistake. Already Mr. Green has done good service to rice-growers in advising about their enemy, the paddy weevil. The palms have their enemies, about which a good deal has yet to be learnt. Many natives are interested in cacao and tea, and many more are likely to try rubber-tree planting when the European pioneers of the 1,600 acres already planted in Ceylon have begun to show profitable returns. A reproach of long standing against Ceylon, of being so far behind Java in respect of a scientific staff to assist agriculture, is thus in a fair way to be removed, and Mr. Chamberlain is likely to have the felicity of sanctioning the appointment of an Agricultural Board in Ceylon on the recommendation of Governor Sir West Ridgeway, just as he has recently appointed an Imperial Agricultural Department for the West Indies, headed by Dr. Morris, C.M.G., so well known for good work in Ceylon and at Kew.

Before leaving the subject of agriculture and planting, I may be allowed to mention that what seems a fair, if not moderate, estimate of the value of the whole of such property in Ceylon, works out to a total of £45,500,000, and when the time comes for getting rid of the present abnormal, one-sided, and unjust tax on imported rice and other food stuffs, and indeed for going a long way towards making Colombo a free port—so that it may still further share the great prosperity of the sister port of Singapore —there should be little difficulty in raising, by means of a general land-levy, a sum equal to the deficiency so created in the customs. As an indispensable preliminary to such readjustment of taxation, Sir West Ridgeway has

VIEW ON THE MAHAWELI GANGA, AT GANGARUWA, NEAR KANDY.

THE DEVON FALLS DIMBOOLA A PEEP FROM THE CART ROAD.

already promised a Commission to consider the Incidence of Taxation ; and although action on the report of such a body (even when made) could not well be taken till after the cadastral survey of the island is further advanced, still it is well to make a start in the proper direction, and to look forward to the day when a more equitable collection of taxes for the Ceylon administration, after the pattern set in India, can be attained. Ever since 1892 there has been a growing conviction among observant officials, as well as other residents of experience, that the million of rupees given up by the Government in the land paddy or rice levy has not gone to benefit the mass of cultivators or poorer class of Sinhalese and Tamil agriculturists, but has passed mainly into the pockets of well-to-do landowners, money-lenders, and other middlemen; while it has been clearly proved that the remaining customs rice-tax is a heavy burden on the poorest class of townspeople, as well as on the estate coolies, who have nothing but imported rice to look to.

My space will not allow me on this occasion to enter on the important Plumbago mining industry, further than to say that the export (likely to be 600,000 cwt: this year) has very largely increased, owing to the price in England and America trebling during the past few years. The promised geological survey to begin in 1900 will do much to develop this industry as well as gem digging ; and we want science (zoologists) also to help us in regard to our pearl-yielding oysters, of which no fishery has been had for several years.

The mention of zoology reminds me of certain branches of Ceylon trade connected with its fauna : the export of elephants, for instance, and the utilisation of tamed elephants in road, railway, and other public works. There is no reason to believe that the number of wild elephants in our jungles in the south-east and north-east of the island is falling off, and in the past thirty-six years no fewer than 2,800 elephants have been exported from Ceylon of a nominal value of £80,000 ; but in reality worth three times that amount if they arrived safely at their destination, whether it be a European or American menagerie, or more frequently a Rajah's court in India. Hunting and fishing give employment to a large number of natives, and the local trade in dried deer flesh, as also the export trade in horns and skins, is a considerable one; while a large portion of the food of the maritime natives (as of the colonists) is obtained from the surrounding ocean, largely by Buddhist fishermen, who tell you they do not kill the fish, but only take them out of the water—they die of themselves ! Nevertheless, a considerable quantity of salt-fish has to be imported for native use in Ceylon, showing there is great room for a local industry of the kind. A Game Preservation Society, lately started by public-spirited planters and a few officials, indicates the fear entertained of the indiscriminate slaughter of deer—of which we have several species in Ceylon—going too far ; and much good will be done for the benefit of the people, as well as of sportsmen and Government, by the close seasons now ordained and other measures of protection afforded.

Of manufacturing or industrial pursuits, apart from agriculture and mining, there is a singular lack in Ceylon. A good many weavers' looms (1,182 in all) are still worked in the Eastern and Northern Provinces. There are 2,216 oil mills reported in the island, and twelve sugar mills still at work in the Southern Province.

THE PEOPLE.

In considering the people of Ceylon I would say that a fair estimate based on the experience of the last census and the impetus to immigration of recent years, justifies my putting the present population of the island at no fewer than 3,400,000, of whom 2,250,000 will be Sinhalese, 800,000 Tamils, 210,000 Moormen (Arab descendants), 11,000 Malays, 1,200 Veddahs with 10,000 of various races, against about 25,000 Eurasians or European descendants, and not more than 6,500 Europeans all told. Altogether in Ceylon we have the representatives of some seventy races or nationalities, so that our native streets and bazaars in the large towns present one of the most varied and interesting assemblages of peoples to be seen anywhere on the face of the globe. As to the advance in material prosperity of the mass of the people during the past sixty years, I need only point to the figures for population ; no community could increase as the Sinhalese and Tamils of Ceylon have done without being blessed with material comfort, peace, and good government. As an old and eloquent missionary has said:
"Were some Sinhalese Appuhami to arise, who had gone down to the grave eighty years ago, and from that time remained unconscious, he would not know his own land or people......... He would listen incredulously when told there is no rajakariya, or forced labour, and no fish tax, and that there are no slaves, and that you can cut down a cinnamon tree in your own garden without having to pay a heavy fine."

Again the same writer has said that the improvement in the homes of many of the people within his time was as great as the contrast between a begrimed native chatty (clay vessel) and a bright English tea-kettle.

What the British Government has done in Ceylon (as in India) in the maintenance of public health alone in medical treatment, hospitals asylums, and dispensaries, in enforcing sanitary regulations, together with provision for water supply in the chief towns, is beyond all praise. No native ruler in Oriental history has any record of this kind to show, and no feature of our administration is more acceptable to the natives than the provision made through dispensaries and hospitals. In this connection I must refer to the successful campaign fought by our present Governor. his executive and medical officers, against the introduction of plague into the island during the past two years. No doubt our proximity to the equator, high rate of temperature, and large amount of sunshine have much to do with our exemption ; but still these did not save Madras or Southern India, and nothing but the constant watchfulness maintained at Colombo and other ports prevented plague cases, with the bacilli which

Ceylon in 1899.

actually appeared in our harbours, from finding a lodgment ashore and spreading throughout the island.

As regards education the natives of Ceylon owe a special debt of gratitude to the various missionary bodies at work in the island since 1814 for giving the first general impetus to the instruction of the people. The Dutch Government, pastors, and teachers did a limited amount of work in their day, but it was not till the time of Sir Hercules Robinson that the British Government awoke to a due sense of its duty and endeavoured to to meet the wants of a rising generation. Even then teachers in the vernaculars of the people could only be got from the mission schools. Within the past thirty years a great advance has been made, and even the Buddhists and Hindus have begun to take advantage of the admirable and equitable system of grants-in-aid provided by the Government. We are ten times further advanced in public instruction in Ceylon than in India, but still only one child in 6 or 7 of a school-going age is being instructed, so that much remains to be done. Let it never be forgotten that female instruction in India and Ceylon was unheard of until the present century. In making liberal grants for public instruction, the present Government of Ceylon has given special attention to technical and industrial teaching and training. A technical college, as lately remodelled, is doing good practical work, while a reformed agricultural school with experimental stations is to form part of the scheme under the new Agricultural Board.

In this connection I may be permitted to refer to the improved appearance of our Ceylonese youth, in the towns especially, under the influence of Western instruction and athletic training. In the favourite English game of cricket many of them greatly excel, and there can be no doubt that public money expended in training and maintaining a Volunteer Infantry Corps, while providing a useful body for supplementary defence, has done much to improve the physique and bearing of many of our young men. Detachments of Volunteer Artillery and "Mounted Infantry" are composed of patriotic Colonists, so that, so far as internal peace is concerned, the British Infantry Regiment now stationed in Ceylon can at any time be spared for service in South Africa, and can be readily transferred from Colombo to Durban. The Colony pays a very considerable military contribution to the Imperial Government, and lately some sharp criticism has been locally applied to the mode and amount of levy; but no Colony is more loyal or attached to the British Crown, or more ready to make sacrifices in any time of the Empire's need, if such should arise, than the first of Crown Colonies, Ceylon.

One of the most practical reforms introduced by the present Governor of Celyon has been a reorganization of the Civil Service, by which not only have the position and prospects of a body of honourable cultured public servants been improved, but greater efficiency of administration has been secured. This is an important matter, for there can be no doubt of the confidence reposed by the mass of the people in our revenue and judicial officers, and it is greatly owing to their labours that the Sinhalese and

Tamils are now in so advanced and contented a position. Some visitors have written of Java as the model Colony, pointing to the unequalled comfort and submission of the Javanese natives. This is very much accounted for by the Dutch Government denying to the natives the equal rights and opportunities for education and advancement which are open to the Ceylonese as to Her Majesty's subjects everywhere in the British Empire. Still further, Sir West Ridgeway's experience of the Indian and home services has been utilised with beneficial effect to place the Survey Department of the Colony on an entirely new footing—a departure which, with an increased staff and far more systematic arrangements, is likely to give us the topographical, cadastral, and trigonometrical surveys of the island within a reasonable period of time, and so to enable long-delayed fiscal and administrative reforms to take effect.

Something has also been done to stir up the Public Works Department of the Colony, but without the same measure of success, for I believe it is a fact that, with abundance of labour available and every encouragement from the Executive, this body, year by year, does not overtake the money voted for useful and often urgent public works. There is evidently room for inquiry, and possibly for weeding out incompetent, while properly encouraging and rewarding really efficient, officers in this department.

ADMINISTRATION OF JUSTICE AND CRIME.

An attempt has recently been made in a portion of the London as of the local press to cast discredit on the administration of justice, and to hint that life and property are not properly protected in Ceylon. There is, in my opinion, no justification for sweeping statements of this kind, and I think the vast majority of Colonists—especially of the older residents— as of intelligent Ceylonese, will bear me out in this view. I am far from saying that our police and judiciary are perfect, or that the laws need no improvement—some people think we have too much "law," and it is a fact that no people on the face of the earth are fonder of litigation than many of the Sinhalese. Indeed, villagers in Ceylon seem, in too many cases, to regard the British law courts established in their midst as affording a laudable means of spending a considerable portion of their time, and many cases in court are started with no desire of settlement, but by repeated postponements to secure a holiday trip with relatives and friends from time to time, while, owing to the subdivision of property under the Roman-Dutch law, litigation is sometimes carried on about the fractional part of a few coconut palms or other fruit trees. An improved and simple system of registration following perhaps on the cadastral survey, which is being energetically pushed on, will be the best check on the many land cases and disputes now prevalent, and will also put the vexed question of waste lands on a proper footing. No impartial person, acquainted with the native propensity to trespass on Crown and even private property, and with the advantage that can be taken of native ignorance by speculators of their own or European race, can say that the action taken by the present Government is otherwise than reasonable and just and in the best interests of the people themselves in endeavouring to secure a speedy adjustment of claims to forest, chena, waste, and unoccupied lands. The Supreme Court found fault with some technical points—since corrected—in the original legislative enactment, but its principle has been most generally approved, and for the administration of the law two of the most qualified and reliable members of the service (true friends of the natives) have been chosen. As regards the general policy of the Ceylon Government towards the natives, I need only mention that, in the past thirty years, free grants have been issued, after inquiry, for 40,000 acres to the people, while a large extent has been granted at half value and a still larger area of clearly proved encroachments has been transferred at a moderate valuation. I have the utmost confidence in the two officials—Messrs. Lewis and Booth—who are working under the Ordinance: they are sure to give careful consideration to all *bonâ fide* individual or village claims, while at the same time firmly resisting dishonest claims and land jobbing.

Returning to the admitted prevalence of crime in certain districts of Ceylon, I am among those who attribute it largely to the spread of two great evils, the drinking of arrack and other intoxicating drinks and gambling. Certain reforms in the administration of the arrack monopoly are urgently required, and some I have formally placed before the Government, as also for checking the spread of an opium habit among a people who never grew, and until this century never used, opium. The hasty use of the knife in quarrels is one of the weaknesses of the rural Sinhalese, and various remedies have been proposed. The most efficient, in my opinion, for this and similar serious crimes would be banishment to the Andaman Islands—the Indian penal convict station. Nothing (not even hanging) is more abhorrent to the Sinhalese Buddhists than transportation across the seas into penal servitude.

It is a striking fact that serious crime is most rampant where ignorance and Buddhism most prevail, and where arrack-distilling is carried on. Recognizing that the prompt administration of justice is one of the first necessities of an advancing community and a deterrent of crime, I think the time may be near—if it has not come—when a fourth judge should be appointed to the Bench of the Supreme Court to aid in appeals and criminal sessions, and for this post I have a very decided opinion that a senior judicial officer from the Civil Service should be chosen, as is so freely done in India. On the whole, I think the jury system, as remodelled of late years, works well in Ceylon, though it involves a very heavy tax on Colonists native prisoners invariably exercising the choice given to them, by asking for an English (rather than a Sinhalese or Tamil) speaking jury, which, of course, includes a proportion of Europeans and Eurasians.

HARBOUR WORKS.

I must now turn to some of the great public works which have benefited Ceylon during the present generation, and though railways should come first,

Ceylon in 1903.

I will first, with your permission, speak shortly of the Colombo Harbour Works. Designed by the late Sir John Coode, and since his lamented death by his firm, Messrs. Coode, Son, and Matthews, these works (when completed, say by 1902) are certain to constitute Colombo one of the largest and best protected harbours in the world, with an enclosed area of 600 acres, a first class graving dock (half the cost of which is to be borne by the Admiralty), and numerous other shipping conveniences. The total cost to the Colony from first to last of harbour improvements, land reclamations, and docks is not likely to be much less than £2,000,000; but the investment is fully justified by the growing importance of Colombo as the great calling and coaling port for mail and commercial steamers in the Indian Ocean, the total tonnage (inwards and outwards) having risen from 446,110 tons in 1869—the year in which the Suez Canal was opened—to 6,200,000 in 1898, while a further steady addition may be anticipated, with the possibility, some years hence, of the naval headquarters being transferred from Trincomalee to Colombo when the graving dock is complete.

RAILWAYS.

I now turn to Railways. Sir Henry Ward gave the first great impetus to railway construction in Ceylon; but it was not till 1867 that the Colombo and Kandy line, seventy-four miles, was opened during the Government of Sir Hercules Robinson, who extended it for seventeen miles, and then proclaimed his belief in his terminus Nawalapitiya spelling "Finality." In the interests mainly of the Uva planting divisions of the country, I began a campaign in 1872 for railway extension from Nawalapitiya to Haputale. which resulted in Sir James Longden getting sanction in 1878 for a first division of forty-one miles through Dikoya and Dimbula, while not till March 1888 did Governor Sir Arthur Gordon (after a series of very trenchant despatches) get sanction for the final twenty-five miles into Uva; while the same indefatigable Governor arranged for the extension of Sir William Gregory's seaside line to Galle and Matara and for the approval of a Kurunegala extension, afterwards carried out by Sir Arthur Havelock. Including the Matale branch of seventeen miles (made during the time of Governor Gregory), the Colony has now 297 miles of first-class railway, 121 of which are the free property of the Colony, while the total income in excess of charges and interest forms a most important part of the general revenue. In this connection I may mention that the Dimbula-Uva extension has well fulfilled the financial expectations of its advocates, notwithstanding that, by an unfair system of accounting, the Departmental Reports up to 1897 appeared to show that the Uva section was worked at a loss. His Excellency Governor Ridgeway ordered this to be rectified in accordance with an appeal I personally ventured to make, and now the traffic, properly divided, shows a very considerable and steadily growing profit from this Uva extension, although justice has not yet been done in opening feeding roads, one fully equipped railway station (Ambawela)

"SENSATION ROCK" ON THE CEYLON RAILWAY INCLINE.

VIEW OF ALAGALLA PEAK FROM THE RAILWAY ON
THE KADUGANNAWA INCLINE.

he King of Kandy sometimes ordered criminals to be flung from the top of this mountain as a mode of capital punishment.

having been left for no fewer than six years without a cart road of any kind leading to or from it.

In this connection I may be allowed to mention that some relaxation of the ordinarily wise policy of reserving Crown lands above 5,000 feet, seems to be required to enable portions, at least, of the waste land between Dimbula and Uva to be utilised, and so to yield traffic to the railway. It seems anomalous for a locomotive line to run for some ten miles through waste land, none of which yields traffic. By-and-by, by a system of leases with conditions as to planting certain portions with timber trees for most of the existing so-called "forest" is no more than scrub—it is possible that the Patana, chena, and "forest" might be made available to private enterprise, either for plantations or for a series of gardens for the cultivation of fruit and vegetables for the Colombo market.

I now turn to the important revival of enterprise in Railway Extension which has marked the administration of the present Governor of Ceylon. Agitation for a railway to Jaffna, the populous peninsula in the north of the island, commenced some thirteen years ago; but successive Commissions of Inquiry could show nothing to justify action until early in 1897, a joint Commission of officials and unofficials saw their way to recommend a light broad-gauge extension from Kurunegala to Anuradhapura, with a feeding line on a 2½-feet gauge from the latter town to Jaffna. Of this Governor Ridgeway approved, and so recommended to the Secretary of State; but Mr. Chamberlain, acting, it is supposed, on the advice of the Consulting Engineer, refused to make any change of gauge at Anuradhapura, and decided that this Northern Railway must be on the broad gauge all the way.

Realising, some years before that the home authorities were very unlikely to sanction any northern extension scheme that involved a "break of gauge," as they had always resisted that policy in respect of our mountain line, I endeavoured to demonstrate the wisdom of crying "finality" for the broad-gauge at Kurunegala. I pointed out to the late Sir C. Hutton Gregory that the existing heavy traffic of the inland districts of Ceylon was almost entirely served by the existing broad-gauge system, that the chief problem now was how to send locomotive lines through the northern and eastern divisions of the island, and that, having regard to the absence for hundreds of miles of both population and traffic, it would be wise to devise the very simplest and cheapest form of locomotive line. In connection with a proposal to unite the Indian and Ceylon railway systems *viâ* Adam's Bridge, fathered by Mr. Shelford and Sir George Bruce, I became a strong advocate for starting afresh from Colombo on a metre-gauge up the western coast, which for sixty miles had population and traffic—such a line passing from Puttalam to Anuradhapura, to Jaffna, and eventually to Trincomalee and perhaps Batticaloa. A new interest was later on given to the introduction of a narrow-gauge, by the adoption of a 2½-feet line by Sir West Ridgeway (with Mr. Chamberlain's sanction) for a Colombo Kelani Valley Railway of some fifty miles to traverse one of the most populous low-country districts (through Cotta and Avisawella) in the island, and with very heavy planting traffic at several of its stations. The anomaly, therefore, became all the greater of having a 5½ feet broad-gauge (more costly in working than in first construction—a big waggon to do a wheelbarrow's work), through one of the poorest districts in Ceylon north of Kurunegala, and for eighty miles north of Anuradhapura, where there was no cultivation and where none giving adequate results could be mentioned as capable of introduction unless water by irrigation works was first provided. Accordingly steps were taken in England to urge on Mr. Chamberlain, by deputation, the advisableness of reaching the north by way of the west coast with a smaller railway; but the Secretary of State adhered to his decision for a broad-gauge all the way from Kurunegala to Jaffna, or rather to the northern port, Kangesanturai, of nearly 200 miles, involving a total cost exceeding 11,100,000 rupees; and (although part of this is to be taken from surplus revenue), without much prospect of the working expenses, interest, and sinking fund for the required loan being provided by the traffic for many years to come.

Before I go further, let me admit that there is something to be said for a broad-gauge to Anuradhapura and Mannar in view of the possible future change of the South Indian line to Paumben to the standard gauge, and His Excellency Sir West Ridgeway has always been a firm believer in the future connection of the railway systems of our island and the continent. Had the broad-gauge been adopted only to Mannar, the feeding lines in the north and east of Ceylon on the 2½ feet gauge could have been connected through Puttalam with Colombo.

RESOURCES OF THE NORTH-CENTRAL PROVINCE.

But it is clear now that the time for speculation as to what should or might be in regard to Railway Extension to the north is past, and we must face the inevitable; and although I have been among the most persistent opponents of the policy adopted—a policy which, for the first time, sends a Ceylon Railway for over 150 miles through a country almost devoid of population and traffic—I am nevertheless now ready, as an old Colonist with a warm interest in the land of my adoption, to make the best of what must be, and to endeavour to find out how the evils anticipated may be mitigated, and all possible advantages be ensured and, if possible, strengthened. Our present Governor, it is understood, returns to Ceylon, with instructions and full power to carry a locomotive line—a "light broad-gauge railway" it is called—from Kurunegala to the extreme north of the island forthwith. Every possible economy, I believe, is to be observed both in the construction and the working of this line; there are to be no extravagantly built stations, and old rolling-stock from the existing lines is, as far as possible, to be utilised. I have been unable to get from practical planters any encouragement as to the possible occupation and cultivation of the country between ten miles north of Kurunegala and the neighbourhood of Anuradhapura. It is said to be too dry and poor for palm

SCENE OF THE NILWALAGANGA, SOUTHERN PROVINCE.

Ceylon in 1899.

cultivation ; but I am glad to learn that certain Crown forests are likely to be benefited by this section, and that their value should be increased by it There is first of all Kalugalla forest, said to cover 10,000 acres, and to contain fine palu, ebony, and halmilla timber trees ; and next, before the railway enters the North-Central Province, it should touch the great reserve known as Palekelle, of some 35,000 acres with ebony and halmilla. Our present experienced Conservator of Forests (whose Indian training and personal ability have in my opinion, met with rather scant official recognition in Ceylon) is, I believe, of opinion that the railway may foster the development of an industry in charcoal-burning, according to the latest approved methods. The demand for fuel is rising in Colombo, and charcoal is easy of transport, and can, I am told, be made of very suitable first-class woods. As regards the North-Central Province, any one who travels along the roads would be apt to think that the bulk of the country is "forest" ; but in reality there is no more than a belt, and inside there is only low chena or scrub, and only here and there are blocks of forest with palu, ebony, and satinwood to be found. Once past Madawachchi, however, and into the Northern Province, and we get again into good timber in ebony and satinwood with the finest palu (a specially hard, durable wood), in the island. Of course, what is really wanted to make these forests more valuable is an increase of population and a consequent larger and cheaper supply of labour Whether the railway will induce this to come from what is generally termed "overcrowded Jaffna," or whether coolies can be got from Southern India, remains to be seen. At present, owing to the want of labour, forest work is very expensive ; but undoubtedly this northern railway must have a beneficial effect in regard to timber utilisation and forest management. Still, it will be a poor look-out if "timber" and charcoal should be the only articles to look to for 150 miles or so until Jaffna is reached. And this makes one deeply regret that the advice of an old missionary to the Tamils (the late Rev. J. Kilner) given thirty years ago, was not adopted. He advocated the planting of palmyra nuts along the north road all the way from Jaffna to Dambulla. If this had been attended to by the road coolies, it must have cost very little, and avenues of this slow-growing but useful palm—so well suited for a dry country—would have done much to induce village settlements in this unoccupied land. I have just been reading of the wonderful change the roadside cultivation of fruit trees has wrought in the past twenty years in many parts of Europe, particularly in Belgium, Southern Germany, and France. In little Belgium alone, according to statistics for 1894, over 2,875 miles of roads planted with 741,571 fruit trees are yielding a very large value per annum. There may be a lesson here for Ceylon, in the districts which we want occupied and opened up; but when all is said, one thing must precede occupation and cultivation, and that is a water supply, or means of securing water. It is, therefore, the opinion of many thoughtful observers that irrigation works should have preceded railway expenditure. But if it be true, as at present rumoured, that Mr. Chamberlain has empowered the Governor of Ceylon to simultaneously go

Ceylon in 1903.

ahead in these dry northern districts, with a liberal restoration and repair of irrigation tanks, a good deal no doubt may be accomplished by the time the Jaffna Railway is opened.* Of course, the cultivation of rice, the staple food of the people, now so largely imported, is the first consideration. Some people think cotton should be profitably grown; but with Tinnevelly cotton at present abundantly produced at so cheap a rate, one is not sanguine of much profit here. But I have what is perhaps a more startling suggestion to make. It was my fortune to travel home this time from Colombo with a fellow-countryman (a Scot from the far north) with large and varied experience in sugar cultivation—sixteen years in Demerara first, and later ten years in the Straits Settlements—and he surprised me as to the profitable nature of the crops of sugar now being grown in Penang, although the yield per acre was far less than in Java; and, further, that a good market for all the sugar produced was found in China, through reliable Chinese merchants buying the crop in advance on the spot. Conversation turned on waste land in Ceylon, and the north and east being referred to, my friend, who represents large English capitalists, expressed himself as resolved to visit the country to be traversed by this northern railway. I have collected for him all the meteorological information available, and embodied it for different stations along the route and for others at the mouth of the Mahaweliganga, in a table which will be found in an appendix to this paper. The question of rainfall is an all-important one to the sugar cultivator; but at the same time, if irrigation is made available to supplement a deficient supply, the industry might do well.

Now, I am quite prepared for an incredulous smile as to sugar cultivation ever paying in Ceylon. It has been tried, I will be reminded, and many thousands of pounds sunk in the south, west, and centre of the island by men of experience in Mauritius and elsewhere; but all to no avail. Let me, however, recall the fact that, because of an unfortunate experiment by the Messrs. Worms in the "forties," it was firmly believed among Ceylon planters for thirty years that *Tea* cultivation could never be properly carried on in the island! It is just possible, therefore, that, tried by skilful men with all modern appliances and greatly increased experience, sugar may still be found a profitable crop in some parts of our island, and not the least in the North and East. One advantage the pioneer cultivator would have would be a local market with the protection of our present import duty. Ceylon imports at present as much as 100,000 cwt. of sugar, most of which pays a customs duty of three rupees per cwt. Of course, a great

---

* Since writing the above, news has come from Ceylon that at the opening of the Legislature the Acting-Governor announced that of a total of 20,640,000 rupees to be spent on the Jaffna, Kelani, and Udapussellawa Railways, and on Irrigation Works, half must be provided from the General Revenue. This will mean an unfair burden, in my opinion, on the consumers of imported rice (who contribute largely to the surplus—rather less than half our people eating free rice, while more than half pay a customs tax), and it may seriously interfere with reproductive public works required to maintain the present prosperity of the island—the railway to Puttulam being one.

Ceylon in 1899.

attraction to any one beginning in Northern Ceylon would be the prospect of a cheaper and steadier labour supply than can be commanded in the Straits.

Competition in the labour market, whether by railway contractors or sugar cultivators, will probably disturb the minds of our tea and other planters; but when it is remembered that there are some ten or twelve millions of natives next door to us in Southern India never far from the verge of scarcity, to whom two rupees a week per family of four (father, mother, and two children) is contentment, there ought to be abundance of coolies for all our work in Ceylon if proper agencies are used to secure and import it.

I have only one further suggestion to make in this connection, and that is the need of fish culture in the tanks and even in the rice fields, not only in the north but all over Ceylon. In Java I have it on good authority that the native farmers reckon the "harvest" of fish gathered from their rice fields as scarcely inferior in importance to that of the harvest of grain; while fish in tanks are fed in Java with masses of hibiscus (or shoe) flowers and pieces of oilcake.

Let me, in conclusion, repeat that the responsibility of saddling Ceylon with this northern railway as designed is a serious one, and that it must lie with the Colonial Office rather than the local Government. At the same time, as it has to be, we must make the best of it and endeavour to devise means of mitigating loss and gradually securing a profit. As for the narrow locomotive line from Colombo to Kelani Valley, there can be no doubt it will pay handsomely from the first day of opening, and the same may be said of the similar line likely to be made simultaneously from Nanuoya through Nuwara Eliya to Udapussellawa. To secure still more railway profits and so to compensate for loss on the northern line, I would strongly recommend the Government to extend the 2½-feet line through the Northern portion of the city of Colombo to Negombo and Chilaw and even to Puttalam. Such a railway would pay handsomely on its own merits, would serve a teeming, prosperous population on the first half, and would develop much fresh coconut land along its second section.

I must now draw this discursive account of recent and prospective progress in Ceylon to an end. I hope I have left the impression that the principal industries of the island are in a sound and promising condition; that the administration is decidedly progressive; and that the people are advancing in comfort and intelligence. I know it is the opinion of its present Governor, of leading Colonists and officials, that Ceylon only requires to be better and more widely known to be still more appreciated. Sir West Ridgeway, who came to us from the Isle of Man (an island that prospers mainly through its visitors), fully shared the opinion long felt by us old colonists that Ceylon ought to be regarded as a show-place for travellers from all parts of the globe. As a winter resort it has much to recommend it, and we have now the finest hotels in the East in Colombo,

Mount Lavinia, Kandy, Hatton, Nuwara Eliya, Bandarawela, &c., with every variety of climate between—as extremes—90° and freezing point, but in which snow and fogs are unknown. The sanatarium is being especially made attractive, with a view to meeting the requirements of visitors as well as of local residents, and here nearly all home outdoor sports can be enjoyed.

CONCLUSION.

In conclusion, may I briefly indicate what the ordinary visitor may anticipate as likely to interest him in Ceylon? The ancient and modern names applied to the island raise high expectations when they include Lanka the Resplendent, a pearl-drop on the brow of India, the Eden of the Eastern Wave, and so on : but they are fully justified when we find that, from whatever side it be approached, Ceylon unfolds a scene of loveliness unsurpassed if it be equalled by any other land in the universe. There is no more interesting and beautiful town than the capital, Colombo, and the variety of race and dress in its bazaars, and the delightful drives in its "Cinnamon Gardens," never disappoint the stranger. Coco palms fringe the shores until they seem to kiss the waves breaking over the coral reefs, and each has its owner and often its mark, so that Dr. Norman MacLeod, when he landed at Bombay, exclaimed :—" Oh, India, that the very hairs of thy head should be numbered "! Inland, as the visitor travels by the comfortable railway train to Kandy, he may note cinnamon and fruit-tree culture; a wide expanse of glistening rice-fields dotted with gardens and villages on knolls surrounded by trees, in which the arrowy slender areca and the graceful kitul, jaggery or sugar palms may be noted ; while he may have the good fortune to see that finest of tropical floral displays, a talipot palm in flower (the palm which only flowers once in its life, after sixty to eighty years of growth, sending a column of cream-coloured wheat-like blossom some 20 feet above its own stem of 50 to 80 feet, which lasts for three months and then the whole tree dies down).

As the visitor approaches the hills he will be enabled to mark the cultivation of cacao (the chocolate or cocoa yielding plant) with its large pendent scarlet pods, of Liberian coffee with dark red cherries, possibly of one or other of the india-rubber yielding trees, and even of tea. Climbing the Kadugannawa Pass excites interest in ever-varying mountain and lowland scenery, in the terraced rice-fields of the Kandyans, in the first glimpses of the far-famed Royal Botanic Gardens at Peradeniya, and in the approaches to the uniquely beautiful and historically interesting little mountain capital of Kandy. Then comes the farther railway trip to Matale and a visit to the caves of Dambulla : the ancient rock fortress of Sigiri or the buried cities of Anuradhapura and Polonnaruwa, with monuments of antiquity almost rivalling those of Thebes. Or, starting from Kandy upwards

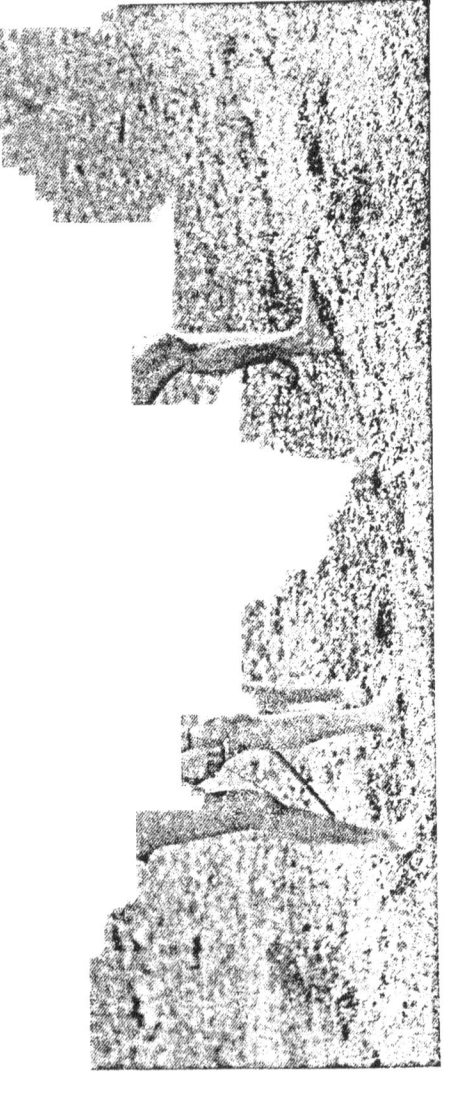

VEDDAHS AT KALLODAI.

Ceylon in 1899.

by train, the visitor rises from Gampola and Nawalapitiya to Hatton, whence an excursion can be made to the top of Adam's Peak, and an unequalled view of the Peak's shadow and the country got from the summit; while continuing in the train he passes through the largest continuous scene of tea cultivation in the world, the plantations of this evergreen shrub being diversified by groves, belts, or shade of eucalypti, grevilleas, and other introduced ornamental trees, while streams and waterfalls lend life to the valleys, and cultivation is everywhere framed by the forest-clad everlasting hills. Here Sir Samuel Baker hunted for eight years in his youthful prime, when as yet there was scarcely a single plantation between Great Western and Adam's Peak, while now there are 300 tea estates, as many planters, and some 150,000 coolies and dependent natives. Nuwara Eliya is reached from Nanuoya in a short journey by coach (soon to be superseded by rail), and from the Grand Hotel or Hill Club, the highest mountain top in the island (8,296 feet) can easily be attained in a morning's walk, while a drive to the Hakgalla Gardens is only second in interest to the visit to Peradeniya. Continuing the railway journey from Nanuoya (where a full mile in altitude above the sea has been attained) summit level is reached at 6,240 feet, and soon after the grand Uva amphitheatre with its rolling patanas and circlet of hill ranges bursts into view, and twenty miles of a wonderful descent is made by the train. If so inclined the visitor can pursue his journey by coach to Badulla, and onwards by a good road to the east coast at Batticaloa with its lake of singing fish, visiting the Veddahs, or wild men of the jungle, on the way, or having some sport with wild elephants. A steamer service round the island affords ready communication with Batticaloa, Trincomalee, Jaffna, &c. Altogether there is no more wonderful or interesting railway journey for its length in the world (and personally I have been able to compare a good many famous railway lines in Europe, America, and Australia) than this Ceylon ride of 143 miles from Colombo to Bandarawela on our first-class mountain railway ; and the intelligent traveller will remember that it is not alone for its scenic beauty, natural vegetation, or cultivated gardens and fields that interest should be aroused, but that all around are places and spots full of historic memories —that, in fact, in Sinhalese annals every valley has its battle and every stream its song—that from the peak of Allagalla the prisoners of the Kandyan King were hurled to execution—that Kandy itself is the centre of many centuries of royal rule that controlled the fate of scores and hundreds of European prisoners, Portuguese, Dutch, French, and British, many of whom lived, married, and died in the country—that at Gampola we are passing through ancient royal domains, and that, as we rise to the mountain plateaux, we enter a region consecrated in Sinhalese legend and Hindu epic poetry to the adventures of Sita and Rama, whose names still remain in stream and plain to testify to the connection with far-off if not prehistoric times. And yet the interest and mystery to the stranger now is not more of the past than of the present, and must find vent in some such words as those so well expressed in the tribute of an English poetess who visited the island about the middle of the present century :—

> Ceylon! Ceylon! 'tis nought to me
> How thou wast known or named of old
> As Ophir, or Taprobane,
> By Hebrew King or Grecian bold.
> To me, thy spicy-wooded vales,
> Thy dusky sons and jewels bright,
> But image forth the far-famed tales—
> But seem a new Arabian night.
>
> And when engirdled figures crave
> Heed to thy bosom's dazzling store,
> I see Aladdin in his cave :
> I follow Sindbad on the shore.
> Yet these, the least of all thy wealth,
> Thou heiress of the eastern isles,
> Thy mountains boast of northern health,
> Where Europe amid Asia smiles.

APPENDIX.

METEOROLOGICAL CONDITIONS IN NORTH-CENTRAL AND NORTH-EAST CEYLON.

WITH REFERENCE TO THE REQUIREMENTS OF SUGAR CULTIVATION.

Altitudes, Rainfall, Distribution, Periods of Drought, and of average Temperature at certain selected stations.

REVISED UP TO DATE.

1. MANKULAM, marked in map at two places, one with "Railway Station," R.S., &c. &c. Height above sea, 167 feet. Rain observations, nine years ; an average annual fall of 58·21 inches on seventy-two days average. Greatest fall in twenty-four hours, 9·70 inches. In 1901 total fall was 31·57 inches. Average rainfall each month :— January, 3·15 ; February, 1·24; March, 1·19 ; April 2·50 ; May, 1·30 ; June, 0·57 ; July, 0·86 ; August, 1·54 : September, 4·82 ; October, 8·83; November, 16·34 ; December, 15·87 inches.

2. VAVUNIYA (also R.S.), 318 feet up ; observed two years ; fall, 50·36 on 93 days ; greatest fall in twenty-four hours, 3·90. Average mean temperature, 80·3°. Greatest drought recorded, 101 days, June–September, 1891. Average monthly fall :—January, 4·40; February, 0·92 ; March, 2·05 ; April, 6·75 ; May, 4·79 ; June, 0·01 ; July, 1·03 ; August, 0·86 ; September, 2·11 ; October, 8·69 ; November, 12·06 ; December, 7·61 inches. (In 1901 the total fall was 46·88 inches.)

Ceylon in 1899.

3. MADAWACHI (R. Station), 285 feet high; observed eleven years; total fall, 49·91 inches on seventy-four days. Greatest fall in twenty-four hours, 6·70 inches. Monthly fall :—January, 2·68 ; February, 1·28 ; March, 1·80; April, 5·18; May, 2·68; June, 1·18; July, 1·09; August, 2·62 ; September, 2·15 ; October, 7·34 ; November, 9·99; December, 11·92 inches. (In 1901 the total fall was 25·10 inches).
4. ANURADHAPURA (R.S.)—295f eet high; observed thirty-three years; 54·41 inches on 104 days ; 9·32 inches greatest fall in twenty-four hours. Greatest drought, 121 days, May-September, 1884. Average annual mean temperature, 80·2°. Monthly fall :—January, 3·04 ; February, 1·42 ; March, 2·78 ; April, 7·56 ; May, 3·70 ; June, 1·51 ; July, 1·01 ; August, 1·76 ; September, 3·00 ; October, 8·46 ; November, 11·04 ; December, 9·12 inches. (Total fall in 1902, 60·71 inches).
5. TRINCOMALEE, 12 feet above sea ; 33 years observed ; rainfall, 63·45 inches average on 110 days; 8·21 inches greatest fall in twenty-four hours. Longest drought 104 days, February-May, 1884. Average annual mean temperature, 81·3°. Monthly fall :—January, 5·73, February, 2·20 ; March, 1·65 ; April, 2·08 ; May, 2·30 ; June, 1·38 ; July, 2·02 ; August, 4·32 ; September, 4·64 ; October, 7·92 ; November, 14·04 ; December, 15·17 inches. (In 1902 the total fall was 77·31 inches).
6. KANTHALAI, 150 feet up ; twenty-five years observed ; 65·26 inches average annual fall on sixty-two days ; 8·50 inches greatest daily fall. Monthly fall :—January, 7·16 ; February, 2·59 ; March, 1·66 ; April, 3·53 ; May, 4·06 ; June, 1·11 ; July, 1·93 ; August, 3·14 ; September, 3·51 ; October, 7·89 ; November, 13·75 ; December, 14·93 inches. (Total fall in 1901, 21·07 inches).
7. ALLAI, 95 feet above sea; observed twenty-five years; 72·37 average annual fall on fifty-seven days; 8·25 inches greatest daily fall. Monthly fall :—January, 7·87 ; February, 2·67 ; March, 2·31 ; April, 2·04 ; May, 3·15 ; June, 1·98 ; July, 1·83 ; August, 4·80 ; September, 4·79 ; October, 9·18 ; November, 15·37 ; December, 16·38 inches. (Total fall in 1901, 75·82 inches.)

APPENDIX VI.

TYPES OF RACES AND AMUSING CHARACTERS IN CEYLON.

(BEING SKETCHES AND CARICATURES GIVEN IN THE "SOUVENIRS OF CEYLON," BY A. M. FERGUSON.)

THE KANDYAN ADIGAR ("the supreme one") represents a dignity next in rank to the Kandyan Sovereign. These were the first, second, and third Adigars, conjoint Prime Ministers, Commanders in Chief, and Judges of the Appellate Court. After being long extinct, the dignity has been revived of late years. The folds of stiff muslin worn by the Kandyan Headmen give them an odd appearance, and led a late facetious Judge of the Kandy District Court to place to their credit the invention of crinoline. At Pavilion *levées* and on other state occasions the Kandyan Chiefs still appear in full dress, and their coronet-like caps relieve the effeminate effect of "all this muslin," and show to advantage when compared with the comb-adorned heads of

The MARITIME SINHALESE MUDALIYARS.—The figure represents one of these, the highest Native Chiefs in the low country; for the rank of Maha Mudaliyar (Great Mudaliyar) is the very highest in the Maritime Districts. Mudaliyar, or Mudiyanse, is a military term about equivalent to the rank of Captain of a district, and in the olden days, even in the Dutch times, each Mudaliyar had his guard of Lascoreens or native soldiers. Originally there was a Korala, the highest civil authority, and a Mudaliyar, the highest military power, in each korale or county. But collisions of authority led to the suppression of the civil rank in the Dutch time, and the concentration of all power, civil and military, in the Mudaliyar—whose sword, worn conspicuously at *levées* and on other full-dress occasions attests the origin of the rank. The effect is not more ludicrous than the sword which forms an essential part of the court-dress of England; though here, in Ceylon, every interpreter of the Supreme Court or of a Government Agent's Kachcheri (office), and of a District Court, with all Secretaries of District Courts who are natives, are *ex officio* Mudaliyars. The Mudaliyars of Korales are the Government Agents' right hands in matters of revenue, title to lands, &c.; and the Government can reward meritorious servants of Government, or natives in private life who distinguish themselves by acts of public spirit, with the much-coveted distinction of Mudaliyar of the Governor's Gate. For instance, Mudaliyar of the Gate, de Soysa of Moratuwa, received his higu rank for opening a road in Hewaheta. In former days the different castes had each its headman, but these are now abolished and officers for the different districts only are appointed, irrespective of caste; the offices being open

Sketches and Caricatures.

indeed, to all competent natives, as is the use of velvet, a fabric which was once restricted to Maha Mudaliyars by a sumptuary law. This law regulated the most minute particulars of the dress of headmen, and rendered it penal for private individuals to ape their betters in such matters. All such laws have now been swept from our Statute Book. The representative of the Sovereign can still make a belted Mudaliyar, but the meanest in Ceylon may dress like the highest if he chooses. In our "Ceylon Directory" for 1863 we wrote respecting the female comb and European coat of the Sinhalese, in noticing the figures of the bridegroom and bride, that "the singular adoption by the rougher sex of an article elsewhere peculiar to females, is by some traced to the influence of the wife of a Portuguese Governor." [As a cure for the untidiness of long and loose tresses, she made presents of combs, the use of which soon spread.] The full-dress coat which covers the Sinhalese "Comboy" is undoubtedly of Portuguese origin. But different in appearance as the men of the broadcloth and comb and those of the muslin and the cornered cap are, they are merely representatives of sections of the same Sinhalese race, the Highlander differing in his bearing from the Lowlander, as all Highlanders do, and differing, moreover, in having longer retained his independence of foreign domination.

The figure of a LAMA ETENA, or Sinhalese lady of rank, is somewhat too European to be characteristic ; and the reproduction of a photograph of a Kandyan lady does but scant justice to the original. What the Kandyan notions of beauty are may be gathered from the following description supplied to the late Dr. Davy by a Kandyan Chief :—

"Her hair should be voluminous, like the tail of the peacock, long reaching to the knees, and terminating in graceful curls ; her eyebrows should resemble the rainbow ; her eyes the blue sapphire and the petals of the manilla flower. Her nose should be like the bill of the hawk. Her lips should be bright and red, like coral or the young leaf of the iron-tree. Her teeth should be small, regular, and closely set, and like jasmine buds. Her neck should be large and round, resembling the benigodea. Her chest should be capacious ; her breasts firm and conical, like the yellow coconut ; and her waist small, almost small enough to be clasped by the hand. Her hips should be wide ; her limbs tapering ; the soles of her feet without any hollow ; and the surface of her body in general soft, delicate, smooth, and rounded, without the asperities of projecting bones and sinews."

The full-dress costume of a Sinhalese lady is well represented in the figure of the bride ; the ordinary female dress is shown on the coffee-picker and ayah, and in the two figures, especially that to the left in the illustration of Demonolatry.

Whether the Sinhalese were "always here," as some think, or whether they came over with Wijayo five centuries or so before the Christian era, certain it is that they are the people of the country, speaking a language spoken nowhere else, except in the roots which are common to all the Indo-Germanic tongues.

Very different are the cases of the two races represented by other figures. "THE CHETTY," who is kin to the great Tamil family of Southern India, and the so-called "MOORMAN" [see engravings of Trader and Mason], who traces his origin, however remotely, to Arabia, are each a sojourner in the land, and were, in historic times, strangers to it. The Tamils [see engravings of Jaffna Tamil, Tamil Females, and Roman Catholic Tamil and his wife, with that of the Natucotta Chetty], offshoots from the great Scythian race of Southern India, made themselves a footing by war; the "Moors" are said to have sought an asylum from persecution, but both have distinguished themselves in the walks of (Oriental) enterprise and commerce. Indeed, the word "Chetty" signifies merchant, and much of the native and intermediate trade of Ceylon is carried on by the "Nattucotta Chetties." But these are men from the Coast of Coromandel, turban-wearers, and bearers of the insignia of heathenism, while the figure with the Portuguese cap and huge jewelled rings distending his ear lobes, is a representative of the "Christian Chetties of Colombo"—a class largely employed as brokers, shroffs, bill collectors, and clerks. More strictly native are the Tamil man and his wife, but these also being Christians (as the emblem worn by the male figure shows) there is a good deal of European modification in the man's dress. An unsophisticated Tamil would content himself with three pieces of cloth : one bound round the loins ; one thrown over the shoulders, like the Highlander's plaid; and the third worn on the head. [See engraving of Jaffna Tamil.] The Moormen equally with the Chetties speak Tamil, which would seem to show that they came directly to Ceylon from Southern India. The tradition is that seven wifeless Arabs, fleeing from their enemies, settled and married in Alutgama and so spread. The Mohammedans of Ceylon are bigoted, but not aggressive. They are the Jews of Ceylon and are found everywhere, as pedlars, lapidaries, jewellers, masons, and shopkeepers. In the Kandyan country they have devoted themselves with much success to the pursuits of agriculture.

A PETTAH SHOPKEEPER, such as we have represented in full dress, may often be seen driving as fine a horse and waggon as can be sported on the Galle Face—the "air-eating" resort of Colombo society. There is no mistaking our old friend "TAMBY," the Master Mason, in the corner. The dress in this case, including the absurd funnel-shaped calico cap, is most truthful and characteristic. In the Kandyan country the Moormen are industrious agriculturists, and in former times much of the inland traffic was conducted by them by means of *tavalam* or pack bullocks.

"Papa ! don't the Moormen marry ?" was the question put by a rather sharp child, when he first saw the page of engravings and his eye rested on the solitary Tamby. The fact is that these Mussulmans have a great repugnance to allowing their women to be seen ; and an artist whom we asked to represent a Moor lady said he could only draw a female figuer completely draped with no part of the body visible, save the ring-adorned ankles. For the present, therefore, we cannot gratify the curiosity of those who would wish to see what a Moorwoman looks like, but we trust to add a Ceylon Mussulmanee on a future occasion.

Time was, when with British merchants the word of a Moorman, but especially that of a Chetty, was deemed as good as his bond. There was a species of "socialism" which prevailed amongst the Chetties especially, which gave the European merchant additional security. But with the wild speculation of the cotton crisis and the extension of commerce, things have altered rather for the worse. The native who contracts to deliver cotton or coffee insists on heavy money advances, while he gives a promissory note at a long date for the Manchester goods he buys—a note not invariably honoured.

Akin to the Moormen in religious profession, though widely different in race, are the MALAYS, who have found their way to Ceylon from the Straits of Malacca, mainly as soldiers of the Ceylon Rifle Regiment. Let us hope that the female sweetmeat-seller is anything but a representative of Malay beauty. The Malays have been highly prized for their soldierly qualities, and it becomes now more than ever a matter of anxiety to recruit the Ceylon Rifles, as a wing of the corps is to form a portion of the garrison of the Straits. There were formerly several Ceylon regiments, one of which was made up of Kaffirs from the Mozambique coast.

The PARSEES—descendants of the Ancient Persian race, and still fire worshippers—are mere sojourners in Ceylon, their headquarters being Bombay and Surat in Western India. The few residents here are, without exception, engaged in commerce. In physique and fairness of skin, they can scarcely be distinguished from Europeans proper.

The "APPOO," or head Sinhalese servant, in full dress of snowy white, in going to market is not likely to neglect the sacred duty of the brotherhood, that of charging a percentage on the purchases made for "master." The Ceylon servants differ from those of India in that the majority of them speak English very well indeed, far better than most Europeans can speak any native language. Their masters, especially young men who may have an old servant, generally shout "boy!" (properly Bhaee, the Hindustani for brother) when they want attendance, there being no bells hung in the Ceylon houses; but the servants greatly prefer to be called "appoo," which signifies gentleman. The Ceylon servants are not faultless, but there are worse in the world. The Sinhalese seems to have little aptitude for equestrianism as they show for navigation, and a Sinhalese groom is as rare as a white crow or a perfectly straight coconut tree. The "HORSEKEEPERS" employed by Europeans are universally Tamils from Southern India, and so are the grass-cutters, who are usually the wives or female relatives of the horsekeepers. The grass-cutters forage for natural grasses, which they take from the ground, roots as well as leaves, and after washing the grass, bring a bundle twice a day to their employers. Of course, those who have Guinea grass plots can dispense with grass-cutters; but Guinea grass, while luxuriant in wet weather, is apt to fail in seasons of drought. As the best grass grows on the roadsides, and as the road officers wish to preserve this sward, while the grass-cutters seize every occasion to pare it off, the relations between the two classes is that of chronic warfare. It would be unjust not to acknowledge the natural talent of eloquence possessed by this class of people, eminently by the females. Their vocabulary may be limited, but for emphasis of tone and energy of gesture they can bear comparison with the orator who

"Shook the Senate and fulmined all Greece."

As their discussions are usually carried on in the open air, they can never put in the plea, " Unaccustomed as I am to public speaking."

The cheapness of arrack in Ceylon does not improve the character of the horsekeeper class in Ceylon, and a drunken horsekeeper is a spectacle as common as that of a drunken Sinhalese house servant is rare.

The IMMIGRANT LABOURERS who work on the tea, &c., plantations are of the same race with the horsekeepers, but they rarely take spirits to excess ; and the large majority of them succeed in the object for which they come to Ceylon,—that of saving rupees to enable them to return to their "country"; that country being amongst the rice lands of Tanjore, Trichinopoly, and Madura, the palmirah groves of Tinnevelly or the coconut "topes" of Travancore, rich enough to clear away encumbrances on their patrimonial fields, to add to those fields, or to become for the first time landholders on their own account. Immigration, carefully regulated as it is in the interests of the weaker and less intelligent class, is an equal blessing to sparsely peopled Ceylon and the overcrowded population of Southern India. Happily no plantation in Ceylon has ever been opened by means of slave labour (the mild prædial slavery which existed amongst the natives was finally abolished in 1844), and consequently the relations between the European planters and their Tamil labourers are generally of a happy character. The Tamils are not strong (many of the poor creatures come to Ceylon resembling locomotive skeletons), but they are docile and good-tempered, and soon learn to perform very fairly all the details of estate work,—their small, lithe hands giving them eminent facilities for the important operations of pruning and handling the coffee bushes. Large numbers of these people are settling in Ceylon, acquiring competence as cart drivers, landowners, small traders, &c.

To return to the Sinhalese. The DHOBY or WASHERMAN (there are no native washerwomen) is as invariably Sinhalese (except in the purely Tamil districts of the north and east of the Island) as the attendants on horses are Tamils. These dhobies wash clothes beautifully white, but they require careful looking after, or they will lend out articles of clothing or exchange bad for good. They must be warned, also not to "Europe" the clothing too much, or they will beat them on flat stones in waterpools until cotton clothing is better fitted for the use of the paper-maker than that of the owner. "Fast colours" very often yield to the bleaching of these dhobies. The BARBER is a welcome daily visitor to young gentlemen, who, though they may not boast of much beard, delight in receiving, and by means of the barber retailing, such gossip as that "The Dutch have taken Holland," that "Smith is going to get married to Brown's wife," &c. The services of the WATERMAN will be required in a large portion of Colombo to boat over and distribute the drinking water from the wells in "Captain's Garden" (a peninsula jutting out into the lake opposite the Pettah), until the projected works for bringing the waters of the Kelani into Colombo are in operation. The Queen's House LASCOREEN, clad in scarlet jacket and plumed hat, is one of the half-dozen attendants provided for the Governor, to receive visitors, go messages, accompany the vice-regal carriage, &c. The lascoreen survives as a reminder of the abortive attempts made to convert the Sinhalese into soldiers. A former Colonial Secretary said that you never could be certain that they would not fire the ramrod at you. Whatever they may have been in the time of the great Raja Singha, the Sinhalese are not now distinguished for military instincts or aspirations Of the BUDDHIST PRIEST and the TODDY-DRAWER we have already spoken; but we must not overlook the useful and industrious FISHERMAN, remarkable for his broad-brimmed straw hat and thick military coat, contrasting so strangely with his nude lower limbs. He represents a class composed very largely of Roman Catholic Christians, Xavier and other early missionaries having found ready converts amongst the fisher caste all over India. In a MS. note attached by Mr. Vandort to *his* sketch of the fisherman, he writes:—" Being a dovout Catholic, the fisherman dedicates a portion of his earnings to his patron saint, St. Anthony. He also gives up, according to old usage,'an unlimited quantity of fish to the members of the barbers' community, who thus levy a tax on the fishermen for assisting them at weddings, funerals, &c. Like all sailors, the fisherman is very superstitious ; a certain public Government functionary in the employ of the Fiscal of Colombo [the executioner] derives a handsome profit (whenever he has assisted in turning off any unfortunate gallows bird) in selling pieces of the cord used on such occasions, the lucky possessors of which attach them to their nets to ensure miraculous draughts of fishes." The liberality with which these people support the faith they profess is calculated to put to shame more enlightened and richer Christians. Besides extraordinary contributions, the fishermen have almost universally agreed to bestowt he tenth of the produce of their labour, which Government reliuquished about a score of years ago, on the churches of their persuasion.

The cry of "Kaddela! kaddela! kaddelay?" which the Tamil pulseselling woman sends forth is dear even to European children in Ceylon, who, however, listen with still greater delight to the cry of the sweetmeat-seller, " Seeni-sakeree-metai!"

On the Malay " PASONG WOMAN " Mr. Vandort writes :—" Chiefly met with on Thursdays (the day before the Mohammedan sabbath), ' Pasong ' is a sort of sweet pudding made with rice-flower and jaggery, with a frothy head of coconut milk, and rolled up in conical envelopes of plantain leaf, very difficult to be procured on any day except Thursdays. Malay women wear a dress similar to that worn by Moorish women; the only difference is that the wrapper or overall is worn much more open by the Malays, and the material is not muslin, but a thick checked camboy or sarong. The nose-rings, necklaces, anklets, and the rest of the dress is the same as those worn by the Moorish women. Having already noticed the musical mechanic, we would simply say in regard to the "minstrel priest," so called, that Hindoo sacerdotal beggars are, by the laws of Ceylon, exempt from the penalties with which those laws visit other able-bodied vagrants: just as those professional (but well-to-do) mendicants, the Buddhist priests, are put in the same category with the Governor, the military, and immigrant labourers as exempt from the six days' labour on the roads, or their money equivalent enacted from the adult males, of all other classes in the colony.

The truth as well as the cleverness of the LAW COURT ODDITIES will be recognized by those who know what law and litigation are in Ceylon. The whole population, men, women, and even children by their representatives, would seem to be engaged in endless lawsuits. The law of inheritance, as it exists amongst the natives, has a good deal to do with this. The people dearly prize land and fruit-bearing trees, and most of the litigation refers to such matters as the title to "undivided shares" of land and the right in an almost infinitesimally fractional part of a coconut tree. The following statement, by a party to a land case, will show what is the nature of the questions which bewildered English magistrates have to hear and decide:—

" By inheritance through my father I am entitled to one-fourth of one-third of one-eighth; through my mother also to one-fourth of one-third of one-eighth. By purchase from one set of co-heirs I am entitled to one-ninety-sixth; from another set, to one-ninety-sixth more; from another set, to one-ninety-sixth more; and from a fourth set of co-heirs to one-one-hundred-and-forty-fourth."

Caste and class distinctions are not now recognised by the laws of Ceylon. In the period of Dutch rule the case was very different, and even in the early years of the British Government caste distinctions were not only upheld but enforced. One of those worthy Dutch magistrates whom the British continued in office after the capitulation, was in the habit of mixing up legislative and judicial functions after the fashion illustrated by the following decisions, in which Mynheer's English must not be too severely criticised:—

" Pautura Magistrates' Court, 15th March, 1815.

"Sentenced Dinetti Carolis Silva Cangan to pay a fine of Rds. 10, that he, being a Chalia, allowed a married fisherwoman to remain in his garden without the foreknowledge of her husband, nor of the police vidan of the

Sketches and Caricatures. clxxi

village. And his son Dinetti Siman Silva do bail himself in Rds. 25, and two sureties for Rds. 25, that he shall not go to the house of complainer's wife, neither talk with her.

"Saturday, 25th Feb., 1815, appeared Paniloewege Nicholas, of Labugama, 28 years old, headen [heathen, F.]; and requested to marry with Punchy Hamy. Appeared Punchy Hamy, of Labugama, old 18 years, headen, and complains that she cannot remain at the Police Vidan, Ritiellege Don Juan; because he beats her she went out of his house to t e above Paniloewege Nicholas. as she is acquainted with him from a long time; and requested to marry with him. Ritiellege Don Juan, Police Vidan, admitted that he had bated Poentjee Hamy. Ordered that Paniloewege Nicholas, of Labugama, do marry according to their law, with Punchy Hamy of Labugama."

The laws of Ceylon are now administered after a different fashion.

The bar affords an attractive field for the educated burgher and native youth, and the profession would be overcrowded, but for the inveterate litigation mania of the people. The Honourable Mr. Morgan, the able Queen's Advocate of Ceylon, tells with great glee, a story of a native client of his, whom he had not seen for some time, and who apologised for neglecting to visit him by saying, "Oh, Sir, I was ashamed to see your face, as I had no case to bring to you!" The figures, as freely limned by Mr. Vandort, tell their own tale. There is—

"———the Justice
In fair round belly with good capon lined,
With eyes severe———
Full of wise saws and modern instances."

His dignified position (flanked by "sword" and "mace, with registrar, marshall, and crier in attendance), the envy and the hope of the contemplative student, who sits listening to the opposite counsel, as they quote "Archibald's Reports, "Taylor on Evidence,"·The Principles of the Roman Dutch Code, as laid down by Voet (pronounced Foot), or Van Leuwen," or "The Mysteries of Kandian and 'Country' Laws." The absorbed native jurymen (who keenly appreciate the difference with which they are appealed to as "gentlemen," and who, on the whole, give fair verdicts), remind one of the question to which Thurlow's personal appearance gave rise, "I wonder if ever human being was as wise as Thurlow looks"; while the terrified expression with which the bewildered witness regards the stately interpreter (who never—no never—receives visitors and gifts, and never settles cases at his private residence), is a striking contrast to the impudent air of the well-conditioned criminal, with whom prison fare and gentle exercise have evidently agreed. If the prisoner's garments are somewhat scanty, the same cannot be said of the dark policeman, tortured and made hideous by the incongruous uniform, introduced by a former superintendent, who brought with him to the island implicit faith in the effect even of the dress of the Irish constabulary. While we are writing Mr. Campbell, the present superintendent, is superseding this stiff and inappropriate dress by one better suited for Asiatics and a tropical climate. The relations of a proctor in full practice to a client destitute of a full purse are significantly indicated in the figures of the two characters ; while all the penalties of the law of libel staring us in the face prevent our even hinting at the possibility of an argentine argument having influenced the *non est inventus* of the fiscal's peon or messenger. It is a curious fact, however, that some of the best known men of the community are, by some mysterious process, "not to be found," when sought for, at the instance of disconsolate creditors, although they placidly dwell in their usual abodes and pursue their ordinary avocations visible enough to the eyes of their neighbours. But the crier, in stentorian tones, adjourns the Court in the name of "My Lord, Queen's Justice ! " and we shut up—our book.

BADULLA: THE CAPITAL OF THE ANCIENT PRINCIPALITY OF UVA: VIEW FROM THE FORT.

APPENDIX VII.

UPPER UVA, CEYLON, AS A STATION FOR BRITISH TROOPS.

(*By* "*Anopheles*," *in United Service Magazine.*)

The transport by sea of a large body of troops after the experience of the South African War, excites little comment, and with our extensive mercantile marine now presents comparatively few difficulties, provided careful arrangements have been previously made. The ease and celerity with which the British troops were dispatched from India to Natal was a momentous movement, the wide-reaching consequences of which are not yet, perhaps, fully appreciated. But it is well known in military circles that the Indian contingent prevented the Boers, on the outbreak of hostilities, from carrying their victorious arms to the Indian Ocean. At the same time it is fully recognised in the same circles that the Indian Government was reducing the number of white troops to an extent which would be dangerous or impracticable if any unruly native population or harassed frontier had been engaging its attention.

In the recent Chinese troubles (and further troubles in the near future are likely to again arise) the Indian Government was called upon for aid; thus in our last two campaigns India has on each occasion been called upon for troops, and on each occasion she has gallantly responded to the call. It is the opinion of all thoughtful men that to rely on India for troops in an emergency is a dangerous proceeding. More particularly at the present time when our restless Northern neighbour is pursuing his usual tractis in Manchuria and Thibet. From her geographical position India is admirably situated to deal with any crisis in the Oriental region; on the one hand she can strike rapidly to the west, and on the other equally rapidly to the east; but when by so doing she renders herself open to attack, and a staggering blow delivered to her would have such far-reaching consequences, it is as a matter of serious moment to weaken her, unless the point at issue is one of vital moment. It is with diffidence that I, a non-combatant, mention the word strategy, or deal even in a cursory manner with questions of that military science; but I think even a layman can grasp the strategical importance of the geographical position of India when he considers that officers still on the active list have seen India sending troops to Persia, Cyprus, Egypt, the Soudan, the Cape, and China more than once. Granted that she has done this with impunity in the past, it by no means follows that it would be good policy to do so in the future. What would have been the condition of Natal, and indeed the state of affairs at the Cape at the present moment, if India from internal causes had been prevented from sending a contingent to South Africa? The point I wish to bring to notice is this—that judging by our recent military history it is not only advisable, but perhaps vitally important, to have ready at hand, to send in any direction, and at the shortest possible moment, a well-equipped, healthy body of men, complete in every detail, to those portions of the globe where hitherto India has been called upon to send her troops. Now, what are the conditions necessary to fulfil the above?

(1) A favourable geographical position.
(2) A country not liable to either external or internal attack.
(3) Proximity to a good harbour with sufficient shipping.
(4) Proximity to a railway.
(5) An extensive country fit for military purposes.
(6) Adequate local supplies, such as cattle, fodder, etc., etc.
(7) A healthy climate for the troops.

A glance at an atlas will, without argument, satisfy conditions 1 and 3.

The geographical position of Ceylon is practically the same as India. Colombo is the Clapham Junction of the East, where all the large Orient liners of the P. & O., Orient, Clan, and other Companies call regularly, and where, consequently, the shipping necessary for the dispatch of troops could be obtained and collected. The new breakwater and batteries, now under construction, will make Colombo secure from the elements and the enemy.

Condition 2 is amply fulfilled. The insular position of Ceylon does not allow of its invasion as long as we command the sea, and the loyalty of the native population is such that the present Governor, Sir West Ridgeway, unhesitatingly offered the services of the only English regiment in the colony for duty at the Cape during the dark days of 1899.

The Ceylon Government Railway meets my fourth condition. It passes close to the country I am about to describe, and has stations at Diyatalawa and Bandarawela, in close proximity to ground in every way suited for a military camp, and within ten hours' journey of Colombo.

With regard to 5; Ceylon, to the majority of people, conveys the idea of a hot, moist, tropical country, enervating to a high degree, if not actually unhealthy. But the hill station of Nuwara Eliya, at any rate, is now becoming known, and it will not be strange to many to learn that other parts of the hill districts of Ceylon boast of an almost English climate. I may remark, parenthetically, in many respects a good deal better? I am not, however, advocating the claims of Nuwara Eliya. It is far too enclosed for the manœuvres of any but a very small body of troops, and even the open country in its near neighbourhood (the Barrack and Moon Plains) is so studded with bogs and morasses that the movements even of a company would be largely confined to the high road. At the present some thirty or forty sickly men regain their stamina there, after the enervating climate of the low country. Hitherto the Sanatorium has been open from the middle of September till the burst of the south-west monsoon at the end of May, or beginning of June. Nuwara Eliya,* from a social point of view, with its race-course, golf links, club, and so forth, is a pleasant place enough in fine weather, but can scarcely become a station for practical, serious soldiering. In the neighbouring Province of Uva can, however, be found all the conditions necessary for the military training of 10,000 or more infantry in a healthy country, and with unrivalled climate. This appears such a startling statement, that I propose to enter somewhat fully into the physical characteristics

---

* Nuwara Eliya has a rainfall of 99·37 inches, and 212 rainy days; average of 26 7.12 years.

FALLS ON THE DIYALUMAOYA, NEAR NAULA,
EASTERN HAPUTALE, 535 FEET HIGH,
(From a Photograph by the late E. F. Grigson.)

of the Province, its climate, and the health of the troops at present stationed there.

I cannot better describe the scenery of Upper Uva than by quotations from an account of a prolonged tour made through the Province in March, 1819, by Dr. John Davy (brother of the famous Sir Humphrey Davy), taken from his 'Account of Ceylon,' published in 1821. Dr. Davy was on the medical staff of the Army in Ceylon, with the title of Physician to the Forces. He travelled from Colombo to Uva *via* Ratnapura, and entered the Province from the Haputale (south) side, over the Idalgashena Pass, and from no point of view is the glorious scenery of Upper Uva seen to better advantage.*

He says :—

"The next stage is to Velaugahena, eight miles distant across the Idalgashena, the summit of which is about 4,700 feet above the level of the sea. This is the principal pass from Saffragam (Ratnapura) into Upper Ouva. The weather being fine, the feeling of the fatigue was lost in the enjoyment of the magnificent scenery of the mountains. . . . On the top of the pass the path takes a turn, and brings one suddenly in view of Upper Ouva, consisting of an extensive surface of green, grassy hills, walled round by lofty blue mountains, laid out like a map at one's feet. The sight of such a country was quite a treat, and the eye at liberty wandered with delight from hill to hill, and from mountain to mountain. . . . On looking round the country it has the appearance of a magnificent amphitheatre, sixty or eighty miles in circumference, formed of a succession of steep, smooth, green, conical hills, and of deep, narrow glens, remarkably free from wood, enclosed on every side by mountains varying in prependicular height from 4,000 to 6,000 feet,

Dr. Davy visited Uva again later in the year 1819. His first tour was in March. On the second occasion he made his trip from the Nuwara Eliya side (about twenty miles north-west of Diyatalawa), and proceeded only as far as Fort MacDonald, six miles north of the camp. He says :—

"About three o'clock in the afternoon we emerged entirely from the forest, and had immediately, from our commanding height, a most extensive view of Upper Ouva, which appeared laid out before us like a magnificent map. The first object in the prospect that arrested attention was Naminacoole-Kanda, rising in the eastern horizon, of a light blue colour, and surpassing every other mountain in the circle that surrounds Upper Ouva as much in massive form as its apparent height. With the general appearance of the country I was disappointed: its surface was not fresh and green as when I viewed it the first time from the Idalgashena, reminding me of the hills in England in spring, but of a light yellowish-green colour, as if parched and withered; nor were its mountains of the intense blue which I then so much admired, but of a dazzling aerial hue. This appearance of the country having suffered from a long drought was greatly heightened by the clouds of smoke in which many parts of it were enveloped, and which, driven before the wind, had a singularly wild effect giving the idea that the ground was not only parched, but in a state of conflagration. . . .

---

* The camp of the Boer prisoners at Diyatalawa is six miles from Haputale at the southern edge of the plateaux.

There is another and striking peculiarity of Upper Ouva that deserves notice and requires explanation. I mean its undulating surface of hills and valleys, rounded and smoothed as equably as if, instead of primitive rock, they consisted of chalk and clay."

The amphitheatre of hills surrounding the plains of Uva on the west and north effectually prevent the clouds and rain of the south-west monsoon from reaching them. Sir Samuel Baker, in his 'Eight Years in Ceylon,' gives the following account of this curious phenomenon seen during the south-west monsoon, when, while the western side of the island is enveloped in mist and rain, the wet weather terminates abruptly at Hakgalla, and the panorama of Uva is seen in all its beauty. He says:—

"From June to November the south-west monsoon brings wind and mist across the Newara Eliya mountain. Clouds of white fog boil up from the Dimboola valley, like the steam from a huge cauldron and invade the Newara Eliya plain through the gaps in the mountains to the westward. The wind howls over the high ridges, cutting the jungle with its keen edge, so that it remains as stunted brushwood, and the opaque screen of driving fog and drizzling rain is so dense that one feels convinced there is no sun visible within at least 100 miles. There is a curious phenomenon, however, in this locality. When the weather described prevails at Newara Eliya, there is actually not one drop of rain within four miles of my house in the direction of Badulla (Uva). Dusty roads, a cloudless sky, and dazzling sunshine, astonish the thoroughly soaked traveller, who rides out of the rain and mist into a genial climate as though he passed through a curtain. The wet weather terminates at a mountain call Hakgalla. This bold rock, whose summit is about 6,500 feet above the sea, breasts the driving wind, and seems to command the storm. The rushing clouds halt in their mad course upon its crest and curl in sudden impotence around the craggy summits. The deep ravine formed by an opposite mountain is filled with vanquished mist, which sinks powerless in its dark gorge; and the bright sun, shining from the east, spreads a perpetual rainbow upon the gauze-like cloud of fog which settles in the deep hollow. This is exceedingly beautiful. The perfect circle of the rainbow stands like a fairy spell in the giddy depth of the hollow, and seems to forbid the advance of the monsoon. All before is bright and cloudless: the lovely panorama of the Uva country spreads before the eye for many miles beneath the feet. All behind is dark and stormy; the wind is howling, the forests are groaning, the rain is pelting upon the hills. The change seems impossible; but there it is, ever the same, season after season, year after year, the rugged top of Hakgalla struggles with the storms, and ever victorious the cliffs smile in the sunshine on the eastern side; the rainbow reappears with the monsoon, and its vivid circle remains like the guardian spirit of the valley.

I can do little more than refer to a very interesting paper on "The Botany of the Ceylon Patenas," by Mr. Pearson, B. A., published in the proceedings of the Linnæan Society, vol. xxxiv. page 300, which will repay perusal. He enters very fully into the origin and present condition of this open country, and draws a somewhat close comparison between it and the savannahs of South America. He roughly estimates the extent of this patana, savannah or down country, as extending over 300 square miles, the far greater portion of which

FALLS OF RAMBODA.

VIEW OF ADAM'S PEAK FROM WOODSTOCK ESTATE, AMBEGAMUWA.

is in Upper Uva. He summarises his conclusions as follows:—

"An examination of such evidence as exists with regard to the origin of the patanas of Uva, and their western extensions of the slopes of the central ridge, leads to the following conclusions. On the Uva slopes below 4,500 feet (the lower limit of the Rhododendron) the peculiarities of the climate have co-operated with the periodically recurrent grass-fires to transform an open forest, low xerophytic trees with an undergrowth of grass (i.e. a savannah forest such as is still found on the eastern boundary of the plateau) into barren grassy plains. These plains, being almost completely denuded of soil, must be regarded as being of the nature of a permanent savannah, the natural reafforestation of the greater part of which is impossible under the present climatic conditions."

The above descriptions, written years ago by Davy and Baker, apply equally well to the present condition of the country. I may say that its general appearance is very similar to the South Downs of England, more particularly their steep escarpments in the neighbourhood of the well-known Berkshire White Horse. In place, however, of the elastic turf which makes those downs the finest galloping ground in the world, the hills are covered with a short, coarse grass which frequently grows in clumps, which makes progression on horseback somewhat difficult. In the convolutions of the hills where the ground is marshy, small clumps of trees and jungle grow thickly, preserved by the wet from the summer grass-fires. These marshes, unless the country is well known, likewise impede the horseman, who is liable to be badly bogged if he endeavours to ride over them. In spite of these difficulties and drawbacks a flourishing pack of foxhounds (the Errebodde hunt) holds its annual meets on these downs, and many a good gallop is enjoyed by the sporting planters in pursuit of the wily "Jack." The hills are composed of gneiss, for the most part unstratified, but in many places convoluted and distorted. Above this is the mica-schist, occasionally garnetiferous, in many sections on the hill sides it lies beautifully stratified directly on the underlying gneiss; in other places quartz is interposed, and its presence has no doubt given rise to speculation as to its being auriferous. Bands of iron pyrites are not uncommon. The soil is composed of these disintegrated rocks with outcrops of gneiss. It is a little difficult to say how far Government rights extend, for as far as I can gather no complete survey of the country has as yet been made. But the question of the destruction of crops by the movements of troops is one of no great moment as there is but little cultivation, and the few paddy fields in the folds of the hills are of limited extent, and can be easily avoided.

I am told by competent authority that the country cannot be surpassed for instructional purposes in scouting and outpost duties. If anything it is too difficult, owing to the irregular and confused character of the ground. I am informed that many parts of the surrounding amphitheatre of hills, with their rocky, steep and frequently precipitous sides, closely resemble the kopjes of South Africa. As a country for infantry, both mounted and dismounted, it is unrivalled, but owing to the absence of roads and other drawbacks it is at present not suited for artillery.

The climate is a decidedly good one, certainly for nine months out of the twelve. From October to January the north-east monsoon brings very wet weather with violent thunder-storms; towards the end of January the weather clears and becomes fine and warm in the daytime and very cold at night, hoar frost being probably not unknown on the patanas. The burst of the south-west monsoon in May, which brings wet weather to the Colombo side of the island, only produces a few showers, but a persistent wind blows from this direction until September and the gradual setting, in of the other monsoon. From the middle of June to the end of September men would take little harm from bivouacking in the open air, as the nights are perfect and not too cold. The maximum shade temperature in summer is probably not more than eighty-four degrees, and the minimum fifty degrees. The rainfall is between fifty and sixty inches,* the far greater quantity falling in October, November and December. In such an ideal climate and situation, 4,000 feet above the level of the sea, at the present is the camp for the Boer prisioners at Diyatalawa in the Province of Uva. And in this camp some 6,000 men have lived a healthy but monotonous life for the last twelve months; monotonous because 5,000 of them are prisoners, and the remainder British soldiers occupied in the deadly monotonous duty of looking after them. If Diyatalawa can justify itself as one of the healthiest stations in the East when its occupants are prisoners and jailors, how much more is it likely to justify it were it occupied by men in the full enjoyment of their liberty?

By the time these lines are in print it is possible that the war will be over and the prisoners, or many of them, will be returning to their own country.

What is to become of Diyatalawa camp, with everything now ready for the occupation of some 6,000 troops? Will it be sold for old iron or bekep t permanently as a station for British troops? It would be a real boon if only the English regiment in the island was stationed here instead of being broken up into fragments at Colombo, Kandy, Trincomalee and Nuwara Eliya where the routine duties of a garrison inevitably tend to mental stagnation and professional deterioration.

When dealing with the sanitation of an area, the most correct method of coming to a right conclusion regarding it is by enquiring into the diseases of the native population, and discriminating between the preventible diseases and those that are dependent on local conditions. This method should be followed in preference to that frequently adopted of judging of a locality by the health of those newly arrived in it. In this instance the latter method would be particularly fallacious, inasmuch as of the two British regiments stationed here, one came from the hardships of the investment of Ladysmith, and the other from the malarious district of Dum-Dum, after long service in India. In spite of these drawbacks, the medical officer in charge of the former of these regiments writes in most enthusiastic terms of the physique and healthiness of the men after they had had four months' experience of the place, i.e. after they had got rid of the diseases they had brought with them or contracted from the Boers. The latter regiment has been here for nearly nine months, and was in a very sickly condition on arrival. Some seventy men have been either invalided home or sent away for change, but how far their complaints were due to local causes or were legacies from Dum-Dum and elsewhere is difficult to say, but India has probably most to answer for. With regard to malaria, which was rife in the regiment on arrival, it is noteworthy

* Bandarawella, three miles from Diyatalawa and with a similar climate has a rainfall of 64·89 inches; 40·81 of which falls in the north-east monsoon. It has 127 rainy days; average of twenty-five years. Compare Nuwara Eliya.

that an examination in August of 600 men, which included a draft of 150 men direct from home, showed that only two men had had an attack of malarial fever for the first time here, one of these was a man of the draft. It is interesting in this connnection to note that only three specimens of the genus *Anopheles* have so for been captured here; one by Mr. Green, the Government Entomologist, and two by myself. If the species had been abundant, many more of the fresh arrivals would surely have been infected with the malarial parasite, with such a large number of malarious cases open to the attacks of the mosquito.*

The native population is remarkably free from disease: the Colonial surgeon informs me that malarial fever is not endemic in the villages round Diyatalawa camp, but it is frequently introduced by the villagers who go on pilgrimages to such malarious places as Tissamaharama and Wellawaya. He also states that the last quarter is the most unhealthy time of the year. Cholera is occasionally imported from the low country, and venereal diseases are not uncommon.

A final word as regards supplies. The camp is about half a mile from the railway, from which supplies are sent into the camp by means of an ærial train. Wood in adundance is obtained from the neighbouring Government forests; the water is good, and can be obtained in reasonable quantity even in the dry weather. Slaughter cattle and vegetables can be obtained to a certain extent locally. The country is suitable for mounted infantry, but fodder is scarce, even the grass which springs up after the periodical burning is very coarse and lacks nourishment; it could be used for bedding, but some method would have to be found to rid it of the ticks of which there are a great number. To buy up the paddy fields and cultivate them with guinea grass (*P. maximum*) or Mauritius grass (*P. muticum*) would be a serious question. But a trial on an extensive scale on the hill sides should be made of (*Paspalum dilatumat*), which grows well at Ootacamund and is a valuable grass for cattle. It is supposed by many to be of Ceylon origin and flourishes on any poor soil, provided it has plenty of water, and at a suitable elevation it will stand the extremes of heat and cold. It is thought very highly of by the farmers of Victoria and New South Wales.

---

* In the month of August, with an average strength of 862, the average number of sick was twenty-seven, one-third of which were venereal cases. These figures tend to show that the sickness in the regiment was not due to local conditions.

APPENDIX VIII.

TREE-GROWING AT A HIGH ELEVATION IN CEYLON.

THE BEST-WOODED PLANTATION IN THE ISLAND.

We suppose we may, without presumption, speak of the Tea and Cinchona plantation (Abbotsford) identified with the name of the late Mr. A. M. Ferguson—and with that of his son, the present proprietor,—as without exception, "the best-wooded" private estate in the island. The late proprietor took a special delight in getting seeds and plants of trees likely to grow in the soil and at the elevation of Abbotsford from every quarter he could hear of in India, Australia, Java, the Straits and England or Scotland. There were, of course, many failures; but also many successes in his introductions and for the last six years of his life he had the great advantage of the counsel and aid of the present Manager of the Estate who knew a great deal about Forestry before ever he came to Ceylon. The result is that, so far as the introduction and cultivation of a great variety of Australian Eucalypts and Acacias, Javanese "Albizzias," Himalayan Toons, Birches and other trees, Japanese and English Firs, with pines and oaks; and a considerable variety besides,—Abbotsford presents an "experimental plantation" in Upper Dimbula, comparable —*longo intervallo*—to even the "Hakgala Gardens" on the other side of the range facing Uva. Indeed the experienced and enthusiastic Superintendent of Hakgala was, some time ago, astonished and delighted to see the conjunction in Lower Abbotsford of so many palms—Australian *Coryphas* and even *Caryota* flourishing: difficult if not impossible to grow in his colder climate—along with English, Himalayan and Japanese introductions. One of the finest English oaks we have seen in the island is here—a tree of, perhaps, 25 feet high; but, curiously enough, it practically stopped growing six years ago and does not now make an inch a year in growth. An oak and a palm, within a few yards of each, form an interesting conjunction. We have not seen the Gangaroowa "Albizzias"—which are realising R15 each, no doubt greatly because of their proximity to the Kandy timber market—but it would be hard, we think, to beat the trees of this description on Abbotsford, some of them 17 to 18 years old and great giants. *Auracarias* here and there diversify the outlook. One of the most strikingly handsome trees, scattered over the plantation, is the Himalayan Birch tree (*Betula Acuminata*)* which, though not tested yet,

---

* We only identified the tree on our return to Colombo and from what is said by Dr. Watt in his "Economic Products," it will be seen that we are a little wide of the mark as to the value of the timber :—

"Betula acuminata, Wall; Brandis, For. Fl., 458; Gamble. Man. Timb., 372. Habitat.—A large tree, met with in the Himalaya, from 6,000 to 8,000 feet, in the Khasia Hills, the mountains of Manipur and the Naga Hills to Martaban.

must offer a very substantial timber, perhaps too hard to work by the carpenter (in a land where bobbins are not in request)—but at any rate invaluable for rough building work on an estate and for firewood if the necessity should arise.*

EUCALYPTS.

Along the roadside, too, there are some magnificent trees of *Eucalyptus pauciflora;* while there is one specimen of the attractive *E. Ficifolia* (rare in Ceylon) with its peculiar scarlet blossom: while higher up we noted grand specimens of *E. Calophylla.* Very striking also is the giant Eucalypt —*E. Amygdalina* or white gum—to which species in Australia belong the highest trees in the world. Here they grow to, perhaps, 100 feet; and the contrast is interesting between the red (*E. Rostrata*), and the other two gums growing alongside:—

THE RED, WHITE AND BLUE!

Of blue gum (*globulus*) not many trees remain; for the reason that they have chiefly supplied firewood for the Factory tea driers (power is got from the river fortunately) during the past ten years, so that there has been no trenching on the forest reserve.† A curious discovery about the blue gum was that, while flourishing apace on the lower division up to 5,500 feet, it did not grow at all well on Upper Abbotsford—although strangely enough there are magnificent trees in and around Nuwara Eliya still higher up. The late Mr. Ferguson and his Manager were so convinced as to the comparative failure of this tree that they gave special warning to the Government Forest Officers not to waste time and money by trying plantations of it in the adjacent jungle clearings; but their advice was not heeded, with the result that today the five-acre clearings planted with blue gums in the jungle by the old road to Nuwara Eliya

"*Properties and Uses*:—Fibre.—The bark when mature peels off in larger slabs than in any of the other species, and is therefore not so serviceable for the purposes to which the others are put.

"Food —On the mountain tracts of North-East Manipur, bordering on the Naga Hills, the Lalupas cut off the bark in large slabs just before the leaves appear, The inner layer of these slabs is carefully separated from the liber and sun dried. This is either eaten like biscuits, or it is reduced to flour and cooked as an article of food. The tree is much prized by these naked savages, and in early spring yields a considerable portion of their diet. This remarkable fact does not appear to have been observed by any traveller, previous to my exploration in 1880 of the hill tracts of Manipur, and apparently the nutritious properties of the bark have not been discovered by other Indian hill tribes. (See remarks under B. alba.)

"Structure of the Wood.—White, moderately hard, close-grained. Weight 41 lb. per cubic foot.

"It is very little used, but Wallich says it is hard and esteemed in Nepal for all purposes where strength and durability are required. "The wood is close-grained and takes a fine satin polish. It is particularly good for door panels, and the examples in the Government House at Naini Tal show that it is a valuable acquisition for ornamental work." (Atkinson's Him. Dist. X., N.-W.-P. Gaz., 818.)"

* This is as true in regard to timber planking. &c., as for fuel—all the timber required for buildings, lines, &c , has been got for many years by cutting and sawing introduced trees without touching original reserves, and we fancy the Abbotsford Manager could more than confirm the useful figures sent for publication lately by Mr. Maclure of Maskeliya.

are poor affairs—and stand as exhibitions of stunted failures. The blue gum tree serves well for factory (fuel) purposes save that the exuded gum is apt to fix on the flues and in the case of steam-engine boiler-flues, especially, to choke up the channels. Even in a domestic stove, the flue has been found blocked up after a time and has required hammer and chisel to cut out the adhering gum which had become almost as solidly fixed as if it were part of the iron!

One of the most attractive of the Eucalypts is *E. Citriodora* (the lemon-scented gum tree, from the pleasant odour of the crushed leaves or broken stems). Several fine specimens (as indeed of all the Eucalypts) are to be seen at Hakgala, and with us at Nuwara Eliya; but we hear that the finest show of the lemon-scented, perhaps, on a private estate, is found at Mr Gordon's bungalow on Rappanhannock, Udapussellawa. Altogether there must be over a score of different Eucalypts—many of them strikingly handsome trees—in the plantation; but curiously enough there is no specimen of *E Pilularis* which attracted attention some time ago on Carlabeck, for its size and good timber. It is curious to notice the resemblance and the difference between the barks of three prominent Eucalypts—Jarrah (*E. Marginata*), Red gum (*Rostrata*) and Iron Bark (*E. Crebra*)—all doing well as growing trees.

Some of the Grevilleas here vie in size with the other large trees mentioned, and they. and the "toons" (*Cedrela toona* of the Himalayas) are freely scattered over the property. But the former (the "silky oak" of Queensland) may be taken to have reached the limit of successful cultivation, if regard be had to its full growth as a timber tree, on the neighbouring estates—Maha Eliya and Calsay—and again on Tangakelle, Ouvahkelle and Elgin which present a wonderful sight in the uniform and numerous interesting belts of grevilleas, where we can recall the wide expanse of cultivation being without a tree some years ago. Perhaps *E. Robusta*—which has become a favourite in these parts as at Nuwara Eliya—is a quicker grower than the Grevillea; while it also supplies a substantial timber. A grove of these between Abbotsford and Tangakelle shows very regular and successful growth; but the striking fact here is the way in which self-sown cinchonas have sprung up among the gums, groups of fine healthy plants showing how well shade agrees with the far-famed Peruvian introduction. Had cinchona originally been grown under shade in Ceylon, we might even now rival Java in our exports.

A SPECIAL FAVOURITE.

But we must not forget to notice what is, in our experience, the best timber tree to grow in and around Nuwara Eliya and perhaps (judging by the specimens here) lower down, *Acacia Melanoxylon*. It is really a valuable cabinet wood, when fully grown; and we recall the late Rev. W. Oakley, the veteran Church Missionary, showing us with pride a book-case and other cabinet-work he had made out of some Melanoxylon trees, having all the markings and dark colouring of Nadoon or Walnut. No straighter or more handsome tree in our opinion grows about Nuwara Eliya, nor one which better resists monsoon bursts and windstorms, apt to level or break the tops off a good many gums and other trees. On Abbotsford, and especially on adjacent Dessford, there is a large number of the finest specimens (for growth) we have seen of Melanoxylon; but, alas, for the exigencies of the situation—as well as

.because of distance from market and absence of demand—a good many are being levelled and cut up for fuel purposes. It is a fact, however, that this tree, like most of the Acacias, is not a favourite with tea planters, because of its tendency to spread and throw up suckers, especially where the soil is stirred for cultivation purposes. On a piece of land reserved for timber trees this propensity does not so much matter : in fact it constitutes an economical means of planting up waste bits of land in or near the Sanatarium, where the tree flourishes apace, and in its lofty as well as, symmetrical, pyramidal shape, it offers an attractive feature as an avenue tree, or in groups at certain vantage points.

ORNAMENTAL AND FRUIT TREES.

A very attractive-looking tree in its youthful prime—seed got from Java—is *Acrocarpus grandis*; as also *Swietnia macrophylla*, Mahogany plants from Peradeniya, but of slow growth up here; while Dr. Thwaites' favourite *Pehimbiya* (Sinhalese name of *Filicium decipiens*, which he used to recommend to planters is not much more than a shrub at an elevation which not only sees certain palms but a fine *jak tree* come to fruit; as also mango-trees in full bearing!

Of "Cupressus" and "Cryptomeria" there are many fine specimens on Abbotsford—though Hakgalla Gardens are the true show-place for giant trees in great variety of these. A tree which is encouraged as a good and handsome grower, especially suited as a windbelt, is the Himalayan *Bucklandia* splendid specimens of which in huge well-formed trees (80 feet high or so), we observed on our way to Darjeeling from the *terai* upwards. It is very much used at Darjeeling for planking and for doors and windows.

BAMBOOS.

A feature on Abbotsford—and one which could be turned to mercantile account if a town like Colombo were near at hand—is the numerous groups of bamboos, of the giant variety especially, along the riverside and in many of the ravines, varied with the tiny (and medium) varieties useful for basket making. The present Manager had to clear out a great many clumps of bamboos from ravines as not so useful as water or Mauritius grass.

CINCHONAS.

Revisiting Abbotsford after an interval of two or three years, one of the most pleasant sights was the number of healthy vigorous-looking cinchona stems rising above and diversifying the tea fields, chiefly Succirubra and Hybrid. The smoother velvety leaves in some cases denote an approach to the more delicate and richer varieties. Altogether there must be quite 100,000 of these healthy stems from the old roots and from self-sown plants; while one of the original plants left to grow by the roadside, which was measured in our presence, is 72 feet high by 36 inches in girth at a foot above the ground. The age of this giant is 19 years.

APPENDIX IX.

NORTH-CENTRAL CEYLON:

HOW IS THE WASTE LAND OPENED BY THE RAILWAY TO BE UTILISED?
CATTLE STATIONS AND STOCK-RAISING SUGGESTED BEYOND THE TANK-SERVED RICE-LANDS.

The question will soon come up before Government as to what is to be done with the vast extent of jungle-covered waste land in our North-Central territory, outside the limits of tank-benefited areas, or land capable of being asweddumised? We are indebted to Mr. Duncan Skrine for some thoughts and suggestions on the subject, which, we think, are well worthy the consideration of Government. In addition to his prolonged experience in Ceylon, as planter and merchant, Mr. Skrine adds a thoroughly practical acquaintance with English farming and stock-raising. Now, interested as Mr. Skrine was, through his late friend, Mr. Bowden Smith, in Railway Extension to the North, he has during his present stay of fifteen months in the island, endeavoured to make himself acquainted with a considerable part of the country to be traversed.

For this purpose, he has twice visited the North-Central Province and he has been struck by the fact that even at the end of the dry season there, when every blade of grass seemed to be burnt up, the live-stock did not appear to be suffering, and in fact looked in better condition than the cattle in the wetter South-West portion of the island. This, to some extent, corresponds with our experience of Southern India whence, indeed, a great number of cattle, goats, so-called sheep, and poultry are annually imported into Ceylon, a great portion of which, we believe, might be reared in the North-Central regions of our island. That is a consummation devoutly to be wished! How to attain it is the question, and Mr. Skrine is of opinion that if clearing work is done in regard to the chena and scrub, leaving the big trees alone, cattle, and goats especially, will thrive amazingly and *greatly improve the grass and other provender* in the country beyond and around Anuradhapura. The question is, who is to begin the work? Well, it is not unnaturally suggested that Government should lead the way. For purposes of health and sanitation alone Government would do something around each railway station; and if, while about it, 200 acres are cleared in each such case, and stock introduced, an object lesson of special value could be offered to native capitalists and others. Besides, Government will probably be obliged to provide large stocks of firewood for locomotive use, along the route; and the clearing work will, in this way, be profitable in itself. Indeed, it is no doubt the intention of the Forest Department to utilise the Railway to carry valuable timber to market from the jungles of the North, and this will mean a good deal more clearing, with resulting profits from such marketable timber as well as from firewood,

North-Central Ceylon.

But in view of the suitableness of much of the North-Central country, when cleared, for stock-raising, it is possible that Government may be approached in another way. We will know how terribly large divisions of Australia—nearly all the interior districts in fact—have suffered from drought of late years; and yet there are never wanting capitalists "to take up land" in the Southern colonies for sheep or cattle, as the case may be, and to spend large amounts on their "home stations," on artesian wells for watering their flocks or herds, and on buildings for their employees. Now, if the Government of Ceylon were prepared to lease some blocks of 10,000 acres each for stock-raising, on easy terms, we think it very probable that Australian "Squatters" would be attracted. The great attention to them of our North-Central country would be proximity to a railway; cheap and willing labour in Tamil immigrants; plenty of timber—too much indeed, but the value of firewood would probably repay cost of clearing, even if it were stipulated that large trees should be untouched; facility for introducing suitable stock (in cattle and goats) from India to live on and improve the fodder, until gradually by crossing, better breeds were secured, acclimatized and established; and, lastly, possible facilities for watering stock in connection with tanks. Whence would come the squatter's, or rather Stock-owner's, return, it may be asked? Not likely from wool, even if sheep were tried; but rather from the local market for cattle, sheep and goats we should say. Here are the imports into Ceylon of live stock for some years taken from our "Directory":—

		1895.	1900.	1901.
Horses...	... No.	627	534	453
,, Nominal value	...	R179,290	199,190	154,850
Cattle ...	... No.	18,381	26,530	29,093
,, Nominal value	...	R410,550	613,230	650,940
Sheep and Goats ...	... No.	66,940	96,330	111,733
,, Nominal value	...	R332,570	544,520	683,260

This is apart from the import trade in frozen meat from Australasia which, however, would probably be unaffected for many long years, if at all. In view of the successful experiment on the island of Delft, it is quite possible that the breeding of horses or good ponies would enter into stock owners' calculations; but, in any case, they will see from the above figures that there is ready for them a local trade demand, for close on 30,000 cattle and over 100,000 sheep and goats per annum, of a nominal value as entered at the Customs (there being no import duty of nearly R1,400,000—in reality, as sold in the local market, of probably double that amount or certainly not under two million rupees or £133,000. Such a local market is surely good enough to secure the attention of some enterprising Australian stock capitalists accustomed to cattle or sheep runs in the hot and often arid regions of Central or Northern Australia, in Queensland, New South Wales, &c. We shall endeavour to bring the matter under the notice of some of these gentlemen as well as of the Australian press. The first question they will ask, of course, will be:—How is it known that cattle, &c., will thrive in your North Central country? Our answer is based on the experience of Mr. D. W. H. Skrine (with the training and observation of an English farmer as well as a Ceylon planter) namely, that he has seen cattle looking better at the end of the dry season in Anuradhapura district than in the comparatively wet South-Western division of the island;

and further that a great deal of North-Central country is probably better fitted for cattle, sheep and goats than is much of the country in Southern India whence we now import 140,000 head per annum.—*Ceylon Observer*, Aug., 23, 1902.

FARMING IN THE NORTH-CENTRAL PROVINCE.
Editor, Ceylon Observer.

Sept. 4, 1903.

DEAR SIR,—I was glad to read that article of yours, setting forth the capabilities of the territory along the Northern Railway route for the rearing and fattening of stock. I have long been of opinion that there is a great future for the country which is being gradually reclaimed from the decadence into which it had fallen for centuries, before the sagacity and political humanity of Sir William Gregory stepped in to arrest the decimation of its inhabitants and to rescue them from the sufferings induced by bad and insufficient water and ill-nourishing food. The cattle I have seen in and about Anuradhapura were of the sleekest; and Mr. (afterwards Sir Græme) Elphinstone told me that he sent the cattle, for which he could not find food and accommodation enough on his upcountry estates, to graze and fatten in the Bintenne country, until they were wanted for milk and for draught, when he sent away a new batch to make place for them. Even better suited than for cattle should the climate be for sheep and goats, which notoriously breed fast and which also revel in dry and arid tracts. There is always a market for these, as the annual imports you have quoted show; but while the idea of inducing stockbreeders of Australian experience to come over is an excellent one, I do not think the new enterprise need be wholly, or even greatly, dependent on their aid. There are men in our midst, European and Ceylonese, who will take up the industry, as soon as the line is open, and there is practical demonstration of the accessibility of suitable reserves. But the Government must adopt a liberal policy towards them. Perhaps some of the older planters will be able to say whether others than Elphinstone, adopted the plan I refer to above.—Yours truly, BOS.

Made in the USA
Monee, IL
03 May 2026

49438402R00277